Postgraduate Medical Education and Training:
the System in England and Wales

# Postgraduate Medical Education and Training: the System in England and Wales

Robin Dowie

King Edward's Hospital Fund for London

Printed and bound in England by Redwood Burn Ltd, Trowbridge, Wiltshire

Distributed for the King's Fund by Oxford University Press

ISBN 0 19 724641 9

Although this book was prepared under the auspices of the Council for Postgraduate Medical Education in England and Wales and with financial support from the Department of Health and Social Security, the views expressed are those of the author.

King's Fund Publishing Office
2 St Andrew's Place
London NW1 4LB

# Foreword

A truly remarkable feature of British medicine during the past 40 years has been the development of postgraduate medical education. Certainly postgraduate degrees and diplomas have been in existence for a very long time but structured arrangements for prescribing, dispensing, monitoring and assessing training are of recent origin. They have been generated by and have in turn spawned a bewildering nexus of commissions, councils, colleges and committees. These have taken the stage and have published their advice, requirements and demands to cover all branches of medical training. Since the NHS is the principal employer of doctors the whole field of education has become inextricably bound up with issues of medical manpower.

The man from Mars observing and analysing this concatenation may well experience mental indigestion but help is at hand. Robin Dowie collected a vast amount of information relevant to the whole scene in the course of her feasibility study on the possibility of establishing an information system for hospital medical and dental training posts and trainees in England and Wales.

She now offers a most valuable by-product of that enquiry in presenting a masterly review of the postgraduate scene describing the system and the workings thereof. The relevant organisations and the consumers of training including women and overseas doctors are all considered. Financial aspects and manpower are discussed. She writes with clarity and with authority springing from her own survey of the current scene. The book will be of interest to all who are in the business of regulating, delivering or receiving postgraduate medical training.

Ken Rawnsley
Professor Emeritus in Psychological Medicine
University of Wales College of Medicine

# Acknowledgements

In the autumn of 1984 the Council for Postgraduate Medical Education in England and Wales commissioned a one year study to examine the feasibility of establishing an information system for hospital medical and dental training posts and trainees in England and Wales. A working group of Council members, under the chairmanship of Professor Ken Rawnsley, steered the study and I was appointed as the researcher. Although I had carried out research in health services for a number of years I was not familiar with the complex organisation of the system for postgraduate medical education and training in the United Kingdom. So the first few months of the study year were spent making many visits to national bodies concerned with education and training to learn of their roles and the information held on trainees and training posts. Visits were made later to the 14 health regions in England, Wales, and a number of health districts.

As the fieldwork for the study progressed it became obvious that the material being collected was more extensive than could be covered in a single report on the feasibility exercise. The Council – under the chairmanship of the late Professor R F Whelan – agreed, therefore, to extend my appointment after the completion of the feasibility study. This book is the outcome.

During the fieldwork for the feasibility study many people were interviewed or provided help. They were thanked individually in the report on the study and I would like to express my gratitude to them again. Both during the study year and in the following months when the book was being prepared I was given copies of published and unpublished documents by the royal colleges and faculties, joint committees on higher training, the offices of the regional postgraduate deans, the Council for Postgraduate Medical Education, the Department of Health and Social Security, the General Medical Council, the Medical Research Council, the regional health authorities, certain special and district health authorities and by other bodies. Unpublished statistics were supplied by the British Council, the Defence Medical Services Directorate of the Ministry of Defence, the National Advice Centre and the Medical Directorate of Her Majesty's Prison Service. The examination departments of the royal colleges also provided some information on successful examination candidates. The General Medical Council gave permission to reproduce statistics published in its annual reports and *The Medical Register*.

Dr George Mogey and Dr Ray Brotherwood of the Council for Postgraduate Medical Education answered many questions and they, together with Professor Michael Warren and Professor Philip Rhodes, read all or most of the manuscript. I am particularly grateful for both their comments and encouragement. Dr Jack Dowie advised on the framework used for structuring the material. Valued typing and secretarial assistance was provided by Mrs Lavinia Harvey, and Mrs Barbara Wall carried out some computing.

A number of people who helped with the fieldwork also read relevant chapters of the manuscript: Sir David Innes Williams of the British Postgraduate Medical Federation and now Chairman of the Council for Postgraduate Medical Education, Dr J D Crowlesmith recently retired from the British Council, Miss Kathryn Riley of the City and Hackney Health Authority, Dr Michael O'Brien of the East Anglian Regional Health Authority, Mr Stanley Alan of the Faculty of Anaesthetists, Dr P J Taylor of the Faculty of Occupational Medicine, Mr R Beers, Miss Wendy Cogger and Mr P L Towers of the General Medical Council, Mrs Hilla Gittens and Dr Douglas Price of the Joint Committee on Postgraduate Training for General Practice, Miss Joy Greenfield of the Joint Committee on Higher Psychiatric Training, Air Commodore M A Pallister of the Defence Medical Services Directorate of the Ministry of Defence, Mrs Linda Williams of the National Advice Centre, Miss C M Swarbrick of the Royal College of General Practitioners, Mr John Lawson of the Royal College of Obstetricians and Gynaecologists, Mr D P Essame, Dr John Lister and Mr Michael Tibbs of the Royal College of Physicians (London), Dr J L T Birley of the Royal College of Psychiatrists, Mrs S G Nawrocki and Professor W B Robertson of the Royal College of Pathologists, Mrs Irene Stephenson of the Royal College of Radiologists, Mr John Lambert and Mr Wilfred Webber of the Royal College of Surgeons of England, Miss Ellen Sample of St Bartholomew's Hospital Medical College, and Dr T M Hayes and Dr D H Makinson (recently retired) of the University of Wales College of Medicine. I am most appreciative of the time spent in reading and preparing comments on the text. Many other people in the health regions and in the British Medical Association, Department of Health and Social Security, Medical Research Council and other organisations kindly answered queries. The views expressed in the book are, however, my own and also the errors.

During the time of my employment with the Council for Postgraduate Medical Education in England and Wales I was on secondment from the Health Services Research Unit of the University of Kent at Canterbury. Later, in the months when the book was being finished, I was on the staff of the British Postgraduate Medical Federation of the University of London. The financial support throughout, however, was provided by grants from the Department of Health and Social Security and a supplementary grant from the Publications Panel of King Edward's Hospital Fund for London. Naturally, I am grateful to these employing and funding bodies.

My friends and colleagues gave encouragement and showed understanding when the pressure of completing the work rose in the final months and my sons, Sean and Craig, were the best of companions at all times.

Robin Dowie
1987

# Contents

FIGURES

# 1 Introduction

The organisation of postgraduate medical education in the National Health Service (NHS) has been reviewed on various occasions since the Royal Commission on Medical Education reported in 1968.[1] Three inquiries were set up by Parliament: the Inquiry into the Regulation of the Medical Profession[2], the Royal Commission on the National Health Service[3] and the inquiry into medical education by the Social Services Committee of the House of Commons[4] which was followed up by the Committee four years later.[5] One of the most recent discussion documents has come from the Education Committee of the General Medical Council (GMC).[6] All of these bodies recommended or proposed changes affecting the structure of training undertaken by junior hospital doctors and the roles of the institutions involved in postgraduate medical education. None, however, discussed in any detail the administrative and financial resources needed if the recommended changes to the training grades were to be implemented. Furthermore, none of the proposals made by the parliamentary inquiries for restructuring the training grades has been adopted. The document from the GMC was welcomed by many bodies concerned with postgraduate education and training provided the proposals reflected non-mandatory developments.

There are two reasons why changes to the training grades will be difficult to implement: first, the complicated organisational arrangements for overseeing post-graduate medical education might also need to be restructured and second, large numbers of doctors would be involved. In England and Wales in September 1984 there were approximately 22,400 doctors – including honorary contract holders – in the four training grades in the hospital medical service, 1865 trainees in general medical practice and 265 in community medicine.[7,8,9] (The same training grades apply in the hospital dental service and in England and Wales in September 1984 there were 675 dental trainees.[10])

This book describes the organisation of postgraduate education in England and Wales for junior doctors planning careers in hospital medicine, general medical practice, community medicine and occupational medicine. It identifies the various areas of responsibility and the financial commitments of the Department of Health and Social Security (DHSS) and the Welsh Office, the regional health authorities (RHAs), district health authorities (DHAs) and special health authorities (SHAs), the universities, the royal colleges and faculties and higher training committees (HTCs), the research bodies and of the trainees themselves. The roles of the General Medical Council and the Council for Postgraduate Medical Education in England and Wales are – the uncertain future of this body notwithstanding – covered also.

Estimates of expenditure are included wherever possible. An attempt has not been made, however, to quantify the total expenditure on postgraduate medical education. Systematic research is required to obtain the necessary costings. The book shows how improved information on trainees in the registrar and senior house officer (SHO) grades is needed by regional bodies involved in education if the success of the postgraduate education system is to be properly evaluated. A change in the organisational arrangements is also proposed, namely, that the responsibility for inspecting general professional training posts (registrar and SHO posts) in hospitals should be transferred from the royal colleges and faculties to the regional postgraduate medical education committees (RPGMECs).

Much of the source material used was collected during a twelve-month study to investigate the feasibility of collecting and providing on a national basis information on NHS medical and dental training posts and trainees in England and Wales. The study was set up by a working group of the Council for Postgraduate Medical Education in England and Wales (CPME) and the funding was provided by the DHSS. The report of the study was published late in 1984.[11]

Early in the fieldwork visits were made to the royal colleges and faculties and the joint committees on higher training (JCHTs), to the General Medical Council and to other national bodies concerned with medical and dental trainees. At a later stage, the regional health authorities, the Welsh Office, and the offices of the regional postgraduate medical deans were visited. Semi-structured interviews were held with the deans. The main purpose of the fieldwork was to find out what information on doctors and dentists in the training grades and on training posts is held by the collegiate bodies, and by the health regions and universities, and whether it is stored in manual or computerised record systems. A great deal was learnt on the regional visits about the local arrangements for educational activities, in particular the procedures for reviewing the progress of trainees in the different grades. Many documents were collected during the fieldwork. Later other documents were collected for analysis, notably the examination regulations for the higher qualifications awarded by the royal colleges and faculties, the 1982 pass lists for the final higher qualifying examinations, and the 1983/84 statutory accounts of the regional health authorities and some district and special health authorities.

During another fieldwork phase of the feasibility study information was recorded about the training posts and medical and dental trainees employed in two health districts – City and Hackney (a London teaching district) and Bradford (a northern non-teaching district). The data sets used were the minimum data sets recommended by the Steering Group on Health Services Information that was chaired by Mrs Edith Körner.[12] The information collected on the trainees included items on qualifications and career progression. The data for the training posts covered the approval status granted by the royal colleges, faculties and JCHTs. The exercise provided an opportunity to learn how medical staffing activities are carried out in health districts and to observe the relevance of some of the activities to postgraduate education.

*Framework of the book*

The next chapter provides the background by reviewing the proposals for restructuring the training grades made by the various royal commissions and committees of inquiry starting with the Royal Commission on Medical Education which sat between 1965 and 1968. It is suggested in the chapter that one reason why the various proposals were never adopted is that the inquiries did not take fully into account the administrative arrangements and financial resources needed to implement the proposals.

The other chapters are organised within a broad 'demand' and 'supply' framework: demand for postgraduate education from employers notably the NHS, and from individual doctors; and supply provided by the various institutions – the NHS, the universities and the Medical Research Council, all of which are financed by central government, the royal colleges, faculties and joint committees on higher training, and by other agencies supporting research. The advisory role of the Council for Postgraduate Medical Education in England and Wales and the regulatory functions of the General Medical Council are also discussed. The simple framework does not, however, overlook the substantial interdependence both within 'demanders' and 'suppliers' and between them. A significant part of the demand from individual doctors is clearly a derived demand (from the NHS demand). Many linkages exist between supplying institutions (for example, the universities and the NHS have joint advisory responsibilities) and the 'suppliers' are able in various ways to influence the demand for their services. The final two chapters within the framework – chapters 19 and 20 – discuss the financial arrangements operating between the universities and the health service and draw attention to the lack of information on the expenditure by the health authorities on postgraduate education and training.

An account of recent reports on medical manpower planning in the NHS is given in the penultimate chapter. The final chapter makes suggestions for improving the organisation of the system for postgraduate education and training in England and Wales and reasons are given as to why the career and training grade structure in the hospital service should be urgently reviewed.

In the chapter on medical manpower planning, a ministerial working group formed in October 1985 to examine the medical staffing structure for the hospital service is mentioned. The report from the group[299] containing recommendations for the reform of the staffing structure was published in July 1986, shortly after the manuscript of

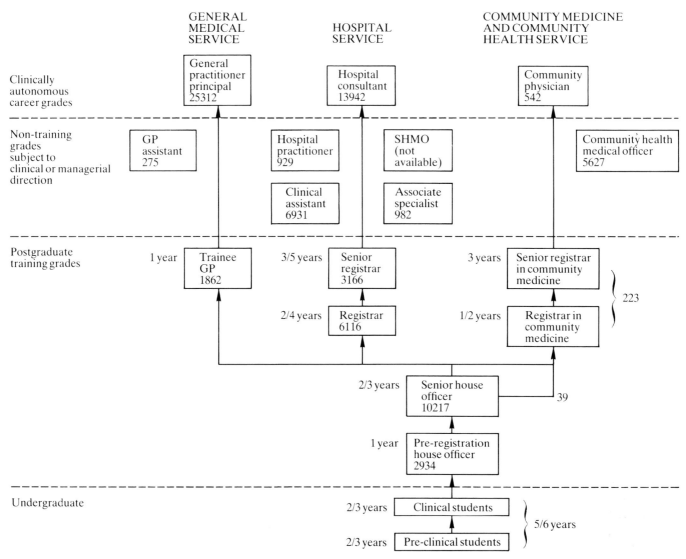

Figure 1 Medical career structure in the National Health Service and
the numbers of doctors in the grades in England and Wales, 1984

SHMO = senior hospital medical officer

1 The numbers for the hospital service apply to 30 September 1984 and include doctors with NHS permanent paid whole-time and part-time appointments and doctors with honorary appointments. Information on honorary appointment holders is given in Table 8. The number for hospital consultants includes SHMOs with allowance.

2 The numbers for doctors in the general medical service apply to 1 October 1984. All hospital practitioners and most clinical assistants are also principals in general practice and are included in the general practitioner number for unrestricted and restricted principals.

3 The numbers for the community medicine and community health service apply to 30 September 1984. The community health service has its own career structure and over half of the doctors have part-time or sessional contracts (see Table 14).

4 The indicated lengths of training in the various grades represent the periods doctors would normally expect to take. A range is given as length of training will vary according to specialty.

Sources: Fourth Report from the Social Services Committee, page xvii[4] (with amendments) and DHSS 1984 censuses of medical manpower.[7,8,9]

---

this book was completed. References to the recommendations in the report have, however, been inserted in the text.

Presented in the chapters is statistical and descriptive material from very many sources and the majority of sources are not routinely available in academic and public libraries. Sections of the text may, therefore, be found useful for reference purposes by a variety of readers – medical students; doctors of all grades working in the NHS or in other services in Britain; doctors trained overseas who are planning to visit this country; administrators, health authority members and others working in, or concerned with, the NHS; and academics and researchers with an interest in postgraduate medical education and medical manpower.

The book does not provide an historical account of the institutions associated with postgraduate medical education. The chapters are chiefly concerned with the organisation of the system in the mid-1980s although they contain references to past events (which mostly happened after the Royal Commission on Medical Education reported in 1968) that helped to shape the present system. For a detailed account of the emergence, particularly in the two centuries to 1965, of the characteristic patterns of English medical practice, institutions, staffing and training, readers are advised to consult the book *Medical practice in modern England* by Stevens.[13] A shorter and more general account is provided in chapter 11 of *An outline history of medicine* by

Figure 2  Geographical location of the English health regions and Wales, and numbers of hospital medical trainees including honorary appointment holders, 30 September 1984 (LPGTHs=London postgraduate teaching hospitals)

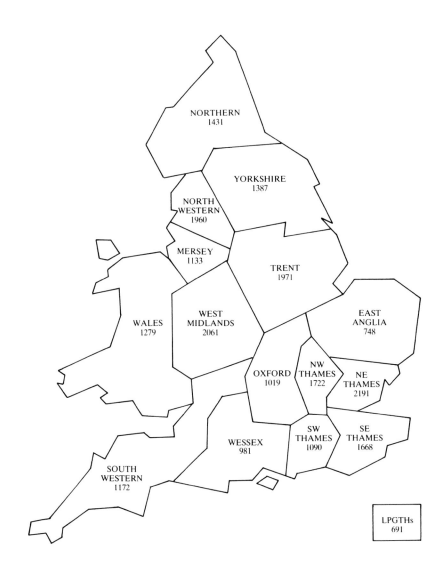

**Table 1**  Organisation and administration of the training grades for medical staff in the NHS hospital service in England and Wales

| Grade | Senior registrar | Registrar | Senior house officer | Pre-registration house officer |
|---|---|---|---|---|
| No of hospital medical staff England and Wales 30 September 1984* | 3166 | 6116 | 10217 | 2934 |
| Employing authority for the trainees | RHAs SHAs | DHAs SHAs | DHAs SHAs | DHAs SHAs |
| Usual duration in grade in mid 1980s** | 3–5 years | 2–4 years | 2–3 years | 1 year |
| Qualifications (experience) and registration required for entering grade | At least four years postgraduate experience and a higher qualification in most specialties. Full or limited registration with GMC | At least two years postgraduate experience. Full or limited registration with GMC | At least twelve months postgraduate experience. Full or limited registration with GMC | University medical degree or diploma from non-university licensing bodies. Provisional, limited or full registration with GMC |
| Establishment control (in England) | DHSS on advice of Central Manpower Committee. Numbers closely relate to expected consultant vacancies | DHSS on advice of Central Manpower Committee | RHAs, although a freeze on new posts was imposed in 1982 | 'Target' number for each region set centrally and related to number of graduates |
| Training status | Higher specialist training | General professional training† | General professional training† | Pre-registration |
| Educational approval for posts granted by: | Joint committees on higher training or equivalent college committees | Appropriate royal college or faculty | Appropriate royal college or faculty | Universities with medical faculties or medical schools |

\* Including doctors with honorary contracts.
\*\* The usual duration varies according to specialty – see Fifth Report from the Social Services Committee (page 10).[5]
†Some posts are 'selected' as being appropriate for vocational training for general medical practice.

Sources: Report on Hospital Medical Manpower in the South East Thames Region[15] (with amendments) and DHSS 30 September 1984 census of hospital medical staff.[7]

Rhodes.[14] The introductory chapters of the reports of parliamentary inquiries on medical manpower matters usually contain a summary of relevant inquiries held, reports published and government decisions taken since the National Health Service Act was passed in 1946.

Readers who are not thoroughly familiar with the National Health Service may find helpful the diagram of the medical career structure in Figure 1, the map of England and Wales showing the boundaries of the health regions and the number of medical trainees working in hospitals in each region and Wales in Figure 2 and the summary in Table 1 of the organisation and administration of the training grades for medical staff in the hospital service in England and Wales.

# 2 Proposals for restructuring the training grades

The practice of hospital care being provided by consultants or specialists each supported by a 'firm' of doctors of junior status was well established – at least in the teaching hospitals – by the time the National Health Service came into existence in 1948. The unification of the various hospital administrative systems under the new service meant that a single hospital staffing structure was also needed. Thus in 1947 a committee under the chairmanship of Sir William Spens was set up to look at the career structure and levels of remuneration for hospital doctors in the NHS. It reported the following year.[16]

The Spens committee observed that there existed already a hierachical structure of three well-defined grades leading to the consultant or specialist grade, although the titles given to doctors in each grade differed across the country. Grade III was the most junior grade, the posts being normally obtained not less than one year after registration and usually held for one year. Post holders were known as senior house officers, resident medical officers, and so forth. Grade II posts were obtained normally not less than two years after registration and were held usually for two years. The titles given to the holders included assistant and junior registrar. Grade I was the most senior, the posts being obtained normally not less than four years after registration and usually held for three years by doctors called chief assistant, first assistant or senior registrar. The Spens committee recommended that these three hospitals grades should continue within the NHS and, furthermore, that they should be recognised as training grades.

No recommendation was made about the year spent in the hospital service immediately following graduation – the pre-registration year – partly because it was viewed as experience which completed a graduate's medical education. An interdepartmental committee on medical schools chaired by Sir William Goodenough had recommended in 1944 that medical graduates should spend a compulsory extra year of hospital training before becoming registered practitioners.[17] The Spens committee, the General Medical Council and the profession were also of this opinion and a regulation to this effect was incorporated in the Medical Act of 1950. It was enforced in January 1953.

The three junior grades of limited tenure envisaged by the Spens committee were accepted by the profession and implemented at the beginning of the new health service. The grades were called junior registrar (later renamed senior house officer), registrar and senior registrar (SR). However, the concept of the grades being primarily for training future consultants was not adopted. Discussions between the health departments and the profession over the committee's recommendations led to two additional grades of unrestricted tenure being introduced: the senior hospital medical officer (SHMO) grade which was immediately under the grade of consultant, and the junior hospital medical officer (JHMO) grade.

Thirteen years later a review of developments in the staffing structure of the hospital service since the inception of the NHS was carried out by a government-established Joint Working Party chaired by Sir Robert Platt. The report which was published in 1961, pointed out that serious imbalances between training and service needs had arisen.[18] It recommended that the grades of senior registrar, registrar, SHO and house officer (HO) (fully registered) and house officer (provisionally registered) should be retained and these grades have continued until the present time (see Figure 1, page 22) apart from the post-registration HO grade which was phased out in 1983/84.[7] The Joint Working Party believed, however, that the SHMO grade needed to be replaced by a medical assistant grade for doctors who would work as 'assistants' to, and under the supervision of consultants, and that the JHMO grade should be discontinued. The recommendations of the Joint Working Party were adopted: the two grades of unrestricted tenure were closed to new entrants in 1964 and the medical assistant grade was introduced. (The medical assistant grade became the associate specialist grade in 1981.)

During the 1960s there was an accelerated increase in the number of junior doctor posts, the stimulation coming from the widespread adoption of the staffing model of the 'firm' in general hospitals across the country. Concern over the content of training offered in many junior posts was expressed by various professional groups. This was also a period when overseas doctors were entering Britain in increasing numbers to undertake postgraduate training.

PROPOSALS FOR RESTRUCTURING THE TRAINING GRADES FROM 1968

The next body to review the hospital staffing structure in the United Kingdom (UK) was the Royal Commission on Medical Education established in 1965. It was followed by three more parliamentary inquiries into medical education and the health service, all of which recommended that the training grades be restructured although along different lines. The Education Committee of the GMC would also like changes to be introduced. The names and dates of these commissions and committees are shown in Table 2. The most recent recommendations to be presented were contained in a discussion document from a working group which had been established following an initiative from the Minister of State for Health, Mr Barney Hayhoe, in October 1985. The document was circulated for comment in July 1986.[29]

Table 2  Royal commissions and committees concerned with postgraduate medical education since 1965–68

| Title | Chairman | Date when inquiry began | Date of report |
|---|---|---|---|
| Royal Commission on Medical Education[1] | Lord Todd | June 1965 | April 1968 |
| Committee of Inquiry into the Regulation of the Medical Profession[2] | Dr A W Merrison | November 1972 | April 1975 |
| Royal Commission on the National Health Service[3] | Sir Alec Merrison | May 1976 | July 1979 |
| Social Services Committee of the House of Commons*[4] | Mrs Renée Short | November 1980 | July 1981 |
| Education Committee of the General Medical Council[6] | Professor A Crisp | February 1982 | December 1983 |

* A follow-up inquiry was held by the Social Services Committee of the House of Commons in 1985.[5] Mrs Renée Short was still the chairman of the Committee but the membership had changed substantially.

The reports on medical education from the royal commissions and committees listed in Table 2 share five characteristics. First, as mentioned above, all contain proposals for restructuring the training grades with the purpose of improving standards in postgraduate training. Second, these proposals appear to be based on an implicit assumption that the majority of doctors, if given suitable training and career guidance, are capable of passing through the junior training grades at a similar rate of progress. Third, the reports do not provide estimates of the numbers of doctors that would be covered by each of the new grades if the proposals were introduced. Fourth, the financial resources which were available for postgraduate education at the time of the inquiries are not reviewed and there are only brief references to those resources needed to implement the proposals. Finally, none of the proposals made prior to 1986 for altering the hospital training grades has been adopted.

The various proposals for restructuring the training grades are reviewed in the remainder of this chapter and, for ease of comparison, those made before 1986 have been summarised in Figure 3. Included in this review are estimates of the numbers of doctors who could be affected if some of the proposals were introduced. These

Figure 3  Proposals for restructuring the training grades made by five commissions and committees, and the existing grades since 1953 and intended duration for doctors obtaining a consultant post at the age of 32-33 years

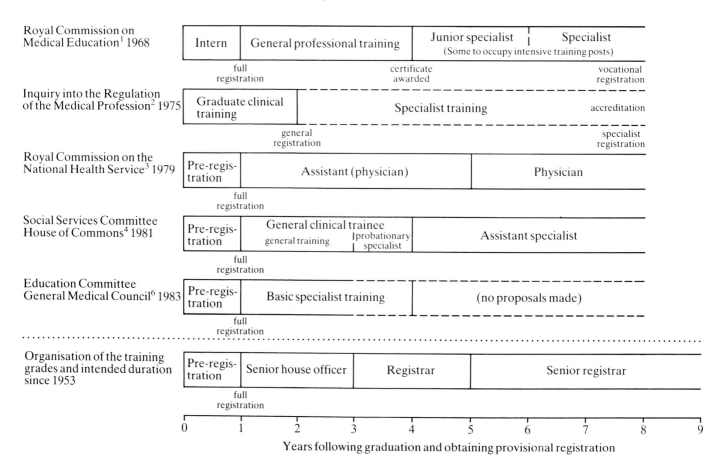

estimates are based on the DHSS 30 September censuses of hospital medical staff.[7] There have been many other reports from working parties established by the professional bodies, the departments of health and by other agencies that have discussed the career imbalance in the hospital service and offered possible solutions. These are not covered here. A review of this material is, however, contained in a book on the subject of medical manpower by Parkhouse.[19]

In 1965, a Royal Commission chaired by Lord Todd was asked 'to review the whole field of medical education and to make proposals "in the light of national needs and resources"...'(para 18).[1] With regard to postgraduate training, the Commission recommended that after an 'intern year' (the pre-registration year) of training was completed, trainees should enter a period of general professional training normally lasting three years. The prospective trainees would be matched with a suitable series of appointments, this being best done at regional level. During the training period they would be assessed progressively, the assessments being based on reports by supervisors (consultants), on standard tests of knowledge and skill, and possibly by external assessment for borderline trainees. The responsibility for overseeing the appointments and progress of the trainees in the regions was to fall on the regional postgraduate committees representing the NHS, the universities and the professional bodies. These committees were to receive regular reports from the supervisors and statistical information about the overall level of the trainees' performances. Clinical tutors and/or area organisers appointed in the district hospitals would coordinate the supervision of trainees at the local level.

Once the general professional training phase was satisfactorily completed, the trainees were to be given a certificate. The Commission believed that if the proposal of planned programmes of appointments and progressive assessments was introduced, a very high proportion of doctors would receive the certificate after three years of training. Those seeking a career in the hospital service would then enter the grade of junior specialist progressing to the specialist grade to complete their training.

All certificate holders could enter the junior specialist grade. However, a proportion of more capable trainees selected on the basis of their performance as general professional trainees, would be appointed to intensive training posts (in effect, senior registrar posts). These posts would offer accelerated promotion through the junior specialist and specialist grades. The time spent in these posts before the trainees might reasonably be considered for consultant appointments would generally vary between two and four years according to the specialty.

The Commission was less specific on the training and career prospects of the junior specialists who were not in intensive training posts and, numerically, comprised nearly two-thirds of the junior specialists. It simply suggested that they should be given appropriate supervision and further vocational training. In due course, these trainees along with those in intensive training posts would become eligible for inclusion in a vocational register which the GMC was encouraged to set up. The responsibility for seeing that junior specialists, whether or not in intensive training posts, received appropriate training would be held by the regional postgraduate committees. The Commission did not believe, however, that junior specialists would need such close supervision as general professional trainees.

Criticism of the higher qualification examination systems administered by the royal colleges and the newly established colleges was expressed by the Commission. The timing and nature of the examinations – even those of the newer colleges – were not related as closely as they should to the existing arrangements for postgraduate training in British hospitals and even well prepared candidates often failed. There was also a lack of complete reciprocal recognition of the primary examinations administered by the English and Scottish royal colleges of physicians and surgeons. After reviewing statistics of pass and failure rates provided by the colleges, the Commission adopted the principle that doctors in general professional training should be assessed on a progressive basis throughout the three-year period. There was 'no place for a single major "pass or fail" examination' (para 93).

Although the Commission was asked to make proposals in the light of national needs and resources, it did not discuss in any detail the financial implications of its recommendations for postgraduate education. Rather, it took the wider view that any increase in the costs of providing professional training should not be borne by the universities. They were already devoting a significant part of their resources to professional training which was not a part of their primary academic function. The NHS, as the main employer of doctors, was seen to be the appropriate provider of medical training that was not academic. Where universities provided teaching and facilities for professional training, the cost was to be 'repaid' by the NHS. Although the Commission identified responsibilities to be borne by the professional bodies (royal colleges and faculties), in particular the inspection and approval of training posts, it made no reference to the financial resources that would be needed by them.

Little progress was made in reorganising the structure of professional training along the lines recommended by the Royal Commission except at the senior level. The royal colleges and faculties created the joint committees on higher training or equivalent committees with the purpose of regulating training in the senior registrar grade or, in the case of general practice, during the three-year vocational training period. The JCHTs then set up specialty advisory committees (SACs) to oversee training standards within individual specialties. In most regions, the training of senior registrars is now monitored by specialty training committees that report to the regional postgraduate medical education committee (see chapter 13). However, the proposal that doctors should systematically enter three-year general professional training programmes and be progressively assessed has not been introduced except for doctors joining vocational training schemes for general practice.

The next inquiry to propose radical changes was the Committee of Inquiry into the Regulation of the Medical Profession chaired by Dr (later Sir) Alec Merrison.[2] This Committee was particularly critical of the training in the pre-registration year that follows after a doctor has graduated and become provisionally registered with the General Medical Council. Under the present GMC regulations, during the pre-registration year a doctor must spend at least four months in medicine and at least four months in surgery to become eligible for full registration. The remaining time can be spent in medicine or surgery or in another clinical hospital discipline (including laboratory medicine). Up to four months experience in a health centre may also be counted as part of the pre-registration year but only if the health centre posts have been recognised for this purpose.[20] At the time when the Committee met, however, the GMC regulations governing the content of training required that six months be spent in medicine and six months in surgery with six months in midwifery counting as either medicine or surgery. Six months of health centre experience was also permitted.

The Committee of Inquiry took the view that a new approach to postgraduate training was required along with a new organisational structure. It proposed a three-tier medical education system: undergraduate training, graduate clinical training, and specialist training.

Graduate clinical training would replace the pre-registration year. Its normal duration was to be 'something like two years' and the trainees would occupy a series of posts providing a wide range of general clinical experience. They could also do some specialty work. At the conclusion of this training phase a doctor would be eligible for general registration – the equivalent to full registration.

The responsibility for controlling the education of the doctors during graduate clinical training was to rest with the trainees' own university. As there would need to be closer overall supervision of the trainees than already existed, the Committee recommended that additional resources be given to the universities to set up tutorial systems whereby trainees would be personally guided and advised by members of the medical faculties. The resources would have to be made available by the government through the University Grants Committee (UGC).

Once a doctor had general registration, he or she would enter specialist training. The Committee of Inquiry believed that every doctor should receive a specialist education but the requirements and duration of the training would vary according to the nature of the specialty. This would also be the time for doctors to prepare themselves for membership or fellowship of the appropriate royal college or faculty. At the conclusion of their training, the doctors would be 'accredited' and thus entitled to registration in a specialist or 'indicative' register to be set up and maintained by the GMC.

The Committee recommended that the GMC should control the standards of specialist medical education as well as those of undergraduate and graduate clinical training and, subsequently, the responsibilities of the Council were extended to cover all stages of medical education and training under the Medical Act of 1978. The Committee believed, however, that the monitoring of training standards and the accreditation of individual trainees within each specialty would best be carried out by bodies to which the GMC delegated the responsibility – notably the royal colleges and joint commitees on higher training.

Needless to say, the proposed three-tier training structure was not adopted. If a tutorial system had been set up to closely supervise the 5000 or so doctors who would have entered graduate clinical training in the late 1970s, the additional resources provided by the UGC would have been considerable. The same point applies to the proposal for specialist training. At the time of the inquiry which lasted from late 1972 to 1975, the JCHTs and equivalent college committees were overseeing higher training in 30 or more specialties and covering over 2500 senior registrars. If all the general registered doctors (about 14,500) were to have received specialist training organised in the same way as that provided for the senior registrars, the higher training bodies and RPGMECs would have needed greatly supplemented resources. These monetary issues were not discussed in the Committee's report.

### Royal Commission on the National Health Service

Thirteen months after the Committee of Inquiry reported, the Royal Commission on the NHS was set up. It was also chaired by Sir Alec Merrison. In the terms of reference the Commission was asked to consider 'the best use and management of the financial and manpower resources of the National Health Service'.[3] With medical manpower, the Commission found that one of the few subjects on which the evidence was unanimous was the need for improvement in the hospital career structure. There were too many doctors in training grades below senior registrar for the number of consultant posts that became available annually, and in some places, the training given to junior doctors was unsatisfactory because there were too few consultants to supervise their work properly. The Commission chose, therefore, to suggest (rather than recommend) an alternative training/career structure.

There should be a hospital staffing structure made up of three post-registration grades: assistant physician (or surgeon or psychiatrist or other specialist), physician, and consultant physician. The grade of assistant would be a training grade with tenure being equivalent to four years whole-time. A trainee would have a single contract to cover the period. A one-year extension could be granted on educational grounds. During the period a doctor would receive a generalist training and a substantial amount of specialist experience. It would also be the time to obtain a higher qualification.

The higher grade of physician would be both a training and a career grade. Entry would be by competition and the contenders would normally hold a higher qualification. At least three years would normally be spent in the grade before a person could enter the grade of consultant physician. Alternatively, once a doctor had completed the necessary training, he or she could occupy a career post within the physician grade. Such a post would carry clinical responsibility for patients matched to the individual's abilities and seniority. The final grade of consultant would be the same as before.

The report provided only a brief outline of the suggested career structure. No administrative issues were raised about, for example, who was to assume responsibility for organising the general and specialist posts that doctors would occupy during their four-year assistantship. Also, it did not suggest the criteria by which the successful completion of this training phase was to be assessed and what would happen to those who failed to meet the criteria after five years.

For a body that was asked to consider the best use and management of NHS financial and manpower resources, the Commission made surprisingly few references to the funding of postgraduate medical training. It did point out that the cost-sharing relationship between the universities and the NHS was complex, and the escalating costs (which were large) and the demands of postgraduate education had added to the strain on NHS/university relationships, although the NHS met the bulk of the costs. It believed, however, that a 'grey area' of obligation and accounting between the NHS, the UGC and the universities was acceptable if good relationships and efficiency were to be sustained. No references were made to the contributions provided, and the resources used by the royal colleges and faculties.

### Fourth report from the Social Services Committee

Fifteen months after the report from the Royal Commission on the NHS was presented to Parliament, the Social Services Committee of the House of Commons began its inquiry into 'medical education with special reference to the number of doctors and the career structure in hospitals'.[4] The chairman was Mrs Renée Short. This Committee shared the concern of the previous inquiries over the duration of postgraduate training and the limited career opportunities for those who are fully trained. It was also concerned by the narrow content of training required by the specialties. The members favoured instead a concept of a period of general clinical training as part of all postgraduate medical education. 'It is important that all of those [doctors] who intend to practise medicine, in whatever specialty, should have the opportunity to gain insight into the problems of old age, child health and development, general practice, the role of medicine in the community, and the psychological aspects and effects of illness' (para 190).

The Committee looked to the royal colleges and faculties to take the lead in achieving this aim. Thus it recommended that 'all specialties, through their Colleges and Faculties, should require post-registration trainees to spend periods totalling at least one year in other disciplines' (para 191). The Committee was also convinced that organised training programmes were needed: they would lead to an improvement in training standards and to a reduction in the length of training needed before a doctor became eligible for a consultant appointment. The structure of the proposed training arrangements was as follows.

The pre-registration year would continue unchanged. Once a doctor was fully registered, he would be known as a registered doctor or general clinical trainee and two to three years would be spent in this grade. In the first and possibly the second year he would receive a 'general clinical training' in, for example, paediatrics, psychiatry, geriatrics or general practice, to be followed by one year of probationary training in a specialty of choice. On the satisfactory completion of both the general clinical training and the probationary year in the specialty the trainee would be eligible for promotion to the assistant specialist grade. The grade would encompass the present registrar and senior registrar grades. The trainees would enter a designated specialist training scheme of three to four years duration which might incorporate experience in an academic department. The organisation and administration of these proposed training arrangements would be carried out at regional level and the Committee recognised that additional administrative resources and information would have to be made available to the various regional committees responsible for education and manpower. Two other related recommendations made by the Committee were that there should be an increase in the number of consultants and a decrease in the number of junior doctors in most specialties, and that the contracts of all junior doctors should be issued by the regional health authorities. (At present, the district health authorities employ junior doctors below the grade of senior registrar.)

The load carried by the regional committees and the regional postgraduate deans as chief executive officers to the RPGMECs would be considerable if all the recommendations in the 'Short report' were implemented. The Social Services Committee believed that the availability of career guidance would help to reduce the number of situations where trainees became disappointed with their specialty choice or found themselves in 'dead-end' training posts. The central role in providing this guidance and counselling especially to overseas doctors, was to be played by the deans and clinical tutors. It was also envisaged that the regional deans – of whom there are fifteen in England and Wales – would be involved in the procedures for selecting the assistant specialist trainees who could number 6000 or more.

The Short report did not say who was to assess whether general clinical trainees had satisfactorily completed their general and specialty training and what would be the criteria for making the assessments. There was no mention either of the higher qualifying examinations and diploma examinations that are administered by the royal colleges and faculties and their level of importance in the training of doctors. Again, there was no reference to what would happen to doctors who failed to satisfactorily complete the specialty training year or failed to be accepted on to a designated training scheme. Finally, the report did not discuss the finance needed to implement the improvements to the organisation of postgraduate medical education, even though finance was seen to be one of three obstacles which might hinder progress. (The other obstacles were logistics and organisation.) There was some discussion, however, about the additional costs that would be incurred in providing higher salaries if the number of consultant appointments was increased and there was a corresponding reduction in the number of trainees. The Committee hoped that the costs would be offset by savings from an increased efficiency in the hospital service because, it was assumed, consultants are more efficient than junior doctors in the manner in which they diagnose and treat patients.

The Social Services Committee held a follow-up inquiry into medical education in the spring of 1985. Mrs Renée Short was still the chairman but the membership of the committee was substantially changed. In its report[5] the Committee did not pursue the proposals on restructuring the training grades contained in the earlier report. Instead it expressed the view that there are at present too many training grades in the hospital service and there should be an elision of the registrar and SHO grades into a single early specialist training grade and the registrar grade be eliminated in due course. The process of losing registrar posts or transferring them to the senior registrar or SHO grade would be gradual and there would need to be a parallel extension of the pre-registration period – which the General Medical Council was discussing (see below) – and a general expansion in the number of consultant posts. The response of the government to this and other recommendations was published in February 1986.[21] The Committee was criticised for not explaining how this elision of the training grades would help either to improve patient care or doctors' careers.

## Discussion document from the General Medical Council

Under the Medical Act of 1978 the Education Committee of the General Medical Council was given the function of coordinating all stages of medical education. At a conference on postgraduate training held by the Council in February 1982, the

Education Committee was encouraged to consider first the 'general professional training' stage which covers the grades of senior house officer and registrar. Late in 1983 the Committee circulated a discussion document, Basic specialist training, which contained proposals relating to the content of training given to most doctors in the two to three years after full registration, that is, whilst senior house officers in the hospital service.[6] (The proposals did not apply to vocational training programmes for doctors wishing to become general practitioners.)

A fundamental concern of the Committee expressed in the document was the practice of many newly registered doctors of restricting their experience to the specialty of their career choice, although the regulations for the higher qualifying examinations administered by the royal colleges and faculties permit candidates to spend six months or more in other disciplines after full registration. The years immediately after full registration should be a time for understanding the broad base of many diseases and disabilities and for appreciating the importance of being able to communicate with patients and colleagues. The Education Committee suggested, therefore, that in the two to three years following the pre-registration year doctors should extend the general training received in the pre-registration year and begin some specialist training. A period could also be spent in general practice. The trainees would occupy hospital posts for six to twelve months and the Committee hoped that the royal colleges and faculties together with employing authorities and the RPGMECs would identify a proportion of the training posts as being available for 'general experience' for doctors not yet committed to any particular specialty. The posts would form a pool of general, post-registration, vocational training posts that would allow the uncommitted trainee to develop his or her broad skills and at the same time, provide a suitable foundation if the trainee decided later to specialise in the discipline. 'Basic specialist training' as outlined in the discussion document is, therefore, very similar to 'general clinical training' which was proposed by the Social Services Committee in the 1981 report, except that the earlier proposal divided the training into defined periods of general training for one to two years followed by one year of specialist training.

The Education Committee did not explicitly state that the progress of the trainees should be monitored during basic specialist training but it suggested the regional deans and clinical tutors 'may have a special role in monitoring progress and contributing to decisions about the appointment of young doctors to the multipurpose posts'. The Committee also recommended that the deans should consider how best to ensure there was general career guidance available to all young doctors. The discussion document did not, however, contain any clearly formulated ideas on how to implement the basic specialist training proposals within the NHS nor were there any references to additional administrative resources that might be required.

The document on basic specialist training was circulated to bodies associated with medical education and training and written comments were submitted to the Education Committee. On the whole the proposals were welcomed provided they reflected a non-mandatory development. The Committee had to accept that proposals of this kind will not become effective unless the procedures for the higher qualifying examinations are modified to require all candidates to have experience outside the examination discipline, and there is a change in the negative attitudes of some appointment committees towards applicants with broadly-based experience.[22] The Education Committee is now looking at the content of general clinical training which trainees receive in the pre-registration year.

*Proposals from the ministerial working group*

The working group formed following the initiative from the Minister of State for Health, Mr Barney Hayhoe (referred to in detail on page 310), was concerned to bring hospital medical staffing into balance so its recommendations applied to both the training grades and the career grades (see pages 48 and 54). The recommendations for the training grades did not actually propose restructuring the grades apart from a long-term aim of reducing the length of time spent in the registrar and senior registrar grades to the point at which the two grades could be combined into a single higher training grade. Rather, the group recommended that posts in the registrar grade should be classified into two groups – regional posts and district posts – with the aim of meeting the pressing need for a satisfactory relationship between the number of graduates from UK medical schools entering the registrar grade to the expected number of senior registrar – and hence consultant – opportunities.[299]

Regional registrar posts with the contracts being issued by regional health authorities would be filled by doctors who were eligible to seek a consultant career in this country. The post holders would expect to spend around three years in the grade and would have to complete at least two years before appointment to senior registrar posts. District registrar posts would be reserved for overseas graduates in training and their contracts would be held with district health authorities. A central body – similar in function to the central body responsible for advising on national quotas of senior registrar posts (the Joint Planning Advisory Committee (JPAC) (see page 61)) – would be asked to advise the DHSS on quotas for regional registrar posts, by region and specialty. Regional health authorities acting on the advice of their medical manpower and education committees would identify suitable posts or rotations to fill the regional quota in each specialty. Those registrar posts not identified as regional posts would be designated as district registrar posts. Some posts might be converted to consultant posts in due course.

Training at SHO level, the group believed, should provide doctors with an opportunity for a period of general professional training in a variety of disciplines followed by some basic training in the specialty of their choice. Thus, the group did not wish to change the overall nature of training in this grade. It was proposed, however, that all senior house officers should receive formal careers counselling shortly after entering the grade and regularly thereafter. Trainees applying unsuccessfully for registrar posts in their chosen specialty should receive further careers counselling with a view to changing their specialty. Further basic experience at SHO level in the revised specialty of choice might then be needed. To accommodate this proposal, it might be necessary in the terms and conditions of service of hospital medical staff to extend the scale of annual salary increments payable to trainees spending longer periods in the SHO grade.

The working group was provided with technical assistance (such as the preparation of special analyses of information collected in the DHSS 30 September censuses of hospital medical staff). The document from the group did not, however, give any indication of the estimated numbers of registrar posts, and trainees (registrars and senior house officers), region by region, that would be affected by the proposals. Nor did the document identify those who would assume the responsibility for providing career counselling at intervals to senior house officers, and the administration and resources needed to ensure that there would be continuity in the nature of the advice provided to each trainee. The working group believed, however, that there is a pressing need to correct the career imbalances and it hoped that implementation of the proposals could begin by 1 January 1987.

# 3 Demand for hospital doctors

HOSPITAL DOCTORS EMPLOYED BY THE NHS

The demand for consultant and trainee doctors in NHS hospitals in England and Wales is centrally controlled and planned, although the regional, district and special health authorities* are the employing authorities. The DHSS supervises the deployment of hospital medical manpower in England in four main ways. First, it issues directives on the overall rates of expansion to be achieved in the career and training grades and the specialties in which new posts are to be concentrated. Second, it instructs the health authorities to prepare short-term programmes and longer-term strategic plans containing medical manpower target numbers which have been formulated in accordance with the policies contained in the directives. These plans are then submitted to the DHSS. Third, it sets regional target numbers of posts to be created annually in the pre-registration house officer grade. Finally, in consultation with advisory bodies, notably the Central Manpower Committee for England and Wales (CMC), the Department grants approval for new senior registrar and registrar posts to be advertised. In certain specialties this has applied also to the advertising of established posts that are vacant. The CMC also advises on the deployment of any new SHO posts in the special health authorities.† (The origins, terms of reference and procedures of the CMC are described in Volume II of the Short report.[4])

In Wales the overall responsibility for the NHS and thus for hospital medical manpower is held by the Secretary of State for Wales, and the task of advancing his policies rests with the Health and Social Work Department within the Welsh Office. The day-to-day administration of the service is undertaken by nine health authorities. Bids from the authorities for new consultant and senior training posts are approved by the Welsh Office on the advice of the Welsh Manpower Committee (WMC) and the Central Manpower Committee on which the Welsh Office is represented.

---

*SHAs were created in 1982 to manage many of the London postgraduate teaching hospitals previously managed by boards of governors. There are now eight including the Eastman Dental Hospital. Management of the remaining postgraduate teaching hospitals was transferred to teaching DHAs. Table 45 (page 278) identifies the SHAs and the postgraduate teaching hospitals that they administer.

† Until 1986, annual guide lines were issued on the establishment of new consultant posts in the various specialties. However, for the year 1987/88 a limit on the number of new posts available was set only in relation to mental handicap. RHAs and SHAs were still expected to inform the DHSS of amendments to their consultant establishment.

The following pages examine the trends in England and Wales since 1970 in the employment of consultants and doctors in training posts in NHS hospitals. The government's present policies relating to the hospital grades are also examined. The statistics used are from the 30 September censuses of hospital medical staff administered annually by the DHSS.[7] Honorary appointment holders working in NHS hospitals have been omitted from the tables and figures. Growth rates in the numbers of honorary doctors are discussed later in the chapter. (It should be noted that the tables on medical and dental staffing in the NHS which are published annually in *Health Trends*[23] include honorary appointment holders.)

### Trends in the expansion of the consultant and training grades 1970-84

In February 1982 the government published its response to the recommendations on the career structure and training of doctors made by the Social Services Committee of

Table 3  Number of NHS employed hospital doctors by grade, England and Wales, 1970–84

| 30 September | Consultants** | Senior registrars | Registrars | Senior house officers† | House officers | Total training grades |
|---|---|---|---|---|---|---|
| 1970 | 8957 | 1515 | 4503 | 5466 | 1938 | 13422 |
| 1971 | 9156 | 1638 | 4552 | 5741 | 2031 | 13962 |
| 1972 | 9411 | 1753 | 4647 | 6356 | 2077 | 14833 |
| 1973 | 9762 | 1843 | 4709 | 7045 | 2020 | 15617 |
| 1974 | 10106 | 1922 | 4653 | 7410 | 2129 | 16114 |
| 1975 | 10365 | 1977 | 5003 | 7995 | 2216 | 17191 |
| 1976 | 10687 | 2012 | 5081 | 8159 | 2353 | 17605 |
| 1977 | 10770 | 2097 | 5183 | 8479 | 2486 | 18245 |
| 1978 | 10961 | 2133 | 5387 | 8787 | 2634 | 18941 |
| 1979 | 11139 | 2236 | 5491 | 9360 | 2755 | 19842 |
| 1980 | 11355 | 2314 | 5550 | 9704 | 2814 | 20382 |
| 1981 | 11628 | 2437 | 5606 | 10007 | 2863 | 20913 |
| 1982 | 11828 | 2499 | 5752 | 10104 | 2866 | 21221 |
| 1983 | 12106 | 2603 | 5766 | 10204 | 2974 | 21547 |
| 1984 | 12408 | 2560 | 5715 | 10181 | 2927 | 21383 |

The header spans: *NHS-employed hospital doctors**

\* Doctors holding permanent paid (whole-time or part-time) appointments in NHS hospitals, and four special hospitals 1982–84.
\*\* Including senior hospital medical officers with allowance.
† Including junior hospital medical officers and post-registration house officers until these grades were withdrawn.

Source: DHSS 30 September censuses of hospital medical staff.[7]

Figure 4 Trends in the numbers of NHS permanent paid medical staff in the consultant and training grades in the hospital service, England and Wales, 1970-84

*3 Demand for hospital doctors*

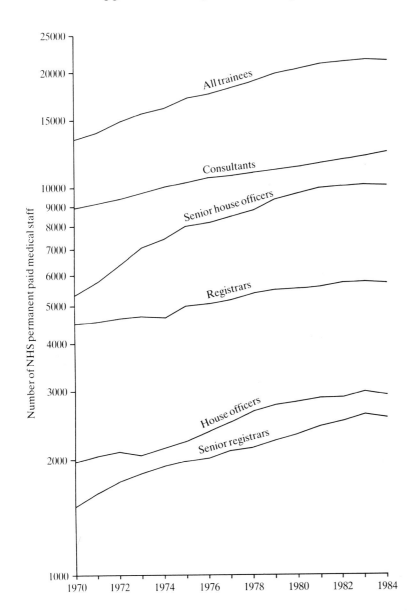

the House of Commons.[24] At the same time the DHSS issued a circular giving guidance on the implementation of two particular recommendations: that senior house officer numbers should stand still, and the imbalance between the numbers of consultants and the numbers of doctors in the training grades should be reduced. The regional health authorities were asked to draw up plans so far as resources permitted, to achieve a 1:1 ratio between consultant and training grade (senior registrar, registrar, SHO and pre-registration HO) numbers by 1988 and a doubling in the numbers of consultant posts by 1996.[25] Before considering the progress made so far in achieving this overall balance, the trends in the expansion of the numbers in the individual training grades and the consultant grades from 1970 are reviewed. These are shown in Figure 4 and the numbers on which the figure is based are given in Table 3.

a. *House officers* As indicated in Chapter 2, medical graduates from universities in the United Kingdom and doctors holding equivalent licentiate and membership (English Conjoint or Scottish Triple) qualifications awarded by the royal colleges of physicians and surgeons or by the Society of Apothecaries of London (refer to page 261), must have a total of twelve months pre-registration experience to become eligible for full registration with the General Medical Council. At least eight months are to be spent in hospital medical and surgical house officer posts that have been recognised as giving a satisfactory pattern of experience. (The term pre-registration house officer was simplified to house officer in the 1984 DHSS census tables. The revised name is used in the remainder of this chapter and in the following chapters.)

Figure 4 indicates that between 1970 and 1983 the number of house officers increased by over 50 per cent with the steepest rates of growth occurring between 1974 and 1979. The direction of the trend was determined by government policy. The Royal Commission on Medical Education recommended a substantial increase in the number of medical school places for British students[1] and in November 1970 the government responded by announcing that the number of entry places in medical schools and faculties in Great Britain should be increased to 4100 by the late 1970s.[26] Two new university medical faculties were due to accept their first students – Nottingham in 1970 and Southampton in 1971 – and the existing institutions increased their capacity over the decade. The government also agreed in 1970 to establish a medical faculty in the University of Leicester. (It opened in 1975.) Since 1980 the rate of expansion has plateaued and this situation will continue until late in the decade. The 1985-87 regional target numbers for HO posts set by the DHSS indicate a possible average annual growth rate of 1.5 per cent per annum[27] and the 1988 target number does not allow for any growth.[28] These posts will be filled by United Kingdom graduates and by a small but growing number of overseas qualified doctors (154 in 1984[29]) who requalify in the United Kingdom in order to obtain full registration with the GMC (see page 95).

b. *Senior house officers* In the 1982 circular which recommended freezing SHO numbers, it was suggested that the appropriate baseline for the size of the grade might be the number of doctors in the grade at the time of the 30 September 1981 census together with any substantive vacancies on that date.[25] The relevant census figures were 10,007 doctors in permanent paid NHS appointments and 136 or more vacant posts.[7] The regional health authorities were asked to cooperate by freezing their numbers of SHO posts but they could redistribute existing posts between specialties and geographical areas.

The need for intervention can be appreciated from Figure 4. Between 1970 and 1981 the numbers of doctors in the SHO grade increased by 83 per cent overall with the steepest rate of growth occurring in the first five years.* Consequently, by 1981 the ratio of NHS consultant posts to SHO posts was in the order of 1:0.9. The other more senior training grades had, from 1972 when the CMC first met, been subjected to central manpower controls. The SHO grade – apart from posts in the hospitals managed by boards of governors – was excluded because in the early 1970s, it was not generally recognised as a training grade. The situation has now changed and all SHO posts should have approval for training purposes granted by a royal college or faculty and be filled by trainee doctors.

Although the regional health authorities agreed in principle to freezing the SHO grade, there was a marginal increase in the number of senior house officers over the next two years equivalent to 1 per cent per annum. The first sign of a downturn in the numbers occurred in 1984 (see Figure 4). There were 23 fewer doctors in post on 30 September 1984 compared with the previous census. The total numbers in 1984 were 10,181 SHOs (excluding locums) in NHS posts and 139 or more vacant posts. Around 3500 of the 1984 doctors would have been in the hospital phase of their vocational training for entry into general practice (chapter 4). (Note: the ministerial working group which reported in mid-1986 proposed that the 'ceilings' on SHO posts should be lifted to allow a modest increase in the number of SHO posts in each region.[299] This would be necessary to accommodate the breadth of training required by some doctors for entry to the registrar grade (refer to page 39).)

c. *Registrars* In comparison with the other training grades, the registrar grade had the slowest rate of expansion between 1970 and 1984. Figure 4 indicates that the rate was steadily controlled throughout the period at an average annual increase of 1.7 per

---

*Until 1983 two other grades of junior doctors were recognised: post-registration house officer and junior hospital medical officer. (Entry to the JHMO grade was closed in 1964.) In the text and the tables, the annual numbers for these grades have been added to the figures for the SHO grade.

cent. The 1974 dip in the trend is probably artificial – in the 1974 reorganisation of the NHS, the newly created (and now disbanded) area health authorities (AHAs) assumed responsibility for the employment of registrars. It is thought that the number of registrars was under-recorded in the census for that year. What Figure 4 does not show, however, is the growth in the numbers of registrars with honorary appointments although they comprise less than 10 per cent of all registrars (page 55).

One reason for introducing central manpower controls over this grade was the relative imbalance between the numbers in the two senior training grades. In 1970 the ratio of senior registrars to registrars was 1:3.0. A paper published in *Health Trends* around that time showed that appropriately qualified registrars wishing to obtain an SR post in four medical specialties (diseases of the chest, cardiology, general medicine and neurology), or in eight surgical specialties or in obstetrics and gynaecology would face very strong competition.[30] The overall situation has improved. There are now 2.2 registrars in NHS posts for every senior registrar but there is still 'fierce' competition for SR posts in these 'popular' specialties.[23]

d. *Senior registrars*   There was a relatively steady average annual increase of 4.3 per cent in SR numbers between 1970 and 1983 (see Figure 4) and this growth rate contributed to the improvement in the ratio of senior registrars to registrars in NHS posts. In the 1984 census, however, there were 43 fewer senior registrars than in the previous year. The Central Manpower Committee's decision to close certain vacant posts in general medicine and general surgery was one reason for the decline, although the number affected by the decision was tiny.[31]

For planning purposes it is necessary to take account of both the number of persons with permanent paid appointments and the number of approved posts without a permanent holder. Table 4 gives the two sets of figures for senior registrars from 1980. It is noteworthy that in September 1984 there were many more vacant approved posts – almost all being whole-time posts – than at the same time in 1983. (The procedures for obtaining CMC approval to advertise vacant posts may have contributed to this situation.) So when the number of vacant posts in 1984 was added to the number of persons in post, it gave an overall annual increase of at least 1.2 per cent.

e. *Consultants**   Figure 4 shows that consultant numbers in NHS posts increased at a relatively constant rate from 1970 to 1984. The average annual increase across the period was 2.4 per cent and the rates for the last two years matched this average increase. When vacant posts are taken into account the rates of increase for 1982–83

---

* A small number of senior hospital medical officers with allowance are included in the consultant numbers (see page 53).

Table 4   Vacant posts as a percentage of all NHS posts, and percentage increases in all NHS hospital posts for consultants and senior registrars, England and Wales, 1980–84

| 30 September | Consultants | | | | Senior registrars | | | |
| | Vacant NHS posts* | NHS staff in post** | Vacant posts as % of all NHS posts† | Annual increase in all NHS posts† | Vacant NHS posts* | NHS staff in post** | Vacant posts as % of all NHS posts† | Annual increase in all NHS posts† |
| --- | --- | --- | --- | --- | --- | --- | --- | --- |
| | | | % | % | | | % | % |
| 1980 | 1163 | 11355 | 9.30 | | 235 | 2314 | 9.22 | |
| 1981 | 1070 | 11628 | 8.43 | 1.4 | 211 | 2437 | 7.97 | 3.9 |
| 1982 | 1050 | 11828 | 8.16 | 1.4 | 177 | 2499 | 6.61 | 1.1 |
| 1983 | 1003 | 12106 | 7.65 | 1.8 | 144 | 2603 | 5.24 | 2.7 |
| 1984 | 978 | 12408 | 7.30 | 2.1 | 220 | 2560 | 7.91 | 1.2 |

  * All approved whole-time and part-time posts without a permanent holder.
 ** Staff in post holding permanent paid whole-time or part-time appointments.
  † Vacant posts and posts filled with permanent paid staff.

Note: The 1984 census figures for vacant NHS posts are under represented because returns were not received from South East Thames RHA and Bristol and Western DHA.

Source: DHSS 30 September censuses of hospital medical staff.[7]


Table 5   DHSS approval for new consultant posts to be advertised 1978/79–1984/85

| Posts to be advertised in | Number of new posts |
| --- | --- |
| 1978/79 | 290 |
| 1979/80 | 297 |
| 1980/81 | 339 |
| 1981/82 | 325 |
| 1982/83 | 361 |
| 1983/84 | 364 |
| 1984/85 | 320 |

Source: On the State of The Public Health.[32]

and 1983–84 were still around 2 per cent – see column 4 in Table 4. This table also shows that the number of approved whole-time and part-time posts that were vacant at the time of each census since 1980 fell annually, although the 1984 figure is under-represented because returns were not received from one health region and a teaching health district.

As mentioned earlier, central manpower approval given on the advice of the CMC – and in Wales on the advice of the WMC – has had to be obtained before a new consultant post could be advertised. Table 5 shows that 364 consultant posts could have been advertised during 1983/84 and 320 posts in 1984/85. For some years there were limitations placed on the number of consultant posts created in certain specialties because of a shortage of trained senior registrars who would be eligible candidates. The specialties affected in 1983/84 were anaesthetics, geriatric medicine, radiology, accident and emergency, chemical pathology, histopathology, medical microbiology, mental handicap and forensic psychiatry.[32] By 1984/85, however, the situation had vastly improved and for the next few years it was only necessary to restrict approvals in the specialty of mental handicap.

*Correcting the imbalance between the consultant and training grades*

The progress made towards meeting the goals set in the 1982 health circular on career structure and training[25] has been slow. The circular recommended that the number of consultant posts be doubled by 1996. To achieve this target figure of approximately 25,400 whole-time and part-time posts, an average annual growth rate of around 3.3 per cent would be needed. In 1984/85, if this rate had applied, more that 440 new posts would have become available. Clearly, the current rate of expansion in consultant numbers falls well below this target rate.

Another goal in the circular, to achieve an overall 1:1 ratio between consultant and training grade numbers by 1988, also appears to be unrealistic at this point in time. Nineteen eighty-four was the first year in which there was not an increase in the total number of doctors in the training grades (see Figure 4). The imbalance between doctors in training posts and consultants was almost 9000, giving a rate of 1.7 junior doctors to each consultant.

Mindful of the very slow progress being made in altering the consultant/junior doctor ratio, the ministerial working group which reported in July 1986 (page 310) proposed the following measures to boost the rate of consultant expansion, especially in the acute specialties:

1. central funding to be provided for additional new consultant posts in general medicine and related specialties and in general surgery and traumatic and orthopaedic surgery;

2. senior registrar posts identified as surplus to training requirements to be converted to consultant posts;
3. registrar staffing within consultant firms to be reviewed prior to each impending consultant retirement with a view to converting a registrar post to a consultant post if appropriate on service grounds;
4. a scheme for early voluntary retirement of consultants, and arrangements to facilitate the partial retirement of consultants over 60 years, to be introduced.[299]

REGIONAL VARIATIONS IN NHS HOSPITAL STAFFING RATES

There are very wide variations in the number of NHS hospital doctors employed in the regions relative to the size of the regional populations. Table 6 shows the 30 September 1984 census figures for consultants and doctors in training grades (excluding honorary appointments) in each region and Wales. It also gives the regional rates of doctors per million population (based on the 1984 mid-year estimates prepared by the Office of Population Censuses and Surveys (OPCS) in these grades.[33] Account has not been taken of doctors who are employed in more than one region. The scattergram in Figure 5 shows the regional population rates for consultants related to the rates for trainees in the post-registration grades. In general, there is a positive relationship between the number of consultants employed in a region and the number of trainees ($r=0.676$, $p<0.01$).

The remarkable feature in the table is the very high level of staffing in the North East Thames region. The rate of NHS consultants employed per million population in 1984 was 321 and this was 52 per cent greater than the lowest rate of 211 which was in the Trent region. The rate was in the order of 230 per million in four regions – Yorkshire, Wessex, Oxford and West Midlands – and in South Western it was marginally higher at 235. For post-registration trainees (that is, excluding house officers the great majority of whom have provisional registration), the North East Thames figure of 467 per million exceeded the lowest regional rate (285 in Wessex) by 64 per cent. South West Thames and South Western also had relatively low rates of trainees (excluding house officers) – 305 per million.

The proportion of NHS consultants who hold part-time contracts varies geographically and this is one of the reasons for the imbalance in the regional staffing levels. Column 1 of Table 7 gives the percentage of NHS-employed consultants whose contracts are for nine sessions or less per week in each region. In 1984 there were more part-timers than whole-timers in the four Thames regions and in Oxford. When the population rates for consultants were recalculated using whole-time equivalent (WTE) figures (column 2, Table 7), the position of North East Thames compared to the other regions was not so extreme. It employed 36 per cent more WTE consultants per million population than Trent which had the lowest rate. Table 7 also gives the regional WTE rates for trainees (excluding house officers). Since there are relatively few part-time trainees except in the SR grade, the regional WTE rates in 1984 were only slightly lower than the rates for the combined training grades given in Table 6.

The major London undergraduate teaching hospitals are concentrated in three of the four Thames regions (North East Thames, five hospitals; North West Thames,

Table 6   National and regional numbers of NHS-employed consultants and doctors in hospital training grades, and rates per million population, 30 September 1984

| Health region | Number of NHS-employed doctors* | | | | | | Doctors per million population** | | | | | |
|---|---|---|---|---|---|---|---|---|---|---|---|---|
| | Con-sultants | Senior registrars | Registrars | SHOs | HOs | Total trainees (exclud-ing HOs) | Con-sultants† | Senior registrars | Registrars | SHOs | HOs | Total trainees (exclud-ing HOs) |
| Northern | 837 | 136 | 337 | 709 | 182 | 1182 | 270.6 | 44.0 | 109.0 | 229.2 | 58.8 | 382.1 |
| Yorkshire | 826 | 161 | 321 | 669 | 152 | 1151 | 229.5 | 44.7 | 89.2 | 185.9 | 42.2 | 319.8 |
| Trent | 972 | 234 | 480 | 927 | 241 | 1641 | 210.8 | 50.8 | 104.1 | 201.1 | 52.3 | 355.9 |
| East Anglia | 483 | 90 | 162 | 372 | 89 | 624 | 249.0 | 46.4 | 83.5 | 191.8 | 45.9 | 321.7 |
| North West Thames | 929 | 202 | 478 | 693 | 251 | 1373 | 267.6 | 58.2 | 137.7 | 199.7 | 72.3 | 395.6 |
| North East Thames | 1198 | 271 | 579 | 894 | 325 | 1744 | 320.5 | 72.5 | 154.9 | 239.1 | 86.9 | 466.5 |
| South East Thames | 1021 | 182 | 381 | 757 | 255 | 1320 | 284.0 | 50.6 | 106.0 | 210.6 | 70.9 | 367.1 |
| South West Thames | 789 | 117 | 310 | 475 | 154 | 902 | 267.1 | 39.6 | 104.9 | 160.8 | 52.1 | 305.4 |
| Wessex | 656 | 107 | 306 | 392 | 136 | 805 | 232.2 | 37.9 | 108.3 | 138.8 | 48.2 | 285.0 |
| Oxford | 557 | 130 | 273 | 408 | 123 | 811 | 231.6 | 54.0 | 113.5 | 169.6 | 51.1 | 337.2 |
| South Western | 734 | 121 | 232 | 603 | 174 | 956 | 234.9 | 38.7 | 74.2 | 193.0 | 55.7 | 305.9 |
| West Midlands | 1195 | 219 | 553 | 962 | 273 | 1734 | 230.9 | 42.3 | 106.8 | 185.9 | 52.7 | 335.0 |
| Mersey | 587 | 103 | 319 | 525 | 149 | 947 | 241.8 | 42.4 | 131.4 | 216.2 | 61.4 | 390.0 |
| North Western | 1082 | 193 | 412 | 1015 | 262 | 1620 | 270.7 | 48.3 | 103.1 | 254.0 | 65.6 | 405.3 |
| London postgraduate hospitals and special hospitals | 386 | 201 | 230 | 157 | 0 | 588 | — | — | — | — | — | — |
| Wales | 688 | 109 | 345 | 628 | 161 | 1082 | 245.1 | 38.8 | 122.9 | 223.7 | 57.4 | 385.4 |
| England and Wales | 12408 | 2560 | 5715 | 10181 | 2927 | 18456 | 249.3 | 51.4 | 114.8 | 204.6 | 58.8 | 370.9 |

* Doctors holding permanent paid (whole-time or part-time) appointments in the NHS hospital service and four special hospitals.
** Estimated home population, 30 June 1984.
† Including senior hospital medical officers with allowance.

Note: Some doctors are employed in more than one region.

Sources: DHSS 30 September 1984 census[7] and OPCS 1984 population estimates.[33]

Figure 5  Relationship between numbers per million population of NHS permanent paid consultants and trainee doctors (excluding house officers) in the hospital service in the English health regions and Wales, 1984

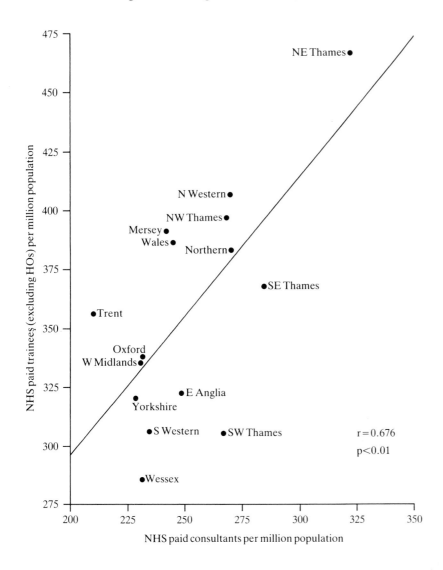

Table 7    Regional and national rates of NHS-employed consultants holding part-time contracts, and whole-time equivalent rates per million population for NHS-employed consultants and trainees (excluding house officers), 30 September 1984

| Health region | % of all NHS consultants* with contracts for 9 sessions or less  % | Whole-time equivalent consultants* per million population† | Whole-time equivalent trainees** per million population† |
|---|---|---|---|
| Northern | 27.5 | 253.2 | 372.8 |
| Yorkshire | 42.0 | 225.0 | 316.8 |
| Trent | 38.1 | 201.8 | 351.1 |
| East Anglia | 41.8 | 242.6 | 315.0 |
| North West Thames | 60.5 | 228.9 | 390.3 |
| North East Thames | 63.0 | 274.1 | 460.6 |
| South East Thames | 56.4 | 260.1 | 363.6 |
| South West Thames | 58.6 | 236.8 | 300.2 |
| Wessex | 44.5 | 221.9 | 278.9 |
| Oxford | 51.9 | 222.5 | 323.6 |
| South Western | 45.1 | 221.9 | 301.3 |
| West Midlands | 41.5 | 227.5 | 333.9 |
| Mersey | 39.4 | 231.1 | 386.8 |
| North Western | 42.7 | 260.8 | 402.3 |
| London postgraduate hospitals and special hospitals | 60.4 | — | — |
| Wales | 29.1 | 235.9 | 383.7 |
| England and Wales | 45.7 | 241.7 | 365.5 |

  \* Permanent paid consultants including senior hospital medical officers with allowance.
 \*\* Excluding house officers.
  † Estimated home population, 30 June 1984.

Sources: DHSS 30 September 1984 census[7] and OPCS 1984 population estimates.[33]

three hospitals; South East Thames, three hospitals). This helps to explain their relatively high to very high medical staffing levels. Also there are greater opportunities for clinicians to undertake private practice in the south east of England. But consultant and trainee levels similar to North West Thames and South East Thames are to be found in two of the regions in the north of England – Northern and North

Western. Indeed, the North Western region has the highest senior house officer level of all. What the regional figures mask, of course, are intra-regional variations particularly between teaching and non-teaching districts.

Included in Tables 6 and 7 are doctors employed in the eight London postgraduate teaching hospital groups administered by the special health authorities and four special hospitals for psychiatric patients requiring special security. The special hospitals, which are under the direct control and management of the Secretary of State for Social Services, employ relatively few doctors – 52 in 1984 of whom 29 were consultants or SHMOs with allowance and only six were trainees. (Rates per million population cannot be calculated for the SHAs because the London postgraduate teaching hospitals do not serve defined catchment areas.) What is noteworthy in Table 6 is the size of the figure for senior registrars: there were more NHS senior registrars in the postgraduate hospitals than in 11 of the regions including Wales in 1984. The high percentage figure for consultants with part-time contracts in Table 7 is in line with the rates for North East Thames and North West Thames. (Six of the eight SHAs are sited within the boundaries of these two regions.)

NON-TRAINING GRADES SUBJECT TO CLINICAL DIRECTION

There is another group of NHS hospital medical staffing grades: senior hospital medical officer, associate specialist, clinical assistant and hospital practitioner. They are non-training grades and appointment holders are subject to consultant clinical direction.

a. *Senior hospital medical officer*   The grade was established in the early 1950s for doctors who were not trainees and whose experience and standing did not justify appointment to the consultant grade. From 1959 to 1964 post holders could ask to be considered for an allowance which, if granted, made them nearly equal in status to their consultant colleagues. (Those occupying an approved consultant post could have their personal grading reviewed.) On the recommendation of a working party on medical manpower chaired by Sir Robert Platt[18] the grade was closed to new entrants in 1964 because of the closeness of its status to the consultant grade. By 1984 the number of doctors still working as senior hospital medical officers was relatively small although up-to-date statistics are not published. Those with an allowance are added to the statistics on consultants in the DHSS 30 September censuses. The number of SHMOs without allowance may be fewer than 50. (There were 62 in England and Wales in September 1980.[7])

b. *Associate specialist*   The SHMO grade was replaced by the medical assistant grade to which admission was normally restricted to doctors with two or more years of service as a registrar and who had worked in hospitals for three or more years since full registration. The grade was renamed 'associate specialist' in 1981 but the level of experience needed for appointment remained the same. Tenured posts are established on a personal basis for those who do not wish, or are not able, to complete higher training. Candidates are expected to have all or part of a higher qualification and to show reason why they are unable to proceed further to the consultant grade. Employing authorities require approval of the DHSS – granted on the advice of the CMC – to establish a post. In 1984 there were 982 associate specialists in England and Wales; few were under the age of 40, 44 per cent were women and over one-third of all doctors worked on a part-time basis.[7]

c. *Clinical assistants*   Around 7000 doctors, mainly general medical practitioners or women doctors who wish to work part-time, are engaged as clinical assistants on a sessional basis under paragraph 94 of the Terms and Conditions of Service of Hospital Medical and Dental Staff.[34] The maximum number of sessions for which a clinical assistant can be contracted with a health authority is nine. The contracts can be held indefinitely but more commonly they are given on a one to three-year renewable basis. There are no manpower controls over the number of clinical assistant posts and in 1985 there were suggestions in the medical press that health authorities were creating nine-session posts as a device to avoid the controls on new consultant and training posts.

d. *Hospital practitioner*   This grade is available only to general practitioner principals who have undertaken some appropriate training in the specialty concerned. It is a more highly paid grade than that of clinical assistant but the contractual commitment is limited to a maximum of five sessions or notional half days per week. Nearly 90 principals were employed in the grade in England and Wales in 1984.[7]

e. *Proposed intermediate-level service grade*   The ministerial working group (page 310) would like a new non-training grade introduced, but with strict controls to prevent its use at the expense of new consultant posts being created. The features of the grade would include a sessional (whole-time or part-time) contract, entry normally being direct from the SHO grade after a minimum of three years in the grade, appointment by competition to an advertised post, and regional manpower approval to be obtained before a post could be first established by a district. Post holders would be eligible for regrading to associate specialist, and they might compete for regional registrar posts. If such a grade was introduced then, the working group believed, there should be no further clinical assistant appointments of six sessions or more.[299]

A proportion of the doctors working in NHS hospitals are not employed directly by the health authorities (HAs). Rather, the HAs have issued an honorary contract to them to cover their hospital service. In the consultant grade, honorary contract holders are usually doctors employed as professors, readers or senior lecturers by universities with medical schools or faculties. At senior registrar or registrar level, honorary doctors may hold university teaching contracts as lecturers or tutors, or they can be employed on research contracts which are funded by the Medical Research Council (MRC) and by other research agencies, or by trust funds administered by special trustees and health authorities. Honorary contracts are also granted to doctors in supernumerary training posts or who are funded independently to carry out research. The procedures for issuing honorary contracts to junior doctors are discussed in chapter 14.

Naturally, the amount of time the majority of these doctors spend on NHS duties is limited. In the 30 September 1984 census there were 1534 honorary consultants in England and Wales but together they formed a WTE figure of 828.2; that is, overall they spent an average of 54 per cent of their time on NHS activities. The WTE rate for the 606 honorary senior registrars* was 340.1 and for the 401 registrars, the WTE rate was 257.8.[7] There are very few honorary doctors in the SHO and HO grades. Those that are appointed are usually on secondment from the armed services or they are NHS doctors employed temporarily as demonstrators or assistants in university departments.

*Trends in the expansion of the honorary consultant and training grades 1970–84*

Table 8 (columns 4–6) shows that in 1984, 11 per cent of all consultants working in NHS hospitals held honorary appointments. Moreover, this proportion has remained almost constant over the past decade. In contrast, the proportion of senior registrars who held honorary contracts grew steadily from 10 per cent in 1970 to 22 per cent in the years 1978 to 1980. It then fell slightly to 19 per cent over the next four years. Registrars with honorary appointments form a much smaller proportion of the total registrar numbers (7 per cent in 1984) and this proportion has changed relatively little since 1978. The fluctuations in honorary senior registrar and registrar numbers between 1981 and 1984 (columns 2–3 in Table 8) were probably caused by the cutbacks

---

* This number includes 43 honorary senior registrars in the Yorkshire region who were not covered by the 30 September 1984 census. (Yorkshire RHA, personal communication 1985) The 1984 number of NHS-employed and honorary senior registrars combined quoted elsewhere in the book includes these 43 doctors.

Table 8   Numbers of consultants, senior registrars and registrars holding honorary appointments, and honorary doctors as a percentage of all hospital doctors, England and Wales, 1970–84

| 30 September | Honorary doctors* | | | Honorary doctors as % of all hospital doctors** | | |
| | Consultant | Senior registrar | Registrar | Consultant† | Senior registrar | Registrar |
|---|---|---|---|---|---|---|
| | no | no | no | % | % | % |
| 1970 | 858 | 164 | 71 | 8.7 | 9.8 | 1.6 |
| 1971 | 925 | 193 | 104 | 9.2 | 10.5 | 2.2 |
| 1972 | 986 | 232 | 84 | 9.5 | 11.7 | 1.8 |
| 1973 | 1063 | 285 | 125 | 9.8 | 13.4 | 2.6 |
| 1974 | 1078 | 287 | 120 | 9.6 | 13.0 | 2.5 |
| 1975 | 1134 | 340 | 118 | 9.9 | 14.7 | 2.3 |
| 1976 | 1207 | 434 | 173 | 10.1 | 17.7 | 3.3 |
| 1977 | 1244 | 506 | 251 | 10.4 | 19.4 | 4.6 |
| 1978 | 1324 | 585 | 303 | 10.8 | 21.5 | 5.3 |
| 1979 | 1392 | 613 | 291 | 11.1 | 21.5 | 5.0 |
| 1980 | 1423 | 654 | 329 | 11.1 | 22.0 | 5.6 |
| 1981 | 1437 | 637 | 383 | 11.0 | 20.7 | 6.4 |
| 1982 | 1475 | 591 | 367 | 11.1 | 19.1 | 6.0 |
| 1983 | 1525 | 632 | 417 | 11.2 | 19.5 | 6.7 |
| 1984 | 1534 | 606†† | 401 | 11.0 | 19.1 | 6.6 |

&ast; Doctors holding honorary appointments in the NHS hospital service.
&ast;&ast; Doctors holding pernament paid and/or honorary appointments in the NHS hospital service.
† Including senior hospital medical officers with allowance.
†† Including the number of senior registrars in the Yorkshire region which was supplied by the Regional Health Authority.

Source: DHSS 30 September censuses of hospital medical staff.[7]

in the funding of the university budgets.[35] There are, however, reasons to suspect that not all junior doctors holding honorary contracts are covered in the annual censuses. This matter is discussed in chapter 14.

REGIONAL VARIATIONS IN RATES FOR HONORARY DOCTORS

The regional breakdown of honorary doctor numbers for 1984 is shown in Table 9 and

Table 9 National and regional numbers of honorary consultants and doctors in hospital training grades, and rates per million population, 30 September 1984

| Health region | Number of honorary doctors* | | | | Honorary doctors per million population** | | | |
| | Consultants | Senior registrars | Registrars | Total trainees† | Consultants | Senior registrars | Registrars | Total trainees (excluding HOs) |
| --- | --- | --- | --- | --- | --- | --- | --- | --- |
| Northern | 48 | 37 | 27 | 67 | 15.5 | 12.0 | 8.7 | 21.7 |
| Yorkshire | 48 | 43†† | 39 | 84†† | 13.3 | 11.9 | 10.8 | 23.3 |
| Trent | 120 | 67 | 21 | 89 | 26.0 | 14.5 | 4.6 | 19.3 |
| East Anglia | 46 | 17 | 17 | 35 | 23.7 | 8.8 | 8.8 | 17.5 |
| North West Thames | 201 | 58 | 38 | 98 | 57.9 | 16.7 | 10.9 | 27.9 |
| North East Thames | 278 | 81 | 37 | 122 | 74.4 | 21.7 | 9.9 | 32.6 |
| South East Thames | 154 | 21 | 68 | 93 | 42.8 | 5.8 | 18.9 | 25.9 |
| South West Thames | 95 | 25 | 2 | 34 | 32.2 | 8.5 | 0.7 | 10.5 |
| Wessex | 61 | 32 | 6 | 40 | 21.6 | 11.3 | 2.1 | 14.2 |
| Oxford | 81 | 37 | 41 | 85 | 33.7 | 15.4 | 17.0 | 34.9 |
| South Western | 58 | 26 | 16 | 42 | 18.6 | 8.3 | 5.1 | 13.4 |
| West Midlands | 77 | 33 | 18 | 54 | 14.9 | 6.4 | 3.5 | 10.4 |
| Mersey | 65 | 20 | 15 | 37 | 26.8 | 8.2 | 6.2 | 15.2 |
| North Western | 98 | 46 | 28 | 78 | 24.5 | 11.5 | 7.0 | 19.3 |
| London postgraduate hospitals | 266 | 78 | 30 | 109 | — | — | — | — |
| Wales | 70 | 24 | 12 | 36 | 24.9 | 8.5 | 4.3 | 12.8 |
| England and Wales | 1534 | 606†† | 401 | 1050†† | 30.8 | 12.2 | 8.1 | 21.1 |

\* Doctors with honorary appointments working in the NHS service.
\*\* Estimated home population, 30 June 1984.
† Including 36 honorary SHOs and 7 HOs.
†† Including the number of senior registrars for Yorkshire which was supplied by the Regional Health Authority.

Note: Some doctors with honorary contracts work in more than one region.

Sources: DHSS 30 September 1984 census[7] and OPCS 1984 population estimates.[33]

it is worth noting that there were more honorary consultants and senior registrars working in the London postgraduate hospitals than in all but one of the regions. Regional rates of honorary doctors per million population are also given in Table 9 while displayed in the scattergram in Figure 6 is the relationship between the rate for consultants and the rate for post-registration trainees in each region. In common with

Figure 6  Relationship between numbers per million population of consultants and trainee doctors (excluding house officers) with honorary appointments in the hospital service in the English health regions and Wales, 1984

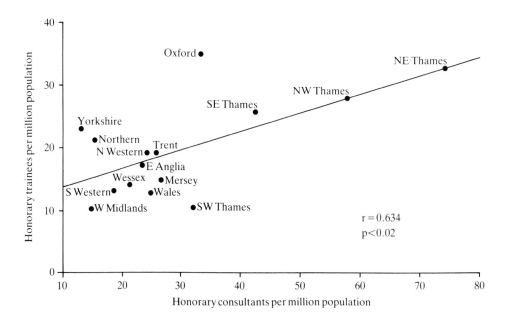

the pattern for NHS-employed doctors, a positive relationship exists between the number of honorary consultants in a region and the number of trainees with honorary contracts (r = 0.634, p‹0.02).

The variation between the regions in the population rates for honorary doctors is even more pronounced than the variation for NHS doctors. The presence of the long-established medical schools in three of the Thames regions (North East, North West and South East) has had a weighting effect on their honorary consultant rates, although the rates are far from uniform. The North East Thames figure of 74 honorary consultants per million population in 1984 was almost 75 per cent greater than the South East Thames figure. The situation in the West Midlands, Northern, Yorkshire and South Western regions was markedly different – they had fewer than 20 honorary consultants per million population. Nine regions including Wales had between 10 and 19 trainees (excluding house officers) with honorary contracts per million population and in six regions there were between 20 and 35 per million, with

Oxford and the Thames regions (apart from South West Thames) having the highest rates.

The regions, when preparing medical manpower targets for their short-term programmes and ten-year strategic plans have to take into account doctors holding permanent paid (whole-time or part-time) appointments and doctors with honorary appointments.[36] Thus regions with relatively high percentages of honorary WTE appointments in their total WTE hospital staffing levels are in a slightly advantageous financial situation since the salaries for honorary doctors are paid from non-NHS budgets (except in occasional circumstances when a university will employ a doctor on behalf of a health authority). This point is illustrated by a regional comparison for senior registrars. In North East Thames, honorary senior registrars made up 16 per cent of the overall WTE figure in 1984; in the Northern region the comparable figure was 11 per cent.[7]

*Honorary training posts and career prospects*

Around 1964 the DHSS set up a system to record information on medical staff appointed to NHS consultant and senior registrar posts. The purpose of this 'fields of recruitment' exercise was to monitor the competition for these senior posts. The system was discontinued in 1982/83. Information, including copies of candidates' curriculum vitae, was supplied by the employing authorities responsible for filling the

Table 10   Previous grade of candidates appointed to NHS consultant and senior registrar
posts in England and Wales, 1978/79–1981/82*

| | *Previous grade of successful candidates* | | | | | |
|---|---|---|---|---|---|---|
| | *Consultant appointments*** | | | *Senior registrar appointments*** | | |
| | *Consultant* | *Senior registrar†* | *Other* | *Senior registrar* | *Registrar†* | *Other* |
| | % | % | % | % | % | % |
| 1978/79 | 14.4 | 60.5 | 25.1 | 5.7 | 69.2 | 25.1 |
| 1979/80 | 11.7 | 64.7 | 23.7 | 8.3 | 69.7 | 22.0 |
| 1980/81 | 11.5 | 64.9 | 23.6 | 4.9 | 72.5 | 22.6 |
| 1981/82 | 12.4 | 67.4 | 20.2 | 7.5 | 69.2 | 23.3 |

* Based on returns received.
** Hospital medical specialties.
† Permanent paid NHS appointments.

Source: DHSS fields of recruitment annual returns.[23]

posts. The overall coverage over the years was in the order of 70 per cent[23,37] but the response rates for individual specialties could be above or below this figure and the teaching hospitals were under-represented. Summary tables derived from the returns were published annually from 1975 in *Health Trends*. The tables for the four years 1978/79 to 1981/82 showed a consistent pattern which suggested that doctors in honorary registrar posts may have enhanced promotion prospects.[23]

It was shown in Table 8 that no more than 5 to 7 per cent of all registrars were in honorary posts in the years 1978–82. The fields of recruitment data in Table 10 indicate, however, that during those years well over 20 per cent of new appointments to the SR grade were by persons who were not in permanent paid NHS appointments. A summary table covering 1979–83 in a 1984 article in *Health Trends* suggests, however, that the previous appointment of one-third of the doctors in the 'other' category in Table 10 was in a post overseas.[23] Many would have been British trainees gaining experience abroad. The survey of junior doctors employed in Bradford HA, and City and Hackney HA in 1984 found that 25 per cent of the senior registrars in both districts had been appointed from academic, research or other non-NHS employment.[11]

Honorary senior registrars may have less chance of obtaining a consultant post than their NHS colleagues. In 1982, 19 per cent of all the doctors in the SR grade were in honorary posts (Table 8) while 20 per cent of the consultant appointments made over the previous year were filled by doctors who were not in permanent paid NHS appointments, and the proportion had been higher in the previous three years (Table 10). However, the previous appointment of one-fifth of those appointed from outside the NHS between 1979 and 1983 was held overseas.[23]

Another analysis carried out by the DHSS using different data sources – and published in 1983 – found that of the senior registrars who were appointed to permanent paid NHS posts over 12 months in 1981/82, slightly under half (47 per cent) were not permanent paid registrars on 30 September 1981. The proportion of NHS consultants appointed in that year who were not permanent paid senior registrars at the time of the 1981 census was 38 per cent.[23]

Data on senior registrar appointments suggest that many of the doctors entering SR posts are academically well qualified. Indeed, when a chest and general medicine SR post in Trent was advertised in 1984, applications were received from 23 United Kingdom or Irish graduates of whom 12 had held a research post at registrar level, and 13 had obtained a doctorate or were working on a thesis.[38] A similar pattern of academic qualifications and experience was observed in the application documents of 49 candidates for a SR post in general surgery that was advertised in Wessex in 1982; 35 per cent had completed a thesis or were preparing one. When the post was readvertised three years later 66 persons applied and the level of research and academic attainment was even higher among the candidates.[39]

Honorary training posts (clinical lectureships, research fellowships, and so forth) are not subject to manpower controls. In recent years the DHSS and its manpower advisory committees have become increasingly concerned that an uncontrolled expansion in honorary posts could worsen the imbalance between the numbers of doctors in training and the permanent career outlets. So in July 1984 the Department circulated for discussion a document which proposed that a mechanism for the joint planning of training grade numbers be established. After consultations between the Department and the Welsh Office and the Joint Consultants Committee (JCC), the Committee of Vice-Chancellors and Principals of the Universities of the United Kingdom (CVCP) and the Medical Research Council, a small central committee – the Joint Planning Advisory Committee – was established. It is made up of representatives of the professions, academic and research interests, dental interests and the NHS, with coopted members and observers from the four health departments in the United Kingdom and from other bodies attending. Its remit is to advise the DHSS and the Welsh Office on the total number of posts required nationally in the training grades, both NHS and honorary, for specialty groupings commencing with the senior registrar grade. It is to advise also on quotas to be allocated jointly to the regional health authorities and their associated university or universities, to the special health authorities, to Wales and for research. The apportionment of the regional posts will, however, be determined by appropriate 'machinery' within the regions.[40] The Committee met for the first time in December 1985.

# 4  Demand for doctors in the community-based services

Other careers within the National Health Service for which the postgraduate education system trains doctors are general medical practice and community medicine. However, trainees usually spend two or more years in hospital training posts as part of the postgraduate training programmes for these specialties. Another group of doctors is employed in the community health service. There are no specialist training programmes available for this service but the matter is under review (see page 67). Finally, a relatively small group of doctors work as ophthalmic medical practitioners under the general ophthalmic service.

GENERAL MEDICAL PRACTITIONER PRINCIPALS AND TRAINEES

General practitioner (GP) principals hold individual contracts with the family practitioner committees (FPCs) and they act as independent contractors. Machinery exists, however, to control the setting up of new family practices, especially in areas considered to be 'over-doctored'; that is, where the average list size is 1700 patients or less. An independent body – the Medical Practices Committee – exercises this function in England and Wales. An allowance is available to a doctor if he or she practises in a 'designated' (under-doctored) locality. In 1983, a designated area was an area where the average list size was 2500 patients or more.[41]

In October 1984 there were 25,132 unrestricted principals in general practice in England and Wales and this figure was double the figure for NHS hospital consultants (12,408). The rate of expansion in general practitioner numbers between 1970 and 1984 was slower than for hospital consultants; the average annual percentage increase for unrestricted principals was 1.5 compared with 2.4 for consultants. Table 11 gives the numbers of unrestricted principals and the annual percentage increases across the 15-year period. There is another very small group of general practitioners who are restricted principals (180 in 1984). These doctors can only hold a list of limited size or provide a restricted range of services (maternity and/or family planning services). There is another small number of doctors employed as assistants by unrestricted principals (275 in 1984).[8] A report *General practice: a British success* published by the British Medical Association (BMA) contains a series of tables giving statistical trends for general practice manpower, list sizes and so forth.[41] Many of the statistics were collected in the surveys of general medical services in England and Wales conducted annually on 1 October by the DHSS.[8] The information is provided by the family practitioner committees.

Table 11    Numbers of unrestricted general practitioner principals
and annual percentage increase, England and Wales,
1970–84

4   Demand for doctors in
the community-based
services

| 1 October | Number of principals | Annual % increase |
|-----------|---------------------|-------------------|
| 1970 | 20357 | — |
| 1971 | 20633 | 1.4 |
| 1972 | 21044 | 2.0 |
| 1973 | 21266 | 1.1 |
| 1974 | 21510 | 1.1 |
| 1975 | 21667 | 0.7 |
| 1976 | 21837 | 0.8 |
| 1977 | 22100 | 1.2 |
| 1978 | 22363 | 1.2 |
| 1979 | 22696 | 1.5 |
| 1980 | 23184 | 2.2 |
| 1981 | 23701 | 2.2 |
| 1982 | 24217 | 2.2 |
| 1983 | 24719 | 2.1 |
| 1984 | 25132 | 1.7 |

Source: DHSS 1 October surveys of general medical services[8] (and, for
the years 1970–81, reproduced in General medical practice: a British
success[41]).

Entry into general practice as a principal within the NHS is regulated. From 16
August 1982, intending family doctors have been obliged to undergo a period of
'prescribed' training of at least three years, which includes one year at least spent as a
trainee general practitioner with an approved trainer. Alternatively, a doctor may
undergo medical training which is deemed to be 'equivalent' to prescribed experience.
Applicants for equivalent experience also spend one year in a training practice unless
there are exceptional circumstances.[42] Certificates of prescribed experience or equivalent experience are issued by the Joint Committee on Postgraduate Training for
General Practice (JCPTGP). The procedures for vocational training in general
practice are described in chapters 12 and 13.

Reliable data on the total number of trainees in hospitals wishing to enter general
practice are not obtainable from hospital medical staffing records.[11] Information only
exists on the number of trainees who are working with approved general practitioner
trainers, of whom there were 2610 in England and Wales in 1984 (see page 157).

Approximately 215 vocational training (VT) schemes provide training in three-year programmes and 730 trainees were in the general practice phase of these programmes during 1984. Another 1100 or more trainees were in general practice, having made independent arrangements to join a GP trainer. So on 1 October 1984 the total number of trainees in general practices was 1862. This number was 5 per cent higher than the number for the previous year (1769).[8] (Note that in some VT schemes, trainees spend time in general practice during the first and/or second year of their programme as well as in the third year.) Other trainees planning to enter general practice who are in NHS hospital posts on 30 September are covered by the annual census of hospital medical staff[7] but they cannot be separately identified.

At present the total number of unrestricted principals in England and Wales is increasing by 400-500 per year (Table 11). There is no compulsory retiring age for general practitioners, but if 4 to 5 per cent cease to practice each year because of death or retirement, the annual take-on rate of principals will be in the order of 1500-1700 although some will be principals re-entering general practice. (Five per cent of unrestricted principals are 65 years or older.[8]) In 1985, 2031 certificates of experience – 1513 for prescribed experience and 518 for equivalent experience – were issued by the JCPTGP to doctors throughout the United Kingdom who had undergone training with approved trainers.[43] (The total number of certificates issued in 1984 was 1762.) These various figures suggest that overall the 'supply' of newly trained general practitioners may now exceed the 'demand'. Certainly competition for vacancies in many geographical areas is becoming fierce. (New principals usually enter general practice by applying for a vacancy in an existing practice partnership or for a vacant single-handed practice or by establishing a new practice.)

## COMMUNITY MEDICINE SPECIALISTS AND TRAINEES

The specialty of community medicine and the career structure was established at the time of the 1974 reorganisation of the National Health Service. The specialty incorporated three established branches of medical activity: public health, including preventive medicine and health education; administration and planning of hospital services; and teaching and research in university departments and research departments.

Many medical officers of health chose to take early retirement after reorganisation in 1974 rather than apply for the newly created community physician posts at district, area or regional health authority level. This meant that there was a serious shortage of manpower within the specialty. Moreover, the level of recruitment over the remainder of the decade was insufficiently high to improve the general situation – there were never fewer than 100 vacant posts out of an establishment figure of around 730.[44] So in 1979 the DHSS, the Welsh Office and the profession set up a Joint Working Group to look at the recruitment situation in England and Wales. One recommendation made in the Group's report was that the rate of recruitment to the specialty should be doubled from its existing level to about 80 recruits a year. This rate would need to be sustained over 15 years.[44]

Three years later there was another reorganisation in the structure of the National Health Service. The area health authorities were abolished and with them the area community medicine posts. Also some health districts were restructured causing certain existing posts to be abolished and new ones created. About 60 area and district medical officer posts were lost.[9] (There are no posts equivalent to district medical officer (DMO) or specialist in community medicine (SCM) in the special health authorities for the London postgraduate hospitals.) A second wave of community physicians (79) were granted early retirement following the 1982 reorganisation.[32]

Table 12   NHS and honorary community medicine staff by grade, England and Wales, 1974–84

| 30 September | Regional/area/ district medical officers NHS paid*,** | Specialists in community medicine NHS paid* | honorary | Senior registrars and registrars NHS paid* | honorary | Senior house officers NHS paid* |
|---|---|---|---|---|---|---|
| 1974 | 274 | 257 | — | 20 | — | — |
| 1975 | 288 | 319 | 5 | 59 | — | — |
| 1976 | 283 | 327 | 13 | 76 | — | — |
| 1977 | 281 | 336 | 40 | 95 | 8 | — |
| 1978 | 279 | 324 | 45 | 104 | 13 | — |
| 1979 | 276 | 311 | 51 | 116 | 12 | — |
| 1980 | 267 | 319 | 53 | 126 | 15 | 6 |
| 1981 | 252 | 332 | 53 | 138 | 14 | 6 |
| 1982 | 195 | 306 | 52 | 172 | 14 | 15 |
| 1983 | 202 | 325 | 53 | 191 | 12 | 20 |
| 1984 | 196 | 299 | 53 | 212 | 11 | 39 |

  * Doctors holding permanent paid (whole-time or part-time) appointments.
** Including a tiny number of special salary scale staff (6 in 1984).

Notes:   i. Area medical officer posts were abolished in 1982 and the grade of district community physician was replaced by district medical officer.
ii. There is another grade, senior medical officer (community health) which is closed to new entrants. There were 43 in the grade in 1984.

Source: DHSS 30 September censuses of community medicine and community health service medical staff.[9]

Table 13   NHS community medicine posts without a permanent holder,
1980–84

| | NHS posts without a permanent holder | | |
|---|---|---|---|
| 30 September | *Area/district medical officer** | *Specialist in community medicine* | *Senior registrar and registrar* |
| 1980 | 21 | 124 | 50 |
| 1981 | 23 | 79 | 31 |
| 1982 | 21 | 120 | 20 |
| 1983 | 13 | 127 | 21 |
| 1984 | 18 | 108 | 11 |

* Area medical officer posts were abolished in 1982 and the grade of district community physician was replaced by district medical officer.

Source: DHSS 30 September censuses of community medicine and community health service medical staff.[45]

Table 12 gives the numbers of NHS and honorary doctors in community medicine in England and Wales from 1974. NHS posts without permanent holders are covered in Table 13. The establishment of NHS filled and unfilled career posts (regional medical officer (RMO), area medical officer, district community physician and SCM) recorded in the 30 September 1981 census of community medicine staff was 686; after reorganisation it fell and the lowest number of 621 was recorded in the 1984 census. Furthermore, 20 per cent of the 1984 posts were without a permanent holder at the time of the census.[9,45] More losses in the numbers of doctors in the career grades are likely to have been recorded in the 1985 census because when the new management structure for the National Health Service was implemented during 1984–85[46] a small number of specialists in this discipline were appointed as regional or district general managers.

On the training side in this specialty, unlike other specialties, trainees are appointed to a single training grade covering both registrar and senior registrar periods, although progression to SR posts is not automatic (page 175). The total number of NHS-employed senior registrars and registrars in 1984 was 212, nearly double the number for 1979 (Table 12), and the annual rate of growth in the last two years was 11 per cent in each year. The specialty started to appoint trainees in the SHO grade in 1980/81 and by September 1984 there were 39. (A handbook outlining the training for a career in community medicine has been prepared by the Faculty of Community Medicine (FCM).[47]) According to the annual reports from the Chief Medical Officer of the DHSS, during 1983 58 doctors were recruited to the specialty compared to 46 in 1982 and 53 in 1981.[32] So the goal of an annual take-on rate of 80 suggested by the Joint Working Group in 1979/80[44] is gradually being reached.

COMMUNITY HEALTH DOCTORS

There are no formal training programmes for doctors who enter the community health service, although the matter has been considered by various working parties or bodies over the past few years: by a joint working party set up in 1980, by six bodies representing general practice, paediatrics, community medicine and community health and each concerned with standards of training in child health[48], by a working party of the Community Health Doctors Subcommittee of the Central Committee for Community Medicine and Community Health that met in 1981[49], by the Joint Paediatric Committee of the Royal Colleges of Physicians and the British Paediatric Association in 1982[50], by a Faculty of Community Medicine working party in 1983 and, even more recently, by a small group of representatives of the Royal Colleges of Physicians, the Faculty of Community Medicine, the Joint Paediatric Committee, and the British Paediatric Association. One reason for the difficulty in obtaining a consensus over training requirements is the broad definition of community health and, in particular, child health. There are already various specialties which provide care for

Table 14 Community health medical staff holding permanent paid (whole-time or part-time) appointments by grade, England and Wales, 1980–84

| 30 September | Senior clinical medical officer | | Clinical medical officer | | Other medical officer and sessional clinical officer | | Total community health staff | |
|---|---|---|---|---|---|---|---|---|
| | Whole-time | Part-time | Whole-time | Part-time | Part-time* | WTE | Whole-time | Part-time** |
| 1980 | 619 | 394 | 676 | 926 | 2873 | 419.5 | 1301 | 4187 |
| 1981 | 628 | 435 | 710 | 899 | 2837 | 404.5 | 1338 | 4176 |
| 1982 | 627 | 455 | 715 | 880 | 3021 | 415.6 | 1344 | 4357 |
| 1983 | 618 | 494 | 715 | 819 | 3151 | 425.8 | 1334 | 4465 |
| 1984 | 614 | 477 | 719 | 784 | 3033 | 395.8 | 1337 | 4290† |

\* Including 6 whole-time doctors in 1980, 0 in 1981, 2 in 1982, 1 in 1983 and 4 in 1984.
\*\* Including 5 honorary doctors in 1980, 5 in 1981, 3 in 1982, 2 in 1983 and 3 in 1984.
† Part-time sessional contracts were held by 2686 doctors in 1984.

Source: DHSS 30 September censuses of community medicine and community health service medical staff.[9]

children and so the underlying problem is whether there is a role for community health as an independent specialty. Some health authorities are starting to integrate the community child health service with the hospital paediatric service and with general practice.[51]

Comparable statistics on doctors employed in the community health service in England and Wales are only available from 1980 (see Table 14). The service is dominated by persons working part-time. Three-quarters of the doctors hold part-time contracts and within this group around two-thirds work on a sessional basis with many of them doing less than one session per week. The officers with sessional contracts include doctors who are also principals in general practice. There is a preponderance of women doctors in this service. In the 30 September 1984 census of community health service medical staff[9] they comprised three-quarters of both the senior clinical medical officers and the clinical medical officers, and just under half of the sessional clinical officers.

To supplement the information collected in the annual census of community health service medical staff the DHSS undertook an ad hoc survey in May 1983.[51] Employing authorities in Great Britain were asked to make returns on staff holding whole-time or part-time appointments and on staff working regularly on a sessional basis. Four-fifths of the authorities responded. Seventy per cent of the total number of whole-time equivalent staff covered by the survey in England and Wales were working in child health, 14 per cent were in family planning, and the other areas of work included occupational health, environmental health and care of the elderly. Over 1400 general practitioners were surveyed; the great majority worked on a sessional basis, usually one session per week, with one-third of the sessions being in family planning. Some employing authorities reported that clinical medical officers of high calibre were now being recruited and generally the level of recruitment to the community health service was adequate.

OPHTHALMIC MEDICAL PRACTITIONERS

Ophthalmic medical practitioners (OMPs) are medically qualified doctors who hold prescribed qualifications which, together with their experience, have been approved by the Ophthalmic Qualifications Committee.* An applicant should hold an appointment with the health service with the status of consultant ophthalmologist or have held an appointment of appropriate seniority and experience in an approved ophthal-

---

\* Under The National Health Service (General Ophthalmic Services) Regulations 1974 for England and Wales. Statutory instruments 1974 no 287.

mic department for not less than two years. The Diploma in Ophthalmology awarded by the Royal College of Surgeons of England (page 132) or any approved higher degree or qualification should also be held. Once an application has been approved by the Qualifications Committee, the doctor can then apply for inclusion in the Ophthalmic List held by the FPC in the area in which the doctor wishes to practise. (There are three parts to the list – the first relates to OMPs, the second part to ophthalmic opticians and the third part to dispensing opticians.)

As contractors within the general ophthalmic service, OMPs undertake the testing of sight usually on a peripatetic basis, and having made arrangements with one or more dispensing opticians or ophthalmic medical centres to use their premises and equipment. A standard fee for each sight test is claimed from the FPC. The level of the fee is reviewed annually by the Review Body on Doctors' and Dentists' Remuneration (refer to page 71) and included in the fee is a nominal amount to cover the use of the facilities and other expenses. Some consultant ophthalmic surgeons and other experienced doctors working in hospital ophthalmology departments are also ophthalmic medical practitioners.

# 5 NHS salaries, allowances and hours of work

It could be argued that one reason why trainee doctors invest their own resources – time and money – in postgraduate education is the prospect of having enhanced earning opportunities within the NHS when a career grade appointment – hospital consultant, general practitioner principal, specialist in community medicine – is eventually obtained. This proposition is explored using a time series which compares the minimum salaries for the hospital consultant/SCM grade and the individual training grades in the years 1975–85 with the situation in 1975.

Table 15 gives in the first five columns the minimum whole-time salaries for the grades excluding allowances from 1 April in each year or, in 1985, from 1 June. The sixth column shows the general index of retail prices with the base year of 1975 equal to 100. The remaining columns give the minimum whole-time salaries adjusted to 1975 prices. There are two points of note about the table. First, 1975 was chosen as the base year because in that year hospital doctors received a major pay award of 30 per cent for junior doctors and 39 per cent for consultants. Second, the information in the table is not the same as that in the tables on the short-term movement in doctors' total earnings presented in the annual reports of the Review Body on Doctors' and Dentists' Remuneration.[54-57] An index from the New Earnings Survey based on earnings for full-time non-manual men excluding medical practitioners is used, and the earnings given for doctors include allowances such as Class A and B units of medical time (UMTs) payable to junior doctors. (Increases in allowances are usually calculated at rates similar to the rate of increase in the basic salaries; UMT payments are related to the basic salary.) However, although the data bases used in Table 15 and the earnings tables in the Review Body reports are not the same, the trends derived from the differing data bases are in line.

Nineteen eighty and 1985 were the only years in which the minimum salary in real terms for hospital consultants and the career grades in community medicine exceeded the 1975 salary level (Table 15). The 1980 situation was brought about by a 31 per cent pay rise in current prices between 1979 and 1980. The level fell again over the next two years but then rose annually, with the most substantial increase occurring between 1984 and 1985 (4.4 per cent in current prices). Hospital consultants are, of course, eligible for certain allowances such as domiciliary consultation fees, although the frequency of individual doctors doing domiciliary visits varies widely within the same specialty.[58] Doctors of consultant status in hospitals and community medicine may also receive one or more distinction awards during their careers. There are four

Table 15   NHS minimum whole-time basic salaries for hospital consultant and training grades 1975–85, in current prices and 1975 prices

| 1 April | Minimum whole-time salaries* in current prices | | | | | General index of retail prices** | Minimum whole-time salaries* in 1975 prices | | | | |
|---|---|---|---|---|---|---|---|---|---|---|---|
| | Consultants | Senior registrars | Registrars | Senior house officers | House officers | | Consultants | Senior registrars | Registrars | Senior House officers | House officers |
| | £ | £ | £ | £ | £ | | £ | £ | £ | £ | £ |
| 1975 | 7536 | 4818 | 4152 | 3663 | 2859 | 100.0 | 7536 | 4818 | 4152 | 3663 | 2859 |
| 1976 | 7848 | 5130 | 4464 | 3975 | 3171 | 116.5 | 6736 | 4403 | 3832 | 3412 | 2722 |
| 1977 | 8056 | 5235 | 4569 | 4080 | 3276 | 135.0 | 5967 | 3878 | 3384 | 3022 | 2427 |
| 1978 | 9528 | 5460 | 4767 | 4257 | 3420 | 146.2 | 6517 | 3735 | 3261 | 2912 | 2339 |
| 1979 | 11859 | 6720 | 5829 | 5175 | 4164 | 165.8 | 7153 | 4053 | 3516 | 3121 | 2511 |
| 1980 | 15510 | 8770 | 7600 | 6700 | 5400 | 195.6 | 7929 | 4484 | 3885 | 3425 | 2761 |
| 1981 | 16440 | 9330 | 8070 | 7100 | 5730 | 218.8 | 7514 | 4264 | 3688 | 3245 | 2619 |
| 1982 | 17370 | 10050 | 8730 | 7700 | 6180 | 237.7 | 7308 | 4228 | 3673 | 3239 | 2600 |
| 1983 | 18440 | 10670 | 9260 | 8170 | 6560 | 248.6 | 7418 | 4292 | 3725 | 3286 | 2655 |
| 1984 | 19470 | 11260 | 9770 | 8620 | 6920 | 261.0 | 7460 | 4314 | 3743 | 3303 | 2651 |
| 1985† | 21460 | 12380 | 10760 | 9480 | 7610 | 275.6†† | 7787 | 4492 | 3904 | 3440 | 2761 |

* Excluding additions to basic salary where appropriate, such as Class A and B units of medical time for trainees.
** Annual average.
† From 1 June.
†† Based on an average index for nine months January–September 1985.

Sources: DHSS advance letters on pay and conditions of service[52] and Monthly Digest of Statistics.[53]

categories of award – A+, A, B and C – and in June 1985 the B award was £10,970 and the A award £19,200.[52] These awards are for meritorious service and currently there is about a 70 per cent chance of a consultant receiving an award by the time of retirement.[57]

The minimum salaries in real terms for the four training grades have never returned to the 1975 level. (Trainees in community medicine and general practice are employed on the same basic scales as trainees in hospital.) There was, however, a restructuring in the Class A and B UMT rates payable to registrars, senior house officers and house officers in 1983 (see below) and these allowances now compensate in part for the erosion in the minimum salary levels relative to 1975.

The Review Body on Doctors' and Dentists' Remuneration receives evidence from the departments of health in the United Kingdom, the professional associations and from representatives of NHS regional management, the chairman of the Central Advisory Committee on Distinction and Meritorious Service Awards and from individual practitioners. In its annual deliberations on all aspects of remuneration for doctors and dentists taking any part in the NHS the Review Body has to take into account any government guidelines on pay limits in the public sector, and cash limits set for the NHS. Moreover, the Review Body is an advisory body only and the government does not always accept its recommendations.

UNITS OF MEDICAL TIME

Since 1976, junior hospital doctors and dentists have been employed on contracts which cover a standard working week of 40 hours plus a further commitment for duty which is determined by the employing authority to meet the needs of the service. Both the standard working week and the further commitment for duty are expressed in 'units of medical time' (or UMTs) of four hours. Thus the standard working week of 40 hours for which a doctor receives a basic salary is equivalent to 10 UMTs. There are classes of UMTs available for additional duties. Class A is payable for additional hours worked or for 'standing by' in hospital or at home as if the doctor was based in hospital. Class B UMTs apply if the doctor is 'on call' outside the hospital to give telephone advice and to make non-urgent or voluntary visits to the hospital. Recent research has shown, however, that there are few instances of B UMTs being allocated in contracts for the registrar grade and below.[59]

### Survey of junior doctors' hours of work

In 1981 the Review Body on Doctors' and Dentists' Remuneration asked the Office of Manpower Economics (OME) to conduct a survey of junior doctors' and dentists' working hours to enable it to review the system of payment for additional UMTs worked. At that stage the average number of contracted hours for trainees was in the order of 90 a week – a situation causing deep concern to both the juniors and the Review Body.[54]

The survey covered a representative sample of about 900 junior doctors and dentists in 16 health authorities in Great Britain and there was an 88 per cent response rate. The trainees were asked to make continuous diary recordings over a period of seven days. The surveyed doctors and dentists were on average contracted for 89 hours per week, and spent on average 84 hours on duty. When on duty, the average hours actually worked were about 55. These average figures concealed, however, substantial variations between the different grades and specialty groupings. In general, as the grades increased in seniority, the average number of hours spent on duty and the proportion of duty time spent working were reduced. For example, senior registrars recorded on average 46 hours working out of 78 hours on duty per week, while for house officers the average was 63 hours working out of 89 hours on duty. In the specialty groupings the average weekly hours on duty ranged from 62 in mental illness to 101 in traumatic and orthopaedic surgery, while the average hours worked ranged from 42 for mental illness to 70 in orthopaedic surgery.[55] (On behalf of the Review Body the OME repeated the survey of hospital trainees' hours of work in November 1985 (see page 77).)

The Social Services Committee of the House of Commons in its 1980/81 inquiry into medical education had also expressed concern over the number of hours worked by junior doctors. It recommended that the contracted week should be reduced initially to a maximum of 80 hours, and that the government should study different patterns of shift work and work sharing between different firms in a district.[4]

The combined weight of concern and evidence from the various bodies prompted the government to take two steps. One was to request employing authorities to eliminate rota commitments for junior hospital staff which were more onerous than 1 in 2, and to restrict the number of rotas more onerous than 1 in 3. The second step was to introduce from 1 April 1983 revised rates of remuneration to hospital doctors in the registrar grade and below for contracted Class A UMTs (page 78). (Senior registrars and registrars in community medicine and doctors in the general practice phase of vocational training do not qualify for Class A and B UMT payments. They are eligible instead for an out-of-hours duties allowance equivalent to 15 per cent of basic salary. Payments to senior house officers in community medicine for out-of-hours commitments are based on their availability throughout the year.)[51]

*The system for allocating Class A and B UMTs*

Before commenting on the directives to restrict onerous rota commitments, the system for converting rota arrangements into Class A and B UMTs is outlined. The reference used is the report of a study into the allocation of UMTs in health districts in the Oxford and South Western regions which was carried out by the Management Advisory Service (MAS) in 1982.[59,60]

The distribution of Class A and B UMTs depends on the number of junior medical staff available to share a rota to provide 24-hour daily cover for the patients of one or more clinical firms. Account has to be taken of expected absences from duty by the members of the rota for study leave and annual leave and for regular commitments such as teaching and administrative duties. Junior doctors with honorary contracts can be included in a rota and receive appropriate Class A UMT payment either directly or indirectly from the health authority. Senior medical staff may also join the rota but without receiving additional reimbursement if they are consultants. Associate specialists are eligible for an extra duty allowance.

The calculation of the basic rota is as follows: there are 168 hours in a week which

Table 16   Expected allocations of units of medical time (UMTs) in relation to the number of doctors on rota

| *Expected UMTs with no allowance to cover leave because locums are employed* | | *Expected UMTs with allowance to cover leave of colleagues* | | |
| --- | --- | --- | --- | --- |
| *Number of doctors on rota* | *Expected UMTs per doctor per week* | *Number of doctors on rota* | *Expected UMTs per doctor per week* | |
| | | | HOs | *Other training grades* |
| 2 | 16 | 2 | 18* | 20*,** |
| 3 | 11 | 3 | 12 | 13 |
| 4 | 8 | 4 | 9 | 10 |
| 5 | 7† | 5 | 7 | 8 |
| 6 | 6† | 6 | 6 | 7 |
| 7 | 5† | 7 | 5 | 6 |
| 8 | 4 | 8 | 5 | 5 |

\* Staff working a 1 in 2 rota should be given the option of electing whether they will cover the leave of colleagues.

\*\* A doctor contracting to cover the absence of a senior registrar should receive 19 UMTs because senior registrars have less study leave than other training grades.

† Since the total number of allocated UMTs is 35 or 36 when five to seven doctors are in a rota, it is better if the doctors are contracted prospectively to cover each colleague's absences.

Source: Management Advisory Service report.[60]

represent 42 UMTs. All NHS employed staff in the rota are considered to be on duty for the standard 40-hour working week of 9 am to 5 pm Monday to Friday (or part thereof if employed part-time). This represents 10 UMTs leaving 32 UMTs to be covered by the on-call rota for nights and weekends. The 32 UMTs are divided equally among the number of staff in the rota and they are payable in whole numbers. If the rota members are contracted to cover the expected absences of colleagues rather than having the employing authority appoint locum cover, additional weekly UMTs are allocated to compensate for the extra hours of duty during these absences.

Table 16 gives the expected number of additional UMTs to be paid according to varying numbers of doctors sharing a rota. This table of 'norms' was used by MAS in its survey of UMT allocations and it gives figures both for doctors whose contracts do not commit them to cover for absent colleagues and for doctors who receive extra UMTs for this purpose. It shows that doctors working a 1 in 2 rota are eligible for between 16 and 20 additional UMTs according to their grade and whether they are contracted to cover the leave of colleagues. A 1 in 3 rota gives an allocation of between 11 and 13 UMTs per doctor. Until recently it has also been possible for doctors to be committed to a rota arrangement more onerous than 1 in 2.

## Allocations of UMTs in hospitals and districts

The study carried out in the Oxford and South Western regions relied on district medical officers supplying MAS with information on the number and grade of the junior posts in each specialty within each hospital, the UMT allocations with explanatory notes for the firms within the specialties, and a description of the rota arrangements for the firms.[60] Since a considerable amount of detail was required, the researchers were willing to extract items from copies of contracts to reduce the workload falling on the DMOs if they did not have the full range of information readily to hand. Comprehensive information was provided by the districts in the two regions by November 1982. The returns for each hospital and district were then compared with the expected UMT allocations by rota size shown in Table 16. Also, the variations between the actual UMTs awarded in the districts and the expected allocation were costed using the current basic salary scales.

From these data MAS observed that there were variations in the number of junior staff on duty during each on-call period within a firm or specialty within each hospital. This meant that when the rota commitments were converted into UMTs, doctors in the same grade and specialty received differing Class A allocations. Taking HO posts as an example, the majority were in rotas of 1 in 3 which is equivalent to 11–12 UMTs. But in a few hospitals the house officers worked 1 in 2 rotas and received 16–18 UMTs. The survey team found in at least 20 hospitals that the total number of Class A UMTs allocated to the registrar, SHO and HO grades exceeded the expected number; in four hospitals the weekly excess was greater than 50 UMTs. It was also observed that in some hospitals locums were being employed even though the junior doctors were contracted to cover absent colleagues.

## Memoranda with instructions to reduce rota commitments

During the time of the MAS study the DHSS had been consulting with the professions on how best to make progress in reducing rota commitments to the acceptable level of 1 in 3. These discussions followed from a conference held on this matter in February 1982. Finally in November a memorandum was issued (PM(82)37) requesting each district to establish a small working party to review rota arrangements and to try, if possible, to eliminate all commitments more onerous than 1 in 2 by March 1983. Also, the working parties were to rearrange any 1 in 2 rotas so that the commitments were no more onerous than 1 in 3.[61] This memorandum was followed up in June 1983 by an advance letter which announced changes in the terms and conditions of service of junior medical and dental staff to prohibit regular rota commitments more onerous than 1 in 2.[62]

Working parties were set up in the districts to review and revise demanding rota commitments, and representatives of the trainees were involved in the discussions. However the progress made was slower than hoped for in the 1982 circular. (It had asked that, wherever possible, practitioners appointed after 1 August 1983 and a substantial proportion of those continuing in post at that date should have rota commitments no more onerous than 1 in 3.)[61] For example, when the fieldwork for the study on the feasibility of establishing a national information system on training grades was done early in 1984 it was found that one-third of the trainees in City and Hackney, a London teaching district, were receiving Class A UMT allocations for rotas more onerous than 1 in 3 and in the Bradford district in Yorkshire the proportion was close to a quarter.[11]

There were two main reasons for the difficulties experienced by the working parties in meeting the timetable set by the DHSS. The first was the reluctance of some trainees in post to have their UMT allocations reduced. This was understandable because the financial losses could be considerable (see page 79). But these doctors would, in due course, complete their contracts and be replaced. The contracted UMTs for the new appointments could then be calculated according to the revised rota commitments. The second reason for the working parties' difficulties lay in the differing nature of the specialties. Certain specialties carry a heavier burden of emergency or call-out work than others, although the overall staffing levels across the specialties may be similar. Thus, many district working parties found that there were logistical problems in reducing the rotas to 1 in 3 in these heavy burden specialties. In the South Western region, for example, half the region's districts with 1 in 2 rotas stated that the changes required were quite impractical.[63] At the same time health authorities were being discouraged from employing external locums and this was an additional complication.

The district working parties had been asked to report on their progress and so these difficulties were drawn to the attention of the DHSS. It responded in January 1985 by issuing another memorandum (PM(85)1) offering further detailed guidance.[64] When reviewing the remaining rotas that were more onerous than 1 in 3 the working parties could apply different rules if the posts were in specialties regarded as carrying a heavy burden of call out: general medicine, paediatrics, obstetrics and gynaecology, anaesthetics, and the surgical specialties of general surgery, paediatric surgery, traumatic and orthopaedic surgery, cardio-thoracic surgery, neurosurgery and plastic surgery. Although under the terms and conditions of service it was now inappropriate for a trainee to have a regular rota commitment more onerous than 1 in 2[62], there were still doctors – usually in the senior grades – with this level of commitment in a few districts. The new memorandum recommended, therefore, that in these districts the working party should report on such arrangements to the district health authority and if the authority did not find the recommendations acceptable it could put the case to a regional panel for advice. Junior doctors and dentists could also appeal to the regional panel. These were new panels to be established by the regional health authorities and the membership was suggested as consisting of the regional medical officer, the regional postgraduate dean or deputies, a consultant and two juniors.[64]

Considerable progress has been made across the country to reduce junior doctors' contracted hours to a maximum of 88 per week on average. However, the target level recommended by the Social Services Committee of a maximum of 80 hours is still a long way from being achieved. The 1984 Review Body on Doctors' and Dentists' Remuneration was told that between November 1982 and August 1983 there had been a 15 per cent reduction in the number of posts in England with rotas more onerous than 1 in 3 and more reductions were planned. However, the proportion of posts with rotas more onerous that 1 in 3 was still over 20 per cent. There were also considerable regional variations in the improvements achieved. A major obstacle to progress had been the need in many instances to provide cover in a district at two or more hospital locations which could be miles apart.[57] Moreover, the time spent in negotiation by clinicians and administrators within districts was incalculable. Some disputed rota arrangements had even been referred to the British Medical Association for guidance. The results of the 1985 survey of junior doctors' hours of work (published in the 1986 report from the Review Body) were in accordance with the movement to reduce rota commitments. In general, doctors were being contracted for fewer hours per week (around three hours less) than in 1981.

By working less onerous rotas, trainees now have more time available for private educational activities. There is, though, an element of 'catch 22' in this situation. At least one professional body is anxious that the shorter working hours may have adverse effects on clinical training. The experience of junior staff might fall below a minimal acceptable level. As for the trainees, there could be some who feel that the loss of earnings under the revised rota arrangements (see below) is not really compensated by the increase in time available for private study and research.

*Remuneration for UMTs*

It was mentioned on page 73 that one outcome of the OME survey of hours on duty

Table 17    Gross payment per annum for one UMT calculated on
the minimum basic salary for each grade, June 1985*

| Grade | *One Class A**
UMT per annum* | *One Class B†
UMT per annum* |
|---|---|---|
| | £ | £ |
| House officer | 289 | 76 |
| Senior house officer | 360 | 95 |
| Registrar | 366 | 108 |
| Senior registrar | 371 | 124 |

  * The minimum basic salary for each grade is given in Table 15.
 ** Payable at 38% of standard rates for house officers and senior house
     officers, at 34% for registrars and 30% for senior registrars.
  † Payable at 10% of standard rates for all grades.

Table 18    Gross salary of a doctor employed on a minimum basic
salary* (10 standard UMTs) plus 13 Class A UMTs**,
June 1985

| Grade | *Gross salary
per annum* |
|---|---|
| | £ |
| House officer | 11367 |
| Senior house officer | 14160 |
| Registrar | 15518 |
| Senior registrar | 17203 |

  * The minimum basic salary for each grade is given in Table 15.
 ** 13 Class A UMTs is the expected allocation for a 1 in 3 rota to all but
     the HO grade, and where an allowance is included to cover leave of
     colleagues (see Table 16).

and hours worked by hospital junior staff was the introduction of revised rates of
remuneration for Class A UMTs payable to the registrar grade and below. From 1
April 1983, Class A UMTs have been paid at 38 per cent of the standard rate for
UMTs (3.8 per cent of the basic salary) for senior house officers and house officers, 34

per cent of the standard rate (3.4 per cent of basic salary) for registrars, and 30 per cent of the standard rate (3.0 per cent of basic salary) for senior registrars. Previously all grades had been paid at 30 per cent. Class B UMTs are payable to all the grades at 10 per cent of the standard rate or 1 per cent of the basic salary.

Table 17 gives the gross payment per annum of one Class A UMT and one Class B UMT for each grade calculated according to the June 1985 minimum basic salary. For senior house officers, registrars and senior registrars the Class A UMT rate lay between £360 and £371. The rate for house officers was lower at £289. In Table 18 the gross salary of doctors receiving the minimum basic salary and payment for 13 Class A UMTs in each grade has been calculated. This is the UMT rate payable to senior house officers, registrars and senior registrars working a 1 in 3 rota and covering absent colleagues (see Table 16). House officers qualify for 12. If Table 18 is compared to Table 15, it can be seen that 13 Class A UMTs increase the basic salary of senior house officers and house officers by 49 per cent; the increase for registrars is 44 per cent, and for senior registrars, 39 per cent. For those doctors eligible for 18 to 20 Class A UMTs because they work on a 1 in 2 rota, their basic salaries are enhanced by around 72 per cent if they are house officers or senior house officers, by 65 per cent if registrars and 57 per cent if senior registrars. (Until June 1985 – when the basic salaries for consultants were raised substantially – it was not uncommon for a senior registrar who had been in the grade for three or more years to be earning a gross salary which exceeded the basic salary of a newly appointed consultant.) It is understandable from these figures for gross salaries why total support was not given by all trainees to the reviews of rota arrangements.[57] Whether the reduced rota commitments will give rise to higher levels of educational attainment in, for example, the higher qualification examinations administered by the royal colleges and faculties, it is too soon to judge.

## 6  Occupational medicine, Public Health Laboratory Service, Prison Medical Service and Armed Services

Information on the numbers of medically qualified persons employed by government departments and agencies, the nationalised industries and in the private sector is fragmentary in nature. Some of these doctors are not undertaking clinical activities; a proportion are in administration or research. Since sources of statistical material on doctors employed outside the NHS are limited in availability, this chapter deals only with doctors practising occupational medicine and with doctors in the Prison Medical Service which is administered by the Home Office and in the medical services of Her Majesty's (HM) Forces – the Royal Navy, Army and Royal Air Force. There is also a section on the Public Health Laboratory Service (PHLS), although this service is incorporated in the NHS. The information on the numbers of prison medical officers was provided by the Medical Directorate of HM Prison Service and the Defence Medical Services Directorate of the Ministry of Defence supplied the statistics on the three defence medical services.

A general introduction to the employment opportunities for medical officers in various government departments – the DHSS, the Health and Safety Executive, Home Office, Scottish Home and Health Department, Welsh Office and Ministry of Defence – is included in a book *Careers in medicine* that was prepared by the Council for Postgraduate Medical Education in England and Wales.[65] The openings in the DHSS, for example, span a wide range of responsibilities, including administration, environmental health and advice on the medical aspects of war pensions and industrial injuries. Entrants may have initially trained and practised in any of the disciplines in the hospital service, in community medicine, general medical practice or occupational medicine. The book on careers also has sections on career opportunities in the armed services and in various overseas services – Overseas Development Administration (ODA), Voluntary Service Overseas and the medical missionary service.

DOCTORS PRACTISING OCCUPATIONAL MEDICINE

The Faculty of Occupational Medicine (FOM) was established in 1978 by the Royal College of Physicians (of London) but training programmes in the specialty of occupational medicine had been recognised since 1974. The specialty is concerned with all aspects of the two-way relationship between health and work which arise in every type of employment – agriculture, fishing, mining, manufacturing, and the service industries such as transport, education and health.[66] The membership of the Faculty in 1985 was made up of over 1250 fellows, members and associates in the United Kingdom and over 200 based overseas (Dr P J Taylor, personal communication 1985). Around 6 per cent of the United Kingdom members were women. More than 850 of the UK members work full-time and it is thought by the Faculty that they form the great majority of full-time occupational physicians in the country. The members who work part-time form a small minority of doctors – perhaps 2000 – engaged on a part-time basis in occupational health activities. Many of the non-members are general practitioner principals who are doing sessions in factories and for the prison service, police, education services and other public bodies and private employers. Another group of 'part-timers' are women with domestic responsibilities. They may do sessions for local branches of companies employing large numbers of staff in the service industries and retail trades.

Doctors may join the Faculty after obtaining the higher qualification of associateship and the regulations for this examination and the qualification of membership are given in chapter 9. The Board of the Faculty may also elect to membership persons who have made notable contributions in the field of occupational medicine. To prepare general practitioners and other doctors wishing to work in occupational medicine on a part-time basis the Faculty has developed the syllabus of introductory training courses lasting not less than 30 hours to be mounted by local course organisers. The courses will provide an introduction to the subject, act as a stimulus to further training and provide a course of tuition suitable for doctors appointed under the health and safety regulations.[67]

The United Kingdom, unlike many Western European countries, does not have a nationally integrated occupational health service. The Medical Division of the Health and Safety Executive and the Executive's field force, the Employment Medical Advisory Service, give advice on health and safety to the various inspectorates in the Executive and to managers, trades union officials and employees who seek information. Many large private and nationalised industries have their own occupational health service and numerous medium-sized organisations employ part-time occupational physicians. But in general there is an uneven distribution in the availability of services to employees. This matter was of concern to the Select Committee on Science and Technology of the House of Lords when it considered occupational health and hygiene services in 1983. The published report contains a comprehensive overview of the provision of occupational health services in the United Kingdom.[68]

The Faculty of Occupational Medicine presented written evidence to the House of Lords select committee and included was a table giving a breakdown of its membership in Great Britain according to the types of industry in which the doctors worked.[69] This information is reproduced in Table 19 and it shows the wide variety of occupational activities covered by the specialty. The industry orders employing the largest numbers of faculty members are public administration and defence (apart from HM

Table 19    Membership of the Faculty of Occupational Medicine active in Great Britain by
type of industry, March 1983

| Industry order* | | Full-time | Part-time | Total |
|---|---|---|---|---|
| I | Agriculture, forestry and fishing | 4 | — | 4 |
| II | Mining and quarrying | 83 | 13 | 96 |
| III | Food, drink and tobacco | 26 | 21 | 47 |
| IV | Coal and petroleum products | 9 | 1 | 10 |
| V | Chemical and allied | 61 | 22 | 83 |
| VI | Metal manufacture | 30 | 8 | 38 |
| VII | Mechanical engineering | 8 | 10 | 18 |
| VIII | Instrument engineering | 5 | 2 | 7 |
| IX | Electrical engineering | 19 | 12 | 31 |
| X | Shipbuilding | 2 | 1 | 3 |
| XI | Vehicles | 40 | 5 | 45 |
| XII | Metal goods | 4 | 8 | 12 |
| XIII | Textiles | 5 | 3 | 8 |
| XIV | Leather and fur | — | — | — |
| XV | Clothing and footwear | — | 2 | 2 |
| XVI | Bricks, pottery, glass and cement | 5 | 1 | 6 |
| XVII | Timber and furniture | 1 | 1 | 2 |
| XVIII | Paper, printing and publishing | 4 | 7 | 11 |
| XIX | Other manufacturing | 11 | 6 | 17 |
| XX | Construction | 2 | 2 | 4 |
| XXI | Gas, electricity and water | 25 | 8 | 33 |
| XXII | Transport and communication | 96 | 13 | 109 |
| XXIII | Distributive trades | 10 | 2 | 12 |
| XXIV | Insurance, banking and finance | 3 | 3 | 6 |
| XXV | Professional and scientific | 78 | 48 | 126 |
| XXVI | Miscellaneous services | 6 | 1 | 7 |
| XXVII | Public administration and defence (excluding HM Forces) | 125 | 37 | 162 |
| HM Forces | | 147** | — | 147 |
| No main industry | | 47 | 38 | 85 |
| All active members | | 856 | 275 | 1131 |

  * Standard Industrial Classification used by the Department of Employment.[70]
 ** All medical officers in HM Forces who are members of the Faculty of Occupational Medicine are full-time
    employees of their respective service. Not all, however, practise occupational medicine exclusively. Those who did
    in 1985 numbered 66; 23 in the Royal Navy, 13 in the Army and 30 in the Royal Air Force. (Defence Medical
    Services Directorate, personal communication 1985).

Source: Faculty of Occupational Medicine.[69]

Forces), HM Forces, and professional and scientific. The public administration and defence order includes doctors in the Health and Safety Executive who act as consultants to industry and doctors from the armed forces who are Ministry of Defence personnel. Occupational medicine is a recognised specialty in all three armed services and, as the footnote to Table 19 indicates, in 1985 there were altogether 66 medical officers practising occupational medicine exclusively. Other faculty members in the armed services also provided primary medical care. (Some responsibilities for occupational health are held by all medical officers in the three services.) Within the professional and scientific order in Table 19 are physicians employed in academic departments and research units and persons working in educational services and the NHS.

Since the numbers of persons engaged in the industry orders given in Table 19 vary widely, the Faculty calculated the relationship between the number of members in

Table 20 Membership of Faculty of Occupational Medicine active in Great Britain 1983 related to the number of persons in employment in each industry order

| *Persons in employment per doctor** | *Industry orders*** |
|---|---|
| Less than 10,000 | HM Forces†; coal and petroleum products; mining and quarrying; chemical and allied; metal manufacture |
| 10,000–19,000 | Public administration and defence (excluding HM Forces); gas, electricity and water; vehicles; transport and communication; other manufacturing; food, drink and tobacco |
| 20,000–49,000 | Instrument engineering; electrical engineering; professional and scientific; bricks, pottery, glass and cement; textiles |
| 50,000–99,000 | Metal goods; mechanical engineering; shipbuilding; paper, printing and publishing; agriculture, forestry and fishing |
| 100,000 and over | Timber and furniture; distributive trades; clothing and footwear; insurance, banking and finance; construction; miscellaneous services |

  * Part-time doctors are counted as half.
 ** Standard Industrial Classification used by the Department of Employment.[70]
  † When the number of medical officers in HM Forces who were working exclusively in occupational medicine in 1985 (see footnote to Table 19) is related to the total number of persons in the services, the rate is still considerably less than 10,000 persons in employment per doctor.

Source: Faculty of Occupational Medicine.[69]

each order and the number of persons employed in the order as recorded by the Department of Employment. (Part-time faculty members were counted as half.) In Table 20 the industry orders have been grouped according to the sizes of the employment rates per doctor. What is noteworthy is that the orders with the lowest rates – less than 10,000 per doctor, and 10,000-19,000 per doctor – tend to be ones that are or have been nationalised (coal, steel, gas, electricity, water, transport, post and telecommunications, but not shipbuilding), or in which there are high levels of investment by major international companies (chemicals, petroleum products, vehicles, and food and drink).

The career opportunities in this branch of medicine are considered by the Faculty to be good. A high proportion of current members and fellows working full-time are aged 50 years or more and so vacancies caused by retirement will occur. There may not, however, be many more new full-time jobs created. New part-time positions are likely to become increasingly available. New regulations from the Health and Safety Executive on, for example, the control of substances hazardous to health (COSHH) which could come into effect in 1987, may stimulate the setting-up of new posts because they may contain requirements for health surveillance.

PUBLIC HEALTH LABORATORY SERVICE

The Public Health Laboratory Service provides a national microbiology service for the diagnosis, control and prevention of communicable diseases. It also develops applications of biotechnology mainly in the health field. The Service is administered by the PHLS Board and around 80 per cent of the Board's annual income is advances from the DHSS (£32.8 million in 1983/84). Advances are received also from the Welsh Office (£1.4 million in 1983/84) and grants are provided by organisations such as the Medical Research Council and the World Health Organization.[71]

The Service has 52 regional and area laboratories distributed throughout England and Wales and 24 reference and special laboratories or units most of which are grouped in the Central Public Health Laboratory in Colindale, north London or at the PHLS Centre for Applied Microbiology and Research at Porton Down in Wiltshire. Nearly all the regional and area laboratories are situated in or are closely associated with hospitals, providing them with their routine clinical microbiology service and with a reference service when specialised expertise, techniques and facilities are required. The laboratories also serve general medical and dental practitioners, doctors caring for the health of communities and officers responsible for environmental health and for surveilling food and drink. Monitoring the distribution of communicable diseases in the community is carried out in a special unit at Colindale – the PHLS Communicable Disease Surveillance Centre. The surveillance of the effectiveness and safety of many of the immunisation programmes in current use and evaluation of new immunisation procedures is undertaken by the Epidemiological Research Laboratory. The Service has an applied research and development programme with activities being undertaken in nearly every laboratory, and it is involved also in overseas collaborative research programmes and reference services and in consultative and advisory work for international organisations.

The great majority of staff are non-medically qualified scientific officers. Of the medically qualified staff, slightly over 100 in 1984 were consultants and the other doctors numbered around 50.[71] They were employed under NHS terms and conditions of service for hospital medical and dental staff and received the same rates of pay.

PRISON MEDICAL SERVICE

There are more than 100 prison establishments in England and Wales and their facilities include hospitals which provide ambulatory treatment and inpatient treatment and care to inmates. Visiting consultants in, for example, medicine, surgery, orthopaedics and ophthalmology, hold regular sessions at some of the large establishments. Psychological medicine is an important discipline and there are psychotherapeutic units employing part-time specialists in selected centres. The number of males admitted to establishment hospitals in 1983 was around 36,700 and the number of

Table 21  Medical officers by grade in the Prison Medical Service, England and Wales, on 1 April 1984

| Grade | Number of officers |
|---|---|
| Principal medical officer | 4 |
| Senior medical officer | 24 |
| Medical officer | |
| full-time | 64 |
| part-time | 74* |
| Total | 166 |

* 54 worked less than 10 hours a week in the Service.

Source: Medical Directorate, Prison Medical Service (personal communication 1985).

females was nearly 4900. About 1400 males and 250 females were transferred to NHS hospitals. Inmates can also be referred to NHS outpatient clinics – around 15,900 males and 1800 females attended in 1983.[72]

The majority of prison establishments are served by part-time medical officers who are usually general practitioners. At all large establishments – prisons, borstals or remand centres – one or more full-time medical officers are engaged in clinical medicine, court work and supervising the establishment's hospital and nursing staff. The smaller establishments are grouped for the purposes of medical administration under a full-time senior medical officer. The officers in the large establishments also work with a senior medical officer. The most senior grade is principal medical officer. Table 21 gives the numbers of medical officers by grade who were in the service in England and Wales on 1 April 1984. There were 166 altogether of whom 92 were full-time officers.

DEFENCE MEDICAL SERVICES

Each of the three armed services – the Royal Navy, Army and Royal Air Force – has its own medical service offering postgraduate training in most hospital specialties, general practice, occupational medicine including aviation medicine in the Royal Air Force, and community medicine in the Army and Royal Air Force. There are very close relations between the medical services and the National Health Service. The three services rely on the NHS to provide hospital posts for some of their trainees. This happens regularly in the house officer grade. There are about 35 approved pre-registration posts in the Ministry of Defence hospitals in England and Wales[73] but the total number of provisionally-registered doctors with commissions exceeds this figure. At the senior level, all trainees in the senior specialist grade, which equates reasonably closely with the NHS senior registrar grade, spend one or more years in NHS training posts.

Needless to say, standards of training in the service specialties including vocational training for general practice are the same as those in NHS specialties. The hospital training posts and other training posts are inspected and approved by the royal colleges, faculties and higher training committees (chapters 16 and 17). When the regulations for vocational training in general practice were introduced, arrangements for 'selecting' training posts in armed services hospitals for vocational training were made with three regional postgraduate medical education committees, namely Wessex for the Royal Navy, South West Thames for the Army and Oxford for the Royal Air Force.[74] The three services are represented on higher educational bodies such as the royal colleges and faculties and the Council for Postgraduate Medical Education in England and Wales.

Trainees are encouraged to obtain higher qualifications and to enter specialist training programmes. Some doctors obtain higher qualifications and training in more than one specialty, for example in occupational medicine and general practice. This gives them multiple career opportunities if they leave the service young enough to start a second career. Commissions vary in length. In the Army, for example, if a person joins the Royal Army Medical Corps (RAMC) as a medical cadet after the second year of training as a medical student, he or she is committed to serving for a short service commission of six years starting from the date of joining for duty as a fully registered practitioner. Alternatively, a doctor who is already fully registered can join on a short service commission of three years. The doctor may then apply to have the commission extended for a period of up to eight years or converted into a special regular, or regular commission. The regular commission is for those who intend to remain in the RAMC up to the age of 60 whereas the special regular commission is a pensionable commission lasting 16 years. On retirement a doctor can start a second career in civilian practice.[75]

Each of the medical services mounts courses in a variety of specialties. Some courses are open to members of the other services and even to civilians; for example, the Army's courses for the examinations for membership of the Royal College of General Practitioners. The Army has its own Institute of Postgraduate Medical Studies incorporating the Royal Army Medical College and the Queen Elizabeth Military Hospital. The departments in the Institute cover pathology, preventive medicine and medical entomology, military psychiatry, military medicine, military surgery, general practice and dental science.[76]

Table 22   Numbers of hospital consultants, senior specialists and specialists in the Royal Navy, Army and Royal Air Force, April 1985

| Grade | Royal Navy | Army | Royal Air Force | Total |
|---|---|---|---|---|
| Consultants | 59 | 119 | 84 | 262 |
| Senior specialists | 13 | 68 | 32 | 113 |
| Specialists | 24 | 37 | 29 | 90 |
| Total | 96 | 224 | 145 | 465 |

Source: Defence Medical Services Directorate, Ministry of Defence (personal communication 1985).

The names and qualifications, rank and date of promotion to the rank of all medically qualified officers in each medical service are published regularly in the 'List' for the respective services, but the lists do not distinguish between officers who are in clinical practice and officers whose roles are primarily administrative. In 1982-83 the total number of medical officers on the lists was close to 1250.[77-79] However, Table 22 gives the numbers of doctors in the three services in April 1985 who were hospital consultants and trainees. Consultants equate exactly with NHS consultants in qualifications, experience and selection procedures. The senior specialist and specialist grades equate reasonably closely with the senior registrar and registrar/SHO grades. Almost half the total number were in the Army, 31 per cent were in the Royal Air Force and 21 per cent in the Royal Navy.

A feature worth noting in Table 22 is the relationship between the numbers in the consultant and training grades. For every senior specialist and specialist in 1985 there were two or more consultants. So, overall, the ratio of hospital consultants to post-registration trainees was 1:0.8. This was lower than the target recommended for the NHS hospital service by the Social Services Committee of the House of Commons in 1981.[4] Moreover, vacancies occur relatively more frequently in the consultant establishment in the armed services than in NHS hospitals owing to doctors retiring after 16 years of service. This pattern of early retirement must help to maintain the consultant/trainee ratio. It would be interesting, therefore, to learn how the services developed their medical staffing structure.

# 7    Demand from international markets

The international demand for British postgraduate medical education is met in three main ways. The most obvious is the movement of overseas qualified doctors to the United Kingdom for the purpose of receiving further training and education. Most enter hospital training posts or supernumerary posts but some come only to undertake educational courses. A high proportion of the overseas doctors now arriving in Britain must return to their home country in due course. The outward movement of United Kingdom trained doctors is another method by which this demand is met. It is happening at two levels. Senior clinicians are acting as advisers to countries developing medical education systems along the lines of the British model. For instance, the 1984 annual report of the British Council showed that 315 specialists travelled overseas in an advisory capacity on behalf of the Council during 1983/84.[80] At the same time, trainees – usually senior registrars – are spending time in overseas hospital posts. In the anaesthetics specialty it is common for senior registrars to undertake part of their training abroad and, in doing so, these doctors also benefit from the training system of the host country.

Providing overseas qualified doctors with access to the British educational system while still resident abroad is the third way of fulfilling the demand. Several of the royal colleges and faculties hold examinations for the first part of the higher qualifications in overseas centres. The colleges send representatives out to act as examiners. Some even allow overseas trained doctors to take the final examination for a higher qualification without having held a training post in either the United Kingdom or the Republic of Ireland (see chapter 9).

THE MOVEMENT OF OVERSEAS DOCTORS TO THE UNITED KINGDOM AND
IMMIGRATION AND REGISTRATION REGULATIONS

Until 1 April 1985 there were no restrictions on the numbers of overseas qualified doctors and dentists who could enter the United Kingdom. This professional group had been exempt from immigration controls that applied to other immigrants except those from countries in the European Economic Community (EEC). From April 1985, however, newly arrived doctors and dentists from non-EEC countries wishing to practise in the UK have had to be covered by a work permit obtained by their prospective employer. The employer has had to prove there is no suitable candidate for the post from the resident labour force in the United Kingdom or from other member states of the European Community. Alternatively, any doctors or dentists intending to set up in independent practice have needed £150,000 to invest in it and be able to demonstrate a genuine need for their services and investment, and that they will be working full-time and new full-time employment for people already settled here will be created.[81]

An exemption exists in the immigration regulations for overseas doctors and dentists wanting to undertake postgraduate training in or attached to a hospital or to go on educational courses. Permission to enter the United Kingdom for permit-free training will be granted in the first instance for a period of 12 months. The individual may then apply to the Home Office for an extension of stay and, amongst other things, the Home Office will wish to establish whether the applicant is working towards a recognised postgraduate qualification. Four years is the total time allowed for permit-free training and the time can be accumulated in the course of more than one visit. A work permit is needed after four years.[81] Overseas graduates of United Kingdom medical schools must also apply for permit-free status once the pre-registration year is completed if they wish to undergo postgraduate training.

Once admitted to the United Kingdom no doctor is legally entitled to practise medicine in the National Health Service without being registered with the General Medical Council, and there are levels of linguistic skill and clinical experience which must first be reached. The regulations applying to doctors from countries in the European Community are different from those applying to doctors from non-EEC countries. The GMC publishes statistics on the numbers of doctors who are granted all forms of registration in its annual reports[29] and *The Medical Register*.[82] These indicate the approximate size of the international demand for training in the United Kingdom. There is also a demand from several countries which is unmet at the present time. This issue is discussed on page 101.

### Doctors from non-EEC countries

Two types of registration – full or limited – may be granted to doctors newly arrived from non-EEC countries. If a doctor holds a primary medical qualification recognised under section 19 of the Medical Act 1983 and has acquired medical and surgical experience equivalent to 12 months or more as a resident house officer, he or she is eligible for full registration. (Should the doctor lack sufficient clinical experience, provisional registration can be applied for instead. Twenty-five overseas qualified doctors were granted provisional registration in 1984 – see column 1 in Table 23.)

For nearly a century arrangements could exist between the governments of the United Kingdom and individual overseas countries with a medical system whereby each country's responsible body (the GMC in the United Kingdom) recognised for registration purposes the primary medical qualifications of the other country that

Table 23    Numbers of overseas qualified doctors* who registered with the General Medical Council (excluding re-registrations**) by type of registration, 1979–84

| | Provisional registration | Full registration | | | Limited registration | | Total |
|---|---|---|---|---|---|---|---|
| | Doctors holding qualifications recognised under sections 18 or 19† | Doctors holding qualifications recognised under sections 18 or 19†,†† | Doctors on Visiting Overseas Doctors' List | Doctors eligible under EEC regulations | Doctors who passed the PLAB test | Doctors who were exempt from the PLAB test | |
| 1979 | 34 | 1456 | 30 | 124 | 1399 | | 3043 |
| 1980 | 197 | 2990 | 41 | 134 | 1100 | 582 | 5044 |
| 1981 | 74 | 1027 | 35 | 187 | 1094 | 577 | 2994 |
| 1982 | 44 | 774 | 42 | 265 | 960 | 513 | 2598 |
| 1983 | 36 | 867 | 41 | 317 | 690 | 439 | 2390 |
| 1984 | 25 | 929 | 39 | 316 | 643 | 480 | 2432 |

   * Excluding doctors who qualified in the Republic of Ireland.
  ** Excluding doctors whose limited registration was renewed or who transferred from temporary to limited registration or from limited to full registration.
   † Section 18 of the Medical Act 1978 or section 19 of the Medical Act 1983.
  †† Some of these doctors could have held provisional registration in the previous year(s).

Sources: The Medical Register[82] (columns 1 and 4) and General Medical Council annual reports[29] (columns 2, 3, 5 and 6).

were of a satisfactory standard. By the late 1970s, primary medical qualifications of nearly 90 universities in a wide range of countries were recognised for full registration by the GMC. However, on 1 December 1980 (when the relevant sections of the Medical Act 1978 came into force) the number of overseas primary qualifications recognised by the Council was drastically reduced. In 1985/86 only 22 universities in 'old' Commonwealth countries awarded recognised primary qualifications. (The relevant universities are listed annually in *The Medical Register*.[82]) The medical schools are subjected to annual reviews and newly established university medical schools may apply to have their qualifications recognised. (The arrangements between the Council and overseas universities are described in more detail on page 263.)

Column 2 in Table 23 shows the numbers of doctors with recognised overseas primary qualifications who were granted full registration in the years 1979–84. The peak year was 1980 when 2990 were fully registered under the reciprocal arrangements. However, after the revision of the system the figures were substantially reduced – 929 in 1984. Australia is the country from which the largest proportion of doctors who register in this way originate – 43–45 per cent in 1983 and 1984. The other countries in descending order of doctor numbers are South Africa (around a quarter), New Zealand, Hong Kong, Malaysia, Singapore and the West Indies.

There is another section in the 1983 Medical Act which allows the GMC to grant full registration but it is on a temporary basis for no more than 12 months. Visiting specialists can apply and, if successful, they join the Visiting Overseas Doctors' List. Column 3 in Table 23 indicates that the number granted full registration each year is small – 39 in 1984.

The majority of the newly arrived doctors from non-EEC countries who register with the GMC are granted limited registration. The aggregate duration of time over which limited registration can be held is five years. Thus the maximum period that a doctor can hold limited registration is 12 months longer than the permit-free period for postgraduate training under the immigration regulations. Initially limited registration is granted for up to 12 months followed by a period or periods of up to four years. To be eligible a doctor must satisfy the GMC that he or she has been selected for employment, has obtained overseas medical qualifications which are acceptable for the purpose of limited registration (the list is extensive), is of good character, has the necessary knowledge of the English language, and has the necessary professional knowledge, skill and experience.[82,83]

Language skills and professional knowledge and competence are assessed by a five-part test conducted by the Professional and Linguistic Assessments Board (the PLAB test) in various centres in the United Kingdom (occasionally a partial test has been held in an overseas centre). The standards are rigorous. During 1984, 2175 attempts were made to pass the full test and 554 candidates passed (a 25 per cent success rate). Of the successful candidates in the previous year, 47 per cent had qualified in India, 16 per cent in Pakistan, 12 per cent in Sri Lanka, and 5-6 per cent in Iraq and Egypt. The remaining candidates came from 56 other countries.

Some doctors are exempted from sitting the PLAB test. The usual reason is that they have been officially sponsored by the British Council, the Association of Commonwealth Universities, by other bodies acceptable to the GMC or, on occasion, by individual United Kingdom consultants (see page 97). The medical adviser to the sponsoring body or the consultant is responsible for establishing that the doctors' proficiency in English and their professional knowledge is equivalent to those of persons appointed in the United Kingdom to the registrar grade.[83] This may require a further period of English language training in the United Kingdom before a doctor can be recommended for PLAB exemption.

Columns 5 and 6 of Table 23 give the annual numbers of doctors who were granted limited registration having passed the PLAB test or by being exempted from 1979 to 1984. (The regulations for limited registration were introduced on 15 February 1979. Previously certificates of temporary registration had been issued.) In 1980 and again in 1981 more than 1650 doctors were granted limited registration for the first time. Over the next three years, however, the numbers fell by one-third; the 1984 figure was 1123. The fall-off was far greater in the group of doctors obliged to pass the PLAB test – the number dropped by 42 per cent between 1980 and 1984.

Nearly one-third of the doctors granted limited registration between 1982 and 1984 had qualified in India. Sri Lanka, Pakistan, the United States of America and Egypt each trained 7 to 10 per cent of the doctors.[29] Doctors with limited registration can later be granted full registration under certain circumstances. These are discussed on page 95.

### Doctors from EEC countries

Doctors who have qualified in one of the member countries of the EEC and who are nationals of any of the EEC countries can apply for full registration. Alternatively they can apply for limited registration or to join temporarily the list of visiting EEC practitioners.[82] Until 30 April 1985 there were reciprocal arrangements for provisional and full registration between the General Medical Council and the Medical Council of the Republic of Ireland. These arrangements have ceased and persons who qualify in Ireland and who are nationals of an EEC member country can now apply for full registration under the regulations applying to persons from the continental member countries.

There is no obligation for doctors from EEC countries to pass a PLAB test. They are only required to satisfy the employing authorities that their proficiency in written and spoken English is sufficient for the purposes of that employment. Employing authorities can ask for a test of English language skills administered by the Professional and Linguistic Assessments Board to be taken if need be.[84] (Between 1977 and August 1981 EEC doctors had been required as a condition of registration to show that they possessed the necessary knowledge of English. Objections were raised by the EEC Commission and this requirement was abolished.)

The numbers of EEC doctors granted full registration in the years 1979–84 are given in column 4 of Table 23. Although the figures are relatively small compared with those for non-EEC doctors, they rose steeply between 1980 and 1983 – from 134 to 317. Greece joined the Common Market on 1 January 1981 and by the end of 1984 a quarter of the 1529 EEC doctors who had obtained full registration since 1977 held Greek qualifications. A similar proportion had qualified in Italy and one-fifth in Germany.[29]

### Numbers of doctors entering the United Kingdom

The final column of Table 23 shows that in 1983 and 1984 around 2400 doctors holding overseas qualifications were newly registered with the GMC. In both years, 39 per cent were non-EEC doctors eligible for provisional or full registration, 13 per cent held EEC qualifications and were also granted full registration, and 47 per cent were non-EEC doctors given limited registration. During each of the same two years, around 3720 doctors with UK qualifications and 70 who had qualified in the Republic of Ireland were registered for the first time. Thus the annual total figure for new registrations in these years was 6200 and almost two-fifths were doctors holding overseas qualifications. However, an unknown proportion of the overseas doctors who obtained full registration may not have entered the United Kingdom during the period. Doctors eligible for full registration under section 19 of the Medical Act 1983 do not have to be present in the United Kingdom at the time of the registration and some may never practise in, or even visit this country.

*Restrictions on the type of employment*

There are no restrictions laid down under the Medical Act 1983 on the type of employment for which fully registered doctors are eligible. For doctors with limited registration the situation is different. Normally they can only work in hospital posts that have been approved for education and training purposes by one of the royal colleges or faculties or, in the case of Scotland, by one of the regional postgraduate committees. Employment in posts held in the course of training approved by a university department may also be acceptable.[29,83]

Two types of certificates can be issued. One restricts the doctors to a particular supervised appointment or appointments and duration described on the certificate. The other certificate permits the doctor to take up a range of employment in educationally approved hospital posts and under the supervision of a fully registered medical practitioner during a defined period but there may be restrictions on working in accident and emergency departments. In deciding whether to grant limited registration for a particular employment or for a range of employment, the Council takes into account evidence relating to the applicant's professional knowledge, skill and experience. The majority of certificates issued permit the doctors to take up a range of employment, although about half of these certificates place restrictions on working in accident and emergency departments.[11]

The maximum duration of the first certificate issued to each doctor is 12 months. The decision to grant a renewal of the certificate is based on confidential reports supplied by the fully registered medical practitioners under whose supervision the doctor has worked for three months or more. At least two reports are required and the reports are used to monitor the progress of the trainee and his or her suitability for further registration and, more generally, the effectiveness of the PLAB test. Limited registration can only be granted for periods amounting to five years in total. A small number of doctors who held temporary registration on 15 February 1979 have 'preserved rights' and can continually apply to have their limited registration certificates renewed for up to four years at a time.[83]

*Transferring to full registration*

A doctor with limited registration may qualify for full registration. This can be granted in two ways. In the first, the doctor applies to the GMC and he or she will be granted full registration 'if the Council think fit so to direct, having regard to the knowledge and skill shown and the experience acquired' by the doctor.[85] Among the criteria against which the case is considered is the duration of the doctor's clinical experience in the United Kingdom in substantive hospital posts in the grade of registrar or above. The alternative method of obtaining full registration requires the overseas qualified doctor to re-qualify in the United Kingdom. This may be done by passing a university primary medical degree or, more usually, by passing the qualifying examinations administered by the non-university licensing bodies (the Examining Board in England, the Society of Apothecaries of London or the Board of Management of the Scottish Triple Qualification). Successful candidates can then apply for provisional registration in the same way as new graduates from UK universities. Finally, after 12 months of satisfactory experience in recognised HO posts the doctor will be granted full registration. Alternatively, successful candidates can hold limited registration and work in posts in higher grades and, in due course, apply for full registration. It is also possible for candidates to apply immediately for full registration if limited registration experience gained prior to sitting the qualifying examination was satisfactory (page 188).

The numbers of overseas qualified doctors who were granted full registration under the two types of regulations are shown in Table 24. In 1984 the total was 728 and this number was substantially greater than those for the previous two years. The usual method of transferring was by recognition of retrospective experience. Between 1981 and 1984 nearly four-fifths of the doctors were granted full registration this way. The other fifth obtained full registration after requalifying in the United Kingdom.

Nineteen eighty-four was the fifth year following the introduction of the regulations for limited registration on 15 February 1979. Doctors who had first been granted a certificate in 1979 and who had worked continuously since then were obliged to obtain full registration by the termination date in 1984 if they wished to continue in medical practice in the United Kingdom. During the weeks between 15 February 1984 and 31 December 1984, 60 doctors reached the end of their five-year limited registration period. Of these, 24 doctors were granted full registration. Fifteen other applicants were refused and 21 did not apply for full registration. It is possible that they had

Table 24    Doctors with limited registration who were granted full registration 1979–84, and total number of doctors on the Limited Register on 1 January 1980–85

| | *Doctors with limited registration who were granted full registration* | | | |
|---|---|---|---|---|
| | *Doctors whom the Council thought fit*\* | *Doctors who requalified in the UK*\* | *Total* | *Total number of doctors on Limited Register on 1 January* |
| 1979\*\* | 227 | 82 | 309 | — |
| 1980 | 657 | 83 | 740 | 5544 |
| 1981 | 342 | 93 | 435 | 5308 |
| 1982 | 271 | 78 | 349 | 5707 |
| 1983 | 360 | 101 | 461 | 5928 |
| 1984 | 574 | 154 | 728 | 5582 |
| 1985 | na | na | na | 5085 |

na = Not available.
* Under section 25 of the Medical Act 1978 and the Medical Act 1983.
** From 15 February 1979.

Source: General Medical Council annual reports.[29]

returned to their country of origin.[29] Clearly, the transfer to full registration by the 24 doctors nearing the end of their limited registration period formed only a small proportion of the increase in fully registered doctors between 1983 and 1984 shown in Table 24. In point of fact, many doctors move from limited to full registration quite early in their UK careers. The 1985 immigration rules restricting the duration of permit-free training to four years could, however, affect this pattern in the future. Trainees, knowing that they cannot practise in the United Kingdom without a work permit being obtained, may be less motivated to transfer to full registration.

### Numbers of overseas doctors in the United Kingdom

Each January the General Medical Council calculates the total number of doctors with current registration on the Limited Register. (The information is held in a manual record system.) Table 24, column 4 gives the figures for the years 1980-85. The lowest number of 5085 was recorded in January 1985. The figures must, however, be used with caution. The Council does not routinely learn when a doctor has left the country before his or her certificate has expired. The same caveat applies to the statistics on overseas qualified doctors with full registration.

In the years 1980 to 1983, two-thirds of the doctors granted limited registration in each year were obliged to pass the PLAB test because they were not being sponsored by recognised bodies (see Table 23). The General Medical Council, concerned about the standards of training and guidance given to these doctors, decided in 1981 to encourage the royal colleges, faculties and other interested bodies to further develop the practice of setting up sponsorship arrangements. These could be of two types. One involved the provision of funds by the sponsoring body to support the doctors for at least part of their time while in the United Kingdom. There were already programmes of this kind administered by the British Council (page 98), the Association of Commonwealth Universities, the World Health Organization and other agencies. In the other type of arrangement, the sponsoring body and its members acted as 'mentors' to the overseas doctors by offering counselling on examinations and guidance on training and employment while in the United Kingdom. The visiting doctors are not necessarily exempt from the PLAB test. Some medical schools and colleges in the United Kingdom have links with overseas medical schools and hospitals and accept sponsored graduates.

Various ideas on how to select overseas trainees and provide advice and assistance were explored by a working group established by the Council for Postgraduate Medical Education in England and Wales.[86] After widespread consultation, the working group produced proposals for an 'overseas doctors training scheme' for England and Wales which were endorsed by the Council in 1984. The scheme was then recommended to the DHSS for further consideration. In 1985 the Department held meetings with representatives of some royal colleges and the profession and it was agreed that schemes for sponsorship of suitable overseas graduates would be worked out specialty by specialty and based on colleges and faculties. The Royal College of Obstetricians and Gynaecologists (RCOG) already operated a scheme (see below) and a pilot scheme in general surgery and orthopaedics was the next to be developed.[21]

*Sponsorship of overseas postgraduates by the Royal College of Obstetricians and Gynaecologists*

The Royal College of Obstetricians and Gynaecologists for some time had been placing postgraduates financed by funds from overseas in unpaid supernumerary posts. In 1983 the College decided that rather than participate in a centrally-organised overseas doctors training scheme (as proposed by the working group of the Council for Postgraduate Medical Education) it preferred to set up its own double sponsorship scheme.[87] The overseas sponsor of a candidate is normally an overseas national or regional committee of the College, an overseas fellow or member of the College or, exceptionally, a dean of a medical school. The final decision on sponsorship is taken on behalf of the College by the director of postgraduate studies who is also responsible for the placement of sponsored trainees and their subsequent supervision.

To be eligible applicants should have sufficient training both in obstetrics and gynaecology and another subject and have passed the part 1 membership examination of the Royal College of Obstetricians and Gynaecologists (chapter 9) or have gained exemption. The great majority of trainees will want access to patients so, naturally, they must be eligible for registration – limited or full – with the GMC. Training may be arranged in salaried training posts or supernumerary posts. Salaried training posts are made available for college-sponsored candidates by consultants who tend to be in the smaller district general hospitals. The intention is, however, to place sponsored candidates in major district hospitals and teaching hospitals as far as possible. Most candidates are placed at first in SHO posts and once they are familiar with British obstetric and gynaecological practice a registrar post is usually found for them. Supernumerary posts are recognised by the College in about 50 hospitals in the British Isles and as the posts are unpaid they are suitable for trainees supported by scholarships or other official funds. All sponsored trainees are interviewed at the college by the director of postgraduate studies soon after arrival in the United Kingdom. Appropriate programmes of training are mapped out including target dates for sitting examinations. The supervising consultants supply the Director with six-monthly reports on the trainees' progress and the regional college advisers provide support to the trainees when required. All college-sponsored trainees have to keep official log books of their experience. Only very occasionally is sponsorship withdrawn because a trainee has made unsatisfactory progress. During the first two years of operation the double sponsorship scheme placed 26 trainees in salaried posts. The amount of work entailed in administering the scheme was considerable, however.

SPONSORSHIP SCHEMES ADMINISTERED BY THE BRITISH COUNCIL*

Of the agencies which administer funded sponsorship schemes, the British Council is probably the best known.[80] Not only does the Council assist qualified doctors requiring further training and senior clinicians to visit the United Kingdom but, as mentioned at the start of this chapter, it also arranges for UK specialists to act as

---

* The information on the British Council was provided by Dr J D Crowlesmith, Senior Medical Adviser for the Council in 1985.

consultants or advisers in overseas countries. The Council facilitates the exchange of persons (trainees or students, and specialists) in all fields of education.

The Council acts as an agent for a variety of educational and training schemes, the biggest being the Technical Cooperation Training Programme (TCTP)) which is funded by the British Government through the Overseas Development Administration. The ODA identifies countries that it intends to assist and in consultation with each recipient country it prepares a list of agreed priorities. One may be assistance with postgraduate medical education and training as part of manpower development planning, and if the financial allocation for the country in the ODA budget is sufficient to cover this priority, the arrangements are made through the TCTP which facilitates all education and training requirements.

The recipient government nominates doctors and other candidates to receive further training, taking into account each individual's past experience, present circumstances and career prospects. Normally the nominees are government employees and frequently more are nominated than there are places available. Documents are sent to the British Council in London where the training requirements of each doctor are assessed by the medical adviser and advice is given on how the requirements can best be met within the British system. If the training is to be in a clinical field, the doctor's competence in English is assessed and his or her eligibility for limited registration is confirmed with the General Medical Council. The proposed programme of training is finally submitted to the overseas government for approval and agreement. Should a doctor wish to acquire a higher qualification he may have to pass the examination for the first part before starting or continuing training in the United Kingdom.

For doctors entering clinical training the Council arranges one or more supernumerary appointments in NHS hospitals under the supervision of consultants in the appropriate specialty. The training is monitored by the medical adviser of the Council who obtains progress reports as necessary. If a supervising consultant considers a doctor is sufficiently competent to enter an NHS training post the person can apply. (To be eligible to sit the final part of higher qualifications awarded by some royal college and faculties a doctor must have had experience in approved NHS training posts – see page 126.) No changes can be made to an agreed training programme without the prior approval of both the British Council and the doctor's own government. Once a programme finishes the Council's financial and administrative responsibility for the trainee ends.

The training award provides the doctors with a stipend to cover accommodation and subsistence. The award also covers the GMC registration fees, the subscription to a medical defence society and entry fees for appropriate examinations. Bench fees in connection with research and training may be included, as well as allowances for books, travel expenses and so forth. If a trainee obtains a paid NHS training post the stipend is withdrawn for the period of the appointment.

Table 25   Number of overseas doctors undertaking clinical
training in the United Kingdom while on sponsorship
schemes administered by the British Council, 1975/76–
1983/84

| Academic year | Number of sponsored doctors* |
|---|---|
| 1975/76 | 171 |
| 1976/77 | 192 |
| 1977/78 | 234 |
| 1978/79 | 216 |
| 1979/80 | 129 |
| 1980/81 | 126 |
| 1981/82 | 154 |
| 1982/83 | 141 |
| 1983/84 | 155 |

\* Excluding doctors on short visits of one to eight weeks and persons
taking academic courses only.

Source: British Council (personal communication 1985).

In addition to the Technical Cooperation Training Programme the Council has its own fellowship scheme offering yearly awards to visit the United Kingdom for between two months and two years. The scheme is open to applicants of all disciplines and selection is made by a board. The Council also acts as an agent for certain internationally funded sponsorship schemes where training is to be undertaken in the United Kingdom. Two offering training awards to medically qualified graduates were established by the International Atomic Energy Authority and the European Development Fund. The first provides funding for the study of medical and scientific aspects of atomic energy. It accepts applications from all over the world. The second is available to applicants from the African (including Egypt), Caribbean and Pacific countries that signed the Lomé Convention. Both organisations pass the documents of the applicants to the British Council in London which arranges and supervises the required training programmes in the same way as for TCTP candidates.

Table 25 shows the numbers of doctors who undertook a clinical training programme in the United Kingdom while on sponsorship schemes administered by the British Council. The statistics are for the academic years 1975/76 to 1983/84 and they apply to all the schemes. In the last three years the number has averaged 150 per year. (The table does not include doctors who came to this country on short visits of up to eight weeks or persons who did academic courses.)

## UNMET DEMAND FOR POSTGRADUATE EDUCATION

A proportion of the overseas demand for British postgraduate medical education and training is not being met. The workload of the National Advice Centre (NAC) (pages 258–260) supports this assumption. There are a number of reasons. The high failure rates for the PLAB test[29] suggest that many doctors wishing to train in Britain who may be professionally competent, are unable to qualify for limited registration because of inadequate linguistic skills. The list of primary medical qualifications recognised by the GMC for the purposes of limited registration has been criticised for being too restrictive, although there are hundreds of qualifications on the list. A group of letters published in the *British Medical Journal* in 1984[88-91] argued that the regulations under the Medical Act 1983 should be changed to allow the Council to recognise certain postgraduate qualifications for this purpose. At a national level, the government of one middle eastern country with a high national income per capita has expressed concern that graduates from its medical schools who wish to train in the United Kingdom are not eligible for most sponsorship schemes. The government is willing to financially underwrite a suitable scheme if one can be established. Finally, once overseas doctors have entered employment in the NHS, they may have difficulty in obtaining further appointments which offer the level of training that they desire. However, this problem is also being faced by doctors qualified in the United Kingdom.

One course of action open to British-born doctors dissatisfied with training or employment opportunities in the United Kingdom is emigration. There was widespread concern during the late 1950s and early 1960s over the relatively high net migration level of British trained graduates including doctors. As remuneration levels and conditions of service for hospital doctors and general practitioners were improved over the following years the level of net migration fell substantially. The net outflow in the early 1980s of UK-born doctors has been estimated at 120 doctors per year, with most of the movement occurring in the lower ages.[92]

# 8  Women trainees and trainees from overseas in the hospital service

Attention is now turned to the trainees themselves, and in this chapter certain characteristics of two groups in the NHS hospital service – women doctors and doctors from overseas – are examined. Particular attention was paid by the Social Services Committee of the House of Commons in 1980/81 to the training and career opportunities for these groups.[4] One reason why the Committee rejected the suggestion that there should be a sub-consultant grade was a fear 'that if such a grade was available, many women doctors would be shunted into it and much of [the] impetus to improve the career prospects for women would be destroyed' (para 114). With overseas doctors, the Committee observed that they often come in the hope of acquiring postgraduate qualifications but the process can sometimes take many years, 'particularly if the doctor finds him or herself in a post which offers little training and little opportunity to study'. The Committee recommended therefore that 'with the assistance of the Postgraduate Deans, the Royal Colleges should continue to make every effort to advise overseas doctors and to help them achieve their formal qualifications' (paras 231 and 233).

The statistics used in this chapter are from the annual DHSS 30 September censuses of hospital medical staff in England and Wales.[7] The figures showing trends are also based on statistics from the censuses. Some of the tables and figures apply only to doctors in permanent paid NHS hospital appointments; others also include honorary appointment holders. The nature of the data base is, however, stated in every case.

PROPORTION OF WOMEN DOCTORS IN NHS HOSPITALS

Up to five factors can determine the proportion of women doctors employed in each of the hospital grades: the ratio of males to females entering and graduating from British medical schools, the sex ratio of overseas trained doctors entering the grades, the rates for both sexes withdrawing from and re-entering the grades, the rates for working full-time or part-time and, finally, any preferential treatment given to one sex or the other when promoting doctors between grades. Table 26 gives the number of women doctors holding permanent paid appointments in the consultant and training grades in NHS hospitals for the years 1970-84 and Figure 7 shows the trends in the percentages of doctors in these grades who were women. The trends for the five grades need to be interpreted separately because the contributing factors have not exerted an equal influence on each grade. Omitted from the table and figure are

Table 26    Numbers of women doctors in the consultant and training grades (excluding honorary appointment holders)*, England and Wales, 1970–84

| 30 September | Consultants** | Senior registrars | Registrars | Senior house officers† | House officers |
|---|---|---|---|---|---|
| 1970 | 655 | 195 | 672 | 1085 | 435 |
| 1971 | 697 | 217 | 722 | 1146 | 461 |
| 1972 | 740 | 246 | 747 | 1188 | 545 |
| 1973 | 796 | 278 | 785 | 1420 | 518 |
| 1974 | 860 | 308 | 793 | 1507 | 567 |
| 1975 | 918 | 359 | 840 | 1640 | 636 |
| 1976 | 992 | 392 | 876 | 1742 | 749 |
| 1977 | 1041 | 419 | 908 | 1958 | 765 |
| 1978 | 1128 | 416 | 967 | 2116 | 829 |
| 1979 | 1210 | 420 | 1062 | 2343 | 916 |
| 1980 | 1282 | 470 | 1115 | 2424 | 957 |
| 1981 | 1349 | 534 | 1187 | 2560 | 1020 |
| 1982 | 1404 | 587 | 1247 | 2738 | 1057 |
| 1983 | 1481 | 660 | 1276 | 2878 | 1121 |
| 1984 | 1582 | 670 | 1289 | 3056 | 1103 |

_Number of women doctors_

  * Permanent paid (whole-time or part-time) appointment holders in NHS hospitals, and four special hospitals 1982–84.
 ** Including senior hospital medical officers with allowance.
  † Including junior hospital medical officers and post-registration house officers until these grades were withdrawn.

Source: DHSS 30 September censuses of hospital medical staff.[7]

women in the non-training associate specialist grade (page 54). They numbered 428 in 1984 and 60 per cent were employed part-time.[7]

_House officer grade_    During the 1960s the proportion of students admitted to pre-clinical courses in British medical schools who were women ranged between 22 and 26 per cent in each year and this level of intake was governed until late in the decade by limited entry quotas on the number of women admitted to medical schools.[26] From the beginning of the 1970s, however, the annual rates of admission for women students climbed steadily. (The Committee of Vice-Chancellors and Principals

Figure 7 Women doctors as a percentage of all doctors (excluding honorary appointment holders) in the consultant and training grades in NHS hospitals, England and Wales, 1970-84

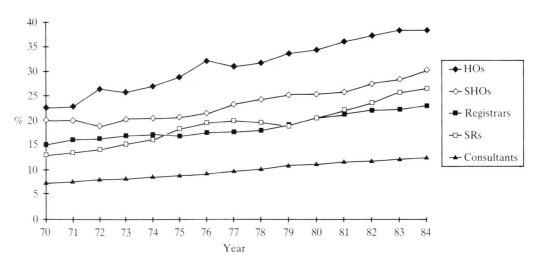

advised in 1974 that any remaining quotas were inappropriate to modern conditions.) At the end of the decade, women comprised almost 40 per cent of admissions to UK medical schools and by 1982/83 the proportion had reached 44 per cent.[32]

The usual duration of study before obtaining a first registrable medical qualification is five years and so the male to female ratio in the house officer grade will not match the admissions ratio until five years later. The effects of this time lag can be seen in Table 26. Women did not start to enter the grade in steadily increasing numbers until 1975 when the proportion rose to 29 per cent, 2 per cent more than the previous year (Figure 7). In 1983 and 1984 the rate was 38 per cent.

*Senior house officer grade*    Doctors normally enter the SHO grade after spending one year as house officers. Thus the proportion of women senior house officers should have started to rise in 1976 and Figure 7 shows that this was the case. Since the early 1970s, however, there have been relatively fewer women in the grade compared to the HO grade. Two reasons account for this. The proportion of women doctors who ceased to work in NHS hospital posts for domestic or personal reasons may have been greater than the proportion of men. A more significant reason, however, is that over the years many doctors entered this grade who had qualified overseas (see a later section) and they were predominantly males. By 1984, 38 per cent of all senior house officers (including honorary appointment holders) in England and Wales were born outside the United Kingdom and Republic of Ireland. Of these, 20 per cent were women. In comparison, 36 per cent of the senior house officers born in the British Isles were women. As this rate was almost on a par with the overall rate for the HO grade, it suggests that the current 'drop-out' rate for women senior house officers is relatively very small.

*Registrar grade*    Figure 7 shows that the lowest representation of women trainees in NHS paid appointments is now in the registrar grade. This grade has absorbed even higher rates of overseas-qualified doctors across the years. By 1984, 46 per cent of all registrars in hospitals in England and Wales had been born outside the British Isles and 16 per cent were women. In comparison, 27 per cent of the British-born registrars were women but this figure was still well below the rate for British-born female senior house officers. Women, therefore, are less likely than men to enter or continue in the registrar grade.

*Senior registrar grade*    The situation was very little different in the senior registrar grade until 1980-81 when the effects of a revised policy to encourage women to continue their training on a part-time basis – described below – became noticeable (Figure 7). Three years later, 26 per cent of the senior registrars in NHS paid appointments were women although over one-third of them held part-time contracts. These part-time doctors will, of course, have to spend longer periods of time in the grade completing their training programmes than their full-time male and female colleagues.

*Consultant grade*    The representation of women in the consultant grade in England and Wales increased very slightly – 0.4 per cent on average – in each year from 1970 (Figure 7). So by 1984 almost 13 per cent of consultants holding permanent paid appointments were women. (They comprised only 10 per cent of consultants with honorary appointments.) The annual rate of change in the overall male to female consultant ratio will continue to be small because relatively few consultant appointments are made each year. For example, on 30 September 1984 there were 12,408 consultants in NHS established posts in England and Wales of whom 679 (5 per cent) had been appointed during the previous 12 months. Twenty-one per cent of these new consultants were women. This rate was slightly higher than the percentages for the previous four years. Since 1970, however, there has been a significant change in the tendency of women consultants to work full-time. In 1970 only one-third held full-time or maximum part-time contracts. By 1984 the proportion was approaching two-thirds.

Research material on women doctors employed in the hospital service and other services in the NHS is reviewed in a monograph by Day.[93] Women consultants are relatively under-represented amongst consultants who have received distinction awards. Also, until recently, women doctors in general have been less likely than men to obtain a higher qualification for membership or fellowship of a royal college. They tended to study instead for diploma examinations that do not lead to college membership – the Diploma in Child Health (DCH) and the Diploma of the Royal College of Obstetricians and Gynaecologists (DRCOG), for example. However, data are provided in chapter 10 (Table 36) on examination success rates for the higher qualifications of membership or fellowship which suggest that women are now obtaining these qualifications in the clinical disciplines, apart from surgery, in numbers proportionate to or greater than their representation in the training grades.

TRAINEES WITH PART-TIME APPOINTMENTS

In 1969 the DHSS issued a memorandum (HM(69)6) asking hospital authorities to create part-time posts for women doctors unable to work full-time because of domestic commitments.[94] Ten years later the scheme was redefined (PM(79)3) and doctors and dentists of both sexes able to work only part-time because of domestic commitments, disability or ill-health became eligible.[95] (One or two small changes were made to the scheme after 1979.) The arrangements by which a doctor – in particular a senior registrar – obtains a part-time post are complex.

*Administrative arrangements of the PM(79)3 scheme*

The principles underlying the arrangements for employing senior registrars on a part-time basis are as follows: there should be opportunities for part-time training in all specialties; there should be manpower control over the number of part-time posts as there is over full-time posts; candidates for part-time posts should be assessed by the same criteria as those for full-time posts and there should be competition between candidates. Finally, the posts should meet the training requirements of the relevant higher training committee or royal college or faculty and they should be at least half-time and include pro rata on-call and emergency duties.[95]

Each year the DHSS obtains advice from the Central Manpower Committee on the number of part-time SR training opportunities which should be made available in each specialty in England and Wales. The DHSS then places advertisements in the medical (and dental) press inviting applications for these opportunities. If the number of applicants in a given specialty exceeds the number of available opportunities, the applicants are referred to a national assessment committee. The membership of the committee is modelled on the usual structure of a regional SR appointments committee (see page 174 in chapter 13).

The applicants selected by the national assessment committee and the applicants in specialties in which there was no competition are given manpower approval and they are then able to approach the regional health authorities or special health authorities to request that personal posts be established for them. Approval for a part-time training programme must also be obtained from the relevant higher training committee or royal college. Before eventually being appointed to a supernumerary post, the trainee should satisfy a local appointments committee as to his or her suitability for the post. Health authorities are not, however, under obligation to establish and fund a suitable post. If, after six to nine months a suitable post has not been created, the manpower approval given to the trainee will normally lapse. Should a doctor already in part-time training move to another region, the manpower approval will move also. The new RHA will have to repeat the process of finding a suitable post, funding, and higher training approval. Finally, employing authorities can establish a personal part-time SR post under the terms of PM(79)3 at any time of the year for a doctor who has previously held a substantive SR post, either whole-time or part-time, in the same specialty.[96]

Employing authorities are free to establish part-time training posts for doctors in the registrar and SHO grades without central approval. The applications are considered at regional level. In the Northern region, for example, applicants are interviewed and the regional advisers for the relevant specialties are consulted about the acceptability of the proposed part-time training.[96] Doctors wishing to enter general practice can undertake both the hospital and general practice periods of vocational training on a part-time basis. Training in community medicine may also be undertaken part-time and central approval is not needed for the establishment of SR posts, but the training content must be approved by the appropriate committee for community medicine (that is, by the Education Committee of the Faculty of Community Medicine).[95]

The royal colleges, faculties and higher training committees have assessed how much training is needed before doctors working part-time can become eligible either to sit the higher qualifying examinations or to complete the higher training programmes (page 242). The various requirements are described in a handbook *Part-time in medicine* which was published by the Council for Postgraduate Medical Education in England and Wales in 1981.[97]

*Numbers of part-time women trainees*

Table 27 gives the numbers of female senior registrars and registrars holding part-time NHS hospital appointments from 1970 to 1984, although not all would have held supernumerary posts under the HM(69)6 or PM(79)3 arrangements. The percentages

Table 27    Numbers of women doctors holding part-time appointments* in the senior registrar and registrar grades,
England and Wales, 1970–84

| 30 September | Numbers of women doctors holding part-time appointments | |
| | Senior registrars | Registrars |
| --- | --- | --- |
| 1970 | 23 | 48 |
| 1971 | 32 | 66 |
| 1972 | 47 | 91 |
| 1973 | 59 | 123 |
| 1974 | 76 | 150 |
| 1975 | 91 | 140 |
| 1976 | 103 | 125 |
| 1977 | 110 | 157 |
| 1978 | 137 | 183 |
| 1979 | 133 | 222 |
| 1980 | 170 | 218 |
| 1981 | 189 | 222 |
| 1982 | 216 | 235 |
| 1983 | 229 | 224 |
| 1984 | 241 | 209 |

* Permanent paid appointment holders in NHS hospitals, and four special
hospitals in 1982–84.

Source: DHSS 30 September censuses of hospital medical staff.[7]

of all women in the two grades who were part-time appointment holders are shown in
Figure 8. For senior registrars the percentages of women who held part-time contracts
rose from 12 per cent in 1970 to 36 per cent in 1980. The figure remained around this
level over the next four years. A smaller proportion of women registrars work on a
part-time basis. The years with the highest percentages (19-20 per cent) were 1974 and
1978-82. Numbers of women part-time senior house officers are not given in Table 27
because relatively few are employed on this basis; in 1984 there were 73 compared to
2983 female whole-time senior house officers in NHS paid hospital appointments in
England and Wales.

*Reports on the part-time training arrangements*

There have been various inquiries into the arrangements for the PM(79)3 scheme.
The DHSS reviewed the scheme in 1981/82 and a small working party set up by the

8   *Women trainees and*
*trainees from overseas in the*
*hospital service*

Figure 8  Women part-time doctors as a percentage of all women doctors (excluding honorary appointment holders) in the senior registrar and registrar grades in NHS hospitals, England and Wales, 1970-84

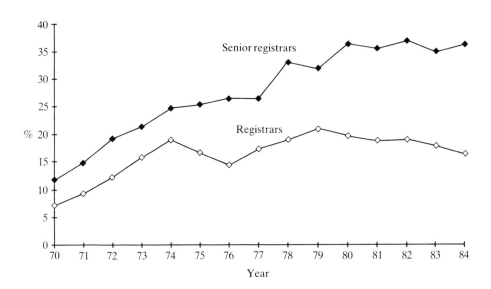

Central Manpower Committee considered both the scheme and the DHSS's review of it.[98] Another working party representing the Joint Consultants Committee and the DHSS met in 1984.[99] In 1980, Day conducted a survey of regional health authorities in England and employing authorities in Wales and Scotland to establish both the level of part-time training activity and the opinions surrounding the administration of the scheme.[93] A year later Burke and Black surveyed doctors holding part-time training posts in general medicine and its sub-specialties in England, Wales and Northern Ireland. Regional advisers of the Royal College of Physicians also participated in the study.[100] In Newcastle, a research team looked at the records of all doctors covered by part-time schemes in the Northern region between 1971 and October 1982.[96] Finally, in 1984 a postal survey of part-time trainees in the Northern, Yorkshire and Trent regions was carried out by Davidson, O'Brien and Roberts.[101]

The research exercises were hampered by a lack of reliable data on the numbers, progress and destination of participants in the part-time training schemes. Without information of this kind it is not possible to monitor the success or failure of the schemes and this was one reason why Davidson and her colleagues decided to carry out the survey of trainees in three regions. The research papers contained a variety of comments on the selection of trainees and the content of their in-post experience. The appointment procedures laid down in the 1979 circular were not always followed in every region and there was doubt if all post holders would have been appointed if candidates able to work full-time had been competing for part-time posts. The progress of trainees in many regions appeared to be inadequately monitored by the regional postgraduate committees. In certain instances trainees were deficient in the acquisition of acute and on-call experience. A proportion had completed their higher training programmes and were now facing problems in obtaining a consultant post – preferably part-time – within the local geographical area.

The reports of the working groups drew attention to the administrative difficulties faced by doctors wishing to work part-time as senior registrars.[98,99] The delays in getting people into post – even after manpower approval was granted – could last up to two years. One reason for the extended delays was the shortage of funds allocated in some regions for establishing PM(79)3 posts. Delays in obtaining educational approval for the posts was another reason. The size of the problem varied from one higher training committee to another. The principle that there should be opportunities for part-time training in all specialties[95] is now incompatible with the manpower policy being followed in some specialties of reducing the total number of senior registrars in training.

The 1984 DHSS/JCC working party proposed that the scheme should continue but with the administration being devolved to the regional and special health authorities. They should be guided on the methods for calculating whole-time equivalents of substantive and supernumerary posts combined, and on the principles for allocating posts for part-time training with the aim of achieving a broad equity of full-time/part-time training within each specialty.[99]

The research team which surveyed trainees in three regions considered that if devolution to the regions did occur there needed to be a central system of review to ensure that the broad intentions of the scheme were being fulfilled. The survey suggested that in the Yorkshire region the guide lines appeared to be interpreted rigidly, with domestic commitment being defined as solely related to child care. The trainees selected were a small number of highly motivated and well qualified senior registrars and registrars (in terms of successes in examinations for higher qualifications) who were intent on training for consultant posts. In the Trent region the guide lines were interpreted in a broader way; scheme members included senior house officers and clinical assistants (who are not trainees) as well as senior registrars and registrars. The overall level of postgraduate examination attainment was lower and relatively fewer members wished to obtain consultant posts. In both the Trent and Northern regions trainees were employed in a wider range of specialties than in the Yorkshire region; there were eight trainees in obstetrics and gynaecology in the Northern region – the highest number in any region.[101]

8   Women trainees and
trainees from overseas in the
hospital service

In 1972 the Government introduced in a memorandum, HM(72)42, a scheme offering a small amount of clinical work to women whose domestic commitments prevented them from taking on regular professional commitments for several years.[102] The scheme was extended to all doctors in this situation in 1977 and the conditions for eligibility are described in an annexe to the memorandum PM(79)3 on part-time training.[95] (A similar scheme operates for dentists.)

To be eligible a doctor must be under the age of 55, currently able to work no more than one day (or two sessions) per week, and intending to undertake more substantial NHS work when domestic circumstances permit. In return the doctor receives an annual retainer (£155 in 1985/86) to help meet expenses and agrees to maintain registration with the GMC and membership of a medical defence organisation, to attend at least seven education sessions each year, to take a recognised professional journal, and to work each year for not less than one half-day a month (with pay) and be ready to work for up to a maximum of one day per week if asked to do so and circumstances permit. Doctors may work in the hospital service at senior house officer or clinical assistant level, in general practice as an assistant, in the community health service as a clinical medical officer or in the Public Health Laboratory Service.

The regional health authorities are responsible for the overall administration of the scheme and for the payment of the retainer fees (apart from fees for persons in the PHLS) but the funding of the fees is provided by the DHSS. Payment for work done under the scheme in a hospital, community health service or the PHLS is made by the employing authority. Doctors working in general practice as assistants are employed by a general practitioner principal or partnership. Prospective scheme members are interviewed and advised by the clinical tutors in the districts and the tutors supervise their progress. Members reapply every year to continue in the scheme and the renewal of membership is normally automatic.

Researchers surveyed the records of the 89 doctors who joined the retainer scheme in the Northern region between 1972 and October 1982 and they concluded that the objective of the scheme was being met.[103] All the members were women and over two-thirds had later left the scheme, the reason in the majority of cases being that the doctor had increased her commitment over the maximum allowed of one day per week. The second most frequently recorded reason for leaving was 'moved'. Of those who had withdrawn, half spent one year or less in the scheme and one-third were members for two or three years.

At the time of the survey in the Northern region there were 27 members in the retainer scheme. In the South East Thames region which covers a larger population than the Northern region, slightly fewer doctors were participating in the scheme in 1982 (23 doctors) and the total number of doctors who had joined the scheme between 1972 and early 1982 was also smaller (82 doctors).[15] The participation of women doctors in the retainer scheme in Wales was, at least until 1980, particularly low. Day in her survey of the health authorities in Wales was informed of only six women who had entered the scheme since it began in 1972.[93]

HOSPITAL DOCTORS FROM OVERSEAS

The place of birth of each doctor (coded as Great Britain, Northern Ireland or the Republic of Ireland, and born elsewhere) is recorded in the annual 30 September census administered by the DHSS.[7] The information entered on the census forms by medical staffing personnel for some doctors may relate instead to their nationality

Table 28   Numbers of doctors born overseas in the senior registrar, registrar and senior house officer grades in NHS hospitals*, England and Wales, 1970–84

|  | Doctors born overseas** | | |
|---|---|---|---|
| *30 September* | *Senior registrars* | *Registrars* | *Senior house officers†* |
| 1970 | 349 | 2620 | 3308 |
| 1971 | 419 | 2602 | 3328 |
| 1972 | 491 | 2619 | 3764 |
| 1973 | 527 | 2698 | 4238 |
| 1974 | 593 | 2716 | 4482 |
| 1975 | 644 | 2942 | 4756 |
| 1976 | 666 | 2981 | 4688 |
| 1977 | 694 | 3046 | 4679 |
| 1978 | 696 | 3168 | 4637 |
| 1979 | 714 | 3198 | 4777 |
| 1980 | 743 | 3148 | 4692 |
| 1981 | 763 | 3053 | 4642 |
| 1982 | 710 | 2996 | 4421 |
| 1983 | 693 | 2901 | 4163 |
| 1984 | 604 | 2810 | 3929 |

 * All staff holding permanent paid and/or honorary appointments.
** Those born outside the United Kingdom and the Republic of Ireland.
 † Including junior hospital medical officers and post-registration house officers until these grades were withdrawn.

Source: DHSS 30 September censuses of hospital medical staff.[7]

Figure 9 Doctors born overseas as a percentage of all doctors (including honorary appointment holders) in the senior registrar, registrar and senior house officer grades in NHS hospitals, England and Wales, 1970-84

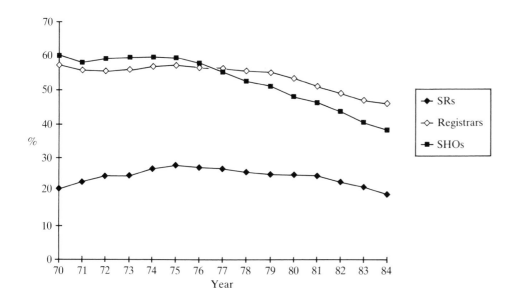

because the personal files do not have place of birth recorded. Job application and appointment forms used by employing authorities are not standardised – they can even differ among hospitals within a health authority – and not all forms ask for country of birth. The evaluation of the items in the minimum data sets recommended by the Health Services Information Steering Group (Körner)[12], concluded that the country of which a doctor is a national differs from his country of birth in about 5 per cent of cases.[11]

The numbers of doctors in the senior registrar, registrar and SHO grades recorded in the hospital censuses between 1970 and 1984 who were born outside the United Kingdom and the Republic of Ireland (that is, born overseas) are given in Table 28. Doctors holding honorary appointments are included in the table but not doctors with locum contracts. Figure 9 shows for each of the 15 years, overseas-born doctors as percentages of all doctors in these grades.

In 1984, 46 per cent of the registrars and 38 per cent of senior house officers covered by the census had been born overseas and, as can be seen in Figure 9, these were the lowest rates recorded for the two grades in the 15-year period. An examination to assess the language skills of many unsponsored overseas qualified doctors applying for registration with the GMC was introduced in June 1975 (the TRAB (Temporary Registration Assessment Board) test which was later substituted by the PLAB test). After that year the proportion of overseas doctors in the SHO grade in every census steadily fell. In the registrar grade, a decline in the annual rates of overseas-born doctors did not become noticeable until after the regulations for temporary registration were replaced by the more restrictive regulations limiting doctors ineligible for full registration, to a maximum of five years registration. This happened in February 1979. The annual percentages of overseas-born doctors in the SR grade have always been much smaller than in the registrar and SHO grades; in 1984 the rate was 19 per cent. The annual numbers and rates for house officers have been even smaller – between 12 to 14 per cent in the last few years – hence their exclusion from Table 28 and Figure 9.

*Trainees with limited registration*

The numbers for overseas-born doctors in Table 28 do, of course, include doctors who obtained their primary medical qualifications in the United Kingdom. Also, a propor-

Figure 10  Doctors born overseas and doctors holding limited or temporary registration as percentages of all doctors (including honorary appointment holders) in the registrar and senior house officer grades combined in NHS hospitals, England and Wales, 1970-84

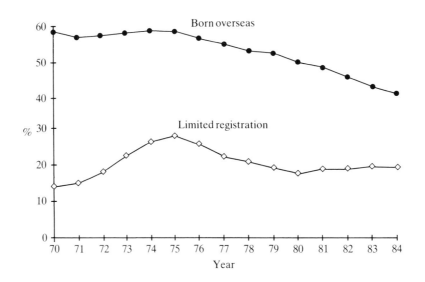

8 Women trainees and
trainees from overseas in the
hospital service

Table 29   Numbers and percentages of doctors holding limited registration in the registrar and senior house officer grades in NHS hospitals*, England and Wales, 1970–84

| 30 September | Number with limited registration** | | Doctors with limited registration as a percentage of all doctors | |
| | Registrars | Senior house officers† | Registrars | Senior house officers† |
| | No | No | % | % |
|---|---|---|---|---|
| 1970 | 471 | 952 | 10.3 | 17.3 |
| 1971 | 533 | 1028 | 11.4 | 17.8 |
| 1972 | 618 | 1381 | 13.1 | 21.6 |
| 1973 | 739 | 1925 | 15.3 | 27.2 |
| 1974 | 895 | 2321 | 18.8 | 31.2 |
| 1975 | 1094 | 2569 | 21.4 | 32.0 |
| 1976 | 1232 | 2191 | 23.4 | 26.8 |
| 1977 | 1274 | 1807 | 23.4 | 21.3 |
| 1978 | 1294 | 1707 | 22.7 | 19.3 |
| 1979 | 1228 | 1657 | 21.2 | 17.6 |
| 1980 | 1108 | 1635 | 18.8 | 16.8 |
| 1981 | 1072 | 1938 | 17.9 | 19.3 |
| 1982 | 1046 | 2005 | 17.1 | 19.8 |
| 1983 | 1119 | 2078 | 18.1 | 20.3 |
| 1984 | 1184 | 1952 | 19.4 | 19.1 |

 * All staff holding permanent paid and/or honorary appointments.
** Temporary registration prior to 15 February 1979.
 † Including junior hospital medical officers and post-registration house officers until these grades were withdrawn.

Source: DHSS 30 September censuses of hospital medical staff.[7]

tion would have held overseas qualifications that enabled them to be granted full registration by the GMC rather than limited registration (or temporary registration until February 1979). So the numbers of registrars and SHOs with temporary or limited registration (including honorary appointment holders) in the years 1970-84, are shown separately in Table 29. In Figure 10 the percentages of doctors holding this type of registration in the two grades combined over the period are plotted as well as the percentages of doctors who were born overseas.

One noticeable feature of Table 29 and Figure 10 is that in 1984 about one-fifth of all senior house officers and registrars held limited registration and this had been the situation for the previous seven years. Moreover, because there had been a gradual decline in the numbers of registrars and senior house officers born overseas over the previous few years (see Table 28), the proportion of these doctors holding limited registration had risen. By 1984, nearly half the overseas-born doctors in these two grades held limited registration (Figure 10). The percentages for the individual grades were: registrars 42 per cent, and senior house officers 50 per cent. The third point applies to the actual data; doctors employed in NHS hospitals on a locum basis are not included. In the 1984 census, 349 registrars were recorded as holding a locum appointment only, of whom 270 (77 per cent) had been born overseas. In the SHO grade there were 505 locums and 313 (62 per cent) were overseas-born.[7] It is not known what proportion of these doctors held limited registration and there would have been others with limited registration who were not in employment on the day of the census.

### Specialties of overseas doctors

In January 1984 *The Times* newspaper carried an item which suggested that 'overseas doctors regularly find themselves in "unpopular" specialities, such as geriatrics and mental illness'.[104] The item was based on analyses prepared by the Commission for Racial Equality. To test whether overseas-born registrars and senior house officers and those with limited registration really are over or under-represented in the broad specialties, the data in the 1984 census were converted into indices and they are shown in Table 30. The two series for each grade were calculated as follows. First, the numbers of doctors in the specialty groupings listed in the table who were born overseas and those who held limited registration were converted into percentages of all doctors in the specialty groupings (the observed rates). Next, the total number of doctors with these characteristics in the grades were converted into percentages of all doctors in the grades (the expected rate). Finally, the observed rates for the specialty groupings were divided by the expected rates for the grades.

Registrars from overseas were noticeably over-represented in the psychiatric and obstetrics and gynaecology specialties in 1984 (Table 30). Indeed, in this second specialty 70 per cent of all registrars were born overseas. They were marginally over-represented in the surgical and anaesthetics specialties and were under-represented in the medical and diagnostic specialties. Within the medical specialties, however, the index for geriatrics was far higher than expected. In fact, overseas-born registrars comprised 80 per cent of all geriatric registrars. In contrast, senior house officers from overseas were noticeably over-represented in the surgical and anaesthetics specialties, were slightly under-represented in the psychiatric and obstetrics and gynaecology specialties, and markedly under-represented in the medical specialties with the

8 Women trainees and
trainees from overseas in the
hospital service

Table 30   Indices for registrars and senior house officers born overseas, and with limited
registration in the specialty groupings, England and Waleas, 1984

| Specialty groupings | Registrars* | | Senior house officers* | |
|---|---|---|---|---|
| | born overseas | with limited registration | born overseas | with limited registration |
| | Index** | Index** | Index** | Index** |
| Medical | 0.88 | 0.84 | 0.71 | 0.70 |
| (Geriatrics) | (1.74) | (2.01) | (1.13) | (1.34) |
| Psychiatric | 1.14 | 1.45 | 0.96 | 0.87 |
| Surgical | 1.08 | 0.92 | 1.24 | 1.30 |
| Obstetrics and gynaecology | 1.53 | 1.58 | 0.95 | 0.93 |
| Anaesthetics | 1.02 | 1.09 | 1.28 | 1.23 |
| Pathology/radiology | 0.54 | 0.47 | 0.84 | 0.95 |
| Total | 1.00 | 1.00 | 1.00 | 1.00 |

 * Including doctors with honorary appointments.
** The method of calculating the indices is given on page 116.

Source: Based on DHSS 30 September 1984 census of hospital medical staff.[7]

exception again of geriatrics. This index was more than 13 per cent higher than
expected.

Many overseas doctors are, of course, in specialties of their own choice. The data
do suggest, however, that some overseas doctors have not been able to exercise their
preferences. (It is possible that doctors from abroad may have higher levels of
preference for training in surgically-related specialties than their British counter-
parts.) British-trained doctors have also felt constrained when exercising their
choices, as has been shown in the surveys of seven cohorts of recently qualified house
officers carried out by Parkhouse and his colleagues[105], and in a postal survey of 6561
doctors conducted in 1979 by the Institute of Manpower Studies.[106]

*Length of time in the registrar and SHO grades*

Doctors commonly spend two to three years in the SHO grade and two to four years
in the registrar grade. In the annual census of hospital medical staff one of the
questions asks for 'the date on which the officer took up his first appointment in his
present grade'.[107] If a doctor entered a grade by holding a locum appointment – and

numerous overseas doctors do – the date taken is the starting date of the appointment. Also, no account is taken of possible breaks in service. The census information is then tabulated to show the years since first entry to the grade.

On 30 September 1984, four years or more had passed since 1006 registrars (both British and overseas) first entered the grade. They comprised 16 per cent of all registrars including honorary appointment holders. In the SHO grade, 1354 doctors (13 per cent) had entered the grade four or more years previously. These numbers and percentages of 'time-expired' trainees were the highest recorded in 15 years. In a study in three regions – Northern, Trent and Oxford – in 1984, information on the time spent in the grade by senior house officers and registrars was extracted from their curricula vitae by personnel staff in the district health authorities. The data showed that 13 per cent of senior house officers (134 doctors) spent more than six years in the grade and the proportion for registrars was even higher – 18 per cent (124 doctors).[108]

Turning to overseas-born doctors in the 1984 national census, 521 registrars (19 per cent) had remained in the grade for over four years. The proportion for overseas-born senior house officers was noticeably higher – 989 or 25 per cent were in the time-expired category.[7] Since doctors with limited registration are restricted to a maximum of five years registration (except in a few cases), the majority of these overseas-born registrars would have held full registration.

Two ad hoc research studies have provided further material on registrars and senior house officers from overseas. Todd and Sheldrick with the help of district medical officers, surveyed doctors in post in the Trent region in 1982.[109] In the non-teaching authorities, over 70 per cent of the doctors in both the registrar and SHO grades had qualified overseas compared to the 1982 national averages for overseas-born doctors of 49 per cent for registrars and 44 per cent for senior house officers. Furthermore, between one-quarter and one-third of all the doctors in these grades held limited registration whereas the national rate is one-fifth. The situation in the three teaching health authorities – Nottingham, Sheffield and Leicester – was the reverse with the rates for overseas-qualified and limited registered doctors being well below the national rates. The Social Services Committee of the House of Commons recommended in 1981 that regional postgraduate deans and the royal colleges should undertake the role of advising overseas doctors.[4] These data suggest that the task in some regions could be daunting in scale.

The other research study, which was carried out by Smith in the Policy Studies Institute, compared and contrasted the professional attributes, experiences, and personal opinions and expectations of overseas-qualified doctors and British-qualified doctors. A sample of nearly 2000 doctors from all NHS medical services in England were interviewed between 1977 and 1978. In his book Smith explored a range of policy options to control the entry of overseas-qualified doctors and concluded that 'probably the best approach is to allow implications for immigration control to flow from the changes in medical training and career structures, rather than vice versa'. A system of training programmes covering the junior training grades should be established and most overseas doctors would need to gain entry to a programme before coming to Britain.[110]

The Overseas Doctors Training Scheme which was commended to the government by the Council for Postgraduate Medical Education in England and Wales in 1984 contained proposals along these lines. Before issuing its response to the recommendation, however, the government announced the decision to impose immigration controls restricting the entry, from 1 April 1985, of medically qualified personnel to four years if the purpose of the visit is for training. Later in the year the Chief Medical Officer of the DHSS established a working party on overseas doctors training schemes[111] and, as mentioned on page 97, the Department with the Royal College of Surgeons of England is working out a pilot scheme in general surgery and orthopaedics. The Royal College of Obstetricians and Gynaecologists has operated a double sponsorship scheme since 1983.[87] Sir David Innes Williams – who was the prime mover behind the Overseas Doctors Training Scheme – has pointed out, however, that it is important that the training objectives of passing examinations for higher qualifications and acquiring specialised clinical skills and experience are reasonably attainable within four years.[112]

# 9 Demand for postgraduate qualifications awarded by the royal colleges and faculties

If a trainee aspires to a hospital consultant appointment in the National Health Service he or she will need to obtain a higher qualification of membership or fellowship of a royal college or an equivalent qualification that is relevant to the chosen specialty. A consultant may be appointed who does not hold such a qualification – the only formal requirement stipulated in the regulations for appointment to consultant medical posts is that appointees must be suitable fully registered medical practitioners[113] – but the occasions when this happens are probably rare. For instance, the Royal College of Surgeons of England issued guidance on the criteria for appointing consultants in surgery to its college assessors who sit on appointment committees. Very exceptionally there may be applicants who possess neither a British or Irish fellowship nor an equivalent qualification from an overseas professional body. Such candidates must satisfy assessors that their education in basic medical sciences and their clinical training in surgery is of a duration and standard comparable to that of candidates who have pursued the normal pattern of experience.[114]

The demand that trainees have for higher qualifications is a derived demand – it is derived from the demand for highly trained specialists in a tightly controlled and, therefore, competitive market. However, as the standards of educational attainment and training in the specialties are set by the professional bodies (the royal colleges, faculties and higher training committees), these institutions which supply educational services (examinations, courses and so forth) also control the level of demand for their services. Parliament has also stimulated the demand for postgraduate training by introducing regulations for the vocational training of general practitioners and by making provision under the appropriate Medical Acts for doctors with limited registration to obtain full registration without having to requalify in the United Kingdom first.

In addition to the qualifications awarded by the royal colleges, doctors may also study for or carry out research for postgraduate degrees awarded by the universities. Many doctors obtain a doctorate in medicine (MD) or philosophy (PhD). Courses for masters degrees and diplomas in a wide range of clinical and medical science subjects are available in various university centres. The Society of Apothecaries of London also offers diploma courses in medical jurisprudence and history of medicine. The Councils for Postgraduate Medical Education in England and Wales, Scotland and Northern Ireland, together with the National Advice Centre, publish annually a guide to postgraduate degrees, diplomas and courses available in the United Kingdom (and Republic of Ireland).[115] It identifies for nearly 100 clinical and medical science subjects, the names of the bodies awarding the degrees and diplomas, the examination dates, the qualifications and experience needed for eligibility, the fees and other relevant information. With the courses, the guide lists under each subject the names of the organising bodies mounting the courses, the nature and duration of the courses, the fees and other comments such as requirements for acceptance.

This chapter is confined to a discussion of the examinations for the higher qualifications of membership or fellowship of the royal colleges and faculties (excluding the Faculty of Homoeopathy (page 230)) and of the college examinations for diplomas such as the DCH and DRCOG. It contains an outline of the regulations and provides information on the current level of fees and the pass rates for many examinations. Presented in the next chapter are data on doctors who obtained higher qualifications relevant to the hospital-based specialties in 1982. There is more material on the educational roles played by the royal colleges and faculties, in particular the procedures for accreditation and the approval of posts, in chapters 16 and 17.

## EXAMINATIONS FOR MEMBERSHIP AND FELLOWSHIP

The Royal Commission on Medical Education expressed criticism in 1968 of the colleges' examination systems for higher qualifications. The timing and nature of the examinations were not related as closely as they should have been to the existing arrangements for postgraduate training.[1] The situation 17 years later seems to have changed very little, at least with reference to timing. Another criticism made by the Commission over the lack of complete reciprocal recognition of the primary examinations of the English and Scottish royal colleges of physicians and surgeons is still valid for surgery. The Royal College of Surgeons of England does not offer exemption to those who passed the primary examination of the other United Kingdom colleges (or overseas colleges) on or after 1 July 1980. The Royal Colleges of Physicians in Edinburgh, Glasgow and London on the other hand, now have a common membership qualification.

It can be seen in Figure 11 that to obtain all but one of the higher qualifications candidates must sit two or three major examinations at intervals of many months and the names given to these examination levels and to the final qualifications vary. Certain colleges award a diploma of membership (usually on payment of a fee) to the successful candidates, these being the Royal Colleges of Physicians of the United Kingdom (RCsP(UK)), the Royal College of Obstetricians and Gynaecologists, the Royal College of Psychiatrists (RCPsych), the Royal College of Pathologists (RCPath), and the Faculties of Community Medicine and Occupational Medicine. (Candidates for the MFOM must first sit an examination of associateship (AFOM).) Members of these colleges may be elected as fellows at some later date. (With the

Royal College of Pathologists membership of the college may be followed, after a 12-year period, by an offer of promotion to fellowship. Also this college permits persons who are not medically qualified to sit the examinations for membership, and membership may be awarded on the basis of published work only.) In order to become a member of the Royal College of General Practitioners (RCGP) an applicant must be successful first in the MRCGP and on payment of an entrance fee a membership certificate is forwarded. The other colleges, in contrast, award their successful candidates with a diploma of fellowship (also on payment of a fee) and soon afterwards the diploma holders are admitted to the college as fellows. This is the practice of the Royal College of Radiologists (RCR), the Royal College of Surgeons of England (RCS Eng), the Royal College of Surgeons of Edinburgh, the Royal College of Physicians and Surgeons of Glasgow and the Faculty of Anaesthetists (FA) of the Royal College of Surgeons of England. (Note that a surgeon is addressed as Mr or Miss or Mrs after he or she has been admitted as a fellow to a surgical college including the RCOG.)

The different requirements over the lengths of time that must elapse before candidates may sit the higher qualifying examinations of the colleges reflect the different roles of the qualifications in training doctors to become specialists. The MRCP(UK) which can be completed in two and a half years after obtaining a primary qualification does not confer specialist status. It is designed to select those suitable for higher specialist training in the United Kingdom and the examination may also be taken by those who do not intend to pursue a career in hospital medicine, hence the shorter training period required in the regulations.[116] The final qualifying examinations in the surgical, anaesthetics, obstetrics and gynaecology and psychiatric specialties may be taken after four years. These too, are aimed at selecting the doctors best suited to become consultants after further training. With diagnostic radiology and radiotherapy and oncology, the final qualifying examinations for the FRCR may be taken after five years. The final part of the MRCPath may be entered after six years and it assesses whether doctors are fully trained and thus suitable for appointment to consultant posts in the pathology specialties. Doctors holding the FRCR but who have not done five years approved training in recognised departments may have to spend an additional period in training before receiving a certificate of accreditation (see page 241).

To complete the MFCM and MFOM, candidates must submit written work of dissertation length for assessment. There is no minimum time period before the candidates for the community medicine part II examination can submit their report or reports, but the preparation of the material is intended to be part of higher specialist training and the material cannot be examined until the MFCM part I has been passed.[123] Candidates for the MFOM are required to complete four years of supervised training having already obtained broad clinical experience normally over a

**Figure 11** Minimum time periods before doctors may sit the examinations for the higher medical qualifications of membership or fellowship awarded by the royal colleges and faculties

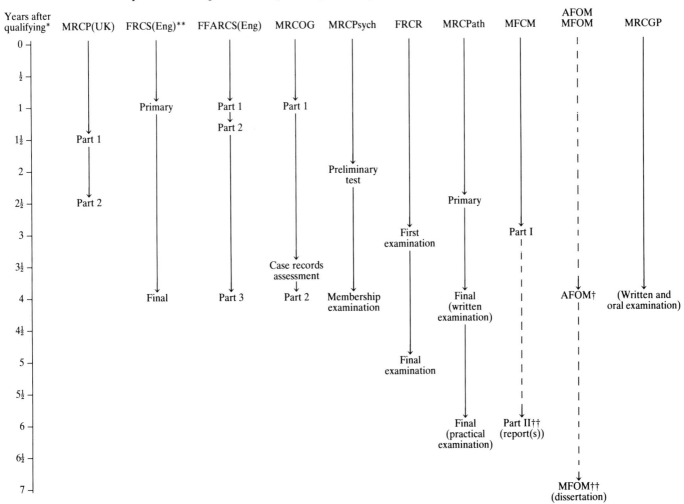

| Years after qualifying* | MRCP(UK) | FRCS(Eng)** | FFARCS(Eng) | MRCOG | MRCPsych | FRCR | MRCPath | MFCM | AFOM MFOM | MRCGP |
|---|---|---|---|---|---|---|---|---|---|---|
| 0 | | | | | | | | | | |
| ½ | | | | | | | | | | |
| 1 | | Primary | Part 1 Part 2 | Part 1 | | | | | | |
| 1½ | Part 1 | | | | | | | | | |
| 2 | | | | | Preliminary test | | | | | |
| 2½ | Part 2 | | | | | | Primary | | | |
| 3 | | | | | | First examination | | Part I | | |
| 3½ | | | Case records assessment | | | | | | | |
| 4 | | Final | Part 3 | Part 2 | Membership examination | | Final (written examination) | | AFOM† | (Written and oral examination) |
| 4½ | | | | | | | | | | |
| 5 | | | | | | Final examination | | | | |
| 5½ | | | | | | | | | | |
| 6 | | | | | | | Final (practical examination) | Part II†† (report(s)) | | |
| 6½ | | | | | | | | | | |
| 7 | | | | | | | | | MFOM†† (dissertation) | |

\* Minimum number of years after obtaining a primary medical qualification.
\*\* The time intervals for the FRCS examinations of the Royal Colleges of Surgeons of Edinburgh and Glasgow are the same.
† Candidates for the AFOM are normally expected to have obtained broad clinical experience over at least three years after the preregistration year.
†† No set time period must elapse before a report(s) or dissertation can be submitted.

Note: The colleges can amend these requirements.

Sources: Regulations for the examinations.[116–125]

Table 31 Minimum experience required in the examination disciplines of the higher qualifications of membership and fellowship, the period available for post-registration experience in other disciplines, and the minimum duration of experience in the United Kingdom or Republic of Ireland needed in the examination disciplines

| Higher qualification | Minimum duration of time* | Minimum requirement of post-registration experience in examination discipline** | Period available for post-registration experience in other disciplines** | Minimum duration of experience in examination discipline in UK or Ireland† |
|---|---|---|---|---|
| MRCP(UK) | 2½ years | 1 year of inpatient care of acutely ill medical patients | 6 months | nil |
| FRCS(Eng) | 4 years | 2 years of approved training in certain surgical specialties | 1 year | 1 year |
| FFARCS(Eng) | 4 years | 2 years of approved training | 1 year | 1 year (in schedule I posts that are normally in the UK) |
| MRCOG | 4 years | 2 years in recognised posts [plus 1 year in another discipline(s)] | 1 year (compulsory) | nil |
| MRCPsych | 4 years | 2 years of approved training | 1 year†† | 2 years (or nil if overseas posts have reciprocal recognition) |
| FRCR | 5 years | 3 years of approved training | 1 year | nil |
| MRCPath | 6 years | 5 years of approved training of which 1 year may be in another discipline | 1 year | Training outside the UK is considered on an individual basis |
| MFCM | more than 3 years | not prescribed | no restriction | nil |
| AFOM | 4 years normally | 6 to 12 months full or part-time | 3 years | nil |
| MFOM | more than 4 years | 4 years of supervised work | 3 years | 2 years in UK |
| MRCGP | 4 years | 2 years or 1 year as a vocational trainee | 2 years | nil |

 * Minimum duration between obtaining a primary medical qualification and sitting the final examination.
** For candidates with a UK primary qualification wishing to sit the final examination in the minimum period of time.
 † For overseas-qualified candidates.
†† In psychiatry the year may be spent in general practice, in a hospital medical post at SHO level or higher or in research in a cognate discipline.

Sources: Regulations for the examinations.[116–125]

period of at least four years following graduation. (Credit can be granted for relevant past experience and suitable academic training.) Candidates must also be associates of the Faculty. A thesis or dissertation that has already been accepted by a university as part of the requirements for a postgraduate degree or substantial published work can be submitted for examination.[124] The higher qualification for general practice has only one phase of examinations – written papers followed approximately six weeks later by an oral examination for candidates who have been successful in the written papers. These examinations may be sat for the first time four years after obtaining a primary qualification and this minimum period is the same as the minimum period in which general practitioner trainees can complete their vocational training.

As mentioned in chapter 2, the Social Services Committee of the House of Commons in 1980/81 was concerned by the narrow content of training required by the hospital-based specialties. It recommended that [the advisory committees for] all specialties through their colleges and faculties should require trainees to spend periods totalling at least one year in other disciplines after they have become fully registered (para 191).[4] Table 31 shows that for most of the higher qualifications it is possible to spend at least one year in other disciplines after obtaining full registration and still be eligible to take the final examination within the minimum time period allowed. The MRCP(UK) is the exception – for United Kingdom candidates with full registration the period available for training in another discipline is six months.[116] For the MRCOG there is a basic requirement of one year being spent in up to four other disciplines; the professional work chosen by the candidates must be approved by the Education Committee of the College preferably before the work is undertaken.[119]

Since most of the membership and fellowship examination regulations for hospital specialties allow doctors to spend one year in other disciplines, why did the Social Services Committee believe that the examination systems were so inflexible? This point was discussed in a paper by Robson which was written on behalf of the Conference of Medical Royal Colleges and their Faculties in the United Kingdom. Robson felt that this complicated question can be answered only partly and on a speculative basis. The trainees are responsible to a certain extent for the situation. They believe that if they stray from the direct NHS career path, even in an approved manner, they will diminish their competitive position on the NHS career ladder. At the same time, many appointment committees prefer candidates with the greatest possible practical experience within the specialty, presumably the reason being that these candidates have decided on their careers and will benefit most from the training.[126] Also, and naturally, experienced doctors when newly appointed require less supervision and instruction than inexperienced doctors.

It was noted in chapter 7 that there is an overseas 'market' for the postgraduate qualifications awarded by the royal colleges. This point is illustrated in Table 31 column 5. Candidates for the final examinations of the MRCP(UK), MRCOG, FRCR, MRCGP, MFCM and AFOM are not required to have trained in the United Kingdom or the Republic of Ireland. The part 1 examination of the MRCP(UK) is held in about 12 centres in Asia, the Middle East, northern, central and southern Africa and the West Indies. The part 2 examination is, however, only held in the United Kingdom and Hong Kong as a very special case. The RCOG also holds its part 1 examination in about 12 centres in North America, northern and central Africa, Asia, the Pacific, the Middle East and the West Indies, while the part 2 examination was held in Singapore in 1983.[127] The Royal College of Radiologists holds the first and final examination for the FRCR in Hong Kong from time to time[128], the first anaesthetics examination for the FFARCS(Eng) and the primary examination for the FRCS(Eng) are held abroad[117,118] and part I of the MFCM can also be taken abroad occasionally.[123] In pathology, it can sometimes be arranged for candidates to take the written examinations for the MRCPath overseas, but they usually attend for the practical and oral examinations in the United Kingdom.[122]

Some requirements are common to the colleges. They all require the candidates to hold an acceptable primary qualification. Each college applies its own criteria of 'acceptability'. Awarding bodies not recognised by the General Medical Council for the purposes of limited registration may be considered acceptable by an individual college. Conversely, a college may not accept the primary qualification from an awarding body which is recognised by the GMC. The Royal College of General Practitioners is the only college which stipulates that candidates must be fully registered with the GMC. Some colleges insist that candidates are sponsored, usually by two senior college members (The Royal Colleges of Surgeons and Radiologists are two exceptions.) Sponsors may have to provide testimonials on the character, ability, training and experience of the applicant. Finally, the basic training in the examination disciplines must be approved by the colleges although they use different procedures for assessing the training done overseas.

The Royal Colleges of Physicians rely on proposers to confirm that the candidates have spent one year in posts involving the care of emergency medical patients, either adults or children. The Royal College of Obstetricians and Gynaecologists in contrast, classifies for examination purposes, posts in both British and overseas hospitals. For example, in Sydney, Australia, there are hospital posts providing obstetrics and/or gynaecology experience suitable for the membership examination; the experience gained in other Sydney posts is appropriate only for the examination for the diploma of DRCOG.[129] In psychiatry, the Royal College will accept one year of overseas training if the candidate provides adequate documentary evidence. However, persons whose training is in posts approved by the Royal College of Physicians and Surgeons of Canada, the American Board of Psychiatry and Neurology or the Royal Australian and New Zealand College of Psychiatrists, will be given credit for the whole of this period of training. The Royal College of Surgeons of England and its Faculty of Anaesthetists partially accept experience in hospitals recognised by the equivalent overseas colleges, faculties and boards, and experience in other categories of hospitals may also be considered. The Royal College of Radiologists also will normally accept overseas training undertaken in departments approved by equivalent overseas colleges, faculties or boards provided candidates comply with the Fellowship regulations in all other respects. Each application is considered on its individual merits.

### Attempts at the examinations and the fees

The Royal College of Surgeons of England does not impose any limitations on the occasions when the examinations may be taken for the FRCS and the FFARCS (see Table 32); the Royal College of Radiologists applies the same policy to the final examination for the FRCR and likewise, the Royal College of General Practitioners for the MRCGP. Unlimited attempts may also be made at passing part II of the MFCM and the two examinations in occupational medicine. The attempts stated in the regulations for the other examinations range between four and six. The Royal College of Pathologists permits six attempts at the final examination and candidates who are still unsuccessful may be allowed to re-enter if there are extenuating circumstances. The Faculty of Community Medicine is also prepared to consider the circumstances of candidates who fail part I of the MFCM on four occasions. Candidates for most final examinations must complete the attempts within a certain time period although the duration of the period varies from college to college.

The scale of fees for 1985 for the various examinations is also shown in Table 32. The fees are set and regularly reviewed by the colleges. There was nearly a three-fold variation between the lowest and highest fees for the first examination – £55 for the preliminary test of the MRCPsych and £160 for part 1 of the FFARCS(Eng). The fees for the final examinations held in the United Kingdom ranged from £105 (MRCPsych) to £200 (MRCP(UK)). The assessment fee for dissertations submitted for the MFOM was far lower at £50. In addition, the colleges – with the exception of the Royal College of Pathologists – ask successful candidates to pay a diploma or registration fee and for some colleges the sum in 1985 was between £50 and £90.

Candidates who are employed by the NHS have to pay their own examination fees. The NHS does not reimburse them. Also, tax relief is not available. Doctors who hold scholarships or bursaries may have their fees paid by the funding body. This applies to doctors who are sponsored under the aegis of the British Council, for example.

Table 32   Number of attempts normally permitted at the higher qualifying examinations for membership and fellowship, and the fees in 1985

| Higher qualification | Examination levels | Total number of attempts permitted | Fees in 1985* | |
|---|---|---|---|---|
| | | | UK centres | Overseas centres |
| MRCP(UK) | part 1 | 4 | £100 | |
| | part 2 | 6 (2 per college) | £200 | |
| FRCS(Eng) | primary | unlimited | £140 | £250 |
| | final | unlimited | £180 | |
| FFARCS(Eng) | part 1 | unlimited | £160 | £250 |
| | part 2 | unlimited | £140 | |
| | part 3 | unlimited | £180 | |
| MRCOG | part 1 | 5 | £75 | £150 |
| | case records | – | £40 | £40 |
| | part 2 | 5 | £150 | £380 |
| MRCPsych | preliminary test | 5 | £55 | |
| | membership | 5 | £105 | |
| FRCR | first | 4 | £100 | |
| | final | unlimited | £100 | |
| MRCPath | primary | 4 | £75 | additional fee of £20 |
| | final (written and practical) | 6 | £150 | |
| MFCM | part I | 4 | £100 UK resident | £120 resident elsewhere |
| | part II [report(s)] | unlimited | £100 | £120 |
| AFOM | examinations | unlimited | £150 | |
| MFOM | dissertation or published work | unlimited | £50 assessment fee | |
| MRCGP | written and oral examinations | unlimited | £155 (reapplication fee £117) | |

* The fees are subject to regular reviews.

Sources: Regulations for the examinations[116–125] and Guide to postgraduate degrees, diplomas and courses.[115]

9   Demand for
postgraduate qualifications
awarded by the royal
colleges and faculties

Table 33   Pass rate levels for the first and final examinations of the higher qualifications of membership and fellowship, 1982–84

| | Percentage pass level* | | | |
| Examination stage | 20–29% | 30–39% | 40–49% | 50% and over |
|---|---|---|---|---|
| First | | MRCOG | MRCPsych | FRCR (radiodiagnosis) |
| | | | MRCPath FRCR (radiotherapy) | |
| Final | FRCS(Eng) FFARCS(Eng) FRCR (radiotherapy) | MRCPath FRCR (radiodiagnosis) | MRCOG MRCPsych | |

* The percentage pass levels are based on examination results for the following years: FRCS(Eng) 1982–84, FFARCS(Eng)1982–84, MRCOG 1981–83, MRCPsych 1983/84, MRCPath 1983/84, and FRCR 1983 for the first part and 1984 for the second part.

Sources: Annual reports and publications of the royal colleges[127–128, 130–132], and a personal communication from the Royal College of Radiologists.

## Pass rates for the membership and fellowship examinations

The royal colleges (with the exception of the Royal Colleges of Physicians) and the faculties inform their members regularly of the numbers of candidates who sit the final qualifying examinations and the numbers who passed. Some also provide details of the success rates for the first examination stage. This information is contained in the annual reports of the colleges or, for surgery and anaesthetics, in the bi-monthly College and Faculty Bulletin that is published as a supplement to the *Annals of the Royal College of Surgeons of England*. Percentage pass rates for first and final examinations for various qualifications in the hospital-based disciplines are shown in Table 33. These rates are based on examinations held between 1982 and 1984. (Most examinations are held twice a year in the United Kingdom; parts 1 and 2 of the MRCP(UK) are held on three occasions.)

Of the four first-part examinations about which data are available, the MRCOG has the lowest overall pass rate (30-39 per cent) and the FRCR in radiodiagnosis the highest – over 70 per cent in 1983. (It is noteworthy that all trainees in diagnostic radiology and radiotherapy and oncology are expected to enrol with the College at the commencement of their specialist training.) It has been reported that usually one in three of the candidates for part 1 of the MRCP(UK) passes.[133]

Of the final examinations, the FRSC(Eng) and the FFARCS(Eng) appear to have considerably lower pass rates (20-29) per cent than the others. The 1984 pass rate for the FRCR in radiotherapy was slightly under 30 per cent. The information on the MRCPath applies to all candidates who entered the two primary examinations and two final examinations in 1983/84 and who successfully completed all parts of the examinations.[130] (Candidates for the Final MRCPath examination may sit the written papers after three years of full-time approved training whereas the final practical and oral examination cannot be taken until five years of full-time training have been completed.)

*The structure of the examinations*

This chapter has emphasised the dissimilarities in the regulations applying to the various qualifications and they need to be borne in mind when interpreting Table 33. The structure of the examinations is more uniform. A multiple-choice question (MCQ) paper forms part of the first examination for eight higher qualifications. For the MRCP(UK) and the MRCOG, candidates complete only MCQ papers. In psychiatry and general practice the examinees also sit an essay paper (or two essay question papers for the MRCGP) whereas in pathology there is a practical and oral assessment. Candidates for the first examinations for the FRCS(Eng), FFARCS(Eng) and the FRCR must sit a MCQ paper, write an essay and be orally examined; in surgery and anaesthetics the candidates progress to the essay and oral stages only if they score a sufficiently high mark in the MCQ paper. (For the FRCS(Eng) there is a MCQ paper, an essay and an oral in each of three subjects – anatomy, physiology and pathology.) For the FRCR, candidates in radiodiagnosis must obtain a sufficient combined mark in the MCQ paper and a film viewing session before proceeding to the oral examination whereas for radiotherapy, a sufficient mark in an MCQ paper only is required. Candidates for the qualifications which do not have MCQ papers in the first level examinations – the MFCM and the A/MFOM – complete instead essay-type written papers. AFOM candidates must also sit clinical and practical examinations and be orally questioned. The subject of part of the oral examination is a journal prepared by the candidate that normally gives an account of occupational medical practice carried out over four weeks within the previous year.

Less reliance is placed on the MCQ examination technique in the final examinations. For almost all the hospital-based qualifications, candidates must complete written and oral examinations and, depending on the nature of the specialty, practical work and/or clinical examinations. For example, part 2 of the MRCP(UK) can be taken in general internal medicine or paediatrics and is a clinical examination consisting of a long case of one hour duration and short cases lasting up to 30 minutes. The candidates have four different examiners for the short and long cases. Candidates for the MRCOG must prepare a portfolio of case records and commentaries of a satisfactory standard before they will be accepted to sit the membership examination. (In 1988 this requirement will be altered and candidates will have to keep a log book.) With the MRCGP, part of the oral examination is based on a log diary in which the candidate has described 50 consecutive patients seen during a normal working week. For the final examination of the FRCS(Eng), candidates may specialise in ophthalmology or otolaryngology.

The colleges are concerned that the curricula for the higher qualifications are appropriate for the disciplines and that the examination standards are maintained. The Faculty of Anaesthetists replaced the two-part examination structure for the FFARCS(Eng) with a three-part structure in 1985. Discussions on the subject of restructuring the fellowship examination started more than a decade earlier when a working party was set up. The new part 1 examination is considered to be more relevant to the vocational training that trainees receive in their first year, usually spent in district general hospitals.[134] In the early 1980s the Royal Colleges of Physicians reformed the part 2 of the MRCP(UK) in response to a feeling that standards were falling. The part 1 MCQ paper contains 'marker questions' which can be used to measure standards of candidates' answers over time.[133] An analysis of the primary examination results for the FRCS(Eng) showed that on average, candidates were scoring a significantly higher mark in the MCQ paper than in the essay or oral examination. The level of the MCQ marking was reset to the standards of the other parts of the examination.[135] (One purpose of the MCQ paper is to identify candidates whose basic understanding of the three examination subjects is insufficient to warrant their entering the essay and oral sections.) This process of review and revision of the content of the examinations and the regulations is continuous. The Royal College of Psychiatrists in 1985, for example, considered how the content of the primary test should be restructured and the Royal College of Surgeons of England introduced amended regulations on the experience needed by candidates for the final examination for the FRCS(Eng) in 1986. To be eligible, candidates in general surgery must now spend six months in general surgery, six months in accident and emergency, six months in a major surgical specialty and six months in any of the above specialties.

## EXAMINATIONS FOR DIPLOMAS AWARDED BY THE ROYAL COLLEGES

Each royal college, apart from the colleges for psychiatrists and general practitioners, holds examinations for one or more diploma qualifications. The education attainments and level of clinical experience required by candidates is often similar to that required for the first part of the examinations for the membership and fellowship qualifications. The diploma examination in anaesthetics (DA(UK)) has been merged with the new part I of the FFARCS(Eng) and pass candidates who have satisfactorily completed one year in approved posts in the British Isles may apply for the award of the diploma.[118] Holders of the diplomas awarded by the Royal College of Pathologists (in pathology, toxicology and cytogenetics) may be exempted from taking the primary examination for the MRCPath.[122] The fees for the majority of diploma examinations in 1985 were around £150 and usually an additional payment was needed to receive the diploma.[115]

The two most commonly awarded diplomas are in obstetrics and gynaecology (DRCOG) and child health (DCH). Both the Royal College of Physicians in London and the Royal College of Physicians and Surgeons of Glasgow award a DCH. Many doctors planning a career in general practice sit the DRCOG or DCH or both examinations while doctors wishing to be approved as ophthalmic medical practitioners may study for the diploma in ophthalmology. In the three years 1981–83, 3949 doctors were examined for the DRCOG and 3138 passed giving a pass rate of 80 per cent (a far higher pass rate than for the first part of the MRCOG).[127] Information on the pass rates for the DCH is not published. The numbers of candidates for the diplomas of the other colleges are tiny in comparison. The single-part examinations for the diplomas in medical radiodiagnosis and in radiotherapy and oncology were first held by the Royal College of Radiologists in December 1983. There were 36 candidates overall and 56 per cent passed.[128] In pathology during 1983/84, 30 candidates entered the examinations for the three diplomas and 37 per cent passed all three stages of written papers, practicals and orals.[130]

This chapter has reviewed the examination procedures for the higher qualifications in the clinical disciplines awarded by the royal colleges and faculties. (Courses for university degrees and diplomas relevant to the medical disciplines are discussed in chapter 15.) In the next chapter the attributes of the candidates who were successful in 1982 in obtaining a higher qualification of membership or fellowship in the hospital-based disciplines are described; that is, the gender of the doctors, the university or country where they obtained their primary qualification and, for UK-qualified doctors, the duration of time between obtaining the primary and higher qualifications. Unfortunately, however, it is not possible to look at the characteristics of those who never succeeded in passing the first or final examinations for these qualifications nor to learn how many of those who finally qualified had to re-take any of the examinations, because the relevant information is not available.

# 10    Higher qualification examination passes 1982

In the mid 1960s the Royal Commission on Medical Education, when collecting evidence, found that none of the colleges had information about the pass rates of British graduates in the higher qualification examinations readily available. The colleges did, however, prepare special analyses for the Commission which appear in one of the appendices of the report.[1] At the same time, Wilson looked at background information on candidates with a primary medical qualification from universities in the British Isles who passed the final examinations for the MRCP(London) and the FRCS(Eng) in 1963, 1964 and 1965.[136] He analysed two items: the length of time between obtaining a primary qualification and passing a final higher qualifying examination and, for candidates who qualified in England and Wales, the university of primary qualification (London, Oxford and Cambridge, and English provincial and Welsh). These two items of information on each successful candidate had been extracted from *The Medical Directory*.[137]

There were two points of note in the paper by Wilson. First, although it was permissible for candidates to sit the final examination for the MRCP(London) 18 months after acquiring a primary qualification, and for the FRCS(Eng) three years after qualifying, few candidates did so successfully. The time taken by the largest group of candidates to pass the MRCP (the mode) was five years between graduation and completion of the examination requirements, and the interval for the FRCS was six years. The second point was that Oxford and Cambridge graduates followed by London graduates tended to pass the MRCP final examination earlier than graduates of the English provincial and Welsh universities. With the FRCS, however, there was little difference between the three groups of graduates, although Oxford and Cambridge graduates appeared to proceed slightly more quickly than the others.

The reports of the Committee of Inquiry into the Regulation of the Medical Profession, the Royal Commission on the National Health Service, and the 1980/81 inquiry into medical education by the Social Services Committee of the House of Commons contain few comments on the examination systems and pass rates for the various higher qualifications awarded by the royal colleges, and yet each one set out proposals for restructuring the training grades (refer to chapter 2). Moreover, there seemed to be an underlying assumption held by these bodies that doctors were capable of proceeding through the grades at similar rates of progress if they have adequate training at every stage.

Since there are no recent data available on the proportions of British graduates who obtain higher qualifications and the duration of time that they take, it was decided to repeat Wilson's 1963-65 exercise for the MRCP (which is now administered by all three colleges of physicians in the United Kingdom) and for the FRCS(Eng). The opportunity was taken also to look at the results for the final examinations for the FFARCS(Eng), MRCOG, MRCPsych, FRCR and MRCPath. Nineteen eighty-two was the survey year chosen and the method was as follows. The pass lists for all final examinations held in that year except those for the MRCOG were taken from the *British Medical Journal*. Copies of the MRCOG lists were supplied by the Royal College of Obstetricians and Gynaecologists. The published pass lists give the surname and initials of each candidate or the surname, first name and initials if the person is known to be a woman. (Most colleges usually send their pass lists to the *British Medical Journal* for publication, although the coverage in the Journal for each year is not always complete. The colleges also publish their own pass lists or lists of new fellows or members in their annual reports or in bulletins that are regularly sent to members. There are only tiny differences between the numbers of pass candidates for the FRCS(Eng) and FFARCS(Eng) and the numbers of names on the published lists of persons admitted as fellows to the college. This suggests that, at least in these disciplines, almost all pass candidates choose to pay the admission fee and join the college membership.)

The names on the pass lists were transferred to coding sheets and then each name was checked in *The Medical Register* for 1982 to see if the sex of the candidate was the same as suggested by the pass list, and to find the name of the university which awarded the doctor's primary medical qualification and the date when the primary qualification was registered with the General Medical Council for provisional registration. (This usually occurs very soon after the date when the qualification is awarded because newly qualified doctors must be registered before they can be employed in the NHS.) If a doctor had qualified at an overseas university, no date was recorded on the coding sheet since the information in *The Medical Register* applies only to the dates of registration to practise in the United Kingdom. The Registers for 1983 and 1984 were also checked if a name did not appear in the 1982 volume. A tiny number of doctors (four) were identified as holding both an overseas primary qualification and a UK primary qualification (awarded by a non-university licensing body in each instance). The country awarding the earliest qualification was coded.

Naturally there was a number of persons whose names were not found in any of the volumes. Some may have held limited registration during these years and the Limited Register is not a published document; others were probably practising outside the United Kingdom and a few may have held a primary medical qualification that is not acceptable by the GMC for limited registration. Also, there were some doctors with the same name and initial as other entries in the Registers while a few married women candidates were thought to have been entered on the pass list under their maiden

Table 34   Numbers of holders of a United Kingdom or an overseas primary medical qualification who passed the final examinations for seven higher qualifications, 1982

| Higher qualification | Holders of a UK primary qualification | Holders of an overseas primary qualification | Total | Holders of an overseas primary qualification as % of total |
|---|---|---|---|---|
| | No | No | No | % |
| MRCP(UK) | 551 | 287 | 838 | 34.2 |
| FRCS(Eng) | 205 | 62 | 267* | 23.2 |
| FFARCS(Eng) | 151 | 72 | 223 | 32.3 |
| MRCOG | 70 | 218 | 288 | 75.7 |
| MRCPsych | 144** | 137** | 281 | 48.8** |
| FRCR | 83 | 43 | 126 | 34.1 |
| MRCPath | 97 | 43 | 140† | 30.7 |
| Total | 1301 | 862 | 2163 | 39.9 |

 * Of these, 26 passed in ophthalmology, 35 in otolaryngology and the remainder in general surgery.
** With the MRCPsych, the number of holders of a United Kingdom qualification may be underestimated and, conversely, the number of overseas holders overestimated.
 † Also 17 persons who were not medically qualified passed the MRCPath final examinations.

Note: Primary medical qualifications awarded in the Republic of Ireland are included in the category of overseas primary qualifications.

Sources: Higher qualification examination pass lists and Medical Registers 1982–84.

name but they were registered in their married name. Letters requesting help with the names not found in the Registers were sent to the examination departments of the royal colleges. All but one supplied the missing details. The Royal College of Psychiatrists was unable to help because it no longer held comprehensive records for 1982. Finally, for each graduate of the United Kingdom universities the time period between the examination month for university finals that preceded the provisional registration date and the month of the higher qualifying final examination was calculated. This time period was coded in months. There were over 2160 entries in total and the data set (but without the names) was entered on a computer of the University of London via the computing centre at the University of Kent at Canterbury and it was analysed using a survey statistical package.

Table 34 shows that the number of passes for the MRCP(UK) ( 838) was about three times larger than the numbers for the MRCOG, the MRCPsych and the FRCS(Eng) which lay between 267 and 288. (To gain an idea of the total numbers of doctors who obtain an FRCS awarded in the United Kingdom it is necessary to add in the results for the FRCS awarded by the royal colleges in Edinburgh and Glasgow.) The FFARCS(Eng) with 223 successful candidates had the fifth largest number of passes and the two diagnostic qualifications – MRCPath and FRCR – had the smallest numbers of passes, 140 and 126 respectively. This was not a surprising finding as these two disciplines are the smallest in terms of numbers of trainees in the NHS. Seventeen non-medically qualified persons also passed the MRCPath final examination.

COUNTRY OF PRIMARY MEDICAL QUALIFICATION

Holders of overseas primary medical qualifications accounted for around one-third of the successful candidates for four of the higher qualifications – MRCP(UK), FFARCS(Eng), FRCR and MRCPath (see Table 34). (Note that primary medical qualifications awarded in the Republic of Ireland are included in the category of overseas qualifications.) With the MRCOG and FRCS(Eng), the situations were strikingly different. Three-quarters of the successes in obstetrics and gynaecology were overseas doctors, and it will be recalled from the previous chapter and chapter 8 that not only does this College have extensive overseas examination arrangements but also a high proportion of registrars in this specialty in the NHS are overseas-born doctors. The situation regarding the FRCS(Eng) was in total contrast; less than a quarter of the doctors who obtained the surgical higher qualification in 1982 had qualified overseas. In psychiatry, almost half the doctors awarded the MRCPsych were thought to be overseas trained doctors. It was not possible to obtain an exact percentage because 58 names out of the 281 on the pass lists were not in the Medical Registers. The spellings of the surnames suggested, however, that many of these doctors were likely to have been on the Limited Register or to have registered with the Irish Medical Council.

In his 1977/78 survey of overseas doctors in the NHS, Smith found that 80 per cent of the interviewed doctors who had received their first qualification in the Indian subcontinent – India, Pakistan, Bangladesh and Sri Lanka – hoped to obtain membership or fellowship of a royal college while in the United Kingdom. The percentage of doctors from Arab countries with this ambition was even higher – 86 per cent.[110] The information from the 1982 final examination pass lists suggests that the levels of achievement of doctors from a few of these countries and from countries in Asia are higher than might be predicted from the GMC registration data.

Countries whose universities award primary medical qualifications, many of which are now recognised for limited registration, are listed in Table 35; also listed are the non-EEC countries whose university qualifications – with one or two exceptions – are fully registrable. Shown for each country is the number of graduates who were

Table 35   Country of primary medical qualification (excluding the United Kingdom) held by candidates who passed the final examinations for six higher qualifications*, 1982

| Countries, many of whose primary medical qualifications are recognised for limited registration | | | Non-EEC countries whose primary medical qualifications are generally recognised for full registration | | |
|---|---|---|---|---|---|
| Country of training | Number of passes | % of passes | Country of training | Number of passes | % of passes |
| India | 155 | 36.2 | Australia | 61 | 26.2 |
| Sri Lanka | 65 | 15.2 | Hong Kong | 56 | 24.0 |
| Iraq | 45 | 10.5 | South Africa | 39 | 16.7 |
| Egypt | 42 | 9.8 | Malaysia | 25 | 10.7 |
| Pakistan | 24 | 5.6 | Singapore | 23 | 9.9 |
| Nigeria | 17 | 4.0 | New Zealand | 18 | 7.7 |
| Other | 80 | 18.7 | West Indies | 11 | 4.7 |
| Total | 428 | 100.0 | Total | 233 | 100.0 |

* MRCP(UK), FRCS(Eng), FFARCS(Eng), MRCOG, FRCR and MRCPath.

Note: Eight doctors who qualified in continental EEC countries and 53 doctors who qualified in the Republic of Ireland were also among the successful candidates for these six higher qualifications.

Sources: Higher qualification examination pass lists and Medical Registers 1982–84.

successful in obtaining one of six higher qualifications in 1982. Figures for the MRCPsych have been excluded because of the incompleteness of the data.

Slightly over one-third of the successful graduates from the 'limited registration' countries had qualified in India. This proportion was predictable because one-third of the doctors from countries in the 'limited registration' category who registered with the GMC for the first time during 1978-82 came from India.[29] The proportions of successful graduates from Nigeria and Pakistan were also in line with the GMC registration figures. The success rates for Iraq and Egypt and, in particular, Sri Lanka were, however, higher than might have been expected. Around 7 per cent of doctors from the 'limited registration' countries who registered with the GMC during 1978-82 were Iraqis and another 7 per cent were Egyptians; in 1982, graduates from Iraq and Egypt each comprised about 10 per cent of the successful higher qualification candidates. With regard to Sri Lanka, 15 per cent of the higher qualifying passes from 'limited registration' countries were graduates from this country, a rate that was two-thirds higher than the 9 per cent predicted from the GMC registration figures.

Furthermore, Sri Lanka produced the second largest number of pass candidates of any overseas country.

Doctors from 'white anglophone' countries (Australia, New Zealand, South Africa, Rhodesia (Zimbabwe), the United States of America and Canada) who were interviewed in Smith's survey of overseas doctors were much less likely to have aspirations of obtaining a higher qualification while in the United Kingdom than doctors from the Indian subcontinent or an Arab country. Only half of these interviewees expressed the wish and Smith concluded that 'a significant proportion of white anglophones came to the UK as part of a "grand tour" rather than primarily for medical training or experience' (page 53).[110] It should be noted, also, that these countries have their own royal colleges or equivalent bodies.

The data on higher qualification passes give some support to Smith's proposition, at least for Australians and South Africans. In the five years 1978-82 Australian doctors comprised over 40 per cent of first-time registrations with the GMC by doctors from non-EEC countries whose universities' primary medical qualifications are now generally recognised for full registration. South Africans formed nearly a quarter. But, as can be seen in columns 3 to 6 of Table 35, the percentages of doctors from 'full registration' countries who trained in Australia and South Africa and who obtained higher qualifications in 1982 were well below these proportions. The rate for New Zealand graduates in Table 35 did match the expected rate from the registration data. In contrast, graduates from Hong Kong, Malaysia and Singapore had more successes in the higher qualifying examinations than expected from the registration figures. The Hong Kong rates were particularly noteworthy: 24 per cent of doctors from 'full registration' countries who passed a higher qualification final examination were from the colony, compared to only 13 per cent of the registrations with the GMC of doctors from this category of countries in the five-year period. Care must be taken when drawing conclusions from these data. If Smith's proposition that many white anglophone doctors do not intend to enter fellowship or membership examinations while in the United Kingdom is true, then the success rates of Asian doctors with full registration cannot be directly compared with the rates for overseas doctors with European origins.

### Women holders of United Kingdom primary medical qualifications

Women formed 26 per cent of the holders of United Kingdom primary medical qualifications who were successful in the 1982 higher qualification final examinations (see Table 36). The percentage of women in the group of graduates from English and Welsh universities was virtually the same. In the years 1976-79, during which most candidates would have undergone their specialty training, the proportion of senior

Table 36    Gender of holders of a United Kingdom primary medical qualification who passed the final examinations for seven higher qualifications, 1982

| Higher qualification | Males | | Females | | Total | |
|---|---|---|---|---|---|---|
| | No | % | No | % | No | % |
| MRCP(UK) | 403 | 73.1 | 148 | 26.9 | 551 | 100.0 |
| FRCS(Eng) | 190 | 92.7 | 15 | 7.3 | 205 | 100.0 |
| FFARCS(Eng) | 111 | 73.5 | 40 | 26.5 | 151 | 100.0 |
| MRCOG | 51 | 72.9 | 19 | 27.1 | 70 | 100.0 |
| MRCPsych | 83 | 57.6 | 61 | 42.4 | 144 | 100.0 |
| FRCR | 56 | 67.5 | 27 | 32.5 | 83 | 100.0 |
| MRCPath | 67 | 69.1 | 30 | 30.9 | 97 | 100.0 |
| Total | 961 | 73.9 | 340 | 26.1 | 1301 | 100.0 |

Note: The percentages apply to the total passes for each qualification.

Sources: Higher qualification examination pass lists and Medical Registers 1982–84.[70]

house officers and registrars employed in NHS hospitals in England and Wales who were women ranged from 20 per cent in 1976 to 23 per cent in 1979. (For SHOs alone the range was 21 to 25 per cent – see Tables 3 and 26.) It would appear, therefore, that women may have been slightly over-represented among the successful higher qualifying candidates in 1982. With the individual qualifications, however, they were unevenly represented.

The number of women who held United Kingdom primary medical qualifications exceeded the expected number among the award holders of the MRCPsych, the FRCR and the MRCPath (Table 36). They comprised over 40 per cent of the successful psychiatry candidates and almost one-third of the candidates in each of the diagnostic specialties. With the MRCP(UK), the FFARCS(Eng) and the MRCOG, their representation was in accordance with that for all successful United Kingdom candidates – that is, around 26-27 per cent. The position was markedly different for the FRCS(Eng). No more than 7 per cent of the United Kingdom qualified candidates who were entitled to a diploma of fellow were women.

SUCCESS RATES AFTER THE MINIMUM LENGTH OF EXPERIENCE

It is uncommon for doctors who have only the minimum post-qualification experience acceptable under the regulations for the higher qualifications of membership or fellowship (refer to Table 31) to pass the final examinations at their first attempt.

Figure 12  Time, in years, after obtaining a primary medical qualification within which
graduates from universities in the British Isles passed the MRCP(Lond) in 1965
(data source Wilson), and holders of a United Kingdom qualification passed the
MRCP(UK) in 1982

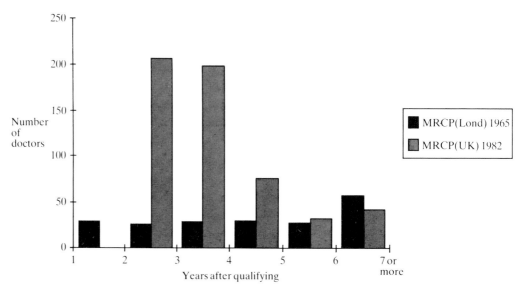

Around one in four of the successful United Kingdom candidates for the MRCPsych
and FFARCS(Eng) achieved this goal in the minimum time period or shortly after,
and one in five of the candidates for the MRCP(UK) and the MRCPath. For the
FRCS(Eng), the proportion of 'high fliers' among the pass candidates was one in eight
and for the FRCR, one in 20. No one obtained a MRCOG diploma in 1982 with only
a minimum amount of training.

### MRCP and FRCS lengths of experience 1965 and 1982

The success rates for the MRCP(UK) and the FRCS(Eng) in 1982 were a vast
improvement on the rates for 1965 published by Wilson[136] (see Figures 12 and 13).
The length of time after qualifying taken by the first half of the successful British
candidates (the median) in the 1965 final examinations for the MRCP administered by
the Royal College of Physicians in London was five years. Moreover, in 1965 doctors
could sit the final examination 18 months after obtaining a primary qualification
unlike now when the minimum time is 30 months. In 1982 nearly three-quarters of the

Figure 13  Time, in years, after obtaining a primary medical qualification within which graduates from universities in the British Isles passed the FRCS(Eng) in 1965 (data source Wilson), and holders of a United Kingdom qualification passed the FRCS(Eng) in 1982

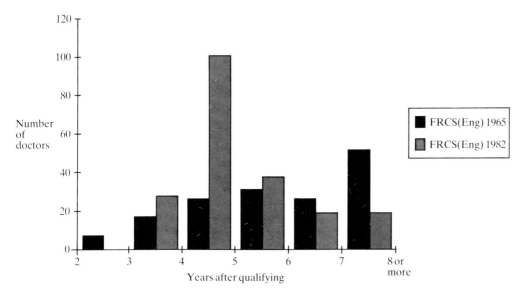

successful UK-qualified candidates for the MRCP(UK) passed within four years of graduation (404 out of 551 doctors). The median was three and a quarter years.

Turning to the FRCS(Eng), for British candidates in 1965 the median time between graduation and passing the final examination was six years even though the minimum duration of post-qualification experience needed under the regulations was three years instead of the current requirement of four years. In 1982 nearly two-thirds of the United Kingdom pass candidates had no more than five years training (129 out of 205 doctors) and the median was almost four and three-quarter years. It should be noted, however, that the regulations for entry to the FRCS(Eng) were amended on at least one occasion between 1965 and 1982 and thus the two samples of pass candidates are not strictly comparable. This point applies also to the two years of results for the MRCP final examinations described in the paragraph above.

*Length of experience for five other qualifications*

Shown in Figure 14 are the time intervals since qualifying of United Kingdom candidates who, in 1982, obtained the three other qualifications that can – according

141

Figure 14  Time, in years, after obtaining a primary medical qualification within which holders
of a United Kingdom qualification passed the FFARCS(Eng), the MRCOG and the
MRCPsych in 1982

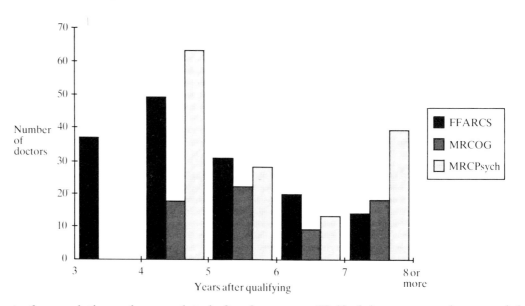

to the regulations – be completed after four years. Half of the persons who passed the
FFARCS(Eng) examinations had been qualified for up to four and three-quarter
years. The median for the psychiatry and obstetrics and gynaecology qualifications
was up to 12 months longer; for the MRCPsych it was almost five and a half years, and
five and three-quarter years for the MRCOG. Moreover, it was quite common for
pass candidates in these two disciplines to have eight or more years of experience.
This was a particular feature of the MRCPsych. One explanation is that doctors
entering this field often reach their decision to specialise in psychiatry after they have
gained experience in other disciplines. For example, 20 of the MRCPsych pass
candidates were listed in *The Medical Registers* as holders of another higher qualification, mostly the MRCP, and this number of dual qualification holders could have
been even higher as doctors do not always submit details of any registrable higher
qualifications that they may hold, for inclusion in *The Medical Register*.

Since the minimum length of experience acceptable by the royal colleges responsible for the diagnostic specialties is five years for the FRCR and six years for the
MRCPath, the time since graduating for the two groups of United Kingdom candidates is shown on the same bar chart (Figure 15). The median time interval between

Figure 15  Time, in years, after obtaining a primary medical qualification within which holders
of a United Kingdom qualification passed the FRCR and the MRCPath in 1982

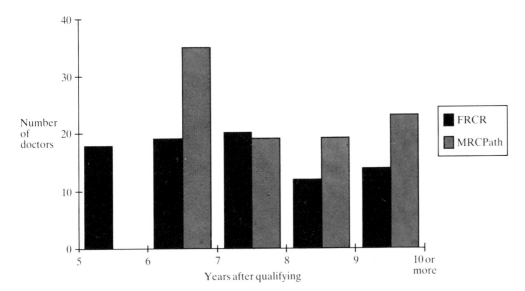

qualifying and passing the FRCR was seven and a quarter years; for the MRCPath it was seven and a half years. At least a quarter of the successful candidates in both disciplines already held an MRCP awarded by one of the royal colleges of physicians in the United Kingdom or by the consortium of colleges.

DIFFERENCES IN LENGTHS OF TRAINING FOR MEN AND WOMEN

When the lengths of training of UK-qualified men and women who passed the MRCP(UK) final examinations were compared, some differences were noted in their rates of progress (see Figure 16). Forty-two per cent of the 148 women candidates who passed did so within three years of obtaining a primary qualification. The percentage of men who passed within three years was lower at 35 per cent (the total number of successful male candidates was 403). At the other end of the time scale, the proportion of all women pass candidates for the MRCP(UK) who were successful seven years or more after qualifying (11 per cent) was almost double the proportion of men (6 per cent), although the actual numbers involved were relatively small.

The results for the MRCPysch – which had the second largest number of women pass candidates with a UK primary qualification – showed a similar trend for some

Figure 16  A comparison of the time, in years, after obtaining a primary medical qualification taken by men and women holding a United Kingdom qualification (shown as percentage distributions) who passed the MRCP(UK) in 1982

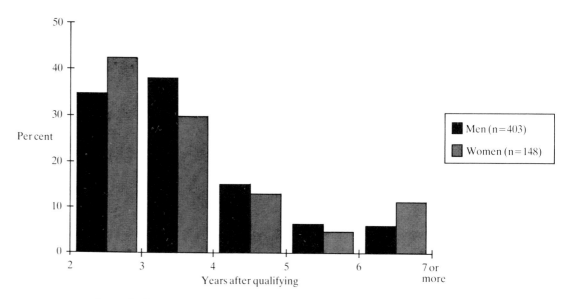

women to take relatively longer than men to complete their examinations. Nearly one-quarter (23 per cent) of the 61 women finished more than eight years after qualifying; for men the proportion with this length of experience among the 83 successful candidates was much smaller at 12 per cent. A study of psychiatrists who passed the MRCPsych in the years 1975-77 suggests, however, that in the mid 1970s women were taking even longer periods of time to obtain the qualification. Nearly half the 104 women respondents did not complete their examinations until at least ten years after graduation and the main reason was that they had interrupted their medical careers.[138] In 1982, in contrast, the median interval for UK-qualified women in the MRCPsych results was slightly under six years.

SUCCESSFUL CANDIDATES FROM UNIVERSITIES IN GREAT BRITAIN

Virtually identical numbers of candidates who passed the final examinations for the seven clinical higher qualifications of membership or fellowship in 1982 were medical graduates from the University of London or the English provincial and Welsh universities excluding Oxford and Cambridge (see Table 37). These two groups of graduates

Table 37   Universities in Great Britain which awarded the
primary medical qualification held by candidates
who passed the final examinations of seven higher
qualifications, and the MRCP(UK), 1982

| | *Pass candidates 1982* | | | |
|---|---|---|---|---|
| *Universities which awarded primary qualification* | *Seven higher qualifications*\* | | *MRCP(UK)* | |
| | *No* | *%* | *No* | *%* |
| London | 456 | 36.5 | 195 | 36.6 |
| Oxford and Cambridge | 142 | 11.4 | 71 | 13.3 |
| Other English and Welsh | 455 | 36.5 | 191 | 35.8 |
| Scottish | 195\*\* | 15.6 | 76 | 14.3 |
| Great Britain | 1248 | 100.0 | 533 | 100.0 |

\* MRCP(UK), FRCS(Eng), FFARCS(Eng), MRCOG, MRCPsych,
  FRCR and MRCPath.
\*\* This figure excludes the numbers for the FRCS awarded by the royal
  colleges in Edinburgh and Glasgow.

Sources: Higher qualification examination pass lists and Medical Registers
1982–84.

each formed slightly over one-third of the total number of pass candidates who
received their medical education in Great Britain. The proportions for these two
university groupings in the results of the MRCP(UK) were also virtually the same.
Candidates who received their medical education in Scotland formed 16 per cent of
the total pass candidates in Table 37, but notice should be taken of the practice of
many Scottish surgical trainees to sit the FRCS examinations administered by the
royal colleges in Edinburgh and Glasgow. The percentage of successful candidates
with Scottish primary qualifications in the MRCP(UK) results was slightly lower at 14
per cent. Indeed, there were almost as many MRCP pass candidates with Oxford and
Cambridge primary medical qualifications as there were holders of qualifications from
the four Scottish universities in this data set. Finally, it is of interest that there were 15
doctors whose only primary medical qualification in *The Medical Registers* was a
qualification awarded by a United Kingdom non-university licensing body. (These
non-university qualifications are described below.) It was not possible to identify the

university at which they received their medical education.

Wilson in his analyses of the 1963-65 data on FRCS(Eng) and MRCP(London pass candidates compared the proportions of candidates holding primary qualifications awarded by the Universities of London, Oxford and Cambridge, and the other English and Welsh universities with the proportion of total graduates from these universities in selected years. Graduates from Oxford and Cambridge were markedly over-represented in the MRCP data and marginally so in the FRCS results.[136]

It was intended to repeat this comparative exercise on the 1982 pass data but difficulties were encountered in obtaining accurate statistics on the total numbers of graduates by university for the years 1975-79. The General Medical Council presents in its bound minutes the numbers of students who pass the final examinations of each university and non-university licensing body in each academic year. If, however, a student passes the examinations for both a university degree and a primary medical qualification awarded by a non-university licensing body (the 'conjoint' awarded by the Examining Board in England, the 'Scottish triple' of the Board of Management of the Scottish Triple Qualification or the licentiate of the Society of Apothecaries of London), he or she is double counted because the GMC statistics represent total passes.[139] Until the early 1980s, it was common for students, particularly those in the London medical schools, to sit both types of examinations. (In the survey of junior doctors employed by the City and Hackney Health Authority in London in 1984, one in ten of the registrars held dual primary medical qualifications.[11])

The Universities Statistical Record also holds statistics on medical graduates. It relies on the universities to make returns under subject headings such as 'clinical medicine', of undergraduates who have obtained a first degree or first degree and first diploma. (It is not clear if the universities include in the returns persons who obtain only a diploma qualification.) There is a difficulty in the data caused by students who do their pre-clinical training at one university, transfer to another university to complete their clinical training and then return to the first university to sit its final examinations. Cambridge pre-clinical students may elect to do this and Oxford students could do likewise until January 1978. Statistics provided by the Universities Statistical Record for the years 1975-79 (personal communication, 1985) showed against Oxford and Cambridge the numbers of undergraduates who completed their clinical training at these universities rather than the total numbers of doctors who passed the Oxford and Cambridge final examinations. Thus the information on the university which awarded the primary medical qualification held by the 1982 higher qualification pass candidates that was extracted from the Medical Registers cannot be related to the Statistical Record's figures.

Another university-related feature for England and Wales observed by Wilson in the 1965 data was that graduates of Oxford and Cambridge tended to spend less time in training before passing the final examination of the MRCP(London) than candidates with a University of London first degree, while the slowest rate of progress was made by graduates of the English provincial and Welsh universities. In the 1982 data, Oxford and Cambridge graduates again had the shortest duration of experience. Eighty per cent of candidates from these two universities passed the MRCP(UK) within four years of obtaining a primary medical qualification. There was almost no difference in the rates of progress of the graduates from the University of London (74 per cent passing within four years) and those from English provincial and Welsh universities (73 per cent), while 68 per cent of the Scottish graduates were successful within this time period.

Turning to the FRCS(Eng), in 1965 candidates from Oxford and Cambridge took marginally less time to obtain this qualification than graduates from the other universities in England and Wales. In 1982, however, it was the group of provincial university graduates including the Welsh that had the fastest rate of progress – two-thirds were successful within five years of qualifying. The rate for London graduates was 61 per cent; the rate for Oxford and Cambridge was even lower but the number of graduates from these two universities was too small to enable a valid comparison to be made.

## Summary of the findings

The main findings from the analyses of the 1982 pass lists for the seven clinical higher qualifications are as follows. First, doctors from Sri Lanka and Hong Kong appeared to be particularly well represented among the overseas candidates. Second, more women graduates from United Kingdom universities obtained the MRCPath, the FRCR and, in particular, the MRCPsych than would have been predicted from the male to female ratio of doctors in the registrar and SHO grades. Their success rates in the MRCP(UK), FFARCS(Eng) and MRCOG were slightly above the predicted rates but they were grossly under-represented in the results for the FRCS(Eng). Third, successful United Kingdom candidates spent shorter periods in training before passing the MRCP(UK) and the FRCS(Eng) than doctors who obtained an MRCP(London) or FRCS(Eng) qualification 17 years previously. Fourth, there was very little difference in the success rates of doctors who qualified in the English provincial and Welsh universities compared with those from the University of London. Oxford and Cambridge graduates appeared to do very well in the MRCP(UK) examinations. If, however, the graduates of these two universities were reclassified according to the university at which they did their clinical training, the level of success for Oxford and Cambridge in the MRCP examinations might be altered. The University of London figures might also be affected because the majority of Oxford and Cambridge pre-clinical students who do their clinical training elsewhere go to a

London medical school. More comparative data is needed to confirm whether the success rates of Scottish graduates, particularly in the MRCP(UK), were lower than would have been expected.

Although it is not possible to calculate exactly the percentage of graduates from British medical schools who later obtain a higher qualification of membership or fellowship in the seven clinical disciplines, the data for 1982 suggest that the proportion could be above 40 per cent. The average number of doctors in each year between 1975 and 1979 who received primary medical qualifications from universities in Great Britain was 3000[32]; the number of graduates with these primary qualifications who obtained a higher clinical qualification in 1982 (excluding those who obtained the FRCS of Edinburgh and the FRCS of Glasgow) was 1248. This suggested proportion of over 40 per cent is supported by survey data on doctors who graduated from Queen's University, Belfast in 1977. By 1983, 40 per cent (53) of the 134 respondents had obtained one of the seven clinical higher qualifications of membership or fellowship. Five had yet to complete their MRCPath examinations and there were others with the first part of a qualification who may have obtained the final part in due course.[140] (Forty-four postgraduate diplomas awarded by the royal colleges had also been received; 30 were the DRCOG.) In any cohort of medical graduates there will also be persons who will enter community medicine, occupational medicine and general practice and, in time, obtain the higher qualifications relevant to these disciplines.

The first circular instructing health authorities to review the rota arrangements for junior doctors was issued in November 1982.[61] It would be instructive to repeat these analyses of the 1982 higher qualification results, or at least those for the MRCP(UK), within the next five years to see if the reductions in rota commitments have been accompanied by changes in the success rates for the higher qualification examinations. More study time may lead to improved pass levels, although benefits of the additional time could be cancelled if, in the examinations, trainees are found lacking in experience because of the reduction in their clinical work load.

## 11  Responsibilities of regional committees and officers for postgraduate education

It was observed by the Royal Commission on the National Health Service in 1979 that the NHS meets the bulk of the costs of providing postgraduate education although there is a 'grey area' of obligation and accounting between the NHS and the other main supplier – the universities.[3] A complex advisory relationship also exists between these two agencies. The responsibilities and activities of the regional health authorities, district health authorities and the universities form the subject matter in this and the following four chapters; financial arrangements are described in chapters 19 and 20. Since many of these activities are shared between the NHS employing authorities and the universities or between the employing authorities and the royal colleges, cross referencing between the chapters is used to avoid lengthy repetition of the material.

The material for the chapters was obtained from various sources: reports and other documents published by the DHSS and the Welsh Office, handbooks and guide lines prepared by health authorities and universities, copies of statutory financial accounts, and so forth. Material collected in interviews with the regional postgraduate deans in England and Wales and with regional specialists in community medicine and other personnel in the health regions and some districts has also been used. These interviews were held during 1984 as part of the fieldwork for the study on the feasibility of establishing a national information system for hospital training posts and trainees.[11]

*Regional advisory machinery*

In most English health regions there are three main medical advisory committees: the regional postgraduate medical education committee, the regional manpower committee (RMC) and the regional medical advisory committee (RMAC). They advise the regional health authorities on education and training, manpower, and general matters. The medical education committee has the longest history. The former regional hospital boards were advised by a health circular issued in 1964 – HM(64)69 – to consider with the universities the need, where such committees were not already in existence, for regional postgraduate education committees representative of university, hospital and general practitioner interests.[141] In addition to these three advisory committees there are other regional committees or subcommittees covering the hospital-based specialties, community medicine, general practice, junior staff and activities such as research and study leave.

The Royal Commission on the National Health Service received evidence from a survey carried out for the 1978 Review Body on Doctors' and Dentists' Remuneration which showed that some 95 per cent of consultants were members of one or more professional committees at district, area or regional level, and about one in six consultants sat on five or more committees. Criticism of the professional advisory machinery was expressed in other evidence supplied to the Commission. Thus, in its report, the Commission recommended that 'the health departments should urgently consider with the professions concerned the best way of simplifying the present structure' (para 20.20).[3] Partly in response to this recommendation a joint working group made up of representatives of the DHSS, the NHS and the medical profession was set up in 1980 to review the role of medical advisory and representative committees and to make recommendations. The Joint Working Group looked at the advisory machinery at both district and regional levels. The regional medical officers assisted by providing details of their regional arrangements.

REGIONAL POSTGRADUATE MEDICAL EDUCATION COMMITTEES

The Joint Working Group suggested that the terms of reference of a RPGMEC should be to advise the regional health authority and relevant university on:
'a. broad policy concerning the promotion of postgraduate medical and dental education;
b. the maintenance of an adequate educational content in all training posts in the light of advice given by the Higher Training Committee[s] (senior registrar posts) and the Royal Colleges and Faculties (registrar and SHO posts);
c. the selection of hospital and community medicine posts suitable for general practice vocational training;
d. the provision of posts suitable for training pre-registration house officers;
e. the approval of GP trainers and [training] practices;
f. the availability and suitability of postgraduate education courses;
g. the provision and working of Postgraduate Centres – responsibility for individual centres rests with district authorities; and
h. provision of a careers advisory service in collaboration with the regional specialty committees.' (pages 10-11[142])

The report of the inquiry into medical education by the Social Services Committee of the House of Commons in 1980/81 listed other related functions that are now being carried out by RPGMECs or their subcommittees: advising on, and coordinating training schemes and teaching facilities; supervising arrangements for assessing the progress of doctors undergoing specialist training; advising the regional health authority and university on study leave allocations and the secondment of individual doctors and the rotation of doctors between posts; selecting and appointing general practice course organisers (in addition to appointing trainers); and advising the university on the appointment of clinical tutors.[4]

The information given to the Joint Working Group by the regional medical officers on the structure of the education committees showed that the regional arrangements were far from uniform; in one region the functions of the RPGMEC were split between two committees. University representatives accounted for less than one-fifth of the members in most of the regions; on one regional committee, however, they formed over 40 per cent of the membership. Five regions included representatives from universities that did not have a medical school. Other regional committees, such as the manpower committee and the medical advisory committee, were infrequently represented on the education committees. The number of specialty subcommittees with members on the education committee was 14 to 15 in half the regions; in the other regions the number ranged from eight to 18. There were hospital junior doctors on all the education committees but general practice vocational trainees and community medicine trainees were infrequently represented. District clinical tutors were on all the committees; in one region they comprised 40 per cent of the membership and in another region a quarter. In some regions, however, the tutors were probably serving as nominees of the district health authorities. The regional postgraduate medical dean and the regional medical officer were represented on each education committee. Usually they were also members of the RMC and the RMAC. Other individuals on the education committee were likely to attend the RMC and RMAC as representatives of a different body or interest. In one region it was estimated that the 72 potential places on the RPGMEC were in fact filled by fewer than 60 individuals.[142] The expenses of the members are met by their employing authorities – the regional health authority or university as appropriate.[143] However, the education committees usually do not meet more than two or three times a year.

Regional variations in the membership of the medical advisory committee and the manpower committee were also reported to the Joint Working Group by the regional medical officers. Not surprisingly, the Working Group recommended that each region should examine its own machinery in order to establish the simplest system for providing advice. To improve the performance of the education committees, it was suggested that small review panels should be set up by specialty committees in conjunction with the RPGMEC to monitor the progress of senior registrars in training. These review panels might also be a suitable body for providing career guidance to doctors in training. Late in 1983, nearly two years after the report on regional management arrangements was published, the 14 regions were asked about the steps taken in response to the recommendations in the report. Information supplied by 11 indicated, however, that the infrastructure of their advisory machinery remained variable and complex.[144]

*Wales*

The National Health Service in Wales does not have a regional administrative tier above the nine health authorities. The HAs are the employing authorities for all grades of medical staff. The role of developing NHS policies that are national in scope lies with the Welsh Office. It is responsible also for the decisions on the financial resource allocations to the HAs and for providing financial support to the University of Wales for postgraduate medical education. Wales does, however, have a committee for postgraduate medical education and the representation on the committee is similar to that of the English regional committees.

REGIONAL POSTGRADUATE MEDICAL DEANS

The chief executive officer for each RPGMEC or equivalent committee is the regional postgraduate medical dean and in at least five regions the dean is also chairman of the committee. The remit for the deans is broad. They are responsible for the overall coordination and supervision in the regions of postgraduate medical training and continuing medical education for hospital medical staff, general practitioners, and other doctors working in the community. They also have a liaison role between the regional committees and national advisory bodies, notably the Council for Postgraduate Medical Education in England and Wales and the royal colleges and faculties. References to the tasks undertaken by the deans are made in the following chapters and the level of their financial support is discussed on pages 301–304.

The appointment of dean in each region is usually made by the university with a medical faculty (or, in the four Thames regions, the University of London) in consultation with the regional health authority. (There are three universities with medical faculties in the Trent region and, therefore, three university postgraduate deans. The dean who assumes the role of regional dean is elected by the three postgraduate deans. The postgraduate dean in Wales is appointed by the University of Wales in consultation with the Welsh Office.) The university issues the contract of employment to the dean, but the salary for some if not all of the sessions or time worked in the capacity of dean is funded by the regional health authority.[143] Many deans also hold part-time NHS consultant appointments or university teaching appointments. At two universities, Newcastle upon Tyne and Southampton, the regional dean occupies a chair in postgraduate education.

The deans are supported by administrative staff usually consisting of an administrative assistant and secretarial support. In most regions the administrative staff are employed by the university but with funding from the regional health authority; in one or two regions they are employed directly by the health authority. (University terms and conditions of service are not the same as those in the NHS.) The location of accommodation for the dean and his staff also varies from region to region. It can be within the medical faculty offices sited in a teaching hospital or in other university premises or in RHA offices. The deans for the Thames regions and their staff are based at the British Postgraduate Medical Federation (BPMF) which is a school of the University of London. (The development of the Federation is discussed on page 274.)

REGIONAL ADVISERS IN GENERAL PRACTICE

The regional deans are assisted and advised by a regional adviser in matters relating to general practice education. The regional adviser also advises the RPGMEC and its subcommittee for general practice and assists in carrying out the committees' decisions. Specific matters of concern for the advisers include the organisation of vocational training schemes for doctors wishing to enter general practice, the selection of general practitioner trainers and trainees, the organisation of day release and intensive courses for trainers and trainees, the provision of careers advice to undergraduates and junior doctors interested in a career in general practice, and the provision of continuing education and arrangements of clinical attachments in hospitals for general practitioner principals. These functions were identified in a 1972 DHSS and Welsh Office memorandum, HM(72)25, in which the regional hospital boards and Welsh Hospital Board were commended to appoint regional advisers. The government departments were acting on a recommendation received from the Council for Postgraduate Medical Education in England and Wales.[145]

Regional advisers are general practitioners whose appointment as adviser is made by the university in consultation with the RPGMEC and its general practice subcommittee. The appointments are part-time and the level of remuneration is the same as the maximum point on the salary scale for hospital consultants.[145] The regional health authorities reimburse the universities for the salary payments. Nearly all the regional advisers are assisted by as many as five to six part-time associate advisers who are also appointed by the universities with the funding being provided by the regional health authorities. In the majority of regions – excluding the Thames regions – the regional adviser and his secretarial staff share the accommodation provided for the regional dean.

REGIONAL SPECIALISTS IN COMMUNITY MEDICINE

Each regional health authority has one or more posts for specialists in community medicine with a responsibility for medical manpower and/or medical staffing. (Not all posts are filled.) The SCMs liaise closely with the postgraduate deans on matters relating to the deployment of medical manpower, standards of training, and the

153

appointment and progress of individual trainees. Information and assistance is also given to the deans by medical staffing departments at regional and district level.

The functions of the RPGMECs that were suggested by the joint working group on medical advisory machinery or listed in the Social Services Committee's report are reviewed in the following pages. They have been grouped according to four types of activity: first, the appointing of 'deputies' (clinical tutors, general practitioner trainers and course organisers) to uphold standards of training. This subject is covered in the remainder of the chapter. The second and third types of activity – monitoring the educational content of training posts, and monitoring the progress of trainees – are covered in the next two chapters. The fourth activity of overseeing the provision of education courses and facilities such as postgraduate centres is discussed in chapter 15.

Handbooks or guide lines or annual calendars are published in many regions. These contain information on the membership of the postgraduate education committees and subcommittees, the areas of responsibility covered by these committees, details of educational arrangements in the districts (postgraduate centres, names of tutors) and, if the publication is a calendar, names, dates and venues of courses. These publications are available from the offices of the regional deans. The four Thames regions are covered in a study guide prepared annually by the British Postgraduate Medical Federation.[146] A national directory published biannually gives the names of the regional postgraduate medical and dental deans, the regional advisers in general practice, the administrators to the deans and other information (see below).[147]

## CLINICAL TUTORS

The Royal Commission on Medical Education in 1965-68 took the view that there should be a postgraduate medical centre in most district hospitals providing a base for an area organiser and/or clinical tutor 'one of whose tasks would be to see that there was a lively programme of meetings and other group activities which would generally be based on the centre' (para 168).[1] The Commission also hoped that there would be close relationships between the local staff concerned with postgraduate education and the regional postgraduate committee and it suggested that the tutors should be appointed by the regional committees. The post of clinical tutor was not a new idea. The 1964 memorandum on postgraduate medical education had proposed that a limited number of hospital consultants – one for each major hospital group or association of small groups – be appointed as clinical tutors.[141]

Clinical tutors (or postgraduate organisers as they are called in Wales) have been described as being the regional postgraduate deans' deputies and representatives in the districts.[148] If, within a district, there are two or more hospitals with postgraduate medical centres (including psychiatric and mental handicap hospitals), then a tutor will probably be appointed for each centre. The tutors – who are usually NHS-employed consultants holding full-time or part-time contracts – are concerned with the educational and training needs of all doctors in the local area in all branches of medical practice – hospital, general and community health. Their specific functions include arranging and developing educational courses and activities (such as journal clubs and clinico-pathological conferences) at the centre in cooperation with colleagues, being available to junior doctors who desire career guidance or counselling, and overseeing on behalf of the university the standards of training offered in the HO posts and the progress of the house officers and of any medical students who take up placements in the local hospital. In many districts the clinical tutors administer the applications for study leave made by the junior hospital staff and some tutors even hold the district study leave budget for hospital medical staff. One other task was mentioned in chapter 8. Doctors who wish to join the Retainer Scheme are interviewed and advised by the clinical tutors. The tutors also supervise their progress.

Clinical tutors are ex-officio members and executive officers of the local postgraduate medical committee and they may also be the chairman. On behalf of the committee they oversee the running of the postgraduate centre and the work of its administrative staff, the purchasing and maintenance of equipment and teaching aids and the service provided by the local medical library. In some regions, Oxford being one, the local committee via the clinical tutor reports annually on its activities to the regional postgraduate education committee.[149] The clinical tutors receive an honorarium for carrying out these responsibilities and, in April 1984, the maximum payment per annum was set at £1105. Psychiatric tutors who are responsible for small numbers of doctors receive a reduced honorarium payment. The level of the honoraria payments are reviewed by the DHSS from time to time and the funding is provided by the regional health authorities.

The universities appoint the clinical tutors in consultation with the RPGMECs, but the procedures followed vary from region to region. It has been the practice in the Northern region for the tutors to be appointed by the university on the recommendation of the postgraduate dean after he has consulted with the medical practitioners in the district concerned. The appointments have been for an initial period of three years and the period could be extended, but only for a limited time.[148] The procedures in the Oxford region are more formal: nominations of candidates for appointment or reappointment accompanied by a full curriculum vitae for each person are submitted to the regional dean (the director of postgraduate medical education and training) by the local postgraduate committee. Appointments are then made by the Regional

Committee for Postgraduate Medical Education and Training and the tutors are responsible to it. The University of Oxford will subsequently confer its title of 'district clinical tutor' provided it is satisfied that the appointee is sufficiently qualified. The appointment is for up to five years in the first instance and a reappointment can be for up to three years.[149] In the South Western region the appointment is normally for four years in the first instance and reappointment may be made every two years thereafter.[150] In at least two regions – Trent and West Midlands – a small number of clinical tutors have been nominated to act as area organisers or directors.

In almost every region the clinical tutors meet together with the regional dean at least twice a year to discuss the content of courses and their administration, new regulations from the DHSS, and other matters of relevance. One meeting may be residential. The regional advisers and possibly the specialty tutors appointed by the royal colleges and faculties (see page 220) may join the tutors once a year. Some regions have a clinical tutors subcommittee of the RPGMEC. The joint working group on medical advisory machinery felt that if regular meetings of clinical tutors within a region were found to be useful they should continue but without being elevated to the status of a formal committee.[142] There is also a National Association of Clinical Tutors which covers the United Kingdom. The Council for Postgraduate Medical Education in England and Wales in association with the National Association produces biannually a directory of postgraduate medical centres in the United Kingdom. Each entry identifies the name, address and telephone number of the centre, the name of the clinical tutor and date of appointment, the name of the secretary or administrator of the centre, and the names of the college and specialty tutors working from the the centre.[147]

GENERAL PRACTITIONER TRAINERS

Although the regulations requiring doctors wishing to enter general practice to undergo vocational training did not come into effect in England and Wales until 15 February 1981, the regional infrastructure of regional adviser, general practitioner trainers and course organisers was already well established. Over the previous ten years many young general practitioner principals had voluntarily followed a programme of vocational training before entering a partnership or setting up in single handed practice.Before a trainee is issued with a certificate of prescribed experience (page 185) he or she will have spent the equivalent of one year full-time in general practice with an approved trainer. Doctors applying for a certificate of equivalent experience are also expected to have undertaken a year in a training practice. (An exception may be made very occasionally if a doctors' previous experience is considered by the Joint Committee on Postgraduate Training for General Practice to be appropriate.[42]) The approval and reapproval of trainers and training practices is the responsibility of the general practice subcommittee of the RPGMEC. Applicants for appointment as trainers are interviewed by the subcommittee or by persons authorised for that purpose and a visit by representatives of the subcommittee to the applicant's practice premises is always made before approval is given. (More than one partner in a practice may be approved as a trainer.) Approval is initially given for up to two years and it may be extended for periods of up to five years. If a new application is rejected or an existing appointment or reappointment is terminated by the general practice subcommittee, the person may appeal to the General Practitioner Trainer Scheme Appeals Committee. The terms of appointment and the appeal procedures are contained in the Statement of Fees and Allowances payable to General Medical Practitioners.[42]

The trainer receives a training grant for the duration of the attachment of a trainee which can be for a period of up to one year unless there are exceptional circumstances. The grant is paid by the family practitioner committee to which the trainer – as a family doctor – is contracted and in June 1985 the grant was £3340 per annum. The trainer can also claim for expenses incurred on behalf of a trainee – for example, the use of an additional motor vehicle and telephone installation and rental charges.[42] The FPCs in England receive moneys from the Treasury through the DHSS to cover the training grants and additional allowances and also the salaries paid to the trainees while in the general practice phase of their training. (Estimates of the total expenditure on items relating to vocational training in England are given on pages 286–290.) The trainers can advertise for a trainee to join their practice or they may prefer to rely on trainees in vocational training schemes to be placed with them by the scheme organisers. (This matter is discussed in the next section.)

The Joint Committee on Postgraduate Training for General Practice has published guide lines to assist the general practice subcommittee of the RPGMECs when selecting trainers. Candidates should have a desire to teach and the ability to do so; they should be clinically competent and have established harmonious relationships with both their patients and their professional colleagues; they should be neither new entrants to general practice nor over the age of 60; and the practice organisation and premises should be of a satisfactory standard.[151] The regional advisers and general practice subcommittees have developed their own selection procedures and methods for monitoring the standards of training provided by the trainers. In the West Midlands region trainers take a written examination and trainees in Devon and Cornwall are asked to score their trainers on a 'value for money' index.[152] In the Oxford region video recordings of previous surgery consultations between the trainer (or prospective trainer) and patients are reviewed during an extended visit to the practice.[153]

In October 1984 there were 2610 approved trainers in England and Wales (of whom

260 or more were course organisers – see below) and they formed 10 per cent of all unrestricted principals. There were, however, inter-regional variations in the percentages of principals who were approved as trainers – in Wales, East Anglia, Wessex and South Western the rate lay between 12 and 16 per cent.[8] The number of trainees who are in the general practice phase of their vocational training in England and Wales at any one time is around 1860. So the supply of trainers exceeds the demand for placements by a considerable margin.

GENERAL PRACTITIONER COURSE ORGANISERS

Vocational trainees are expected to attend a programme of courses on a day release basis during the general practice phase of their training and during the hospital phase if their duties allow. Trainers may accompany the trainees at some of the meetings. Separate intensive courses are arranged for tutoring trainers in teaching and learning skills. As mentioned on page 153, the functions of the regional advisers in general practice identified in the 1972 memorandum included the organisation of day release and intensive courses for trainers and trainees. Mindful of the breadth of the workload proposed for the regional advisers, the Council for Postgraduate Medical Education in England and Wales and a Joint Working Group on Vocational Training for General Practice recommended to the DHSS that vocational training course organisers should be appointed and that they should receive payment. Arrangements to this effect were introduced in 1974.[154]

Course organisers are general practitioners who have been approved as trainers. The designation of trainers to undertake these duties at district or local level is made by the regions' general practice subcommittee subject to the approval by the RPGMEC. The organisers' functions include planning courses in consultation with both trainers and trainees, arranging speakers and providing educational material (audiovisual aids and documents), supervising and evaluating the courses which, naturally, involves attending most of the sessions, and maintaining close contact with the regional adviser in general practice, the regional postgraduate dean and the local clinical tutor or tutors.[154] Another responsibility that they have assumed is the organising of continuing education courses open to all general practitioners. (The financial arrangements and general administration of these 'section 63' courses are discussed on pages 210–213.) Course organisers receive the same grant as trainers (£3340 per annum in June 1985) and it is also paid by the family practitioner committee to which the doctor is contracted and the committee's expenditure is covered by the DHSS. It is not usual for a course organiser to concurrently take on the responsibility for an individual trainee.

The DHSS in its proposals for appointing course organisers anticipated that each organiser would eventually assume responsibility for about ten trainees in the general practice part of their training at one time, and the organiser would also oversee the educational arrangements for trainees in the hospital phase of the schemes. It calculated that there should be eventually one course organiser in each area health authority with perhaps a second in areas with local geographical or other difficulties; the total would be around 100.[154] In early 1986 the number of course organisers in England was 255 and in Wales, 22 (Dr J Bahrami, Association of Course Organisers, personal communication 1986). (There are 200 health districts in England and Wales.)

The great majority of course organisers have been delegated the responsiblity for organising and administering local vocational training schemes by the regional advisers. These schemes are planned programmes of hospital posts and general practice placements through which general practitioner trainees 'rotate' over three years to obtain a comprehensive training. (The criteria for selecting the hospital posts for these schemes are discussed in the next chapter.) The course organiser has to negotiate with hospital consultants to obtain agreement that junior doctors planning a career in general practice will occupy some of their SHO posts and the organiser must also liaise with the local trainers over the placement of trainees in their practices.

The numbers of trainees who participate in the schemes vary; the majority of schemes take between six trainees over three years (two new entrants per year) and 18 over three years (six new entrants per year). Some schemes are much larger with as many as 36 trainees in all and the largest, which is in the Northern region, can take 120 trainees. (A guide on vocational training schemes in the United Kingdom is published by the Council for Postgraduate Medical Education in England and Wales.[155]) A course organiser might be responsible for two or more separate schemes. He will be involved in the appointment of doctors to the vacancies from possibly over one hundred applicants, and he will plan the trainees' rotations between posts and oversee their educational progress. He will also keep in touch with doctors who are known to be developing their own vocational training programmes. Organising vocational training schemes was not in the remit for course organisers drawn up in 1973/74[154] and they do not receive an allowance to compensate for the time devoted to the schemes.

*College and faculty regional advisers and specialty tutors*

The royal colleges and faculties each have a network of regional advisers and district or local tutors covering England and Wales. (The Royal College of General Practitioners is an exception as it does not appoint regional advisers but it does have tutors.) In each region the college and faculty regional advisers liaise closely with the regional postgraduate dean. Each one is normally a member of the relevant regional specialty subcommittee for postgraduate training and they probably attend the meetings of the RPGMEC. At district level the specialty tutors cooperate with the clinical tutors. The colleges and faculties for the hospital disciplines appoint their own members to these positions and the appointment procedures and roles of the regional advisers are discussed in fuller detail on page 220 in the chapter on the collegiate bodies. With community medicine, however, there is regional involvement in the appointment procedures. The nomination of regional faculty adviser is made by the community medicine subcommittee of the RPGMEC in consultation with members and trainees and the nomination is sent to the registrar of the Faculty of Community Medicine for approval by the faculty board.

# 12 Regional postgraduate education committees as monitors of training standards

This chapter covers the roles of the regional postgraduate medical education committees in monitoring the educational content of posts for higher training, general professional training (GPT), vocational training, and pre-registration experience. The universities have been delegated the responsibility for pre-registration posts under the Medical Act 1983. However, in the regions this role is usually carried out by a subcommittee of the RPGMEC, the membership of which represents the university, the regional health authority and possibly the district health authorities. Table 1 on page 25 which outlines the organisation and administration of the training grades in the hospital service may be found useful for reference purposes.

There are considerable regional variations in the numbers of training posts and trainees for whom the RPGMECs and the regional postgraduate deans assume responsibility. The 14 regions and Wales can be classified into three groups according to the numbers of NHS-employed trainees who were recorded in the 30 September 1984 census of hospital medical staff (see Table 6, page 50): regions with 1000 or fewer trainees (including house officers) – East Anglia, Wessex and Oxford; regions with between 1000 and 1500 trainees – Northern, Yorkshire, South West Thames, South Western, Mersey and Wales; and regions with more than 1500 trainees – Trent, North West Thames, North East Thames, South East Thames, West Midlands and North Western. There are also considerable differences in the geographical sizes of the regions as Figure 2 on page 24 indicates.

SENIOR REGISTRAR POSTS AND TRAINING SCHEMES

The majority of RPGMECs have a tier of subcommittees covering the hospital specialties and community medicine and these committees give guidance on the establishment of new SR posts in the region and the organisation of the regional posts into training or rotation schemes. They also oversee the content of the training offered in the posts. In the Trent region which has the second largest number of posts (301 including honorary posts in 1984) these functions are performed not by specialty subcommittees but by a single senior registrar subcommittee that also monitors the progress of trainees.[156] Oxford also has a different arrangement. The specialty subcommittees are not concerned with training; this role in each of 14 disciplines is assumed by a regional postgraduate adviser who, in most cases, has been appointed by the relevant royal college or faculty. Many of these advisers also chair their own specialty subcommittee.[157] These arrangements are considered to work satis-

161

factorily but the region does have far fewer SR posts than Trent (around 170 in 1984).

It is usual for SR posts in a specialty – both established NHS posts and posts for honorary appointment holders – to be linked together in rotation schemes and for the trainees to spend a fixed period of time in one post (for example, six months or a year) before moving to another post and so on. The linked posts may be sited in teaching and non-teaching hospitals and they may offer general training in the specialty or experience in a sub-specialty. (Not all posts are incorporated into rotation schemes.) Most schemes are confined within the boundaries of a single region. In the south east of England, however, it is commonplace for a rotation scheme to include posts in more than one region and posts in postgraduate teaching hospitals may also be incorporated. (The joint working group which reviewed the medical advisory machinery recommended that in the Thames regions, the special health authorities should be represented on the relevent regional postgraduate medical education committees.[142])

*Approval of senior registrar posts*

It was noted in Chapter 3 that new SR posts cannot be advertised until manpower approval has been granted by the DHSS on the advice of the Central Manpower Committee. For some of the 'popular' medical and surgical specialties, authority must also be sought before existing but vacant posts can be advertised. These restrictions apply only to NHS established posts. The negotiations for the manpower approval are undertaken by the regional health authority on the advice of the relevant specialty subcommittee and the regional committee responsible for manpower. Naturally, the RHA as the employing authority must be willing to fund the post holders. The special health authorities – of which there are eight – are responsible for obtaining manpower approval for their own SR posts and for funding them. (This system may be modified when the Joint Planning Advisory Committee sets national targets and regional quotas for senior registrar posts (including honorary posts) in specialty groupings (page 61).) Once manpower approval is granted, the consultant or consultants responsible for the post must arrange for the training programme associated with the post to be approved by the higher training committee responsible for the specialty. This applies to posts in community medicine and occupational medicine as well as to posts in the hospital specialties. Higher training posts (senior specialist posts) in the three armed services are also approved in this way. In the psychiatric specialties, training approval is granted to rotational training schemes providing a comprehensive range of training over three years rather than to individual posts. Posts in anaesthetics are also organised into schemes of higher training often regionally conceived, while in radiology, the Royal College recognises departments for training although posts are assessed individually when being established for full-time training or part-time (PM(79)3) training.

The higher training committees were established by the royal colleges after the report of the Royal Commission on Medical Education which contained a recommendation to this effect was published in 1968.[1] There is a separate HTC covering senior registrar training in seven medical disciplines – medicine, surgery, psychiatry, obstetrics and gynaecology, anaesthetics, pathology and radiology – and the committees cover the United Kingdom and the Republic of Ireland. Medicine, surgery, psychiatry and anaesthetics each have a joint committee on higher training, the membership being made up of the royal colleges for each discipline together with other bodies concerned with training. For pathology, radiology and obstetrics and gynaecology the higher training committee is a committee of the appropriate royal college. The JCHTs for medicine, surgery and psychiatry have specialty advisory committees covering the individual specialties. Community medicine and occupational medicine are represented on the medical joint committee (the Joint Committee on Higher Medical Training (JCHMT)). (The organisation and functions of the higher training committees are fully discussed in chapter 17.)

The procedure for obtaining approval from a higher training committee is a two-stage process. First, the senior consultant with his colleagues completes a schedule providing detailed information on the location of the post and, if it is in a rotation scheme, the location and type of the other linked posts, the staffing of the specialty and the availability of the supporting services, the clinical duties and teaching duties, meetings and opportunities for research and so forth. There are separate application forms for each specialty. Guide lines on these matters – which were prepared for the RPGMECs and specialty advisers by the Councils for Postgraduate Medical Education in the United Kingdom – advise that when the information required by a higher training committee is being assembled the regional postgraduate dean's office should be consulted since the deans have wide experience of the expectations of the higher training committees. Also, their offices may hold on file information that is needed.[158]

The second stage is a visit of inspection usually made by two or more representatives of the higher training committee or relevant specialty advisory committee who will be senior specialists from other regions. The arrangements are made by the secretariat of the higher training committee in conjunction with the consultant named as responsible for the post or training programme. It is usual for the regional postgraduate dean to be informed of the visit, and many endeavour to meet the visitors especially if they are in the same specialty as the dean or if the dean feels that the visitors will find problems with the training programme. On the majority of visits, the visitors meet with all of the consultants involved in the training programme and some teams also like to meet the junior staff who will work with the first holder of the new post. The regional adviser of the relevant college or faculty attends the higher training visit if possible and the visitors may also meet the regional medical officer and district medical officer for the district in which the post is sited. Normally the health authority responsible for the posts reimburses the travel and subsistence expenses of the visitors at NHS rates although now, quite frequently, the visitors' own employing authority covers the expenses.

At the end of the inspection the visitors may informally tell the consultant what the likely outcome of the visit will be and if it is going to be favourable, he may proceed to appoint someone to the post. Many months can pass before the consultant is formally told. The visitors' assessments are confidential to the higher training committee or the specialty advisory committee concerned because they contain value judgments as well as factual information. The steps taken by the higher training committees to formally feed the recommendations back to the consultant and the employing authorities differ. (Note that these committees usually meet no more that three or four times a year.) The Royal College of Pathologists, for example, sends a letter giving a brief summary to the senior consultant in the pathology department and invites him to comment within a certain period of time. The summary is then circulated by the College to other persons such as the regional medical officer and the regional dean. The Joint Committee on Higher Psychiatric Training (JCHPsychT) in contrast, sends multiple copies of a full report on a scheme to the regional dean and relies on him to pass the copies to the employing authorities. Not surprisingly, the systems adopted by the higher training committees sometimes break down (see page 238).

If the post is approved (and the great majority are), it will be for a limited duration. The maximum time period granted by any higher training committee for a totally satisfactory post or training scheme is five years. Should there be serious shortcomings in the training offered – in the view of the visitors – the approval period may be as little as one year during which time the consultants in association with the employing authority will have to upgrade the training standards. For example, the mandatory requirements which a scheme in general psychiatry had to meet if its one-year approval was to be renewed included: the appointment of a tutor for the scheme, the scheduling of regular meetings that all senior registrars could attend, the apportionment of sufficient time for private study and research, and the improvement of the psychiatry sections of the main hospital's library. The report of a visit may recommend that a post in a sub-specialty such as endocrinology should be filled by each occupant for a restricted period of time (one to two years). This is to ensure that the senior registrars do not receive all their higher training in a narrow branch of medicine.

The process for renewing the approval of higher training posts or training schemes or departments is the same as that for new posts. Usually the secretariat of the higher training committee sets in motion the procedures for the revisit – the sending out of the schedule for completion, the arranging of the visitors and visit date. During a five-year approval period, training conditions can alter as hospital beds are closed or services are relocated. If significant changes are made to a training programme before a revisit falls due, the higher training committee or specialty advisory committee expects to be informed. The regional health authorities and special health authorities as the employers of the senior registrars are not obliged by statute to ensure that their higher training posts or schemes have current approval. Trainees in unapproved posts could, however, be disadvantaged as the experience in the posts may not be recognised when they apply to the higher training committees for accreditation (see page 239) or, in the case of the pathology specialties, when they apply to sit the final examinations for the higher qualification of MRCPath. It is for this reason that university lecturer posts and research posts for honorary appointment holders of senior registrar status usually have higher training recognition. Approval for this second type of honorary post is often granted on an ad hominem basis – the approval lapses when the trainee resigns. The same arrangement exists for SR posts created for persons with domestic commitments who are contracted on a part-time basis.

REGISTRAR AND SENIOR HOUSE OFFICER POSTS

Although the terms of reference for the RPGMECs suggested by the joint working group on medical advisory machinery included the maintenance of an adequate educational content in posts for general professional training (registrar and SHO posts), in reality the committees have to rely upon the district health authorities to carry out this task because the districts are the employing authorities for the trainees who occupy the posts. The training experience offered by registrar and SHO posts should also be evaluated and the royal colleges and faculties carry out the assessments and report back to the districts. The procedures for recognising GPT posts are similar to those for higher training posts and they are described more fully in Chapter 16. The travel and subsistence expenses of the visitors are also reimbursed normally by the host authority at NHS rates.

The postgraduate committees in most districts, unlike at regional level, do not formally oversee the standards of training offered in the GPT posts and ensure that the posts have current educational approval. The setting of training standards is left to the consultants in charge of the posts and the overall responsibility for seeing that the posts are approved tends to fall on the district medical officer or unit administrator or even the personnel in the medical staffing department in a few districts. (Vacant training posts should not be advertised unless they are educationally approved.) Some districts, notably those with teaching hospitals, have as many registrar and SHO posts combined as there are senior registrar posts in the smaller of the health regions. For example, in 1984 the London teaching district of City and Hackney which covers St Bartholomew's Hospital and Hackney Hospital had 150 NHS-established registrar and SHO posts[11] and this number exceeded the total number of SR posts (both NHS-established and honorary) in six regions including Wales. The Yorkshire non-teaching district of Bradford had slightly over 100 GPT posts but the usual number of GPT posts in a medium sized non-teaching district is probably around 50.

Posts in the registrar grade can be linked together in rotation programmes and, likewise, SHO posts. In psychiatry, pathology and radiology it is common for doctors to enter a training scheme as an SHO and, after one year to 18 months, to be promoted to the registrar grade to complete their GPT training. (The three colleges recognise schemes (psychiatry) or departments (radiology) or laboratories (pathology) for the purposes of general training rather than individual posts.) The rotation programmes can involve posts in two or more health districts. In the survey of posts in the City and Hackney and Bradford Health Authorities it was found that nearly 20 per cent of the teaching district's GPT posts and 10 per cent of the non-teaching posts were in inter-district rotations. One London surgical SHO programme was based on 20 posts in nine districts including four special health authorities. Twenty doctors spent two years in the programme and they each 'rotated' through four posts at six-month intervals. Another 10 per cent of the City and Hackney posts and 20 per cent of the Bradford posts were in rotations confined to the district and covered posts in either a single hospital or in two or more hospital units.[11] Doctors when appointed to rotations are usually told what their schedule of transfers between posts will be. The normal time spent in each SHO post is six months.

Posts can also be informally linked. Consultants in a specialty will transfer trainees between posts to enable them to gain a breadth of experience, but the timing of the transfers is not necessarily pre-arranged. A quarter of the GPT posts in the London survey came into this category and there were similar posts in Bradford. The specialties which adopted the practice included psychiatry, obstetrics and gynaecology, paediatrics and anaesthetics. Altogether, therefore, three-fifths of the GPT posts in the 1984 survey of two health districts were either in formal rotation programmes or linked for the purposes of extending the trainees' experience.

Regionally-based training schemes incorporating registrar posts are beginning to be formed. In 1984 there were, for example, regional schemes in pathology in Yorkshire, West Midlands and North Western and diagnostic radiology schemes in North Western, Yorkshire and West Midlands, a scheme in obstetrics and gynaecology covering both registrar and SHO posts in about ten districts in the Northern region and a regional programme in the West Midlands, and a scheme for registrars in anaesthetics in Oxford and the West Midlands.

COMPUTERISED INFORMATION ON POSTS

Another reason why most regional education committees and subcommittees have not been able to carry out their remit for general professional training has been the lack of adequate centralised information on the numbers of GPT posts in the districts and the training offered by them. In 1984, only two regions – Trent and South West Thames – had a computerised information system containing details of all registrar and SHO posts including college recognition. The North Western and Wessex regions held information on posts in manual systems and were transferring it into automated systems. The situation in the other regions was on the point of changing. The regional health authorities were either installing computer equipment or enhancing existing facilities to enable information on SR posts and trainees to be entered. Once this task was completed, items on the districts' registrar, SHO and HO posts were to be added to the files.[11,159]

The computer systems adopted by the regions were not compatible. There was a mixture of mainframe computers (three regions), mini computers (four regions) and micro computers from at least six different manufacturers.[11] The regions had been guided in their selection of hardware by the purchasing policies of the regional computer committees. The data sets for the post and person files were, however, reasonably standardised because the regional design teams had taken into account the items included in the DHSS annual census of hospital medical staff[107] and the items in the minimum data sets for medical and dental staff and posts recommended by the Steering Group on Health Services Information chaired by Mrs E Körner.[12]

Entering the data on posts into the regional computers from the districts' records will not be a straightforward task in many regions. Few of the 191 district health authorities in England and the nine health authorities in Wales have automated establishment files holding details of on-call rota arrangements, allocations of Class A and Class B UMTs, educational status and such like for each post. These items are usually held in manual files, and in districts where the medical staffing activities are carried out on separate hospital sites, there may not even be a centralised filing system holding relevant information, including copies of the most recent job descriptions. This situation is likely to change, however, as district and unit managers become increasingly aware of the need to have comprehensive information on their medical and dental manpower establishments when devising and carrying out short-term programmes and long-term strategic plans. Fuller details will also be required by district management accounting departments if specialty costing along the lines recommended in the report on financial information from the Steering Group on Health Services Information[160] is introduced.

POSTS FOR GENERAL PRACTICE VOCATIONAL TRAINING

Doctors wishing to enter general practice must spend the equivalent of three years whole-time after they have obtained full registration in training posts or appointments which provide suitable experience. A total of one year is to be spent in general practice with an approved general practitioner trainer or trainers unless there are exceptional circumstances. At the completion of this experience the trainees apply to the Joint Committee on Postgraduate Training for General Practice for a certificate. Two types of certificates can be issued. A certificate of prescribed experience is awarded to doctors who, during their hospital experience, occupy a combination of training posts 'selected' as suitable for vocational training (see below). Part of this experience can be in selected community medicine posts instead. A certificate of equivalent experience is awarded to applicants who have not spent all their hospital training in selected posts and, therefore, whose experience differs from that prescribed but is considered by the JCPTGP to be equivalent to prescribed experience. (A doctor whose general practice experience has not been entirely with an approved trainer or trainers may be awarded a certificate of equivalent experience[42] although this happens only very occasionally.[43])

The regulations for vocational training in England and Wales and the procedures for selecting posts for prescribed experience are laid down in a statutory instrument.[161] The regional postgraduate medical education committees are obliged to select posts which, on a specific date, are educationally approved by the appropriate royal college or faculty. The date is determined by the Secretary of State and revised from time to time to allow posts that have been approved for specialty training for the first time to be selected for vocational training.[74] In practice, it is the regional subcommittees for general practice that usually select the posts and the RPGMECs endorse the selections.

The criteria used in the selection process differ among the regions. The statutory regulations stipulate that prescribed experience trainees shall spend not less than six months whole-time employment or an equivalent period in each of two of the following specialties: general medicine, geriatric medicine, paediatrics, psychiatry, one of accident and emergency medicine or general surgery, and any one of obstetrics or gynaecology or obstetrics and gynaecology.[161] Many regional committees select all GPT posts with current educational approval granted by the appropriate college or faculty in these statutory specialties. In addition, they also select approved posts in a range of related specialties identified in the Statement of Fees and Allowances

Payable to General Medical Practitioners[42] – chest medicine, dermatology, traumatic surgery, ear, nose and throat (ENT), ophthalmology and anaesthetics. Approved posts in community medicine may also be selected. Other committees adopt more restrictive criteria and will select only those posts that the committee members believe will provide inpatient and outpatient experience appropriate for general practice, and in which the trainees will receive satisfactory supervision by the consultant and senior colleagues and be offered adequate opportunities for attending day release courses and other educational events. In a few regions, notably West Midlands, Oxford and South Western, the regional advisers in general practice have set up their own information systems covering registrar and SHO posts across the region. The advisers relied on personnel in the health districts to provide the data.[11]

Posts in the armed services hospitals in the United Kingdom and overseas can be selected for the purpose of vocational training if they have approval for training purposes granted by the royal colleges and faculties. Arrangements for selecting the posts have been made with the regional postgraduate medical education committees in Wessex for the Royal Navy, South West Thames for the Army and Oxford for the Royal Air Force.[74]

*Vocational training schemes*

A proportion of the selected posts in each health district are 'packaged' into planned programmes or vocational training schemes which provide general practitioner trainees with two years of hospital experience and one year in general practice with one or more approved trainers supplemented by a planned course of academic instruction through day or block release. The order in which the hospital and general practice phases of the training is done depends on the local organisation, but it is usual for trainees to spend the last months of their training in general practice. The programme for each trainee does, of course, include at least two six-month posts in the specialties listed in the statutory regulations and the scheme organisers try, if possible, to make one an obstetrics post. This has not been easy to arrange in some schemes based on hospitals with restricted numbers of obstetrics and gynaecology posts. In a few programmes, one of the four hospital-based posts is an 'elective' or supernumerary post that offers the trainee an opportunity to gain experience in many branches of medicine.

A directory of vocational training schemes in the United Kingdom is available and it lists the location of each scheme, the organising body and scheme organiser, the planned number of new entrants per year and the months in which new entrants start, and special features of the scheme such as the specialties of the hospital posts, the length of time spent in each post, the opportunities for attending courses, whether accommodation is available and whether the posts are recognised for higher qualification examination purposes.[155] The Council for Postgraduate Medical Education in England and Wales prepares the publication from information provided by the regional advisers in general practice. Organisers of some district schemes produce brochures describing not only the programmes of posts but also the size of the district hospital services, the local amenities and even the trainers' practices. Oxford is one region where district brochures are available.

HOUSE OFFICER POSTS

The authorities in the United Kingdom responsible for approving hospitals for pre-registration experience under the Medical Act 1983 are the universities. (They are also responsible for determining whether persons holding their qualifications have completed the required 12 months of pre-registration experience and, therefore, are eligible to become fully registered doctors. The procedures for obtaining full registration are described on page 187.) Under the Medical Act a health centre may also be approved by a university for pre-registration experience if it consists of premises which the Secretary of State for Social Services considers suitable for use in connection with the provision of general medical services under the National Health Service and which he has made available to persons providing such services.

Within the regions the responsibility for ensuring that all HO posts provide an 'acceptable standard of training' is assumed by a pre-registration committee which is usually a subcommittee of the RPGMEC. There is, naturally, a substantial representation of the universities on the pre-registration committees, but the composition of the membership and the extent to which the NHS employing authorities (which provide the funding for the posts) are represented varies from region to region. The pre-registration advisory panel in the Trent region, for example, includes the dean and the postgraduate dean of the three university medical faculties. (Each university also has its own pre-registration committee.) The South Western region, in contrast, has on its pre-registration subcommittee, heads of relevant departments of the University of Bristol, the clinical dean from each of the three main hospitals in Bristol, two representatives of the medical students' association and the person from the medical personnel department who is responsible for running the pre-registration scheme. Although the University of London is the university for the four Thames regions, each region has its own pre-registration subcommittee. The University also has a pre-registration committee – the Standing Committee on Pre-Registration of the Academic Council. The regional postgraduate deans in all the regions normally attend the meetings of the pre-registration subcommittee.

The number of pre-registration HO posts in NHS hospitals in England is closely monitored by the DHSS and in Wales by the Welsh Office. Target numbers of posts in NHS hospitals over four years are set for each region and the targets are reviewed regularly. The total target figure for England on 1 August 1985 was 3010 and for 1 August 1988, 3100.[28] The calculations are based on the numbers of medical students who, it is expected, will graduate in each year and a margin is built in for doctors from overseas who need pre-registration experience to enable them to obtain full registration with the General Medical Council. These doctors will have requalified in the United Kingdom usually by passing diploma examinations administered by non-university licensing bodies. (It is not certain that these doctors will obtain a HO post and the reasons are given on page 191). The regional pre-registration committees are responsible for identifying suitable posts in the teaching and non-teaching districts in a medical/surgical ratio of 1:1 if possible.

The target numbers for each region are calculated using a resource allocation formula and they do not relate to the expected numbers of graduates from the university within each region. Some regions have a great many more HO posts than local graduates to fill them. The West Midlands region is one; it has over 300 posts but the annual output of medical graduates from the University of Birmingham is around 150. The Northern region is another. The situation is the reverse in the Thames regions because of the concentration of medical schools in London. There are about 1025 posts in the four regions[162] and 1100 or more doctors graduate annually from the University of London.[139] Trent, with three medical faculties, also has many more graduates than posts.

Meeting the targets set by the Department has been found difficult in some regions over the last two to three years for educational and financial reasons. The opportunities for creating medical and surgical posts offering an acceptable standard of training in district hospitals have become increasingly limited partly because of the rigorous criteria set by the pre-registration committees. In the South Western region, for example, any potential posts not exclusively in general medicine or general surgery have been excluded by the committee if they could not offer at least three-months general surgical or general medical experience in combination with experience in another specialty.[150] Other regional committees are prepared to recognise posts in a specialty such as orthopaedics or ENT. The house officers may then rotate between general and specialist posts over a six-month period. With finance, the districts in almost every region have to fund established HO posts from their recurrent budgets. Thus there could be occasions when a district prefers not to create a new post or decides not to continue to fill one. Some regions, East Anglia, Oxford and North Western for instance, assist with the costs (salaries) of newly established posts. The

Trent region is exceptional; the regional health authority holds the budget for all pre-registration posts. Moreover, for some years this region has experienced little difficulty in meeting its annual targets for HO posts set by the DHSS.

### Approving standards of training in house officer posts

It is usual for the hospitals in which new posts are sited to be inspected before final approval is given. The posts are assessed on the basis of criteria such as: the number of beds for which cover has to be provided (not normally more than 30 beds); the adequacy of the pathology and radiology services; the medical library facilities; the composition of the clinical team and the availability of the members, including the consultant who should have not less than four NHS sessions a week; and the duty rota commitments.[150] (In the Trent region there has been a policy for rotas for HO posts to be restricted to 1 in 3 which is equivalent to an allowance of 11 to 12 Class A UMTs. Payments slightly above or below this level are permitted.) In the majority of regions and in Wales the visiting team is led by the regional postgraduate dean on behalf of the university. In Mersey, East Anglia and Yorkshire (until October 1986), however, the team leader is the dean of the medical faculty or another person appointed to this role by the university.

House officer posts are reinspected or reassessed at five-yearly intervals, or more frequently if the work content of a post has altered owing perhaps to the closure of beds, or if anxieties have been expressed over the level of the supervision being given by the consultant or on the general conditions of service. Feedback on these matters is often obtained from confidential questionnaires which are sent to most pre-registration doctors. Also, when inspecting a hospital, the visitors meet the house officers and critical comments may be passed.

The universities have authority to recognise posts outside the United Kingdom for pre-registration experience. This is normally done on an ad hominem basis – the recognition lasts for the period that the graduate holds the post. The graduate must supply full details of the conditions of service and the training offered before the pre-registration committee can decide whether to recognise the post.

### Information on house officer posts

The universities are obliged to send information on the recognised posts to the General Medical Council. The Council prepares from its manual records, a 'list' in booklet form of hospitals and house officer posts which are approved or recognised for pre-registration service in the United Kingdom.[163] It covers NHS hospitals and hospitals outside the NHS, most of which are military or naval hospitals. This booklet is revised and republished every two years. Also, circulars showing additions and amendments to the list are produced quarterly. The entries identify the total number of beds for each hospital and the individual posts classified by specialty. If a post is in a rotation, this is footnoted. The lists do not, however, show posts that are recognised but lack funding; so it cannot be assumed that all the listed posts are filled.

In January 1985 there were 2983 recognised posts in England (including about 35 posts in armed services hospitals) and 165 posts in Wales. The English posts were in 350 hospitals and the Welsh posts in 21 hospitals. The ratio of medical to surgical posts was virtually one to one. One post was in a health centre in London.[163] It was first recognised by the University of London for an experimental period of three years starting from August 1981. The experiment was monitored and judged to be successful. So in 1984 it became an established post of four-months duration and subject to the normal five-yearly review. The arrangements made by the general practice of three partners to facilitate the training of the house officers were described in a paper by Harris and colleagues.[164] A previous experimental health centre post in Southampton had faltered – apparently over the issue of prescribing. One other point of note is that the pre-registration year is still almost exclusively based on two six-month posts, in spite of the freedom granted in the 1978 Medical Act for it to consist of at least four months general medicine, four months general surgery and four months in another clinical hospital discipline. The letters from the DHSS to the health regions asking that target numbers of HO posts should be a balance of medical and surgical posts, so far as is practicable, may have partly discouraged initiatives to switch from six-monthly to four-monthly rotational schemes.

# 13 Assessing the progress of trainees employed by the health authorities

The administrative arrangements for appointing trainees in each grade and for overseeing their educational welfare are discussed in this and the next chapter. Doctors employed by the National Health Service are covered in the following pages and the next chapter deals with honorary contract holders.

APPOINTMENT OF SENIOR REGISTRARS TO ESTABLISHED POSTS

Senior registrars in NHS established posts are appointed and employed by the regional health authorities or the special health authorities. In the North East Thames and North West Thames regions, however, the arrangements are slightly different for senior registrars who commence their appointments in a teaching hospital. The appointments are made by the teaching health authorities but the regional health authorities issue the contracts.

The guide lines on the appointment of senior registrars to established hospital posts (contained in health circular HC(82)10) state that the job should be advertised and an appointments committee consisting of at least five members be established.[113] The members should represent five bodies or interests: first, the appointing authority (a lay person to act as chairman); second, the appropriate royal college or faculty (usually the regional adviser); third, the regional postgraduate medical education committee (usually the regional postgraduate dean or his deputy); fourth, the university in the region (by a nominated consultant); and finally, the consultant staff of the hospital or hospitals in which the trainee is going to work. These appointment committees can be quite large if the post is part of a rotation and all the consultants for whom the post-holder will work insist on being on the committee.

Although many of the regional postgraduate deans would like to attend when each appointment is made because this is an opportunity for meeting the new trainees, logistically it is virtually impossible. Even in a small region with a relatively small number of senior registrars – say around 130 – there will be 30 or so appointments made each year. So the deans are usually represented by a deputy. The deans' offices do, however, receive copies of the application documents of the successful candidates and many write a letter of welcome to the senior registrars that includes advice on enrolling for accreditation purposes (page 239) and the letter usually outlines the regional procedures for reviewing the progress of doctors in the grade (see below).

The length of the contract issued to the newly appointed senior registrars is not standardised across the regions. (There is no stipulation in the Terms and Conditions of Service for Hospital Medical and Dental Staff in England and Wales on this matter.

It merely states that 'posts shall be held for the duration of a programme of training typically of three to four years.'[34]) In 1984, two regions (Trent and South East Thames) issued an initial contract of one year to doctors in hospital posts and a further contract was issued subject to the senior registrars making satisfactory progress during the first year. (Wessex has also now adopted this policy.) Four regions (Yorkshire, North East Thames, South Western and Mersey) issued contracts of four years duration. At the end of that period a senior registrar who had not yet found a consultant appointment would be reappointed annually if there were extenuating circumstances. The contracts in all but one of the remaining regions did not specify a fixed time period but indicated that the contract covered the whole of the higher specialist training years. The exception was North Western where the contracts contain no reference to the duration of the senior registrar appointment (Dr J M O'Brien, personal communication 1985).

In community medicine the arrangements for appointing senior registrars are different. Unlike the other specialties there is only one training grade covering registrar and senior registrar experience in England and Wales. Senior registrar posts are not usually advertised and open to competition. They are normally filled by trainees who started as registrars with the authority and who have been closely supervised during their training. The progression to senior registrar is not automatic but is made after rigorous assessment by a senior registrar assessment committee.[47]

SENIOR REGISTRAR REVIEW PROCEDURES

A joint working party on hospital medical staffing, chaired by Sir Robert Platt, recommended in 1961 that joint advisory regional committees should be established in every region to supervise rotation schemes and to advise on the suitability of individual senior registrars for retention in the grade. The members on each committee would represent the regional hospital boards, the board(s) of governors (which, until 1974, administered the undergraduate teaching hospitals as well as the postgraduate teaching hospitals), and the university.[18] The practice of reviewing the progress of senior registrars has been adopted in all the regions and in Wales but the machinery for carrying out this task differs widely.

Using the material collected in the interviews with the regional deans and officers in the regional health authorities during 1984, relevant documents, and recent personal communications, the regions have been classified according to their arrangements – notwithstanding the inherent difficulties in developing classifications – and the classification is summarised in Table 38.

a. *Regions with a standing subcommittee of the RPGMEC or a similar committee which reviews the progress of the senior registrars* The standing committee may be

Table 38    Regional arrangements for reviewing the progress of senior registrars, 1984–86

| *Committees responsible for reviewing senior registrars* | *Regions adopting the arrangements* |
| --- | --- |
| Standing SR subcommittee of the RPGMEC or a similar committee | Northern<br>Trent<br>East Anglia<br>North West Thames<br>South East Thames |
| Standing SR subcommittee but the responsibility being transferred to specialty subcommittees or review panels, or specialty groups undertake interim reviews | South West Thames<br>Wessex<br>South Western<br>West Midlands<br>Wales |
| Specialty subcommittees of the RPGMEC, there being no standing SR subcommittee | Yorkshire |
| Other arrangements:<br>   Specialty subcommittees and college tutors supervise individual trainees | North East Thames |
|    Postgraduate director and regional SCM (medical staffing) | Oxford |
|    Joint Advisory Committee (Senior Registrars) convened as required | Mersey |
|    Dean and Joint Medical and Dental Staff Training Committee (for difficult cases) | North Western |

SR = senior registrar    RPGMEC = regional postgraduate medical education committee

Source: Interviews held with the regional postgraduate deans and officers in the regional health authorities in 1984, and personal communications 1986.

known as the joint advisory committee for senior registrars (JACSR) or by another title. Northern, Trent, East Anglia, North West Thames and South East Thames have this arrangement. The Senior Registrar Subcommittee in Trent, for example, is composed of representatives of the teaching and non-teaching health authorities, the three university medical faculties, the committee of senior registrars, the regional and associate postgraduate deans and the regional medical advisory committee. This subcommittee of 17 members or more meets three or four times a year.[156] Not only does it review the progress of nearly 300 individual senior registrars, including honorary appointment holders, at annual intervals, it also deals with applications for appointment as part-time senior registrars and for fellowships, and approves overseas study leave and locum consultant appointments for more than three months. Finally, it oversees the structure of the training programmes associated with the SR posts. The remit of the Senior Registrar Training Committee in North West Thames is similar, although at present it does not deal with trainees holding honorary appointments. This committee (which has a far wider representation than the Trent committee) meets twice a year and it is the practice for the regional dean to be vice chairman. In addition, a review subcommittee composed of the chairman, vice chairman and members of the main committee in the relevant specialties meets twice a year, the meeting dates falling midway between the meeting dates of the main committee. The subcommittee only reviews senior registrar appointments and it reports to the main committee. The medical staffing personnel in the Trent and North West Thames regional health authorities provide the senior registrar committees with up-to-date compendiums or computerised listings of posts and post holders showing details of planned rotations, dates of appointment, review dates, and so forth. The South East Thames Training Advisory Committee for Senior Registrars differs constitutionally from the other regions in this group because it is not a standing subcommittee of the RPGMEC. Also, it does not take the same interest in senior registrar training programmes as the SR committees in Trent and North West Thames. The committee meets three times a year and the chairman is the regional dean.

b.  *Regions with a standing SR subcommittee which reviews the progress of trainees but where, in some specialties, the responsibility is being transferred to specialty subcommittees of the RPGMEC or to review panels established by the subcommittees* The specialty committees must first show a willingness to assume this role before the responsibility is transferred to them. Wessex and South Western are developing these arrangements. When the specialty committees in Wessex review their senior registrars they have sitting with them a member of the JACSR who is not of the particular discipline under review. Usually it is the dean as chairman of the JACSR who attends. The specialty review committees report to the JACSR. The South Western Regional Committee on Specialist Training reviews the progress of all trainees at the end of the first, fourth and any subsequent years. In certain specialties, however, notably medicine, surgery and paediatrics, annual interviews and group meetings between the trainers and trainees in the rotations are also held. In the West Midlands the JACSR meets three times a year and 17 advisory subcommittees in various specialties report. The progress of each trainee is monitored and problem cases are discussed by the JACSR. The arrangements in Wales also come into this category; the progress of trainees (whose contracts are with the individual health authorities) is monitored at the end of the first year and the fourth year – if still in post – by the Joint Advisory Committee for Senior Registrars in Training. The committee, which meets four times a year, is composed of representatives from all the health districts in Wales, the postgraduate organisers (clinical tutors), the academic departments in the University of Wales College of Medicine, and the Welsh Office. The chairman is the dean of postgraduate studies. However, interim reviews are made by specialty subcommittees who report to the JACSR, and the committee depends heavily on these subcommittees for detailed supervision throughout the training period. In South West Thames the formal monitoring of progress of trainees after the first and fourth and any subsequent years is in the hands of the standing SR committee, but interim supervision of trainees in some specialties is provided by groups of trainers.

c.　*Regions without a standing SR subcommittee and where the review of trainees' progress is done by the specialty subcommittees of the RPGMEC* Yorkshire is the only example. It has 11 specialty committees which carry out reviews; in the specialties without committees – these having relatively few senior registrars – the responsibility for reviewing progress lies with the supervising consultants.

d.　*Regions with other arrangements* There are four. Mersey has a JACSR which is convened whenever an occasion for reviewing the progress of an individual trainee arises – that is, at the end of the first year and as required thereafter. The committee for each meeting consists of a regional representative of the relevant college, university representation, and NHS consultants, and the regional dean and the regional SCM (medical staffing) attend. North East Thames has a senior registrar committee. However, because of the large number of senior registrars working in the region, attention is generally concentrated on those who are time-expired. Individual trainees are looked after by the specialty subcommittees and tutors appointed by the colleges. Finally, in the Oxford and North Western region, specialists in community medicine responsible for medical staffing, in conjunction with the medical staffing departments in the RHAs, arrange for the supervising consultants of the trainees to prepare a report towards the end of the trainees' first year. In Oxford the consultants' reports

---

Note: The responsibility for reviewing senior registrars employed by the special health authorities and working in the London postgraduate teaching hospitals is generally held by the deans of the postgraduate institutes associated with the postgraduate hospitals (page 278). In North West Thames, however, the membership of the regional senior registrar training committee includes a representative from each of three postgraduate teaching hospitals within the region.

are examined by the SCM (medical staffing) and the director of postgraduate medical education and training (the regional dean) and if there appears to be a problem the matter is looked into. The purpose of the third year review is primarily to assess progress towards obtaining accreditation. (The region does not have a senior registrar subcommittee nor specialty subcommittees of the RPGMEC. It does, however, have a Subcommittee for Post-registration Business and the members are the regional postgraduate advisers for each of 14 disciplines and the director of postgraduate medical education and training.[157]) The specialist in community medicine in the North Western region passes to the dean only those reports which are considered to be unsatisfactory. The matter is then taken up by the dean and the chairman of the Joint Medical and Dental Staff Training Committee and if there is a major problem it will be raised at a meeting of the committee. This region has 240 senior registrars and the number of problem cases that arises each year is usually no more than around 12.

The frequency of the reviews and the format of the information provided for the reviews also differs from region to region. Virtually all regions review the personal progress of trainees during the first and fourth years of their programmes; some also assess their professional progress in the intervening years. For the purpose of the reviews the supervising consultants in many regions simply write a letter commenting on the trainee's progress and aptitude. In a few regions, they are asked to provide standardised information. Wessex is one where this happens. Those completing the reports are asked to record for each trainee details on study and research, teaching and administration, career intentions and so forth and the trainee is asked to provide a curriculum vitae which is assessed on its presentation. Finally, in many regions the review procedures are being extended to cover doctors holding honorary senior registrar contracts. (The criteria adopted for issuing these contracts are discussed on page 199.)

*Time-expired senior registrars*

In recent years increasing concern has been expressed over the difficulties facing some fully trained senior registrars in obtaining consultant posts. Health authorities had followed the policy of appointing 'time-expired' senior registrars to locum consultant posts or to supernumerary SR posts and filling the posts that were vacated with new trainees. This practice added more doctors to the pool who would be looking for career posts in due course. So in 1983 the Joint Consultants Committee and the DHSS agreed that, for the time being, each time-expired senior registrar should remain in the post currently occupied assuming that the regional SR committee recommended this course of action and the individual continued to apply for the majority of consultant posts advertised in the relevant specialty.[165] This is now the usual practice in the regions. The majority of regional postgraduate deans interview trainees who have entered a fifth year and again in the sixth year and so on, and the trainees are helped as far as possible in finding a consultant post. Very occasionally a trainee may lack certain professional attributes considered to be necessary for entering the consultant grade. Other arrangements will be made for such persons.

Accurate statistics on the number of trainees who are time-expired have proved difficult to assemble. At the request of the JCC, the regional postgraduate deans collected statistics on the numbers of doctors in this situation in 1985. They adopted the definition of a 'time-expired' senior registrar as 'one who, having completed the training requirements for his specialty, has been unable to obtain a consultant post, normally after a four year contract (WTE) in the senior registrar grade'. Honorary contract holders were included. If a person had spent a period of time abroad this experience was counted in the four years provided the appropriate higher training committee had approved the training. All but one of the regions and Wales were able to make returns for the specified date but three sets were incomplete. This level of response was, however, better than the previous year when only two-thirds of the regions provided returns for the specified date. The problem of inadequate information should diminish in size once all the medical staffing departments in the regional health authorities finish entering on computers the personal records for senior registrars.[159] They will, of course, need to receive routine information on the accreditation status of the trainees or, with pathology, the examination results of candidates who sit the final part of the higher qualification of MCRPath.

Increasingly senior registrars are not obtaining consultant appointments until they have entered their fifth year in the SR grade. The regions are finding, therefore, that although they may have a number of NHS-employed senior registrars who are still in post at the end of their fourth year in the grade, relatively few will still be in post at the end of the fifth year – less than ten doctors in the majority of regions. This pattern is evident in the census statistics on hospital medical staffing. On 30 September 1984, 329 NHS-employed senior registrars in England and Wales had been in the grade for four or more years (13 per cent of the total number) and they would have included persons with part-time contracts under the PM(79)3 arrangements. Half the doctors were in their fifth year and the other half were in their sixth, seventh or subsequent years.[7] Note, however, that the census definition for time in grade (see page 117) is not the same as the definition of 'time-expired' adopted by the regional deans.

The specialty advisory committee for general surgery of the Joint Committee on Higher Surgical Training (JCHST) conducted its own censuses of senior registrars and lecturers in general surgery in December 1983 and June 1985 to find out the number who had completed their training and were accredited and the length of time they had spent in the grade.[166] At the end of 1983, 60 accredited surgeons were 'time-expired' having been in the grade for four or more years. Eighteen months later the number had fallen to 41, a reduction of almost 50 per cent. (The total number of senior registrars and lecturers in the specialty was slightly under 200 in each census.) It was also found in both years that time-expired trainees were fairly evenly distributed throughout the country.

APPOINTING AND MONITORING REGISTRARS

Until the reorganisation of the National Health Service in 1974 the appointing and employing of registrars was done by the regional hospital boards. With reorganisation the responsibility passed to the area health authorities. When the AHAs were abolished in 1982 the district health authorities took over the responsiblity for appointing and employing these doctors. However, in at least one region some registrar appointments – apart from doctors employed part-time under the PM(79)3 arrangements – are now being made by the regional health authorities. It is worth noting that the Social Services Committee of the House of Commons in its 1981 report on medical education recommended that registrar and senior house officer contracts should be held by the regional health authorities.[4] Then, in 1986, a ministerial working group[299] recommended that there should be two categories of registrar posts – regional and district – and the contracts of occupants of the regional posts should be issued by the RHAs (see page 39). The policy, if implemented, would considerably increase the workload of regional personnel officers. (The special health authorities appoint their own registrars.) The development of regional training schemes for registrars in certain specialties was mentioned on page 166. The North Western region is one where pathology and diagnostic radiology schemes are in operation and almost all the contracts of the registrars in the schemes are held by the regional health authority.

Codes of practice to be applied when contracts of trainees (both registrar and senior house officers) who have already been in post for two or more years are extended for a further period have been introduced in a few regions, one being South East Thames. The employing authorities are asked to inform the postgraduate dean before the decision on whether to extend the contract is taken. In Wessex also, the districts contact the postgraduate dean routinely when they wish to extend a registrar contract to cover an additional period in a post and he advises on the educational value of such an extension. However, the deans have no powers to enforce this practice.

Different arrangements for supervising the practice of extending registrar contracts exist in the Northern and South Western regions; guidance is given by regional review committees. There is usually a regional representative on the district appointment committees. In the South Western region district appointment committees are always chaired by a representative who is not in the same specialty as the candidates. In the

Northern region the practice of having a regional representative (often the dean) present at appointments meetings also applies to senior house officer appointments that are part of an SHO/registrar training programme (in psychiatry, for example). The registrars in the two regions are normally appointed for one year and the contract is extended by the district only if a satisfactory report is received by the regional committee which reviews the progress of senior registrars. Contracts are not normally extended after 30 months in the South Western region or three years in the Northern region unless there are extenuating circumstances. East Anglia has also adopted a policy of restricting appointments to a maximum of three years.

Regional subcommittees in certain specialties in the East Anglian, West Midlands and North Western regions also monitor the progress of registrars but they are not so concerned with the contractual arrangements of the trainees. Wessex is another region where this is happening. In the North Western region, for example, there are around 21 specialty training groups primarily concerned with senior registrar training. Increasingly the groups are looking at general professional training; those for anaesthetics and obstetrics and gynaecology are the most heavily involved. In the West Midlands, responsibility for registrar training has been taken over by the specialty advisory subcommittees to the JACSR in pathology, diagnostic radiology, anaesthetics and obstetrics and gynaecology.

A totally different system based on personal interviews has been operating in South West Thames for some years. (This is a small region in terms of numbers of trainees.) A small team, made up of the regional postgraduate dean, the regional specialist in community medicine (for medical manpower and postgraduate education) and the regional adviser in general practice, has been visiting each health district about every 18 months to meet the clinical tutor and staff concerned with medical manpower. Trainees who have been in the registrar and SHO grades for more years than is considered normal have been interviewed and counselled by the dean and the SCM.

In community medicine, trainees of registrar status are closely supervised. There are relatively few trainees in each region compared with the hospital disciplines and this makes the task of arranging supervision easier. Each trainee is supervised by a trainer of specialist status who delegates work of a short and long-term nature and who is responsible for ensuring that the general training objectives are achieved during the training period.[47]

### Information on registrars

To carry out the task of overseeing the progress of registrars, the specialty subcommittees need to be supplied with reliable information on the trainees. In the great majority of regions information of this kind is not readily available. In fact, in 1984, only one regional health authority, South West Thames, held computerised files other than enhanced payroll files on all registrars and senior house officers employed in the region. It was this data base which provided the team which visited the districts with the names of trainees who had spent extended periods in the grades. The office of the regional postgraduate dean in the North Western region did, however, hold comprehensive manual files in 1984 and the system was being computerised.[11] The specialty training groups which chose to monitor the junior training grades were supplied with personal details on the trainees. The group members, together with consultants from districts not represented on the training groups, then collected additional information on, for example, the examination status of the doctors, previous posts held, and career intentions.

In September 1984 probably no more than 1000 to 1500 of the 5450 full-time registrars employed in NHS hospitals in England and Wales were covered by some form of regional system which routinely monitored their progress. Yet, as chapter 8 shows, 16 per cent of all registrars (including those with honorary appointments) had been in the grade for four years or more. The number and the percentages of doctors in this category were the highest in any annual 30 September census of hospital medical staff held since 1970. Furthermore, over half these time-expired doctors had been born overseas, and the majority would have held full registration. There is an underlying issue of even greater concern. What career prospects can be offered to many registrars when the annual intake of doctors to the senior registrar grade (excluding honorary appointments) is only around 650? And, are the registrars who are being refused extensions to their contracts by regional review committees in the Northern and South Western regions simply moving to registrar posts in regions with less rigorous policies over length of time in grade?

The ministerial working group which reported in July 1986 (page 310) proposed that health authorities, with professional advice, should review the position of doctors now in the training grades who are judged unlikely to make any further career progress, and arrange for them to receive appropriate career counselling. The options might include retraining in another specialty or for general practice; appointment to the proposed new intermediate service grade; personal regrading to associate specialist; and, exceptionally, the granting of a five-year rolling contract in respect of the post already held.[299]

APPOINTING SENIOR HOUSE OFFICERS

Senior house officers, like registrars, are appointed and employed by the district and special health authorities. The usual duration of their contracts is six months but there are two exceptions. If the posts are in pathology or psychiatry, the normal duration is

12 months in the first instance and the posts may be incorporated into training schemes that cover both the registrar and SHO grades. (The radiology specialty has very few SHO posts.) Appointments made to rotations of posts are the second exception; the posts may be occupied for six months at a time but the duration of the individuals' contracts will be for 12, 18 or 24 months depending on the schedule of posts to be occupied. Rotations are usually arranged in medicine or in surgery and they offer experience in the various branches of each discipline.

The proportion of SHO appointments which are no longer than six months varies among districts. In the City and Hackney health district in London, for example, 37 per cent of the 92 senior house officers surveyed in 1984 were appointed for a period of six months; 28 per cent held 12-month contracts and 35 per cent were appointed to rotation schemes, including vocational training schemes, of 18 months to two years duration. In the Bradford district in Yorkshire, 58 per cent of the SHO contracts were for six months only and the remainder were appointments to rotation schemes. This district authority did not offer any contracts for single posts of 12 months in the first instance but doctors in certain specialties were likely to be offered extensions to their initial six-month contract if their progress was satisfactory.

There are over 10,000 senior house officers in England and Wales and probably half are seeking a new appointment once or twice a year. The commencement dates for the majority of hospital appointments are 1 August and 1 February but many posts are advertised and filled in the intervening months. It is common for the number of applications received for general medical and general surgical jobs in both teaching and non-teaching hospitals to exceed 100. Glynn and Millington found that graduates of the Charing Cross Hospital Medical School who were appointed to an SHO post before the final six weeks of their pre-registration year in 1983 had applied for eight to nine jobs on average. The number of applications made by the equivalent group in the previous year averaged five to six.[167] Increasingly, doctors in this grade are experiencing short-term unemployment because of the difficulties of obtaining and coordinating appointments to a succession of posts.

Mindful of the time spent by senior house officers in applying for jobs and travelling to unsuccessful interviews (the travel and subsistence expenses are reimbursed by the NHS), and the costs to the health authorities of regularly advertising posts of six months duration and administering the appointment procedures, two regions – North Western and South East Thames – have been exploring the possibility of setting up central processing schemes to appoint trainees to 'packages of posts' organised as rotation programmes. (North Western has slightly over 1000 senior house officers and South East Thames, 750.) The 'UCCA' system developed by the Universities Central Council on Admissions to match school leavers and other intending students with a university and course of their choice is a possible model for an SHO placement scheme.

Occasionally a registrar will be appointed to an SHO post to expand the trainee's experience in a specialty recently entered. Senior registrars may also occupy registrar posts temporarily for the same reason. The employing authority must apply to the regional postgraduate dean for guidance on whether the doctor's grade can be protected – that is, on whether the salary for the higher grade can be paid.

ASSESSING THE PROGRESS OF SENIOR HOUSE OFFICERS AND GENERAL PRACTITIONER TRAINEES

Doctors who are appointed to general practice vocational training schemes are the only group of hospital doctors in the SHO grade whose progress is formally kept under constant review (except for the few who are employed part-time under the PM(79)3 arrangements). The VT scheme organisers and clinical tutors remain in close contact with the trainees during their hospital experience. The trainees are expected, if their hospital duties will allow, to regularly attend the courses arranged for their benefit (refer to page 211). In the general practice phase of their training they are employed by trainers whose duty is to be an 'educational manager'.

There are also formal procedures that doctors who intend to become general practitioners must follow if they wish to be issued with a certificate of prescribed experience (page 168). At the end of each period spent in a hospital post or community medicine post, the trainees must arrange for a 'statement of satisfactory completion of a period of training in an educationally approved post' (form VTR/2) to be signed by the supervising consultant or medical specialist of similar status and endorsed (stamped) by the employing authority. A similar form – 'statement of satisfactory completion of a period of training as a trainee general practitioner' (VTR/1) – is completed by the supervising trainer whenever an appointment in general practice is completed. The signatures of the trainers are verified by the regional advisers for general practice or associate advisers or another person nominated as a deputy. Finally, at the completion of the three-year programme or part-time programme of equivalent whole-time length (see below) the statements are submitted to the Joint Committee on Postgraduate Training for General Practice.[168] The administration of the applications is done by the trainees personally or, in some regions, by the office of the regional adviser on behalf of the trainees.

The need for part-time training for some doctors wishing to enter general practice was recognised when the regulations for vocational training were drawn up.[161] Doctors who wish to train part-time and still be eligible for a prescribed experience certificate must be employed in educationally approved hospital posts and/or training practices not less than half-time. However, the training must have been undertaken not more than seven years before the date on which the application for a certificate is made to the Joint Committee. Persons employed less than half time may be considered instead for a certificate of equivalent experience (see page 246 in chapter 17). The Joint Committee has agreed that the experience should normally be acquired within the ten-year period preceding the application.[168]

Regional arrangements for assessing the progress of all other full-time trainees in SHO hospital posts are very poorly developed. A few specialty subcommittees or training groups, notably in obstetrics and gynaecology, have extended their remits to cover all doctors undergoing general professional training. This is known to be happening in the Northern, East Anglian and North Western regions. In the third region, the specialty training group in anaesthetics is actively concerned with both registrar and senior house officer training – it formed a separate subcommittee for this purpose. (In the specialty of community medicine it is national practise for the small number of senior house officers to be attached individually to a trainer.)

For the vast majority of senior house officers the only points of reference for judging their personal progress are the examinations for the higher qualifications and the level of endorsement given by the consultants for whom they work. The consultants can express their support in two ways: in discussions with the trainees and in the references they write in support of the trainees' applications for further posts. However, whether a consultant is prepared to speak candidly to junior trainees about their aptitude for a specialty and their skills will depend on the personality of the consultant. Anecdotal evidence suggests that many senior house officers are applying for jobs for which they are not suited and part of the reason for the situation is that they are not receiving appropriate counselling. Of course, they may not have consulted their supervising consultant before sending off the applications.

TRAINEES EMPLOYED UNDER THE PM(79)3 ARRANGEMENTS

Chapter 8 contains an account of the PM(79)3 arrangements for appointing doctors who are unable to work full-time because of domestic commitments, disability or ill-health. Doctors in any of the training grades may apply. The chapter also mentions that criticism has been expressed in published papers over the monitoring of the progress of senior registrars by regional postgraduate committees. The criticisms were based on statements made by trainees.

An impression was gained from the interviews conducted in 1984 as part of the study into the feasibility of establishing a national information system on hospital training posts and trainees[11] that many regional postgraduate deans view this group of trainees as a special responsiblity. One recently appointed dean had interviewed all the PM(79)3 post holders in the region over the previous year and a half. Another spoke of his region having never rejected an application for a PM(79)3 post because there was insufficient regional funding available. At least two other regions had not experienced problems over funding. A difficulty that had arisen in at least one region, however, was the reluctance of certain specialty committees, notably in surgery, to create part-time supernumerary posts for persons with domestic commitments.

## MONITORING THE PROGRESS OF HOUSE OFFICERS

Before doctors who have qualified in the United Kingdom can become fully registered, they must spend 12 months as resident house officers in posts which have been recognised for the purposes of pre-registration experience (page 172). A minimum of four months of the period must be spent in medicine and four months in surgery. The remaining months may be spent in a health centre or in medicine or surgery or in another clinical hospital discipline including laboratory medicine.[20]

Each United Kingdom university as a licensing body is responsible for determining whether its graduates have completed the required service satisfactorily in an appropriate combination of posts. (There are no formal criteria for assessing whether a doctor's service has been satisfactory.) A certificate of satisfactory service is issued to the trainees by the employing authorities when the appointment to each HO post has been completed. Before each certificate is issued a preliminary form is signed by the supervising consultant confirming that the service of the trainee has been satisfactory. The appointments are usually of six months duration, but if a trainee during an appointment occupies two posts a certificate is needed for each post. At the end of the 12 months, the two or more certificates are submitted to the university or medical school which then issues a certificate of experience. This certificate is forwarded to the General Medical Council when the house officer applies for full registration. Note, however, that the university may forward the certificate of experience to the GMC on behalf of the house officer. Also, the medical staffing personnel in the health authorities may send completed certificates of satisfactory service direct to the university or medical school.

If a doctor has studied at a United Kingdom university but has qualified by passing only the diploma examinations administered by the non-university licensing bodies, the supervision of his or her pre-registration experience and the administration of the certificates is still carried out by the university or, in London, the medical school. Doctors who have studied overseas and requalified in the United Kingdom by sitting diploma examinations are usually referred to the regional postgraduate dean in the region in which they hope to work. This arrangement is made by the National Advice Centre on behalf of the doctor. When a certificate of experience is issued by a dean for a person holding only diploma qualifications, it must be counter-signed by the secretary of the non-university examining body before being forwarded to the GMC.

(A requalified doctor who has practised for a year or more in the United Kingdom while holding limited registration either before or after requalifying, may ask the GMC to consider whether the experience is sufficient for granting full registration.[169])

In six regions and Wales the regional postgraduate deans are responsible for the day-to-day administration of the certificates and usually for the matching scheme where one exists (see below). The clinical dean of the university or his deputy holds the responsibility in East Anglia, Mersey and Yorkshire (until October 1986); in the four Thames regions the postgraduate sub-deans of the medical schools and colleges of the University of London are responsible, and likewise, the postgraduate deans of the three universities in the Trent region.

APPOINTING HOUSE OFFICERS

In the previous chapter it was noted that the target number of house officer posts in England and Wales closely matches the number of undergraduates who, it is expected, will obtain a primary medical qualification in each year. The allocation for each region is not, however, in accordance with the number of graduates; some regions have many more posts than students but in the Thames regions and Trent there are many more students than posts. Provisionally registered doctors are constrained under the Medical Act 1983 to working only in hospitals approved for pre-registration experience. District health authorities which are the employers of house officers should not appoint them to grades above the house officer grade. The combination of these various factors means that the demand for posts in certain areas of the country is highly competitive and the situation is made more complicated by the requirement that trainees must occupy both medical and surgical posts during the pre-registration year.

*Matching Schemes*

During the 1970s the medical schools were encouraged to establish schemes to assist their graduates in obtaining posts. The majority did develop schemes, although the coverage of the student numbers and the methods for matching students to hospital posts varied greatly. At least four universities – Newcastle upon Tyne, Leeds, Southampton and Birmingham – later abandoned their schemes reluctantly.

When establishing a scheme a university first needs to identify, in hospitals, HO posts in which it can regularly place its graduates. These 'linked' posts will then be reserved by the health authority in agreement with the consultants for the use of the university. A health authority may have arrangements with two or more medical schools even within one specialty. In a hospital in South East Thames, for example, there are three surgical HO posts and each is 'linked' to a different London medical school. Naturally, the hospitals with posts linked to a university may not all be in the same health region as the university. The universities in the Trent region have links with hospitals in East Anglia, Oxford and the West Midlands. The London medical schools rely mainly on hospitals in the four Thames regions, East Anglia, Wessex and South Western. Consultants who supervise posts are not strictly obliged to accept a trainee from the linked university. They may make other arrangements for filling the post from time to time.

Clearly the proportion of graduates covered by each scheme will depend on the availability of the posts. The universities of Oxford and Bristol, for instance, have arrangements for placing their students in hospitals in the adjacent teaching district and in some other districts, but the available posts are too few in number to accommodate the annual output of graduates. The other graduates have to make their own arrangements for finding posts. All the London medical schools have linked posts but in 1983 the proportion of graduates each school could place varied from 60 to 95 per cent.[170]

The administrative arrangements of the schemes vary in a number of ways. In many schemes graduates are allocated only one six-month post at a time; in some they receive in one allocation all the posts that they will occupy over 12 months. Allocations for posts to be filled in August take place between July in the previous year and two months before the appointment starting date. The allocations are normally made by committees which match, as far as possible, the students' ranked preferences for posts with the consultants' ranked preferences for post holders. It is common for the students to have visited the hospitals of their choice and met the supervising consultants beforehand. The consultants may be welcome to attend the meeting when the final matching-up is done. St Bartholomew's Hospital Medical College is one which invites them. Some medical schools have computerised the data bases of recognised posts, linked posts and trainees, and the matching of preferences is done on the computer.

The universities which abandoned their schemes did so mainly because they regularly received a low level of cooperation from the local consultants. Too many were making informal arrangements with students. (Three of the universities that took this decision – Newcastle, Leeds and Birmingham – are in regions which have many more HO posts than doctors graduating annually from the regional university.) Frequently the arrangements for filling posts are made when the students are on 'elective' placements in the hospitals. Some universities allow their students to undertake electives in the fourth year; others delay the students until the fifth year and these students can find that HO posts which they would prefer have already been filled.

Students who are not covered by schemes usually find their own posts through personal contact with consultants or by replying to job advertisements for unlinked posts. The universities usually provide them with a detailed list of recognised posts within the local region. To get around the problem of posts being offered to more than one student by different colleagues – usually unintentionally – a few universities now require the students and consultants to sign a form of commitment when they have made an agreement. The students and graduates are expected to inform the office of the supervising dean of their progress in finding a post. They do not always comply. Some universities may not learn which HO posts certain graduates have held until the doctors submit their certificates of satisfactory service at the end of the pre-registration year.

SAFETY NET

A clearing scheme called 'Safety Net' collects information on the numbers of persons who are unplaced during the three months before the August and February appointment starting dates and on the unfilled posts, and it circulates lists giving details of the vacant posts. The scheme, which covers England and Wales, is run by the Council for Postgraduate Medical Education in England and Wales. It was established in 1977 at the request of the DHSS.[171] There is a similar scheme in Scotland.

The arrangements in 1985/86 were as follows: about four months before August and February two questionnaires were distributed. The first was sent to each undergraduate dean in the medical schools and it asked firstly for the number of students or graduates known to have an HO job for the forthcoming employment period, the number known to be still seeking a job (medical, surgical or either), and the number about whom there was no information. Secondly, the questionnaire asked for the numbers and addresses of medical and surgical posts 'linked' to the medical school that were unfilled. Thirdly, it asked for the date when the final results would be known.[172] The second questionnaire was addressed to the regional and district medical officers. It requested information on the number and type – medical or surgical – of HO posts in each district authority, the number that were already filled, and the addresses, type of specialty and names of persons to contact for posts still unfilled. If they were 'linked' posts, the name of the relevant medical school was to be given.[28] Both questionnaires were returned to Safety Net. (About 90 per cent of the district health authorities responded in the spring of 1985.)

Next, two tasks were carried out. Safety Net prepared a list of all unfilled HO posts (specialty, address and name of person to contact) identified in the questionnaires and distributed it to the medical schools. Then once a fortnight the Safety Net personnel telephoned each medical school and health authority known to have unfilled posts to check on the current situation. Safety Net also received telephone calls from these bodies. At the end of each fortnight the list of vacant posts was revised and redistributed to the medical schools. This task was repeated until just before the starting date of the appointment period (1 August or 1 February).

The second task was the preparation of summary statements, also at fortnightly intervals, on the numbers of graduates or students known to be unplaced or whose circumstances were unknown and the numbers of vacant medical and surgical posts. The figures enabled the DHSS to make predictions on whether there would be a shortfall in the numbers of medical and surgical posts available. As in the previous few years the Department had instructed employing authorities that no post should be filled with a doctor who had not undertaken undergraduate clinical studies at a United Kingdom medical school or by a doctor who did not require the post for registration purposes until it was confident that all UK-trained doctors would be placed. Thus doctors who requalified in the United Kingdom were initially excluded from these posts.

Predictions over the likely availability of posts for August are more difficult to make than for February because of the uncertainty over failure rates for the final examinations which are held late in June or early in July. In the spring of 1984, for example, the Safety Net returns suggested that there would be too few posts available in August for the expected number of UK-trained graduates. The failure rates at some universities were, however, higher than expected and there was a surplus of posts.

# 14   Trainees with honorary contracts

Over 600 senior registrars with honorary appointments, 401 registrars and 36 senior house officers were recorded in the 30 September 1984 census of hospital medical staff in England and Wales (Table 9, page 57) and they would have been engaged in teaching and/or research and been supported by funding from a variety of sources. Each one would have been issued with an honorary contract by a regional, special or district health authority to cover any clinical duties or services that were carried out for the authority.[173] A small number of house officers with honorary appointments are recorded in each census. They are usually provisionally registered doctors with commissions in the armed services who are receiving their pre-registration training in NHS posts.

CATEGORIES OF TEACHING AND RESEARCH APPOINTMENTS

The main employment of honorary contract holders of all grades has been classified into six categories for the purposes of recording information on medical manpower in the Standard Manpower Planning and Personnel Information System (STAMP).[174] (STAMP is a payroll system used in many regions. Wessex and Yorkshire also run a medical manpower information module in conjunction with the payroll system.) The categories are: clinical teacher, university clinical research worker, Medical Research Council clinical research worker, other university, etc appointment, Public Health Laboratory Service, and other. The types of employment arrangements for junior doctors in each category are described in the following pages.

*University clinical lecturers*

The majority of lecturer or assistant lecturer posts are funded from the recurrent grant made by the University Grants Committee to the universities or medical schools and colleges. There are also teaching posts that are wholly or partially funded from endowments, trust funds, charities, and foundations such as The Wellcome Trust, or are funded wholly or partially by health authorities. Persons appointed to posts which are supported by health authority money usually spend part of their time in clinical work and the RHA or DHA may include the clinical sessions in its establishment numbers for manpower planning purposes.

   Junior doctors in clinical teaching posts are appointed on the clinical academic scales. The lecturer scale is a broad scale which ranges from the minimum point on the

NHS registrar scale to the maximum point on the senior registrar scale and it has two extra incremental points. Doctors newly appointed as demonstrators or university clinical assistants or assistant lecturers are usually from the SHO grade. (The terminology used for the different levels of academic appointment varies among universities.)

Lecturers are given fixed term contracts by the universities, usually for four years. The length of the contract is shorter for the more junior grades. The university-employed doctors will probably maintain contact with clinical medicine by sharing the on-call rotas with the NHS doctors in their specialty. This experience is important for doctors who are registered for accreditation or wish to apply retrospectively (page 239). They receive Class A and Class B UMT payments for the on-call work and the payments enhance the basic salaries. The university normally makes the payments although it may recharge the health authority if, for example, a lecturer has a substantial on-call commitment. The opportunities to take on extra remunerated work are not as great for university employees as for their NHS colleagues. (This point was noted in the report of the Royal Commission on the National Health Service.[3])

Traditionally there has been parity in the basic remuneration of NHS hospital doctors and clinical academic staff, even though the rate of increase in the annual pay award for university academics is often lower than that for NHS medical staff. The universities have met the difference. Since 1982 there have been delays in paying the full award to clinical academic staff because the government has been slow in providing the University Grants Committee with sufficient additional funds to compensate the universities. The situation was particularly difficult in 1985 because the government decision that clinical academic staff should be paid the same increases as were given to NHS hospital doctors for the year starting 1 June 1985 was not announced until February 1986. The government also agreed that in future clinical academics' pay should in principle be linked to NHS doctors' pay, which is settled after the recommendations of the Review Body on Doctors' and Dentists' Remuneration have been received (refer to page 71). Six months later, however, there was still no confirmation that the 1986 differential would be met.

Medically qualified staff who are employed by the universities to carry out pre-clinical teaching are on a separate salary scale and their average earnings are substantially lower than those of their clinical academic colleagues. The negotiating body for this group is the Association of University Teachers, but the Medical Academic Staff Committee of the BMA has been requested to represent the group instead when pay is being negotiated. This committee represents clinical academic staff.

## University clinical research workers

Universities receive very little money from the UGC for the purpose of employing medical research staff. Most of the research funds received from central government are channelled through the research councils, notably the MRC, or government departments, in particular the DHSS or, in Wales, the Welsh Office. The universities' other source of income for research is project or programme grants awarded to senior members of the teaching staff. The universities also administer fellowships awarded to individuals by external bodies. The funding agencies are mainly charities concerned with medical research, such as the British Heart Foundation, The Wellcome Trust (see below), the Cancer Research Campaign (CRC) and pharmaceutical companies. The Imperial Cancer Research Fund (ICRF) is a major research charity but the finance covering the majority of its junior clinical researchers is administered directly by the Fund. Regional and district health authorities also fund research – Oxford and Northern are two regions providing resources for elective or 'off service' years for small numbers of senior trainees. The time may be spent on research.

Doctors holding university-administered research posts are usually appointed in competition and they are issued with short-term contracts in accordance with university terms and conditions of service for clinical research staff. The basic salaries are usually equivalent to NHS senior registrar or registrar basic salaries depending on level of experience. The researchers, like the lecturer staff, can participate in the on-call rotas in their specialty and they receive Class A and Class B UMT payments accordingly. Again, the UMT allowances are included in their monthly salary payments and recharge arrangements may operate between the university and the health authority unless the grant-giving body has agreed to meet these costs.

The Wellcome Trust provides resources for both academic teaching posts at senior lecturer and lecturer level, and research fellowships. In 1984, for example, the Trust supported 45 senior lecturerships in medical and veterinary sciences and it provided funding for 21 lecturerships lasting five years for which medical schools in the United Kingdom competed and more were to be provided at the end of the year.[175] On the research side, the Trust offers senior research fellowships in clinical sciences and research fellowships in surgery and in pathology. These fellowships are advertised once a year and nominations must be made by heads of university departments. Candidates for the surgery and pathology research fellowships must have worked continuously for the past three years in British hospitals or universities. Another type of research fellowship lasting two years is available to medical graduates in other disciplines. Nominations of candidates who have worked continuously in the United Kingdom for the past three years must also be made by heads of departments.[176] (The level of the financial contribution by The Wellcome Trust to medical research and by the Medical Research Council, the Cancer Research Campaign and the Imperial Cancer Research Fund is discussed in chapter 19, pages 282–284.)

The Medical Research Council provides two types of research funding for junior doctors: training awards made to individuals, or employment either in a research team supported by an MRC programme or project grant which is held by a senior scientist, or as a member of the Council's own scientific staff. The latter is usually restricted to post-doctoral clinicians.

1. *Training awards*    These are of two kinds – studentships and fellowships. Recently qualified science graduates and medically or dentally qualified graduates wishing to undertake a period of research training usually with the goal of obtaining a PhD, can apply for a research studentship. This is a tax-free stipend or student grant available for up to three years at a level approved by the Department of Education and Science. 'Quotas' of awards are made annually to university departments and MRC establishments. Students who would like to be nominated apply to the heads of these departments. The Council provides the stipend, certain allowances and fees for courses up to a maximum amount.[177] Science, medical and dental graduates may apply instead for advanced course studentships to attend approved formal courses, in subjects relevant to biomedical science.[178] During the academic year 1983/84, 294 research studentships and 124 advanced course studentships were taken up by science, medical and dental graduates.[178] Two years later, however, the numbers of available studentships were substantially reduced (see page 283).

It is more usual for medically qualified graduates to apply for training fellowships. These are available to clinicians up to senior registrar or equivalent grade, and the primary purpose is to provide support for up to three years' research training in the basic subject most relevant to the fellow's particular clinical interest. A training fellowship of shorter duration is available to medically or dentally qualified candidates who wish to attend a research oriented course leading to a master of science (MSc) degree, and who are unable to obtain support from their employers for the purpose. This fellowship may be for one year but weighting is given to candidates wishing to progress from an MSc course to a two to three year fellowship. The competition for both fellowships is held annually. Thirty-six training fellowships were awarded in 1983/84.[178] (The Council also awards a few senior fellowships to senior clinicians each year for the purposes of research.)

The fellowships are administered by the host institution and the holders are covered by the institution's terms and conditions of service. The salaries for clinical fellows relate to the NHS/clinical academic scales. Clinical fellows can undertake on-call rota duties and the UMT payments are met by the Council as long as certain conditions are met, one being that the allocation for the fellows is on the same basis as for staff whose salaries are paid from UGC funds. (Trainees of senior registrar status who wish to have their research experience recognised for accreditation may need to undertake on-call duties.)

2. *Research grants*   The Council will consider applications for project grants from any graduate in a university, medical school, hospital, polytechnic or similar institution. General medical practitioners may also apply. It is unusual for junior doctors to apply directly to the Council especially if a personal salary is required. Normally the application is made by the head of department or another senior colleague. The maximum duration of project grants is usually three years but they can be extended to five years.

The grants are administered by the host institutions and junior staff engaged on projects are employees of the institution and, therefore, subject to its salary scales and terms and conditions of service. Like the fellowship holders, these doctors can receive UMT payments for on-call duties performed and, indeed, the Council asks that before a grant application is submitted, the appropriate authorities are consulted to find out if the necessary NHS facilities and honorary status will be made available. The UMT payments are met by the Council in the same way as it meets the payments for fellowship holders.[179] One reason why the Council is prepared to provide the remuneration for these hospital clinical duties is its concern that MRC-financed researchers do not jeopardise their long-term career development. At the same time, the supply of candidates of high calibre wishing to engage in research is ensured. (The annual handbook of the MRC does not contain statistics on the numbers of junior doctors employed on research grants.[178])

### Other university, etc, appointments

The great majority of undergraduate and postgraduate teaching hospitals and many non-teaching hospitals have trust funds that have accumulated in size over the years. The sources of income are mainly subscriptions and donations, income from investments and property, and legacies. Some of the long established London hospitals are particularly well endowed. The trust funds are managed by the health authorities and boards of governors or by special trustees, and the annual income is a potential source of finance for research. The special trustees or health authorities may also manage through the trust fund accounts, ad hoc research grants and donations from charities, pharmaceutical companies and other agencies. These monies will have been negotiated by individual consultants. The transfer of the responsibility of managing the grant is at the discretion of the grant holder.[180] The holder, if working in a teaching hospital, can ask the university or medical college instead to administer the grant. He might even choose to hold and administer the grant himself. Thus a situation can exist whereby research grants and donations received by one department in a teaching hospital are administered by the university and those of a second department by NHS special trustees. The DHSS has, however, advised trust fund managers not to allow themselves to be used simply as bankers for such deposits.[180]

Altogether in 1983/84, £12,659,000 was spent on research in England from trust funds held by NHS health authorities, boards of governors and special trustees. This sum was £910,000 greater than the expenditure in the previous year. The expenditure on research in Wales from trust funds held by the health authorities was £119,000 in 1983/84, this being two-thirds greater than the expenditure in 1982/83.[181] Of course, not all the money would have been spent employing medically (or dentally) qualified researchers. Scientific staff, secretarial assistance and equipment would have also been covered. (Monies from trust funds are spent on other items, the main ones being patients' welfare and amenities, contributions to staff welfare and amenities, and contributions to hospital capital expenditure. The total assets for all trust funds in England were valued by the Comptroller and Auditor General at £287,933,000 for the year 1983/84, 16 per cent greater than the figure for the previous year.)

Medically qualified researchers financed by money administered through trust funds are not, strictly speaking, university employees. Increasingly, researchers are being employed in non-teaching districts. The contract of employment is issued by the health authority or special trustees, although the terms and conditions of service may be the same as those holding research contracts with a university. These doctors, whose level of experience is normally equivalent to that of registrars or senior registrars, may participate in the on-call rotas and be paid accordingly. For salary purposes they may appear on a payroll or payrolls which are separate from the health authority's payroll for staff holding NHS contracts and the university's academic payroll.

## Public health laboratory service

The work of the PHLS is discussed briefly in chapter 6, page 84. The majority of staff employed in the laboratories or units across England and Wales are scientific staff. Medically qualified staff numbered around 150 in 1984 of whom slightly over 100 were consultants and the remainder were in other grades.[71]

## Other employment arrangements

Researchers who are supported by funding not administered by a university or medical college or by special trustees and NHS health authorities fit into this category. A high proportion are doctors from overseas who are in supernumerary training posts and whose funding is provided by their home government or by sponsorship agencies such as the British Council (see chapter 7). Others include persons employed by pharmaceutical companies and persons holding ICRF fellowships which are administered directly by the Fund or its units (see below). Armed services personnel carrying out research in NHS hospitals also come into this category. Some researchers may hold honorary contracts issued by two or more authorities if their research involves patients in a number of hospitals. The extent to which doctors with other employment arrangements share on-call duties depends on their availability and the NHS staffing levels in the respective specialties.

The Imperial Cancer Research Fund has a network of research laboratories plus seven extramural units. Six of the extra mural units are accommodated in hospital or university premises in London, Oxford and Edinburgh, and the seventh, which was established in collaboration with the Royal College of Surgeons of England, is in Lincoln's Inn Fields, London.[182] The laboratories and units undertake programmes of research and junior doctors can be appointed to the research teams as research fellows. One advertisement in *The Lancet* in 1985 was for a fellowship of three years initially with entry point on the NHS registrar/senior registrar salary scale according to age and experience. The holder would receive payment for extra hospital duties when required. Applications were to be sent to the director of the unit. However, the fellowship would have been awarded by the Council of the Fund on the recommendation of the unit director.[183]

In addition, the Fund offers a limited number of clinical research fellowships. These fellows also participate in the research programmes in the main laboratories or the extramural units. They are normally of registrar or senior registrar status and are expected to register for a PhD or work for an MD. Some NHS clinical or laboratory work (the equivalent of one day a week for example) is performed. The fellowships are advertised twice a year and the advertisement for the round of awards for March 1985 stated that the appointments were for up to four years. Candidates were to apply direct to the Fund.

ISSUING HONORARY CONTRACTS

Health authorities were advised by the DHSS in a 1984 memorandum (PM(84)12) that honorary contracts must be issued to junior clinical academic staff 'if there is a clear understanding that the practitioner is to provide a service to the authority'. This service can be a direct service to patients or an indirect one through a support specialty which forms part of the services provided by the authority. The authority should be satisfied, however, that there is clinical work to be done and the specific duties should be formally recorded.[173] Assisting in outpatient clinics, participating in on-call rotas, and administering procedures and treatments to patients in clinical trials are the types of duties carried out by many honorary contract holders.

If a junior doctor merely requires access to hospital facilities for teaching or research purposes and will not be undertaking procedures or providing any other service, he or she will be issued with a letter of appointment. In comparatively few instances is a letter of appointment likely to be appropriate.[173]

The university on behalf of its teaching and research appointees and the consultants responsible for researchers attached to their departments and for persons filling supernumerary training posts are expected to provide the district medical staffing department with a copy of each appointee's curriculum vitae, a copy of the job description if one has been prepared and details of the duties to be undertaken. The doctor must provide evidence that he or she is registered with the General Medical Council (full or limited registration) and is currently a member of a medical defence organisation. If the candidate is of senior registrar status the appropriate regional training committee will probably be asked to support an application for an honorary SR contract to be issued by the regional health authority. However, this request may not be granted. The progress of those who do receive honorary SR contracts is, in many regions, reviewed in the same way as the progress of senior registrars in NHS posts.

### Criteria for issuing honorary senior registrar contracts

Some regional training committees are unwilling to recommend that the regional health authority issue honorary SR contracts to persons who have not been appointed in competition for advertised teaching posts, research fellowships or research posts funded from grants. North West Thames and South East Thames are two regions where this policy was being developed in 1984 (at the time when the interviews were carried out for the study on hospital medical manpower information systems[11]). South East Thames also requires candidates to have a training programme approved by a higher training committee for the purposes of accreditation (notwithstanding the different policies towards accreditation adopted by the committees (chapter 17)) and for the post to contain a 'significant' amount of NHS commitments. The effects of this restrictive policy could be seen in the statistics from the 30 September 1984 census of hospital medical staff. Only 21 honorary senior registrars were recorded in South East Thames; in the previous year the number was 59.[7] Oxford, East Anglia and Trent also required applicants to have an approved training programme. (Non-NHS posts of senior registrar status can be broadly classified as being either established or 'soft money' posts. Established posts are university clinical lecturer posts and established posts in MRC research units; 'soft money' posts are funded by bodies which do not make a continuing commitment beyond a few years at most.[184])

The desire to impose controls on the numbers of senior registrars with honorary contracts has arisen from the general concern that the supply of senior registrars (both NHS-employed and honorary contract holders) in many specialties greatly exceeds the availability of NHS and honorary consultant posts in these specialties. There are, of course, manpower controls governing the numbers of NHS established SR posts in the specialties. The prospects for honorary senior registrars of obtaining an NHS consultant post do not appear to be better than the prospects for their colleagues in NHS posts. In fact, the fields of recruitment data collected by the DHSS suggested that the prospects are probably poorer when account is taken of the numbers of appointments made of doctors from posts overseas (page 60). The likelihood of being appointed to a consultant post directly from a 'soft money' post is particularly low. The Association of Clinical Professors of Medicine has suggested that only 6 per cent of all senior registrars are in 'soft money' posts and no more than 1 to 2 per cent of all consultant appointments are persons appointed directly from such posts.[184]

The Social Services Committee of the House of Commons in its 1981 report on medical education recommended that 'academic posts should be subject to the same manpower controls as NHS posts'. Moreover, at regional level, the available appointments must be reviewed as a whole.[4] The matter has been widely discussed since then. The universities are independent of the National Health Service and a reluctance has been expressed at local university level towards suggestions that they lose their freedom to create teaching and research posts. The universities have also, since 1981, experienced cutbacks in the financial grants made by the University Grants Committee and clinical academic posts have been lost (pages 270–274).

Discussions between the DHSS and Welsh Office, the Joint Consultants Committee, the Medical Research Council and the Committee of Vice-Chancellors and Principals about the problem of honorary contracts in relation to manpower planning have resulted in a mechanism for the joint planning of training grade numbers being established. It is based on a recognition that although it is wrong in principle to train doctors in greater numbers than the career outlets available, the traditional autonomy of the universities must be respected and the flexibility to develop new avenues of research maintained. To reconcile these aims, national targets and annual regional 'quotas' of training posts in broad specialty groupings starting with senior registrar posts will be set by a small central committee – the Joint Planning Advisory Committee. Separate quotas will be determined for the postgraduate teaching hospitals administered by the special health authorities and separate arrangements will apply to research posts. The bodies represented on JPAC – which met for the first time in December 1985 – are mentioned on page 61. The allocation between academic and NHS posts within the regions will be determined by local discussion between each regional health authority and its associated university or universities. The document circulated to regional and district general managers in November 1985 suggested that when honorary SR contracts are proposed for doctors in non-academic and non-MRC posts, regional training committees will need to be satisfied that normally the posts would be educationally approved and adequate selection procedures have been followed.[40]

### Issuing honorary contracts to other junior doctors

Doctors whose applications for honorary SR contracts have been turned down by a regional committee can be issued instead with an honorary contract by a district health authority. Authorities differ in their procedures for issuing these contracts. One may use the title of 'honorary clinical assistant' for all grades. Another may identify on the honorary contract the equivalent NHS grade of the doctor (honorary registrar, honorary senior house officer). Trainees tend to prefer this arrangement. The length of the contracts can also vary. A district may choose to issue honorary contracts for a maximum of one year in the first instance to doctors whose funding is not administered by the university or special trustees. The consultants responsible for the trainees or researchers have to notify the health authority that the arrangements are unchanged before the contracts are renewed. The new contracts may cover the remainder of the individuals' appointments. Honorary contract holders can receive reimbursement for travelling expenses, subsistence allowances, postage and telephone expenses incurred in the performance of NHS duties.

### INFORMATION ON HONORARY CONTRACT HOLDERS

The annual censuses on medical and dental staff administered by the DHSS ask for information on honorary appointment holders as well as NHS-employed staff. It is likely, however, that the statistics on honorary junior doctors derived from the censuses under-represent the true situation, particularly at registrar level. There are various reasons. First, at the time that the census forms are completed the medical staffing departments in the districts may not have up-to-date records on all junior doctors in post with honorary contracts. Most consultants are familiar with the procedures for obtaining honorary contracts for doctors under their supervision. They do not have a similar responsibility for informing the health authority when a junior doctor leaves, especially if the leaving date is before the termination date of the honorary contract. And doctors in supernumerary training posts and 'soft money' research posts who are looking for NHS posts can leave at very short notice. In a large teaching district which has numerous holders of short-term honorary contracts, the medical staffing personnel may feel the task of contacting the supervising consultants for the purpose of the census to be too onerous. Simply completing the census forms for all NHS-employed medical and dental staff in a large district can be time consuming.

Second, the census asks that the time spent on NHS duties by honorary contract holders be recorded in units of medical time.[107] However, information on time spent may not be held by the health authorities for each doctor. The model contract for honorary appointments, unlike contracts for NHS employed staff, does not include a paragraph stating the amount of time per week to be spent on clinical duties for the authority.[173] Moreover, the time which is worked by some doctors may vary considerably from week to week. If an honorary doctor shares an on-call rota, the allocation of Class A and Class B UMTs should be stated in his or her main contract but if the university has made the appointment, the main contract will be held by the university personnel department. Admittedly, the health authority medical staffing department could arrange to have copies of the contracts of university-appointed staff to be sent to it, assuming the university was agreeable to the arrangement.

Third, numbers of hours of work converted into standard UMTs do not reflect the nature of the work performed. For example, during an outpatient clinic session a research registrar may see two or three patients in a clinical trial, while at the same time an NHS registrar shares the full clinic load. The inability to distinguish for the purposes of the census the nature of the work performed by honorary doctors vis-à-vis the work of NHS-employed staff in the same grade is another reason why district personnel may be reluctant to complete full returns.

Fourth, a district health authority or consultants working in the district may not wish to reveal the total number of honorary doctors, especially as some of the work performed by these doctors cannot be strictly equated with work of NHS-employed doctors. The view may be taken that the district could be penalised in terms of future manpower allocations if the regional health authority or DHSS was fully informed of the local staffing levels.

Finally, it is worth noting, however, that the ministerial working group which reported in July 1986 envisaged that if a regional registrar quotas system was introduced (refer to page 39), there would be a number of clinical research posts with honorary contracts within the regional quotas. District health authorities would not grant honorary contracts at registrar level.[299]

# 15 Postgraduate medical centres, courses and study leave

The majority of teaching hospitals and district general hospitals have a postgraduate medical education centre although the type of premises and arrangements vary considerably. The definition of a postgraduate medical centre used by the National Association of Clinical Tutors when updating the national directory of centres does not, in fact, make reference to physical premises. A centre is defined as 'a place where a programme of postgraduate medical education is organised on a regular basis by a Clinical Tutor appointed for this purpose'.[147] Another definition used by the Council for Postgraduate Medical Education in England and Wales emphasises the nature of the education provided and the groups of recipients: 'a postgraduate medical centre … is a place where facilities are provided for the vocational and continuing education of all doctors and dentists in the area. It should support their individual education and training needs and provide links between all branches of the medical profession'.[185] (Vocational training is undertaken in preparation for a chosen career, and continuing education maintains and expands skills and knowledge after the completion of vocational training.) The Council also holds the view that the centre is intended primarily for the use of doctors and dentists and it should be administered by them, through a clinical tutor, and usually with the help of a local postgraduate medical centre committee.

The reasons for the diversity in the design of the centres date from the 1960s. In 1962 the Nuffield Provincial Hospitals Trust and King Edward's Hospital Fund for London made available 'priming' funds for the promotion of postgraduate medical education (other than training for consultant status). Grants from these sources enabled a number of schemes to be established. Then in 1964 and 1967 the Ministry of Health issued two circulars – HM(64)69 and HM(67)33 – instructing hospital authorities to develop and expand existing arrangements for postgraduate education.[141,186] The 1967 circular contained guide lines on the establishment of postgraduate centres – their location, functions, facilities, administration and so forth. However, the Ministry did not allocate additional resources for the purposes of establishing these centres. Rather, the hospital authorities were encouraged to meet any expenditure from their annual revenue and capital allocations of Exchequer funds and to seek additional financial support from professional and private enterprise. Many followed this advice. Meneces noted in 1969[187] that the capital costs for erecting new centres at local hospitals were being met by three different types of funding arrangements:

203

a. the whole cost being defrayed by voluntary subscription from non-NHS sources;

b. the whole cost being met from NHS funds;

c. a mixture of NHS grants from regional hospital boards, grants from local authorities, donations from the Nuffield Provincial Hospitals Trust and King Edward's Hospital Fund for London, private subscriptions and public appeals and fund raising.

The third type was the most usual pattern of funding. Many centres were not, however, established in purpose-built premises and the accommodation of some of those in alternative forms of premises was later found to be unsatisfactory.

The first edition of the directory of postgraduate medical centres prepared by the Council for Postgraduate Medical Education in England and Wales and the National Association of Clinical Tutors contained information on 211 centres in general hospitals in the United Kingdom in 1972. Nearly half were in purpose built premises, a quarter were in adapted premises and the remaining quarter used 'borrowed' accommodation. Also there were around 40 centres in psychiatric hospitals and some teaching hospitals had a centre. The total number increased steadily over the remainder of the decade; there were 371 centres in all types of hospitals in the 1980 directory. Very few centres have opened since then – the 1986 directory covered 381 centres. The pattern in the type of accommodation has changed over the years. By 1984 only 10 per cent of the centres used borrowed accommodation and the number in adapted premises greatly outnumbered those in purpose-built premises.[147]

The Council for Postgraduate Medical Education in England and Wales identified in 1981 a set of spatial requirements that should be met when designing new centres. They should have space for formal lectures and for seminars and informal discussions; facilities for the presentation of patients; library space and space for individual study; offices for administrative staff, tutors, course organisers and others; space for social facilities, including a bar and catering facilities; a separate entrance foyer; storage space and cloakrooms; and car parking facilities for visitors.[185] The results from a survey of postgraduate centres in the United Kingdom in 1979 suggested that the majority of centres can fulfil these functions, although the design of the premises may not be in accordance with the Council's recommendations. The survey was conducted by the National Association of Postgraduate Medical Education Centre Administrators with assistance provided by the Health Care Research Unit at the University of Newcastle upon Tyne.[188] Usable questionnaires were returned by 208 centres.

Medical library services were provided by 76 per cent of centres. Those that were less likely to offer a service were attached to large hospitals, including teaching hospitals where a medical library was already established. (Many libraries are run by librarians who are fully trained and there are close links between the centre libraries and the regional library services.) There were very few centres in the national survey that did not have any catering facilities, although usually meals and/or refreshments were provided only when meetings were held. (At many meetings the hospitality is funded by pharmaceutical companies.) Fewer than one-third of the centres served lunches daily.

The DHSS and Welsh Office issued a draft health building note on accommodation for education and training in 1985. In an annex to this building note was a list of activities commonly carried out by groups of doctors in postgraduate centres, the usual duration of time spent on each activity and the number of occasions when the activities are held each year. The checklist had been compiled from information gathered by departmental officers and by the Medical Architecture Research Unit of the Polytechnic of North London. Tutorials for hospital specialties, including tutoring for higher qualification examinations and journal club meetings could add up to 630 hours which is equivalent to 180 half-day sessions a year. Divisional meetings and clinical meetings could add up to 87 sessions annually, other meetings and gatherings (films, open days, social events, meetings of the local medical committee and of medical societies, and so forth) 98 sessions, and activities concerned with vocational and continuing education for general practitioners 62 sessions.[189] A centre with this level of use would be occupied for over 425 sessions a year although, of course, the type of room accommodation used for the different activities would vary and more than one activity might be held at a time.

The Council for Postgraduate Medical Education in its 1981 desiderata on post-graduate medical centres saw them as being intended primarily for the use of doctors and dentists.[185] The national survey of centres held in 1979 found, however, that four-fifths provided facilities for nurses. Other health professionals, notably pharmacists and administrators, were also regular users of many centres.[188] The guidance to health authorities contained in the 1985 health building note endorsed the pattern of multiple use. It was based on the concept that the responsibilities of authorities for the education and training of staff are most appropriately fulfilled – for reasons of good management and economical use of space – by facilities in joint-user centres, although authorities may appraise other options. The building note was, however, a draft circulated for consultation with representatives of regional general managers and appropriate professional and other bodies.[189]

CATEGORIES OF COURSES

A 1973 DHSS and Welsh Office memorandum on the financial responsibilities for postgraduate medical and dental education – HM(73)2 – identified three broad categories of courses.[143]

1. *University courses leading to university degrees or diplomas* Students register with the university and pay normal university fees. The remainder of the costs is met by the university.

2. *Other courses* of varying lengths organised by universities normally at the request or with the approval of the regional postgraduate medical education committee. Fees are commonly charged and honoraria or fees are paid to the teachers.

3. *'Section 63' (refresher) courses* for general practitioners that are financed by the National Health Service.

This categorisation is still generally applicable although categories 2 and 3 have a wider coverage, and it provides the framework for the discussion in the following pages.

UNIVERSITY DEGREE OR DIPLOMA COURSES

A reference was made in chapter 9 to a guide to postgraduate degrees, diplomas and courses in medicine which is published annually.[115] It identifies masters degrees and diplomas awarded by United Kingdom universities in nearly 100 clinical and basic medical science subjects, community medicine and public health, and occupational medicine. The courses are usually one year full-time and the candidates are normally assessed by sitting examinations. Postgraduate medical students can enrol instead for higher qualifications – doctorates (MD or PhD) and some masters degrees – that are awarded for completed research.

The fees charged by the universities to students whose home of permanent residence is in the United Kingdom at the start of a course, are standardised. The fee for a full-time course for a masters degree or diploma was £1632 in 1986, unless there was a special feature in the course such as an overseas assignment. Students who were residents of member countries of the EEC were also charged at this rate. Fees for students from non-EEC countries were commonly at least three times greater. Moreover, the fees for similar courses in the same subject often varied among universities. For example, the overseas fee for an MSc in cardiovascular studies run by a university in the north of England was £4350; a diploma course in cardiology run by a school of the University of London had a fee of £8050.[115]

The Universities' Statistical Record publishes statistics on student numbers on behalf of the University Grants Committee. The Record relies on returns made by the universities. The total number of full-time postgraduate students in Great Britain studying subjects in medicine (excluding pharmacology and studies allied to medicine) in 1984/85 was 2553. This figure was slightly bigger than the figure for the previous year – 2503. (The 1978/79 number was 2309.) Two-thirds of the 1984/85 students paid fees set for 'home' students. The number of part-time postgraduate students studying medical subjects was 2150 in 1983/84 and the majority were doing research work for a higher degree. Women formed about 40 per cent of the 1983/84 and 1984/85 full-time postgraduate medical students who were domiciled in the United Kingdom.[190] The National Health Service paid the fees of over 830 full-time postgraduate students in Great Britain and 575 part-time students in 1982/83 but what proportion of the fees were for subjects in medicine is not known.[191]

OTHER COURSES ORGANISED BY UNIVERSITIES AND OTHER BODIES

The great majority of courses attended by junior hospital doctors come into this category. The courses are of two kinds. One prepares candidates for the higher qualification examinations administered by the royal colleges and faculties; the other provides instruction on advanced clinical or laboratory procedures, new methods of treatment and so forth. The courses can be organised by university departments and the offices of the regional postgraduate deans and be held in medical schools and teaching hospitals, or they can be organised by clinical tutors (who are university appointees) with the venues being district hospitals and postgraduate medical centres. Courses are also run by individual NHS consultants and by external bodies such as the royal colleges and faculties. The lengths of the courses vary greatly, some are residential and many are held on a part-time basis such as half a day per week over a number of weeks.

a. *Examination courses* Tuition and refresher courses for the various higher qualification examinations administered by the royal colleges and faculties are normally mounted in collaboration with the regional adviser in the relevant college or faculty or, at district level, with the local specialty tutor. Candidates for the FRCR in diagnostic radiology, for example, are expected to have a thorough understanding of physics and radiological techniques and so most universities with medical faculties in the regions mount two to three-year courses for trainees planning to sit the examinations. The Royal College of Radiologists also holds courses serving trainees in or near London.

The annual guide to postgraduate degrees, diplomas and courses in medicine lists courses of different lengths that provide tuition for the higher qualification examinations.[115] Fees are usually charged. (Whether NHS trainees receive reimbursement for courses attended depends on the decision reached by their district or regional study leave committee (see pages 215-217).) The guide does not, however, provide a

207

total coverage of examination courses mounted by individual hospitals or consortia of hospitals and intended for the hospitals' own trainees. Calendars prepared by the postgraduate deans' offices in, for example, the Oxford and Mersey regions and Wales and by the British Postgraduate Medical Federation for the four Thames regions do contain information at this level of detail. Also, many postgraduate medical centres regularly prepare printed programmes of forthcoming events which can include preparatory courses for examinations, instruction on oral and written examination techniques and even mock exams.

The policy for charging fees for examination courses organised by the medical schools and the regional postgraduate deans' offices is not uniform across the regions. The majority aim to make the courses financially self-supporting and, therefore, charge fees which are normally paid by the employing authorities on behalf of the trainees. In the Northern, Trent and Yorkshire regions, however, fees are not usually charged for trainees who work within the region. In the Northern region, the Regional Postgraduate Institute for Medicine and Dentistry – of which the dean is the director – estimates the costs of the courses planned for the forthcoming year and the regional health authority transfers the amount to the Institute's budget. A similar arrangement exists between the Yorkshire RHA and the office of the dean of postgraduate medical education.

Courses for part I of the membership examination of the Faculty of Community Medicine are organised in a different manner. When the specialty was established in 1974 the DHSS undertook to finance the administrative costs of modular courses of about 20 weeks total tuition spread over two years with an additional one day of study a week between modules. These courses were organised by three consortia of health regions: the Northern Consortium incorporating the Northern, Yorkshire, Trent, Mersey and North Western regions (based at the Trent Regional Health Authority in Sheffield), the Midlands and South Western Inter-regional Training Scheme covering West Midlands, Oxford, Wessex, South Western and Wales (based at the University of Birmingham) and the Thames and Anglian Consortium (based at Guy's Hospital Medical School). In 1985 the central funding of the Thames and Anglian Consortium was withdrawn. A South Eastern Consortium is now operating with the financial responsiblity for the two-year modular course being shared by the South East Thames, South West Thames and North West Thames Regional Health Authorities. Trainees from East Anglia and North East Thames may enrol and their regions are charged on a per capita basis. Central funding is to be withdrawn from the South Western Inter-regional Training Scheme from October 1986. The four participating regions and Wales plan to continue the scheme with the necessary finance being contributed in equal proportions by the participating regions and the Welsh Office (Professor A G W Whitfield, personal communication 1985). The Northern Consortium was disbanded around 1984 and the northern regions now organise courses for their own trainees. In a few centres trainees may enrol instead for an appropriate university MSc degree. They may then complete the requirements for the MFCM.

At the time the specialty of community medicine was established it was felt that continuing education courses were needed for those appointed to career posts. A number of the new specialists had already served for many years in the health service, often as medical officers of health. The DHSS agreed, therefore, to fund centres for continuing education – the Centre for Extension Training in Community Medicine at the London School of Hygiene and Tropical Medicine of the University of London and the Unit for Continuing Education in the Department of Community Medicine at the University of Manchester. However, central funding of the London centre ceased in 1982/83 and the funding for the Manchester unit was withdrawn in April 1986. The Manchester unit, which attracts personnel from many disciplines in the health service, will continue on a self-funding basis and it will be known as the Centre for Professional Development (Dr F Eskin, personal communication 1986).

b. *Courses for advanced training* Attenders at these courses are usually junior hospital doctors who have already obtained the higher qualification relevant to their specialty or, if they are in diagnostic specialties, are progressing towards the final examinations for the MRCPath or FRCR or, in occupational medicine and community medicine, are completing the written work for the MFOM or the second part of the MFCM. Consultants may also attend. These courses are far fewer in number than the examination courses.[115] It is noteworthy that many of the advanced courses are organised in London by the Royal Postgraduate Medical School, the British Postgraduate Medical Federation and the specialist institutes of the Federation.[192]

Attachments for advanced training can also be arranged. These enable doctors who are fully trained or are close to completing their specialist training to spend a period working with a senior specialist. In surgery, for example, a trainee may be taught a new surgical technique during an attachment. If the trainee is an NHS employee, the employing authority will probably meet the fees for the attachment. The guide to postgraduate degrees, diplomas and courses lists various bodies which organise attachments of this kind.[115]

Persons who lecture on examination courses or courses for advanced training may receive fees or honoraria. The level of fees payable to hospital medical and dental staff employed by the NHS is set under paragraph 166 of the Terms and Conditions of Service.[34] On 1 June 1985 the fee was £26.50.[51] Certain conditions must be fulfilled before a lecturer can receive this fee. For example, the activity of the lecture should form part of a planned postgraduate education programme and it should take place outside the practitioner's clinical duties – that is, outside the hours of 9 am and 5 pm during week days – but lectures given during the lunch hour can qualify. Travel and subsistence expenses may be paid where appropriate.[51,193]

Whether the regional or district health authority pays the lecture fees for courses held in the district depends on regional practice. In the South Western region the clinical tutors are expected to send to the regional postgraduate dean a form giving details of a forthcoming lecture. If the dean endorses the lecture as being appropriate for the payment of a lecture fee, the form is passed to the regional health authority for approval and it is then returned to the tutor. After the lecture, the tutor enters the number of attenders on the form and sends it together with the lecturer's expenses claim form to the regional treasurer's department. The costs are charged against the budget allocated to the postgraduate medical centre but which is held by the RHA. (Budget allocations for the centres are made by the finance subcommittee of the RPGMEC.[150]) In some other regions the assessment of whether a lecturer should receive a fee is made by the clinical tutor and the fee is paid from a budget held by the district.

SECTION 63 (REFRESHER) COURSES FOR GENERAL PRACTITIONER PRINCIPALS AND TRAINEES

Continuing education and vocational training courses for general practitioners are familiarly known as 'section 63' courses. Section 63 of the Health Services and Public Health Act 1968 empowered the Secretary of State for Social Services to provide instruction for persons of specified classes who are employed or contemplate employment in certain activities connected with health or welfare. (Before 1968 the relevant section and act was section 48 of the National Health Service Act 1946.) In practice, the employing authorities – regional, district and special health authorities – finance the instruction of their employees, both qualified personnel and trainees. For general medical practitioners, general dental practitioners, pharmacists and opticians the situation is different because they are independent contractors within the NHS. Hence the establishment of separate administrative and financial arrangements for instructing these professional groups and their ancillary staff.

Under the present arrangements for general medical practitioners in England (principals, assistants and trainees who are in the general practice phase of their training) the DHSS allocates money to two budgets. The first budget covers the costs of running courses. It is divided among the regions and each regional budget is transferred to the relevant university and is administered in nearly all regions (from April 1986) by the regional adviser in general practice. He has the responsibility of providing and approving facilities and courses for both the continuing education of general practitioner principals and the vocational training of trainees who are ex-

Table 39  Annual cash limits and expenditures on section 63 courses for general medical practitioners (including trainees in general practice) and travel and subsistence expenses, England, 1979/80–1985/86

| Year from 1 April | Courses | | Travel and subsistence expenses | |
|---|---|---|---|---|
| | Cash limit (£000) | Expenditure (£000) | Cash limit (£000) | Expenditure (£000) |
| 1979/80 | 610 | 584 | 500 | 478 |
| 1980/81 | 768 | 761 | 612 | 751 |
| 1981/82 | 892 | 862 | 742 | 941 |
| 1982/83 | 924 | 902 | 760 | 1137 |
| 1983/84 | 886 | 871 | 1194* | 1235 |
| 1984/85 | 880 | na | 1263 | na |
| 1985/86 | 1000 | na | 1100 | na |

na=not available
* Includes over £400,000 special addition during the year to allow for expected overspending.
Source: Report of the Working Party on Section 63 Courses[194] and Health notice HN(FP)(85)11[195].

pected to attend courses during the general practice phase of their training, and also during the hospital phase if their duties allow (page 185). Previously the budgets were administered by the regional postgraduate deans.

The annual cash limits for courses in England between 1979/80 and 1985/86 and the expenditure until 1983/84 are shown in Table 39 columns 1 and 2. The 1985/86 cash limit was set at £1,000,000. Until 1985/86 the sizes of the regional allowances of course funds had been, to a large extent, historically based, with successive years' allocations being increased incrementally. A Working Party on Section 63 Courses for General Medical Practitioners in England which was set up by the DHSS, recommended in 1984 that the regional allocations for courses should be related to the number of potential recipients – principals, assistants and trainees – within the regions.[194] The recommendation was adopted and it is being implemented over four years. The maldistribution in 1984/85 according to the criterion of recipient target groups was relatively small – the allocations to the 14 regions were over or under the target allocations by no more than 4 per cent in total. Two regions, East Anglia and North West Thames, received considerably more than the others in relation to the target allocations; therefore, East Anglia's allocation will be adjusted downwards by around 25 per cent over four years and the allocation for North West Thames will be reduced by 12 per cent.

The second budget is for travel and subsistence expenses of general practitioners (including trainees) attending section 63 courses. The doctors submit claims for payment to the family practitioner committee to which they are contracted and the committees are reimbursed by the DHSS from this central budget. Until 1985/86 there was no effective machinery for controlling expenditure on travel and subsistence even though annual cash limits had been set on the central budget. Spending rose from £478,000 in 1979/80 to £1,235,000 in 1983/84, an increase of 158 per cent over four years (columns 3 and 4 in Table 39). One reason for the growth rate was the expansion in the number of vocational trainees attending courses. (Vocational training for new entrants to general practice became compulsory in February 1981.) The whole cost of vocational training courses is met from section 63 budgets, apart from payments to course organisers. A survey of 23 family practitioner committees carried out on behalf of the Working Party showed that in 1983/84 nearly a quarter of the total cost of travel and subsistence claims was for trainees.[194]

As an interim measure pending the outcome of the Working Party's recommendations, the DHSS instructed the postgraduate deans in mid-1983 that continuing education courses which were not organised and funded from the section 63 course budget should not be approved for the payment of claims for travel and subsistence expenses made by family doctor attenders. These courses are known as zero rated courses; they are organised by various bodies such as the royal colleges and faculties, the British Medical Association and medical societies, but not by pharmaceutical companies. (Pharmaceutical companies may contribute to the organisation of section 63 courses by providing refreshments and printing programmes or by making a grant for these purposes.) General practitioners and trainees may also attend courses and meetings intended primarily for hospital doctors. The ban on claims for zero rated courses continued in 1984/85 and, in addition, claims for travel of 100 miles or more each way were no longer automatically reimbursed.[196]

The Working Party on section 63 courses felt unable to recommend any new rationally-based criteria for calculating allocations for travel and subsistence. The survey of 23 FPCs had shown wide variations between the proportion of general practitioners (including trainees) covered by each committee who made claims for courses during 1983/84, ranging from 24 per cent for one committee in central London to 63 per cent for a committee in East Anglia. The average amount of each claim received by the individual committees was between £33 and £88. It was not possible to predict the travel and subsistence expenses patterns for FPCs according to characteristics such as size of population, numbers of family doctors, geographical location and so forth. Single handed practitioners did appear, however, to attend less often. The Working Party recommended, therefore, that regional allocations for travel and subsistence should be historically based on the average percentage sizes of the regions' expenditure over the previous three years.[194]

Guided by the recommendation the Department introduced new interim measures for the 1985/86 financial year. General practitioners could once more receive expenses for attending zero rated courses and courses involving journeys of 100 miles of more both ways. To control expenditure, however, a ceiling was set on the amount of money that could be reimbursed to each doctor by the FPCs over the financial year. If, towards the end of the year, there was a surplus in a region's budget for travel and subsistence expenses, the DHSS – acting as budget administrator – would decide the extent to which those doctors, whose claims exceeded the personal cash limit, could receive supplementary payment.[195] The regional cash limits for individual doctors were calculated by dividing the 1985/86 overall cash limit for each region (based on the regional patterns of payments in the years 1981/82 to 1983/84) by the number of general practitioners in the region (principals, assistants, trainees) on 1 October 1984. The average cash limit per doctor ranged from £22-£23 in North East Thames and North West Thames to £69 in the South Western region.[195] The survey of 23 FPCs had suggested that fewer than half the 26,000 family doctors in England make one or more claims each year for section 63 courses expenses. So it was likely that there would be a surplus available for redistribution in the budgets of at least some of the regions. In the event this proved to be the case. At the end of the financial year the DHSS instructed the FPCs to meet in full claims that had been submitted over the year.

The Working Party also recommended that the total budget for section 63 courses and expenses should be devolved to regional level either to the universities or the regional health authorities and that there should be a single budget holder. The most appropriate person, in the view of the Working Party, would be the regional adviser in general practice. The Working Party also believed that the responsibility for setting the policy framework for course approvals and financial control should lie with the regional general practice subcommittee under the overall responsibility of the regional postgraduate dean and the regional postgraduate medical education committee.[194] One of these recommendations was accepted in part when the DHSS agreed that the regional advisers in general practice could be the administrators of the regional budgets for courses for the 1986/87 financial year. The other recommendations were still under consideration.

*Statistics on course attenders*

The Universities' Statistical Record publishes annual statistics for the universities on continuing education courses, the student numbers and student hours. Continuing education courses are defined as 'all courses of less than 9 months in full-time length (or the equivalent in part-time study), whether leading to certifications or not, for which fees are payable (or sponsorship available), whether these courses are offered within university premises or elsewhere'. The student numbers are a retrospective count of the students who have attended each course, and student hours are calculated for each course on the basis of the contact hours recorded for the aggregated student attendance.[190] In general the courses are of short duration with about 90 per cent being less than 50 hours.[191]

The Record received information from the universities on 2965 postgraduate medical and dental continuing education courses held in England and Wales in 1983/84. About 90 per cent were financed mainly by 'government health departments'.[190,191] The average number of students per course during 1983/84 was 26 and the average number of hours tuition per student was 23.

There were, however, significant differences in the 1983/84 entries for individual universities with a medical faculty or medical school. Two – Cambridge and Nottingham – did not make returns. (There were no figures for Cambridge and Nottingham in the table for the previous year either.) Oxford was noteworthy for holding many courses (355) with relatively few students (16 on average) and of short duration (nine hours per student on average). Liverpool, in contrast, held far fewer courses (98) with high attendance rates (over 30 on average) and of considerable length (60 hours per student on average). The average length of courses at Leicester and Southampton was similar – about 58 hours per student. The College of Medicine of the University of Wales returned information on only one course.[190]

This brief analysis suggests that the figures for each university may not be comparable. It is not possible to distinguish between long and short courses; the figures for section 63 courses for general medical practitioners cannot be separated from courses held for higher qualification examinations administered by the royal colleges and advanced clinical tuition, even though the budgeting arrangements are different. The Universities' Statistical Record is reviewing the information contained in its publications. Advice has been sought, presumably from the universities, over the collection and presentation of data on continuing medical and dental education courses.

The British Postgraduate Medical Federation publishes annually statistics on section 63 courses held in the four Thames regions. In 1984/85 791 courses were held altogether: 6 per cent were intensive one-week courses, 71 per cent were extended courses lasting a month, a term or a year and the remaining 23 per cent were weekend or one, two or three-day courses. The total number of attendances by general practitioners including trainees was 88,383. (The number of doctors who were enrolled on the courses was not given.[162])

Finally, some general practitioners and trainees may prefer to be attached to a hospital clinic on a part-time basis for up to three months as an alternative to attending a section 63 course. If the attachment is approved by the regional postgraduate dean, the doctor can claim for travel and subsistence expenses. Thirty-three individual clinical attachments were approved in the four Thames regions in 1984/85.[162]

STUDY LEAVE

Under the terms and conditions of service for hospital medical and dental staff, professional or study leave can be granted by an employing authority for approved postgraduate purposes. The leave may be used for study (usually on a course), research, teaching, examining or taking examinations, visiting clinics and attending professional conferences.[34] The recommended allocation of leave under the terms and conditions is not uniform for the junior grades of staff. (Trainees in community medicine have the same recommended allocations as hospital trainees.[197])

Registrars and senior house officers may receive day release with pay and expenses for the equivalent of one day a week during university terms or leave with pay and expenses within a maximum calculated at a rate of 30 days in a year. The allowance may be accumulated over the period of an appointment. A doctor with an 18-month appointment, for example, may apply for 45 consecutive days' leave but if the leave is granted it cannot be taken until one year of the appointment has been served. Doctors in these two grades may also receive leave with pay and expenses for the purpose of sitting an examination for a higher qualification. (Examination fees are not reimbursed by employing authorities.) Travel and subsistence expenses for examinations are only to be paid when taking the examination is the natural culmination of a course of study approved by the health authority. Doctors in the hospital phase of vocational training schemes are covered by these terms. A number attend courses for the MRCP(UK) and MRCGP and for diplomas (usually the DCH and the DRCOG).

Senior registrars in hospital specialties (apart from the diagnostic specialties) normally hold the higher qualification relevant to their specialty. Thus, the majority have little need of study leave to attend examination courses. The maximum annual rate of ten days with pay and expenses over three years is not, therefore, as generous as that for the general professional grades. (This allowance can also be accumulated.) However, in the terms of their appointment, senior registrars are normally permitted the equivalent of at least one day per week for individual study or work on specific research projects. For house officers there is no recommendation on study leave because the pre-registration year of training is intended to supplement the clinical experience received in the undergraduate years. House officers should, however, be allowed reasonable time within working hours for attending clinico-pathological meetings and ward rounds with other firms within the hospital.[34]

Employing authorities are not bound by the recommendations contained in the terms and conditions of service. The South Western Regional Health Authority, for example, has agreed that because of the geographical position of the region, senior medical staff employed by the authority, including senior registrars, should be allowed two to four extra days of study leave over three years to compensate for the additional time spent in travelling to attend courses and conferences. In contrast, some authorities including teaching districts are finding for budgetary reasons that the amount of leave granted to individuals has to be restricted to less than the recommended annual allowances.

Guided by a 1979 health circular on study leave – HC(79)10 – each regional health authority has established a regional study leave committee or panel and among the members is a representative of the RPGMEC (usually the regional postgraduate dean or his deputy). One duty of the committee is to ensure that appropriate guidance is issued to the employing authorities.[198] Northern, East Anglia, South East Thames, Wessex, Oxford, West Midlands and Mersey are among the regions that have prepared detailed guide lines on study leave allowances for the various grades of medical and dental staff, the procedures for making application, and on regional policies for attending local courses rather than courses held in other regions. The regional study leave committee also decides on difficult applications about which local decisions have not been reached, and on applications for overseas study leave. Individuals whose application for leave has been refused by an employing authority can appeal to the regional study leave committee. The committee hears and decides the appeal.

*District arrangements for considering study leave applications*

The 1979 health circular recommended that decisions on individual applications for study leave from junior medical staff should be considered at a 'service-giving' level, or as closely as possible to it, and that it would be appropriate for routine applications to be approved by nominated officers of the employing authority.[198] Almost every regional health authority has now devolved the responsibility for the registrar and SHO grades to the health districts. (Oxford was one exception in 1986.)

Doctors wishing to apply for study leave complete an application form giving details of the purpose of the leave (course, examination, private study and so forth), the venue, fees, mode of transport, anticipated subsistence expenses and whether the applicant's hospital duties will be covered by colleagues or by a locum employed for the purpose. (The employment of a locum should only happen in exceptional circumstances.) Some forms ask for details of previous study leave granted by the authority and the examination status of the trainee (for example, whether part 1 of a higher qualification awarded by a royal college is held). This is often the only method of recording in the personnel files recent information on the examination status of the trainees. In a few regions a standardised study leave application form is used; elsewhere the districts design their own form. The supervising consultant or consultants sign the forms and in some districts the agreement of the clinical tutor or the chairman of the hospital division for the specialty may also be needed.

The machinery for considering and granting applications is not uniform across the districts. In some, all applications are submitted to a district study leave committee or panel; in other districts, the responsibility is held by the district medical officer or by the clinical tutor and, possibly, the psychiatric tutor for any trainees in psychiatry. There are districts where the personnel officer or administrators of the hospital units assume the responsibility.

Not surprisingly, local decision-making over activities for which study leave with pay and expenses will be granted is not consistent. Some districts are usually prepared to pay travel and subsistence expenses for only two attempts at an examination for a higher qualification; districts in Oxford and Mersey have been encouraged to adopt this policy. Other districts will normally cover the expenses for three attempts. This has been acceptable practice in the East Anglian, Northern, West Midlands and Wessex regions. Some trainees in the south of England who wish to sit examinations held in Scotland – notably for the FRCS awarded by the Scottish colleges and the MRCP(UK) – may receive expenses; others may not. (The MRCP(UK) part 1 examination can only be attempted twice at any one centre.) Although courses for most royal college higher qualification examinations are mounted in each region (and in a few regions course fees are not charged for trainees from within the region), districts may still be prepared to provide fees and expenses for trainees wishing to attend similar courses in other regions.

## Information on applications for study leave

National information is not available on the frequency that study leave is taken. In the survey of trainees in the Bradford, and City and Hackney health districts carried out as part of the feasibility study on a national information system[11], the total number of days or half days granted as paid study leave were recorded from the application forms in each trainee's personal file. All successful applications made since the appointment starting date were covered, and included were days of leave with pay granted for which expenses were not reimbursed by the authorities. (The exercise was time-consuming both in recording the information from the files and in converting the leave for half-day release courses lasting many weeks into full days.) Approximately half the trainees in each of the two districts had not applied for leave by the time of the survey, but these included newly appointed senior house officers who may not have had an opportunity to make arrangements. One-third of the City and Hackney trainees had been granted between one and 20 days leave; the proportion in Bradford was a quarter. However, relatively more Bradford trainees than London trainees had been granted in excess of 20 days leave. It is worth noting also, that the annual study leave budget for the northern district was considerably greater than the budget of the London teaching district.

A survey of study leave applications received by health authorities in the Northern region was carried out by Norton, O'Brien and McEvoy.[199] Records held by the regional health authority showed that 55 per cent of the medical and dental senior registrars had applied for study leave during 1981/82. Two-thirds of both the applications and the days of leave taken were for the purpose of attending conferences and symposia or meetings of societies. To collect information on leave taken in 1981 by junior doctors up to registrar grade, a postal questionnaire was sent to the district health authorities. Only nine of the 16 districts in the region produced full data, and the poor response rate underlines the difficulty of obtaining this kind of information. The analyses showed a four-fold variation between the districts in the average number of days leave granted to trainees who applied for leave – from four days to 15-16 days. Information on the financing of district study leave budgets is equally difficult to obtain and reasons for this are given on page 303 of chapter 20.

# 16 Royal colleges and faculties

This chapter and the following one describe the collegiate arrangements for overseeing training standards. (The examination systems for higher qualifications are discussed in chapter 9.) The functions of the royal colleges and faculties identified in Table 40 for overseeing general professional training are discussed in this chapter; the work of the higher training committees including the Joint Committee on Postgraduate Training for General Practice is covered in the next. The colleges, faculties and joint committees on higher training receive financial assistance from the government for the purpose of monitoring training standards and the procedures for allocating the grants-in-aid are covered in chapter 20. The penultimate chapter contains references to some manpower reports and surveys carried out by the colleges and faculties. The historical development of the individual colleges and faculties is not discussed, even though some variations in current practice can be attributed to historical factors. An account of the development of these professional bodies up until the mid 1960s is contained in the book *Medical practice in modern England* by Stevens.[13]

COLLEGE AND FACULTY REGIONAL ADVISERS

The Royal College of Surgeons of England was the first college to appoint advisers in the English health regions and Wales and the practice began in the early 1960s.[200] Each adviser formed a link between the College, the regional hospital board and the regional university and was available for consultation with the regional board and the postgraduate medical dean. At the same time a small number of surgical tutors responsible for a single hospital or group of hospitals were appointed on an experimental basis with funding provided by the Nuffield Provincial Hospitals Trust. The activities of the tutors were intended to complement those of the 'all purpose' clinical tutors who were starting to be appointed by the universities on the recommendation of the regional postgraduate medical education committees (page 154). The surgical tutor's role was to arrange seminars, joint ward rounds and other educational programmes, establish study facilities and arrange time for junior doctors to study, encourage research and to organise the provision of educational facilities in the local area. The experiment must have been judged a success because by 1985 there were slightly over 200 surgical tutors working from postgraduate medical centres in England and Wales.

The Royal College of Physicians in London did not start to appoint its own regional

Table 40    Royal colleges and faculties which recognise general professional training posts, schemes, laboratories or departments in England and Wales, and number of trainees (permanent paid NHS and honorary contract holders) in registrar and SHO posts, 30 September 1984

|  | *Number of trainees in* | | |
|---|---|---|---|
|  | *Registrar posts* | *SHO posts* | *Registrar and SHO posts* |
| Royal College of Physicians (London) jointly with the Royal College of General Practitioners | 1643 | 3359 | 5002 |
| Royal College of Surgeons of England | 1625 | 3475 | 5100 |
| Faculty of Anaesthetists of the Royal College of Surgeons of England | 835 | 901 | 1736 |
| Royal College of Obstetricians and Gynaecologists | 495 | 1272 | 1767 |
| Royal College of Psychiatrists | 829 | 863 | 1692 |
| Royal College of Pathologists | 345 | 248 | 593 |
| Royal College of Radiologists | 327 | 87 | 414 |
| Faculty of Community Medicine of the Royal Colleges of Physicians | * | 39 | 39 |
| Faculty of Occupational Medicine of the Royal College of Physicians (London) | 1 | — | 1** |

* There is a single registrar/senior registrar grade in community medicine.
** Only one occupational health trainee was recorded in either the registrar or SHO grades in the 1984 census of hospital medical staff. There are, however, posts outside the NHS recognised for training for the associateship examination.

Note: The total numbers of posts covered by the colleges and faculties exceed the figures in the table because vacant posts and posts filled by locums have been excluded.

Sources: 30 September 1984 censuses of hospital medical staff and community medicine staff.[7,9]

advisers until 1969 after a recommendation along these lines was made to the Comitia by a college committee on regional organisation. The other colleges and faculties have also adopted this policy with the exception of the Royal College of General Practitioners; regional advisers in general practice are university appointments (page 153).

The appointment procedures devised by the colleges and faculties and the duties of the advisers are similar. The advice of persons in the regions (senior college members in teaching and non-teaching hospitals and the regional postgraduate dean among others) is usually sought before a new adviser is nominated and appointed. In community medicine, the specialty subcommittee of the regional postgraduate medical education committee makes the nomination and it is sent to the board of the Faculty of Community Medicine for approval. The Royal College of Physicians in its guide lines suggests that advisers should be 'in active practice, preferably not too senior and prepared to devote time and energy on behalf of the College'. (The Councils for Postgraduate Medical Education in the United Kingdom have prepared a booklet on the role of college regional advisers.[201]) The usual term of appointment adopted by the colleges is three years in the first instance and renewable for three to five years. A deputy adviser may be appointed in the larger regions. For the Royal College of Physicians the deputy adviser, where appointed, frequently suceeds to the post of adviser; the usual period of appointment is five years, inclusive of time spent as a deputy adviser.

The advisers are expected to advance in the regions the views of the college or faculty on postgraduate education. They usually serve on the RPGMEC and they are almost always on the appropriate regional specialty subcommittee (frequently in the role of chairman). The adviser or another college representative also serves on appointments committees for senior registrars in the appropriate specialties. Thus, the advisers are kept informed of developments in senior registrar training programmes and of the appointment and progress of the trainees. The extent of their knowledge of registrar and SHO training posts and of the trainees in these grades depends upon the size of the region and the number of trainees in the specialties covered by the respective college.

The Faculty of Community Medicine – which has fewer trainees than most other bodies – expects each faculty adviser and deputy adviser to take a personal interest in all potential entrants to the specialty and to accept a general responsibility for all trainees. In colleges with large numbers of trainees, matters relating to the welfare and progress, including the examination attainments of individual doctors, are normally dealt with by the supervising consultant or specialty tutor with the regional adviser being consulted in special circumstances.

The duties of the advisers are not confined to training and trainees. When a new consultant appointment is to be made the regional adviser of the relevant college or faculty should be given an opportunity to comment on the draft job description and the organisation of the arrangements and facilities for the new consultant in the light of service needs. A consultant in the relevant specialty is nominated by the college to be the 'college assessor' on the advisory appointments committee (AAC) which appoints the consultant. The membership of each AAC is defined under NHS regulations (refer to health circular HC(82)10) and should the post be in accident and emergency medicine, both the Royal College of Physicians and the Royal College of Surgeons can nominate an assessor.[113] A duty of each assessor – who has full voting rights – is to advise the AAC on the suitability of the candidates according to criteria agreed by the college or faculty. (Guidance issued by the Royal College of Surgeons of England to its assessors was mentioned on page 120.) The college assessor must be from outside the region making the appointment; he or she could be a regional adviser from an adjacent region, for example. In anaesthetics, the Faculty of Anaesthetists has designated more than 100 consultants as faculty assessors.

In many colleges and faculties the higher qualification confers membership of the college and elevation to the status of fellow is by election on the basis of esteem. The regional advisers with the help of any local machinery are asked to ensure that the names of members in the region are kept under review. Naturally the advisers keep closely in touch with their college or faculty and regularly attend meetings. The advisers in the colleges which appoint specialty tutors also maintain close contact with the local tutors. The advisers do not receive a stipend from the health service. Claims for expenses may be covered by the health authorities or, but less frequently, by the college.

COLLEGE AND FACULTY TUTORS

The colleges and faculties which have adopted the practice of appointing district-based tutors established by the Royal College of Surgeons, include the Royal Colleges of General Practitioners and Physicians of London and the Faculty of Anaesthetists (and, for dentistry, the Faculty of Dental Surgery). In addition to the 200 or more surgical tutors in England and Wales there are similar numbers of tutors in anaesthetics and general practice. The 1986 *Directory of postgraduate medical centres* in England and Wales[147] identified over 150 tutors in the psychiatry specialties, although a proportion were clinical tutors in psychiatry appointed by the universities to oversee the postgraduate centres serving psychiatric hospitals and units, and others were local appointments or persons self-designated as tutor. They could apply to the Royal College of Psychiatrists for recognition. The College is, however, moving towards a system of having a single regional tutor for each specialty in the discipline and with the tutor having some responsiblity for the teaching of the specialty in the region. There are some specialty tutors in obstetrics and gynaecology.

Listings in the 1986 directory suggest that an imbalance exists in the regional distributions of specialty tutors. For instance, there were 57 tutors (excluding dental tutors) in a wide range of specialties working from nine postgraduate centres in Oxford, and 66 tutors associated with 21 centres in the North Western region. The

Mersey region, in contrast, had 15 centres but only eight tutors serving the various specialties.[147]

POLICIES FOR RECOGNISING REGISTRAR AND SENIOR
HOUSE OFFICER POSTS

The regulations for most of the higher qualification examinations for membership or fellowship of the colleges and faculties stipulate that candidates must undertake part of their training in posts or hospital departments that have been 'approved' (see Table 31 in Chapter 9). Approval is granted on the recommendation of college representatives who inspect the posts. The regulations for the MRCP(UK) are the exception among examinations for hospital disciplines. Candidates for part 2 must have completed not less that 12 months post-registration experience, or equivalent experience in posts involving the admission and hospital care of acutely ill medical patients (either adults or children), and the three colleges of physicians rely on testimonials from two college proposers (fellows or members of at least eight years standing) for assurance that this regulation has been met. The Royal College of Physicians in London in association with the Royal College of General Practitioners does, however, operate a system for approving medical posts in England and Wales for general professional training.[202] Thus, all established registrar and SHO posts in NHS hospitals in England and Wales are covered by some system for assessing the standard of training offered. Moreover, the DHSS has informed health authorities that they should not advertise vacant training posts which are not currently approved. The approval policies of the colleges and faculties are summarised in Table 41.

Table 40 (page 220) shows that the London-based Royal Colleges of Physicians and Surgeons each have responsibility for over 5000 posts in the registrar and SHO grades. The Faculty of Anaesthetists and the Royal College of Obstetricians and Gynaecologists cover between 1700 and 1800 posts in England and Wales. The total number of psychiatry posts in the two grades is also between 1700 and 1800; however, rather than approving individual posts, the Royal College of Psychiatrists recognises training schemes covering one or more hospitals which offer experience in the various branches of psychiatry. The Royal Colleges of Pathologists and Radiologists do not recognise individual posts either. The pathologists grant approval to hospital laboratories and, in 1984, around 600 trainees were working in registrar and SHO posts in England and Wales. The radiologists recognise hospital departments in diagnostic radiology or radiotherapy and the posts for the two specialties when added together exceed 400, three-quarters of which are in the registrar grade. The Faculty of Community Medicine recognises posts, although the numbers involved are considerably smaller than the numbers covered by other the bodies and the responsibility

Table 41   Policies of the royal colleges and faculties for approving training in registrar and SHO posts in England and Wales

| College or faculty | Purpose of recognition | Level of recognition | Maximum length of approval | Recommended length of time spent in posts or schemes |
|---|---|---|---|---|
| Royal College of Physicians (London) | general professional training | posts | 5 years | 3–24 months |
| Royal College of Surgeons of England | FRCS(Eng) | posts | 5 years | 6–12 months |
| Faculty of Anaesthetists | FFARCS(Eng) | hospitals/ posts | 5 years | schedule I posts up to 24 months; schedule II posts up to 12 months |
| Royal College of Obstetricians and Gynaecologists | MRCOG and DRCOG | posts | 5 years | 6 or more months; posts classified as suitable for MRCOG or DRCOG or both |
| Royal College of Psychiatrists | MRCPsych | schemes | 4 years | approved schemes 3 to 4 years; schemes with limited approval 6 to 24 months |
| Royal College of Pathologists | MRCPath | laboratories | 5 years | not stated |
| Royal College of Radiologists | FRCR | departments | 5 years | not stated |
| Faculty of Community Medicine | general training | posts | not stated | SHO posts 6 months, preferably as part of a rotation programme |

Note: The Faculty of Occupational Medicine and the Royal College of General Practitioners do not have independent systems for routinely inspecting posts. General practitioners join teams visiting obstetrics and gynaecology posts and schemes in psychiatry. Visits to medical posts are made jointly with the Royal College of Physicians.

for approving the posts has been devolved to the regional education subcommittees for community medicine.

The two bodies which do not have independent systems for routinely inspecting hospital posts are the Royal College of General Practitioners and the Faculty of Occupational Medicine. Industrial firms may apply to have an occupational medicine post approved for examination purposes before advertising it, although this does not happen often. With general practice, hospital posts selected for 'prescribed experience' (page 168) must be currently approved by the appropriate college or faculty. (Community medicine posts are eligible for selection.) However, it is usual practice for a representative of the Royal College of General Practitioners to join the team of visitors when inspections are made of obstetrics and gynaecology posts and psychiatric training schemes. Inspections of medical posts are normally made by teams jointly representing the Royal College of General Practitioners and the Royal College of Physicians.

### Duration of approval and length of tenure

The maximum approval period is five years except in psychiatry; the Royal College of Psychiatrists has chosen four years as the maximum period. Where an approval is granted for less than the maximum period, the hospital will either be revisited or it will have to provide satisfactory evidence that the target standards have been met. Occasionally the standard of training offered in a hospital or post is considered to be unacceptable and the approval is withheld if it is a new post, or withdrawn if it is an established post. The employing authority is given the opportunity to rectify matters and there have been relatively few instances when posts have been disestablished for this reason.[5] Normally, posts with a maximum length of approval are revisited at the end of the period, although the visit may not take place until after the approval period has ended. The colleges will recognise the experience of persons who occupy posts during these interim periods. (In pathology, the maximum length of approval for laboratories is five years theoretically; in practice, however, the interval between revisits may be much longer for a variety of reasons.) The criteria for assessing training standards developed by each college and faculty cover staffing levels, facilities and opportunities for tuition and private study, supporting clinical and diagnostic services, and workload levels. These criteria are contained in a booklet prepared in 1984 by the Councils for Postgraduate Medical Education.[203]

Many colleges also make recommendations on the length of time individual posts (schemes) should be occupied by doctors planning to sit the examinations for the relevant higher qualification awarded by the college. As Table 41 indicates, they apply different classification systems. In psychiatry, for example, schemes providing experience in the various specialties and with 'full' approval can offer training appropriate for the MRCPsych of three to four years. A scheme with limited approval – possibly because the number of specialties covered by the scheme is insufficient – may provide training from six months to two years. The Faculty of Anaesthetists operates a similar system for classifying hospital departments and their posts. The Royal College of Obstetricians and Gynaecologists specifies instead the college examinations – MRCOG or DRCOG or both – for which each registrar and SHO post is suited (refer to page 126 in chapter 9).

### Procedures for visiting hospitals

When new posts are established the responsibility for obtaining college or faculty approval lies with the supervising consultant and the health authority. Once the current approval period runs out, the responsibility for setting in motion the reapproval procedures lies either with the consultant or the college depending on each college's record-keeping arrangements. The Royal College of Surgeons, for example, has relied on the consultants to notify its secretariat when revisits were due. The College is now computerising its post approval records and the new system will provide the secretariat with listings of posts and the revisit dates. Most of the other colleges and faculties have either recently computerised their records – the Royal College of Physicians being the first – or have plans to do so (see page 228).

Consultants are also expected to notify the college or the regional adviser if the work content of an existing post or scheme is altered or the post is transferred to another unit as part of the reorganisation of local services. The consultants do not always comply and at least two royal colleges – physicians and psychiatrists – now monitor the advertisements for vacant posts in the medical journals to check that the advertised details match information in the approval records. In obstetrics and gynaecology, each hospital department is asked by the royal college to complete an annual statistical return which covers workload and staffing levels. The college secretariat can then check the returns for any posts lacking recognition.

The colleges have slightly different policies for appointing visitors to carry out the inspections. Usually the team is made up of two or more senior members of the college; in obstetrics and gynaecology, psychiatry and radiology they are from regions other than the one in which the visit is held. The visiting teams in psychiatry also include a senior trainee. The Faculty of Anaesthetists appoints only the 20 members of the Board of Faculty to act as visitors – one per visit – to ensure comparability in the assessments. In pathology, the Royal College normally appoints a senior member from each of three disciplines – chemical pathology, histopathology and medical microbiology – and the director of postgraduate studies normally attends as the representative for histopathology. He also assesses general training offered in haematology. The presence of a representative of the Royal College of General Practitioners among team members visiting posts in medicine, obstetrics and gynaecology, and schemes in psychiatry, has already been mentioned. All college visitors may claim reimbursement for travel and expenses from the health authority responsible for the posts.

## Preparation of the final reports

Supervising consultants are usually informally told what the likely recommendations will be at the end of the visit. It may, however, take a few months before the report is finalised and the hospital is formally contacted. Needless to say, the colleges' procedures for processing the reports of the visitors and informing the hospital consultants and the health authorities of the recommendations are not uniform.

The procedures of some colleges for approving the reports are multi-staged. Taking the Royal College of Psychiatrists as an example, the convenors – one of whom leads each team of visitors – prepare the reports of their own visits. The convenors together form a Central Approval Panel which meets three to four times a year and on each agenda are reports from recent visits. The recommendations of the Panel are passed to the Court of Electors for ratification. (The Court meets six times a year.) Once the recommendations are finalised the dean of the college and the secretariat prepare a summary of each report and the summary is signed by the appropriate convenor. Copies of the summarised report are sent to the local clinical tutor for psychiatry, the regional postgraduate dean, the regional adviser in general practice and the professor of the local academic department of psychiatry. The tutor discusses the report with the consultants and trainees involved in the scheme. An extra copy is sent to the clinical tutor with a request that it be passed to the relevant health authority. Some schemes cover hospitals in two authorities and there have been occasions when the second authority has not received a copy.

All the colleges have adopted the practice of preparing an edited version of the visitors' reports or a summary letter for circulation. However, the amount of information contained in the circulated document varies considerably and the identity of the persons on the circulation lists also varies. The regional postgraduate deans routinely receive copies from all but the Royal College of Physicians. This college does, however, inform the regional advisers in general practice and contact may be made with the deans later, particularly when problems arise. Coverage of the health authorities is not as comprehensive – in 1984 the Royal Colleges of Physicians and Pathologists and the Faculty of Anaesthetists did not routinely contact the district health authorities responsible for the posts. Even the colleges that did inform them did not address the reports to the same representative. Two routinely sent a copy to the district medical officer, one addressed each report to the person who counter-signed the hospital recognition application form (perhaps a hospital administrator) and the fourth transferred the decision of who to contact to the psychiatric clinical tutor. The inconsistent practice of the colleges has meant that districts wanting to keep their registrar and SHO post recognition records up to date have had to ask colleges for information on an ad hoc basis. (The policies adopted by the approval bodies for circulating letters or summary reports following visits of inspection are further discussed in the next chapter on higher training committees, page 238.)

AVAILABLE INFORMATION ON RECOGNISED HOSPITALS AND POSTS

Booklets of hospitals and posts recognised for examination purposes are prepared by the Royal College of Surgeons[204], the Faculty of Anaesthetists[205] and the Royal College of Obstetricians and Gynaecologists.[129] The Royal College of Radiologists prepares lists of diagnostic radiology, and radiotherapy and oncology departments and the Royal College of Psychiatrists will supply a list of approved schemes on request. Most of the colleges and faculties are in the process of computerising their hospital recognition records using different kinds of computer hardware and software. In 1984 the Royal College of Physicians was the only college that had a full system running and it now produces regional directories of hospital posts considered for general professional training.[206] The regional postgraduate deans are supplied with a copy of the directory for their region. To simplify the problem of identifying individual medical posts within hospitals the College has developed a post numbering system for identifying each post and the hospital and region in which it is sited. Other colleges, in particular the Royal College of Surgeons, intend to introduce numbering systems but the structure of the systems may not be compatible.

*Coverage of the post recognition systems*

How comprehensive are the post recognition systems? In the fieldwork carried out for the study into the feasibility of establishing a national information system for hospital medical and dental training posts and trainees, the date of the approval and the expiry date were recorded for all training posts in two health authorities – City and Hackney, a London teaching district with 150 registrar and SHO posts, and Bradford, a northern non-teaching district with 103 posts in these two grades.[11] In Bradford all the posts were currently recognised. Ten or so posts in City and Hackney were not identified in the records of the approval bodies, excluding the records of the colleges which do not recognise individual posts (psychiatry, pathology and radiology).

There were various reasons for the situation in City and Hackney and these reasons probably occur in other health authorities with large numbers of posts in various hospital units. In the obstetrics and gynaecology and anaesthetics specialties, departments which have educational approval sometimes create new general professional training posts but do not formally notify the Royal College or Faculty. Both specialties in City and Hackney were due for reinspection and the information collected on these visits would be used to bring the College and Faculty records up to date. There were two medical SHO posts in a small unit that were not known to the Royal College of Physicians. This was an oversight. These posts formed part of a complicated rotation which was organised by a London postgraduate teaching hospital. There were also two medical posts each shared by two hospitals, one in the teaching district, the other in an adjacent non-teaching district. The sessions in the non-teaching district were not recorded by the College. On the surgical side there was a specialised registrar post in an inter-district rotation that was normally filled by doctors holding the higher qualification of fellowship. It was not, therefore, recognised under the FRCS regulations. The College knew of the post. There was also uncertainty over the approval status of two SHO posts in an accident and emergency department. These posts can offer medical training and are approved by the Royal College of Physicians, or surgical training and are recognised under the FRCS regulations.

The colleges and faculties have to liaise with over 200 health authorities – including the special health authorities – in England and Wales and, considering the large numbers of general professional training posts involved (Table 40, page 220), it is not surprising that the systems are not totally comprehensive. The feasibility study fieldwork also identified some problems the health authorities were having in keeping complete records on the current approval status of their general professional training posts. The personnel department in Bradford had all the documents relating to the SHO and registrar posts in the district, but telephone calls had been made to the colleges from time to time to prompt the sending of outcome letters. The coverage of the correspondence on the City and Hackney posts in the district's centralised records was patchy in comparison, and part of the reason for the situation was the procedures adopted by the approval bodies for notifying employing authorities of the outcome of visits and the manner in which the procedures are carried out. The records held in the offices of the respective regional postgraduate deans were also only partially complete. As those colleges and faculties with plans to computerise their hospital recognition records prepare the records for entering in the computer, they may take the opportunity to check the identity of the health authority responsible for each hospital and post. This would be one step towards ensuring that the authorities are always informed of the outcome of visits to inspect their posts.

OTHER MEDICAL FACULTIES

Two other faculties for medically qualified doctors are the Faculty of Ophthalmologists and the Faculty of Homoeopathy.

The Faculty of Ophthalmologists is an independent body which happens to have its offices in the Royal College of Surgeons of England. It is concerned with all matters relating to ophthalmology other than trades union matters and is, therefore, responsible for standards in the discipline. It is the body that is approached by the DHSS and other official organisations whenever advice is wanted on the subject (Professor B Jay, personal communication, 1986). (Inspection of general professional training posts for the fellowship and diploma examinations in ophthalmology is carried out by the Royal College of Surgeons while approval of higher training posts is given by the specialty advisory committee for ophthalmology of the Joint Committee for Higher Surgical Training. Members of the Faculty are also on the SAC.) The Faculty was incorporated in 1949, shortly after the National Health Service came into operation, and it was formed by the Council of British Ophthalmologists (founded in 1918) amalgamating with the Association of British Ophthalmologists (founded in 1938). In common with other colleges and faculties, there are faculty tutors in the regions.

The Faculty of Homoeopathy was incorporated soon after by an act of parliament – The Faculty of Homoeopathy Act 1950. The first national body in the discipline was the British Homoeopathic Society formed in 1844. The London (now Royal London) Homoeopathic Hospital was founded five years later and, in 1877, a school of homoeopathy was opened at the hospital. Under the National Health Service Act 1946, homoeopathic institutions were enabled to provide their own form of treatment, and continuity of the characteristics of the institutions was to be maintained. At present there are specialist homoeopathic hospitals in London, Tunbridge Wells, Bristol and Glasgow, and NHS clinics are held in a few other centres.

Membership of the Faculty is obtained by first passing the membership examination. Candidates must be fully registered medical practitioners and have completed three years post-registration work. The Faculty also has an associateship status and those eligible to apply for election are medical practitioners registered with the GMC (or whose qualifications would be recognised by the GMC), dental practitioners registered with the General Dental Council, veterinary surgeons registered with the Royal College of Veterinary Surgeons, and pharmaceutical chemists registered with the Pharmaceutical Society of Great Britain.*

---

* Refer to The Faculty of Homoeopathy's booklet on courses of instruction in homoeopathic medicine 1986, available from the Royal London Homoeopathic Hospital, London.

# 17 Higher training committees

In 1968 the Royal Commission on Medical Education recommended that junior doctors who satisfactorily complete specialist training should be eligible for registration in a vocational register which – the Commission hoped – would be established by the General Medical Council.[1] Member countries of the EEC already maintained specialist registers and EEC directives required the countries to recognise each other's specialties. The Committee of Inquiry into the Regulation of the Medical Profession also argued that a specialist register should be instituted by the GMC although it knew that the idea of specialist registration caused misgiving within the medical profession.[2] A register has never been instituted.

The royal colleges and faculties responded to the Royal Commission's proposal in different ways. Those responsible for training in medicine, surgery, anaesthetics, psychiatry (and dentistry) in the United Kingdom and the Republic of Ireland, together with the appropriate specialist associations, established a joint committee on higher training for each discipline. The joint committee for medicine covered community medicine and occupational medicine. Separate specialty committees for the major specialties within medicine, surgery and psychiatry were also set up, and these specialty advisory committees report to the appropriate joint committee. Another joint committee was established for general practice but its membership does not include nominations from bodies in the Republic of Ireland.* The royal colleges for obstetrics and gynaecology, radiology and pathology did not form joint committees on higher training in association with other specialist bodies. The functions of overseeing standards of higher training were assumed instead by committees within the colleges. The names of the higher training bodies, the specialty advisory committees and the subcommittees of the SACs in medicine are listed in Table 42. The numbers of trainees in higher training in England and Wales covered by each higher training committee are also given. These statistics are from the DHSS 1984 censuses of medical staff. To obtain the total number of trainees for whom each committee is responsible, trainees in Scotland, Northern Ireland and – for some committees – the Republic of Ireland must be added to the number for England and Wales.

---

* Although the length of specialist training needed for entering general practice is much shorter than the length of higher training for the other disciplines, the work of the Joint Committee on Postgraduate Training for General Practice is covered in this chapter because the structure and functions of the Committee are similar to those of the other joint committees.

**Table 42** Joint committees on higher training and their specialty advisory committees and subcommittees, and royal colleges with responsibility for higher training, and the number of trainees in England and Wales covered by the higher training committees, 30 September 1984

| *Higher training bodies and trainees in England and Wales* | *Specialty advisory committees* | | *Subcommittees of the specialty advisory committees* |
|---|---|---|---|
| **Joint Committee on Higher Medical Training** (1100 trainees approximately, including community medicine, accident and emergency medicine* and haematology**) | accident and emergency medicine; cardiovascular disease; clinical pharmacology and therapeutics; communicable and tropical diseases; dermatology; endocrinology and diabetes mellitus; gastroenterology; general (internal) medicine; (community medicine is served by the Education Committee of the Faculty) | geriatric medicine; haematology; neurology; nuclear medicine; occupational medicine; paediatrics; renal disease; respiratory medicine; rheumatology; genito-urinary medicine | audiological medicine; clinical neurophysiology (subcommittees of neurology SAC); clinical genetics (subcommittee of paediatrics SAC); medical oncology; rehabilitation (subcommittees of general (internal) medicine SAC) |
| **Joint Committee on Higher Surgical Training** (608 trainees, including accident and emergency medicine*) | general surgery; neurological surgery; ophthalmology; orthopaedics; otolaryngology (ENT) | paediatric surgery; plastic surgery; thoracic surgery; urology | |
| **Joint Committee on Higher Psychiatric Training** (468 trainees) | general psychiatry; child and adolescent psychiatry; forensic psychiatry | mental handicap; psychiatry; psychotherapy | |
| **Joint Committee for Higher Training of Anaesthetists** (399 trainees) | | | |
| **Royal College of Obstetricians and Gynaecologists** (134 trainees) | | | |
| **Royal College of Pathologists** (440 trainees including haematology**) | | | |
| **Royal College of Radiologists** (286 trainees) | | | |
| **Joint Committee on Postgraduate Training for General Practice** (1860 trainees in general practice) | | | |

*.** The JCHST is represented on the SAC for accident and emergency medicine and the Royal College of Pathologists is represented on the SAC for haematology, hence the shared responsibilities of these bodies with the JCHMT for the trainees in these specialties.

Note: The figures in brackets represent the number of senior registrars (permanent paid NHS and honorary contract holders) in England and Wales; however, the higher training committees also cover Scotland, Northern Ireland and some cover the Republic of Ireland.

Sources: Various documents and DHSS censuses of medical staff.[7-9]

The joint committees on higher training and their associated specialty commitees are representative of the many professional bodies and associations concerned with specialty training. The Joint Committee on Higher Medical Training arose from meetings held in 1969 and 1970 between representatives of the three Royal Colleges of Physicians of Edinburgh, London and Ireland and the Royal College of Physicians and Surgeons of Glasgow, members of the Association of Professorial Heads of Departments of Medicine and Paediatrics, the Faculty of Community Medicine and various specialist associations for the medical specialties. The Conference of Postgraduate Deans of the United Kingdom was invited to nominate a member in 1971. At approximately the same time, 17 medical specialty advisory committees were formed and each was representative of the appropriate specialist associations. The SAC for endocrinology and diabetes mellitus, for example, included persons nominated by the Society for Endocrinology, the Section of Endocrinology of the Royal Society of Medicine, and the Medical and Scientific Section of the British Diabetic Association. On the SAC for haematology there were representatives of the Royal Colleges of Physicians and the Royal College of Pathologists, as well as appropriate specialist and academic bodies. A SAC for community medicine was not set up; the specialty was served instead by the Education Committee of the Faculty of Community Medicine. For occupational medicine, however, a SAC was created.[207] (The Faculty of Occupational Medicine was not formed until 1978. It is, moreover, a faculty of a single royal college – the Royal College of Physicians in London – unlike the Faculty of Community Medicine whose 'parent' bodies are the Royal Colleges of Physicians of the United Kingdom.) The present members of the SAC for occupational medicine are drawn from the Society of Occupational Medicine and the Faculty of Occupational Medicine.[208]

By 1985 the composition of the Joint Committee on Higher Medical Training had been expanded to include other professional bodies plus a representative of the junior doctors, and observers from the Medical Research Council and the government health departments for England and Wales, Scotland and the Republic of Ireland. The number of specialty advisory committees was now 18 and there were also five subcommittees formed by three SACs (refer to Table 42). The additional advisory committee was for accident and emergency medicine; its members are nominated by the joint committees on higher training for medicine, surgery and anaesthetics, the Royal Colleges of Surgeons, the Royal College of General Practitioners, the British Paediatric Association and the Casualty Surgeons Association.[208]

The Joint Committee on Higher Surgical Training was founded around the same time as the JCHMT and it, too, is representative of four royal colleges (the surgical colleges of England, Edinburgh and Ireland and physicians and surgeons of

Glasgow), the university professors of surgery and the relevant specialist associations.[209] By 1985 there were nine surgical specialty advisory committees plus the joint arrangement with the JCHMT for accident and emergency medicine. Membership of the Joint Committee for Higher Training of Anaesthetists (JCHTA) – which was formed soon after the JCHST – is drawn from the Faculty of Anaesthetists of the Royal College of Surgeons of England and its standing committee for Scotland, the Faculty of Anaesthetists of the Royal College of Surgeons of Ireland, the Association of Anaesthetists of Great Britain and Ireland and the Association of University Professors in Anaesthesia.[210] Representatives of the trainees, the postgraduate deans, the DHSS and even the EEC also attend the meetings. No specialty advisory committees have been formed because the discipline of anaesthesia is treated as a single specialty.

The fourth joint committee, the Joint Committee on Higher Psychiatric Training, was established in 1973 by the Royal College of Psychiatrists and the Association of University Teachers of Psychiatry. The Irish Psychiatric Training Committee is also represented. Attenders at the meetings include nominees from the specialist subcommittees and the college committee for trainees, the government health departments and the Conference of Postgraduate Deans. Five specialist advisory subcommittees cover the specialties within the discipline.[211]

The final joint committee to be established – the Joint Committee on Postgraduate Training for General Practice – was formed in 1975. It succeeded a committee on postgraduate training set up by the Royal College of General Practitioners and the autonomous General Medical Services Committee (GMSC) of the British Medical Association.[212] (This committee deals with all matters affecting general practitioners (page 252).) The membership of the JCPTGP is even more broadly based than the other joint committees; as well as the College, the GMSC, university teachers of general practice, trainees and the postgraduate deans being represented, members are nominated by the National Association of Clinical Tutors, the General Practice Approval Board of the Armed Services and the Joint Consultants Committee.

*Responsibilities of the higher training committees*

The responsibilities which the higher training committees have mostly assumed are three-fold:

a. laying down criteria for training in the individual specialties;

b. approving posts which are suitable for training in hospitals or community medicine or occupational medicine and in academic departments and research units;

c. awarding certificates of accreditation to those who have successfully completed training.

All the committees are concerned with setting standards of training but, as the following pages show, policies differ towards the second and third responsibilities.

POLICIES OF THE HIGHER TRAINING COMMITTEES FOR APPROVING POSTS AND SCHEMES

The Joint Committee on Higher Medical Training oversees the largest number of training posts across the British Isles. The maximum period of approval that can be granted is five years – a policy common to all the higher training committees – but the recommended length of tenure for the majority of specialised posts is only one to two years. Trainees in many of the medical specialties also receive training in at least one related specialty, notably general (internal) medicine, and so the posts with limited tenure recommendations are usually linked with other posts to form rotation schemes. The arrangements to link the posts are made by the employing authorities, possibly on the recommendation of the local specialty subcommittee of the regional postgraduate medical education committee or from the JCHMT on the advice of the relevant specialty advisory committee.

Although the DHSS recognises only one senior training grade in community medicine, the Joint Committee on Higher Medical Training distinguishes between senior registrar and registrar posts and the Education Board of the Faculty of Community Medicine has the responsibility for visiting the senior registrar posts. The visitors may also informally assess the training content of any associated registrar posts. Senior registrar posts in this specialty are often linked to give the trainees wide experience.

The great majority of higher training posts in occupational medicine are in industry or in the armed services. These posts are visited by representatives of the SAC for occupational medicine in the same way as posts in NHS hospitals are visited.

In the surgical specialties and anaesthetics the higher training posts are organised into schemes or programmes which can cover a number of hospitals and the trainees 'rotate' through the posts. Coordinating the approval status of all posts within a scheme can pose problems to the secretariats of these training committees. London provides the greatest number of difficulties because it is common for individual posts in a teaching hospital to be linked to posts in other hospitals and these may be in adjacent regions or in the postgraduate teaching hospitals which are administered by the special health authorities.

Similar difficulties have been experienced by the secretariat of the Royal College of Radiologists when arranging visits to diagnostic radiology higher training posts which are incorporated into London-based rotational programmes. The Education Board of the College is responsible for recognising both departments and newly created whole-time or part-time PM(79)3 posts for higher training and departments for general professional training in diagnostic radiology and radiotherapy and oncology. It liaises closely with the Faculty of Radiologists of the Royal College of Surgeons in Ireland.

The Royal College of Obstetricians and Gynaecologists prefers its senior trainees to spend time in at least two hospital departments under different senior consultants. Senior registrarships (and lectureships and research fellowships for trainees with honorary status) are based on teaching hospitals and the majority of trainees 'rotate' to major district general hospitals for differing lengths of time. The responsibility for approving senior training posts in the British Isles lies with the Higher Training Committee. Subcommittees of the Higher Training Committee have been formed recently to coordinate the development of sub-specialty training in perinatal medicine, gynaecological urology, gynaecological oncology and reproductive medicine.

In pathology the Training Committee of the Royal College of Pathologists is responsible for approving both the laboratories for general professional (primary) training and the higher specialist (final) training posts. Thus only a single visit to each laboratory is needed. The Committee recognises higher training posts in histopathology, medical microbiology, virology, immunology and chemical pathology. In some regions the posts in each specialty are organised in rotation programmes; the Public Health Laboratory Service similarly organises its posts into training programmes. In chemical pathology, if a department lacks a medical consultant, recognition will not be given for senior registrar training (although general professional training for up to six months is acceptable). It is worth noting that although this college grants recognition for general professional training in haematology, at the higher training level the responsibility lies with the Joint Committee on Higher Medical Training and its specialty advisory committee for haematology. The Royal College of Pathologists is, however, represented on the haematology SAC and the JCHMT.

In psychiatry the training posts in each specialty have been organised into schemes, usually regionally conceived, with the purpose of providing a comprehensive range of clinical and academic experience during a three-year period. The sizes of the schemes vary according to the nature of the specialty involved. General psychiatry schemes are the largest, with many schemes incorporating between 12 and 20 or more full-time posts based in hospitals in various health districts. The schemes in the other specialties usually incorporate no more than six posts and there are a few schemes that have only one post – these being in specialties with relatively few consultant posts compared with other psychiatric specialties. Not all regions have schemes in psychotherapy or forensic psychiatry.[211] In the Republic of Ireland the Irish Psychiatric Training Committee is responsible for monitoring higher training in psychiatry. The Irish

Committee has elected to adopt the standards of the Joint Committee on Higher Psychiatric Training and so the Joint Committee arranges the visits to training programmes in the Republic and prepares the reports. The Irish Psychiatric Training Committee can accept or reject the recommendations in the reports, although in almost every instance it accepts.

In general practice the Joint Committee on Postgraduate Training for General Practice is concerned with monitoring the standards of vocational training in the regions rather than having direct responsibility for recognising hospital posts – a task that is carried out by the royal colleges (see the previous chapter) – or for appointing general practitioner trainers, this being the responsibility of the general practice subcommittee of the regional postgraduate medical education committees (page 156). The Joint Committee has a panel of about 70 visitors, mainly regional advisers, associate advisers and course organisers, and the panel conducts a two-yearly cycle of visits to the regions and to the armed forces with the object of assessing the progress in vocational training. It is usual for three visitors to spend three days learning about vocational training schemes in one or two health districts. Trainers, perhaps ten to 12, are interviewed. Meetings are held with the trainees at which their experiences of the hospital posts in the schemes, the day release courses and the training practices are discussed. Whenever possible meetings are also held with the regional postgraduate dean, the local clinical tutors, the course organisers, the hospital consultants associated with the schemes and, naturally, with the regional adviser for general practice.[212] From the information gathered, the visitors are first able to assess the extent to which the criteria published by the region for appointing trainers and for selecting hospital posts for prescribed experience follow the recommended criteria issued by the JCPTGP from time to time and, second, to judge how closely in practice the region is complying with its own declared standards. The visitors report their findings to the JCPTGP together with recommendations, and these are passed on to the regions.

## Procedures for approving posts and schemes

The advisory committees for the individual specialties have drawn up their own criteria for assessing the training offered in NHS established senior registrar posts or schemes, part-time PM(79)3 posts for persons unable to work full-time because of domestic commitments or personal disability, and for honorary posts of higher training status. The committees have also designed their own pro forma for completion by the hospitals when visits are arranged, and the visitors are usually members or nominees of these committees. The procedures of the higher training committees for carrying out visits (excluding those to vocational training schemes) are, however, broadly similar and they are outlined on pages 162-165 in chapter 12. The Councils for

Postgraduate Medical Education in the United Kingdom have also prepared a booklet on this subject.[158]

Since there are inevitable delays in issuing the final report on the visits or a letter containing the recommendations, the senior consultants responsible for the posts or schemes are normally told informally what the likely recommendations will be before the visitors leave. Each visitors' report is considered, first by the advisory committee for the individual specialty (except in anaesthetics, pathology, radiology and obstetrics and gynaecology) and then by the committee with overall responsibility for higher training standards in the discipline.

The higher training committees' lists of persons to whom the final reports or letters should be sent are not standardised. The regional postgraduate deans normally receive copies from all committees, although a 1984 survey of the records held in the offices of two deans found gaps in the coverage, the omissions being mainly information on visits carried out by some of the surgical SACs two to three years earlier.[11] Some of the higher training committees ask the deans to circulate copies of the documents to those health authorities responsible for the training facilities and supporting services. The visits often cover posts in more than one health district and there have been occasions when a relevant district authority has not received a copy.

The circulation of copies of letters on the outcome of visits of inspection for both general professional training and higher training is an item which has been discussed at meetings held under the auspices of the Council for Postgraduate Medical Education in England and Wales. Some of the approval bodies have developed their policy for distributing information in the light of these discussions. Experience suggests, however, that a system that relies on nominated persons in the regions – however willing they may be – to distribute copies to relevant authorities is less reliable than a system where the distribution of all copies is done centrally by the secretariat of the college, faculty or joint committee on higher training.

Finally, it should be noted that the annual numbers of newly established senior registrar hospital posts (or schemes in psychiatry) needing to be visited for higher training recognition are now relatively few in nearly all the specialties and so the majority of visits being carried out at present are to hospitals where the approval period of the existing posts or schemes has lapsed.

AVAILABLE INFORMATION ON HIGHER TRAINING POSTS

Handbooks listing (in the appendices) the hospitals in which there are higher training posts, have been published by the Joint Committee on Higher Surgical Training[209], the Joint Committee for Higher Training of Anaesthetists[210] and the Joint Committee on Higher Psychiatric Training.[211] The Royal Colleges of Obstetricians and Gynaecologists and Radiologists prepare their own lists.

The Joint Committee on Higher Medical Training also prepares listings but these are generated from its computer files. There is a separate computerised record for each post giving the specialty, hospital, date of last approval, period of approval, recommended length of tenure (if relevant) and any additional details such as the location of any other posts which together form a rotation. A post numbering system is used, each number being made up of the regional code and the number of the post within the region. The Joint Committee does not, however, have information identifying the holders of the posts except for those posts that are created on a personal or ad hominem basis for trainees with honorary research contracts or part-time PM(79)3 appointments. The Secretariat prints a list for each region two to three times a year and sends it to the regional postgraduate dean with a request that the entries be checked and any changes notified to the secretariat. For example, ad hominem posts cease to exist when the incumbent resigns; the Joint Committee is not routinely informed if this happens before the scheduled termination date of the post.

The Joint Committee on Higher Surgical Training has numbered the surgical posts using a different system which identifies both the post and the post holder. The Secretariat is computerising the manual records of the nine specialty advisory committees. Hospital recognition records held by the Joint Committee for Higher Training of Anaesthetists, the Joint Committee on Higher Psychiatric Training and the Royal College of Obstetricians and Gynaecologists are also being computerised. (The JCHTA is numbering its posts at the same time.) Each of the higher training committees has developed its own system for automation on different types of computer hardware and software.

ACCREDITATION

A certificate of accreditation indicates that a trainee has completed satisfactorily his or her higher specialist training in approved posts and satisfies the minimum criteria for appointment to a post of consultant status set by the appropriate college or faculty. Employing authorities can (and do) appoint as consultants, British-trained candidates who are not accredited, although this action might go against the advice of the college or faculty nominee on the advisory appointments committee (see page 221). The only formal requirement in the regulations for appointment to consultant medical posts is that appointees must be suitable fully registered medical practitioners.[113]

Two higher training committees do not, in fact, have a system of accreditation. One is the Joint Committee on Higher Psychiatric Training which believes that the practice of accreditation leads to undue rigidity in training programmes. The Joint Committee together with the Royal College of Psychiatrists has, however, issued guidance on the amount and extent of training required before candidates are eligible for consultant appointment. The criteria are applied by college assessors on advisory appointments committees. In pathology, trainees do not normally obtain the final part of the higher qualification of MRCPath until they are virtually fully trained. (The earliest a doctor may sit the final examination for this qualification is six years after graduation.) The Royal College of Pathologists feels, therefore, that success in this final examination is sufficient recognition that doctors have become fully training in their chosen specialty. The situation is different in general practice; doctors being appointed as principals for the first time must hold a certificate of prescribed or equivalent experience. (The procedures for awarding the certificates are described later in the chapter.)

The requirements for higher training in the various specialties (including the psychiatric specialties) are described in handbooks or papers prepared by the joint committees on higher training [208-11], the Royal College of Obstetricians and Gynaecologists[213], the Royal College of Pathologists[214] and the Faculty of Community Medicine.[47] A book, *Careers in medicine*, covering the requirements for all the specialties was published by the Council for Postgraduate Medical Education in England and Wales although some of the training requirements were changed after the revised edition was published in 1980.[65] Lister has also published a paper outlining the general policies of the higher training committees towards accreditation.[215]

### Lengths of training for accreditation

Not only have the specialty advisory committees developed their own training programmes, they also have differing recommended lengths of training according to the level of complexity of the body of knowledge for each specialty and the technical expertise needed. In surgery, all but two of the specialties require four years of higher training in order to qualify for accreditation. The exceptions are ENT and plastic surgery which require three years. (The regulations for the surgical specialties were revised in 1985.) A scheme for dual accreditation in general surgery and urology has recently been agreed by the two specialty advisory committees. The experience expected in the majority of hospital specialties in medicine is around four years but a few specialties, such as cardiology, and paediatrics with a special interest in perinatology or neurology, require four to six years including a year or more in research. It is possible for trainees to be accredited in one, two or three medical specialties. The training needed for single or dual accreditation normally covers a four-year period, whereas six years is required for triple accreditation.[208]

For community medicine, in contrast, higher training in approved senior registrar posts need only take three years, but during this time the candidates will probably obtain part II of the membership examination (which involves the presentation of a report on an original project or a group of reports). The accreditation arrangements for diagnostic radiology and radiotherapy are also framed around the regulations for the higher qualification. The final part of the FRCR cannot be taken until at least three years of training in approved posts has been completed. However, application for accreditation by holders of the FRCR may only be made once they have completed five years of approved training.[121] (The accreditation period was increased to five years in 1983.) Thus doctors who obtain the FRCR relatively early are obliged to continue their training for another year or so. Some take the opportunity to sub-specialise in, for example, neuroradiology or cardiovascular radiology, or in the allied fields of clinical oncology if they hold an FRCR in radiotherapy and oncology. The length of experience required for accreditation by the two other committees – the Joint Committee for Higher Training of Anaesthetists and the Higher Training Committee of the Royal College of Obstetricians and Gynaecologists – is a minimum of three years higher training.

### Retrospective recognition

When considering individual applications for accreditation or, for some disciplines, enrolment for accreditation, the higher training committees – with the exception of radiology – are willing to take into account a certain amount of training done while the candidate was in the registrar grade, as long as the clinical responsibilities and duties were equivalent to those held by a senior registrar in the chosen specialty and the appropriate higher qualification was held. The committees have their own criteria for granting retrospective recognition. In the medical specialties two years (one year in each of two specialties) is the maximum period of training in the registrar grade that can be recognised, and the training should occur after the applicant has completed three years of general professional training following full registration and attained the MRCP(UK), or part I of the MFCM or another acceptable qualification for community medicine, or the primary examination of the MRCPath for haematology. (FRCS, FFARCS and MRCGP are acceptable alternative qualifications for trainees entering higher training in accident and emergency medicine.)[208]

The surgical specialty advisory committees consider that higher training commences once candidates have obtained their FRCS. Since few trainees enter a senior registrar post immediately after receiving the fellowship, the SACs are willing to grant retrospective recognition for at least one post-fellowship year spent in the registrar grade. In obstetrics and gynaecology three years of higher training is required for accreditation, the first of which may be spent in a registrar post after completing the requirements for the MRCOG and the next two years in a recognised post or posts of senior registrar status. Finally anaesthetics: before entering higher training, trainees will have had three years of general professional training in the specialty and higher training normally occupies a minimum of three years, at least two of which must be spent in clinical anaesthesia. The Joint Committee for Higher Training of Anaesthetists is prepared to recognise time spent in the registrar grade after attaining fellowship but the length of the recognition granted to each applicant is at the discretion of the Committee.[210]

Two further points. First, when considering individual candidates for accreditation, the higher training committees will also evaluate training received overseas and time spent in locum senior registrar and consultant posts. In anaesthetics, however, time spent in locum consultant posts is only acceptable if the locum post is held during the final three months of the final year of higher training. Second, higher training in psychiatry commences only after a trainee enters a senior registrar post or a post of equivalent status.

*Accreditation regulations for part-time training\**

The principle of granting accreditation for higher training done on a part-time basis usually under the PM(79)3 arrangements (see chapter 8) has been accepted by the higher training committees. However, the regulations drawn up by some of the committees convey the impression that they are not enthusiastic about the policy. The section on part-time training in the Third Report of the Joint Committee for Higher Surgical Training is prefaced with the statement: 'Although surgery is not regarded as a discipline that lends itself to learning on a part-time basis, Specialist Advisory Committees are prepared to consider on their merits applications for part-time experience. . .'(page 4).[209] To qualify for recognition, a part-time surgical appointment must be equivalent to at least six sessions of working time a week with an appropriate share of emergency duties, and the trainee must fulfil the equivalent of a total whole-time higher training period. The trainee is restricted during the entire period from doing any medical work outside the specialty – this includes work in the General Ophthalmic Service by ophthalmology trainees. Finally, the appropriate specialist advisory committee must approve the training programme, a policy that all the higher training committees hold.

For obstetrics and gynaecology the training should be not less than half-time, the total training period must be equivalent to the whole-time training requirement, and the trainees must not divide their training between obstetrics and gynaecology and

---

\* The regulations on part time training for entry to general practice are described on page 185 in chapter 13.

some other medical work.[213] The Joint Committee for Higher Training of Anaesthetists also expects part-time trainees to undertake a minimum of five clinical sessions per week plus emergency work. They will be recommended for accreditation when they have acquired the equivalent of three years whole-time senior registrar training although they can apply for retrospective recognition for any post-fellowship registrar training that they may have received.[210]

The Joint Committee for Higher Medical Training, unlike the first three bodies, does not stipulate in its handbook the total length of time that part-time appointment holders must train before becoming eligible for accreditation. It merely states that for educational approval, part-time training programmes must cover at least five sessions per week and should include pro rata on-call and emergency duties, and the candidates must be considered suitably qualified and experienced to enter higher training. Indeed it is the philosophy of this joint committee that since the needs of each individual trainee varies according to his or her experience, personal aptitude, interests and expected future career, the personal programme of training requires individual consideration.[208]

### Procedures for accreditation

Usually trainees are first told formally about the accreditation system when they complete their higher qualification examinations for membership or fellowship, although most will have learnt about the system while doing their general professional training. Trainees in medicine and surgery are expected to enrol for accreditation at the beginning of their higher training programme in a senior registrar post or honorary post of equivalent status; the specialty advisory committee for the trainees' chosen specialty then assesses their previous experience to calculate how much retrospective recognition they can receive. Trainees in anaesthetics likewise are expected to enrol when entering higher training. However, not all trainees enrol early in their training programme. The Royal Colleges of Radiologists and Obstetricians and Gynaecologists do not have an enrolment system. The Higher Training Committee of the RCOG has, however, recently compiled a list of those undergoing higher training from information supplied by college regional advisers and professors.

The Joint Committee on Higher Medical Training is the only higher training committee which relies directly on the regions' senior registrar review arrangements (described in chapter 13) for overseeing the general progress of its trainees. The specialty advisory committees normally expect to receive information on the progress or difficulties experienced by trainees from the regional postgraduate deans rather than by direct contact with the trainees. The Joint Committee also takes the view that the trainees should look to the regional postgraduate deans for advice about their training.[208] Candidates are expected to apply for accreditation during the final few months of their higher training programme, any retrospective recognition having been taken into account. They provide details of the posts held including the JCHMT post numbers, and the application form is countersigned by the regional postgraduate dean. The relevant specialty advisory committee or committees consider the applications and a further period of training might be recommended. They are more likely, however, to recommend to the Joint Committee that accreditation be granted.

The Joint Committee for Higher Training of Anaesthetists and the surgical specialty advisory committees base their assessments on formal reports about the trainees. The JCHTA may ask a trainee at the end of each year of training to provide a factual report on the training received.[210] Towards the end of the training programme the Joint Committee asks the candidate's supervising consultant, who may be the faculty regional adviser in anaesthetics, to comment on the adequacy of the candidate's experience. If the report is satisfactory the Joint Committee will recommend to the faculty of which the candidate holds the fellowship, that a certificate of accreditation be awarded. (The Joint Committee itself awards the accreditation certificates to trainees who do not hold the fellowship awarded by the Faculties of Anaesthetists in England or the Republic of Ireland.)

The procedures followed by the surgical SACs are very similar, although one or two committees go further and meet the trainees annually. Trainees in ENT, ophthalmology, cardiothoracic surgery, paediatric surgery and urology are expected to maintain a register of the operations they perform as they acquire experience. A similar requirement for trainees in neurological surgery will be introduced shortly. The SACs also expect to be notified if a trainee plans to spend a period overseas. It has been suggested, perhaps with justification, that these committees are unnecessarily duplicating the activities of the regional committees responsible for overseeing surgical training. (Some of the surgical specialties are very small in manpower numbers – paediatric surgery, plastic surgery and neurological surgery being three examples – so the consultants are familiar with their colleagues in other centres and with the senior registrars, having met them at scientific meetings and other events. The same situation also occurs in the smaller specialties in the other disciplines.)

When trainees in obstetrics and gynaecology apply for accreditation towards the end of their higher training they submit a comprehensive curriculum vitae with the application to the chairman of the Higher Training Committee who then asks two consultants under whom each candidate has trained to supply statements as to the person's suitability for accreditation. If the information is considered to be satisfactory, the candidate's name is submitted to the Council of the Royal College for ratification. The Royal College of Radiologists raised the minimum period of approved training before accreditation can be granted to five years (from four years) in the early 1980s, and although the Education Board believes that appropriate training should be provided in the post-fellowship period it does not have the resources to organise this centrally. It relies, therefore, on the senior registrars to devise their own training with local assistance.[128] At the end of five years the candidates apply for accreditation, supplying details of all training posts held and a small fee.

INFORMATION ON SENIOR REGISTRARS WITH ACCREDITATION

The 1984 numbers of senior registrars including honorary contract holders in England and Wales covered by the joint committees on higher training and equivalent committees of the royal colleges are given in Table 42, page 232. Unfortunately there is no way of estimating the proportion of these trainees who had completed their higher training. The annual censuses conducted by the DHSS only ask for the date when trainees enter a grade. But even if a census included a question on accreditation status, the employing health authorities could not reliably provide the answers as they are not informed when their senior registrars are accredited by either the trainees themselves or by the higher training committees. Also, this information is not supplied to the regional postgraduate deans on a routine basis. The Joint Committee for Higher Training of Anaesthetists is one exception; lists of the names of trainees recommended to the appropriate faculties for accreditation are circulated to the deans.

When the regional postgraduate deans have assembled statistics on 'time-expired' senior registrars in their region they have used a definition of time-expired as 'one who, having completed the training requirements for his specialty, has been unable to obtain a consultant post, normally after a four year contract (WTE) in the senior registrar grade'. However, there has been concern among the deans that the statistics (which they have found difficult to collect – see chapter 13, page 180) take no account of trainees who have spent less than four years in the grade and yet are fully trained, some having been accredited at the end of their second year. The specialty advisory committee for general surgery has twice conducted a survey – in 1983 and 1985 – of senior registrars and lecturers in the specialty to find out the number with accreditation and whether they have been in the grade for longer than four years (refer to page 180). Similar surveys may be made by the SACs for other surgical specialties. The subject of establishing a national register of persons awarded accreditation has not been widely discussed in recent years. It is a matter which the newly created Joint Planning Advisory Committee – whose remit is to set national targets and regional quotas on the numbers of posts in specialty groupings for the senior training grades (page 61) – may wish to consider. An alternative approach would be to set up a national information system for senior registrars that recorded the accreditation or equivalent status of each trainee.[11]

PROCEDURES FOR ISSUING VOCATIONAL TRAINING CERTIFICATES

Doctors planning to enter general practice can either follow a training programme that leads to a certificate of prescribed experience being issued or one which will be considered for a certificate of equivalent experience. The regulations applying to prescribed and equivalent experience are described in chapter 12 and the procedure for issuing to trainees certified 'statements of satisfactory completion' necessary for prescribed experience at the end of each phase of their training is outlined on page 185 of chapter 13. In the last four weeks of their training programme, trainees apply to the Joint Committee on Postgraduate Training for General Practice for a certificate of prescribed experience simply by forwarding the set of certified statements (forms VTR/1 and VTR/2). By applying before the end of the training period, trainees who plan to enter general practice immediately as a principal will not experience a delay in having their names entered on the 'medical list' of the family practitioner committee with which they will hold a contract of service. In order to be considered for a certificate of equivalent experience a trainee is required to complete an application form and supply documents requested by the Joint Committee. The application may take longer to process.

For the Medical Adviser of the Joint Committee and the Secretariat, administering the applications for certificates of prescribed experience is a relatively straightforward although busy task. In 1985, 74 per cent of the 2031 certificates issued to trainees in the United Kingdom came into this category.[43] Applications for certificates of equivalent experience can be more time consuming because the Committee must be satisfied that each candidate's experience and training whether in general practice or in other posts is, overall, educationally equivalent to prescribed experience. An application may include documentary evidence of experience overseas, or in hospital posts for periods of less than six months, or in general practice but not under the supervision of an approved trainer. The booklet *Training for general practice* gives examples of 'exceptional' experience which the Committee will consider, and the criteria by which the experience is judged.[168] The Committee is willing to advise doctors on the future training needed to meet its requirements and, indeed, many inquiries are dealt with by the Medical Adviser.

Doctors who are refused a certificate of either prescribed or equivalent experience are told the reason for the decision and are given guidance on further experience necessary to obtain the certificate. They can appeal to the Secretary of State for Social Services against the decision. The notice of appeal should be sent within 28 days of the

Joint Committee's decision and if the appellant lives in England or Wales the notice is sent to the DHSS. The cases are heard by an appeal board chaired by a legally qualified person. The decision of the appeal board is final.

SPECIALTY RECOGNITION FOR THE EEC

The systems of accreditation in the United Kingdom and specialist recognition within the EEC are not the same. A certificate of specialist recognition or other evidence of formal qualifications in specialised medicine can be issued by a member country to doctors who have attended a full-time course of theoretical and practical instruction or, in certain circumstances, an approved part-time course. The training must be in a university centre, teaching hospital or approved health establishment for at least the specified minimum length of time and must involve the personal participation of the trainee in the activity and in the responsibilities of the establishments concerned. The minimum length of postgraduate training needed for specialist recognition for EEC purposes varies according to the specialty. For the medical specialties, for example, four years is required for the majority, but for endocrinology, diabetes mellitus and haematology the requirement is three years while five years are needed for general (internal) medicine.[216] The certificate enables the holder to move among the member countries of the EEC as a specialist. Specialist recognition has no significance in the United Kingdom but doctors intending to practice in other EEC countries may apply to the General Medical Council for a certificate.

# 18   Other advisory and regulatory bodies

There are, in addition to the royal colleges and faculties and the joint committees on higher training, a variety of national bodies concerned with postgraduate medical education and standards of training. Two notable ones are the Council for Post-graduate Medical Education in England and Wales and the General Medical Council. The origins, membership, functions and responsibilities of the two bodies are, however, quite different. Linked to the CPME is the National Advice Centre from which junior doctors and dentists – mostly from overseas – can receive advice on regulations and opportunities for training in the United Kingdom. These three bodies, the Council for Postgraduate Medical Education in England and Wales, the National Advice Centre and the General Medical Council are covered in this chapter, together with the various professional and educational bodies represented directly or indirectly on the CPME, with particular attention being paid to the British Medical Association and its autonomous committees.

COUNCIL FOR POSTGRADUATE MEDICAL EDUCATION IN ENGLAND AND WALES*

The Royal Commission for Medical Education in its report published in 1968[1] observed that one important reason why postgraduate medical education and training had been 'so inadequate in former years' was that it involved activities and responsibility which, for good historical reasons, had been assigned to different bodies. The resulting situation had been described in evidence to the Commission as chaotic. The Commission believed that the interests of all concerned – the NHS, professional bodies and the universities – lay in cooperation in a comprehensive scheme for postgraduate training (which would include the restructuring of the training grades as described in chapter 2), and establishing machinery at central, regional and local level for planning the scheme and putting it into effective operation.

The Commission recommended that a central body should be set up to exercise general oversight of postgraduate medical education and training in Great Britain. The body was to have the title 'Central Council for Postgraduate Medical Education and Training in Great Britain', it was not to be large and represented on it should be

---

* Note: in 1985 the CPME set up a working group of members to review the functions of the Council. Then in 1986, following the July council meeting, the Council passed to the Secretary of State for his consideration a set of proposals for the future of the Council, one of which was dissolution.

the universities, the main branches of the NHS and the appropriate professional colleges or similar bodies in the main fields of medical practice. The chairman would be independent and appointed, perhaps, by a government minister. The recommendation was acted upon, but instead of there being a single council for Great Britain, two councils were established – one for England and Wales, the other for Scotland. Northern Ireland also has a council.

The Council for Postgraduate Medical Education in England and Wales was established by the Secretary of State for Social Services with the agreement of the Secretary of State for Education and Science and the Secretary of State for Wales. Its first meeting was in December 1970. An unofficial committee known as the Central Committee of Postgraduate Medical Education had met between 1967 and 1970 and its activities were taken over by the new council.[217]

The terms of reference of the Council are:

to coordinate and stimulate the organisation and development of postgraduate medical and dental education and training in England and Wales through maintaining close contacts with professional and educational bodies at a national level and by giving advice to representative regional bodies established in connection with the planning and organisation of postgraduate medical and dental education;

to provide a national forum for discussion of matters pertaining to postgraduate medical education and training;

to provide the Government with an authoritative source of advice on these matters.

The membership is determined by the Secretary of State for Social Services in consultation with the Secretaries of State for Education and Science and Wales; the Social Services Secretary also appoints the chairman. The bodies represented on the Council are the royal colleges and faculties, universities, the profession, National Health Service, the armed services and the Council's Dental Committee whose terms of reference were agreed by the Secretary of State. Other bodies are represented indirectly. The individual bodies are listed on the following pages; some have not been mentioned in any of the previous chapters. The source of the listing is a document prepared by the Council.[218] (Note that as well as nominating a member or members, the bodies on the Council nominate an alternate for each member who attends the meetings when the member is unable to be present.)

BODIES REPRESENTED ON COUNCIL

*Royal colleges and faculties*

The main responsibilities of the colleges and faculties are to maintain standards of practice in the various branches of medicine. As part of these responsibilities they organise postgraduate examinations (see chapter 9), supervise general training in the specialties (chapter 16) and higher training through the higher training committees (chapter 17). Each English college and faculty referred to in Table 40 (page 220) is represented on the Council. These bodies also meet together with the Scottish colleges in the Conference of Medical Royal Colleges and their Faculties in the United Kingdom.

*Joint Paediatric Committee*   This committee was established by the Royal Colleges of Physicians of Edinburgh, Glasgow and London and the British Paediatric Association. Its function is to analyse and state the problems of child health and to recommend courses of action to the parent bodies.

*University bodies*

Individual universities are not represented on the Council but their collective views are available through representatives of the University Grants Committee, the Committee of Vice-Chancellors and Principals of the Universities of the United Kingdom, the regional postgraduate deans, and clinical tutors.

*University Grants Committee*   The UGC is responsible for advising the government on the financial support needed for university education and for deciding on the allocation of government grants to universities.

*Committee of Vice-Chancellors and Principals*   The CVCP is a forum that prepares a collective view of the universities on matters of common interest and offers advice to the government, the UGC, research councils and other bodies concerned. In addition to nominating its own representative on the Council, the CVCP also nominates one undergraduate and three regional postgraduate deans and two clinical tutors (see below).

*Regional postgraduate deans*   As chief executive officers of the regional postgraduate medical education committees (see chapter 11) the regional postgraduate deans in England have a liaison role between the Council and the regional committees. The regional deans, together with the postgraduate dean for Wales, the director of the British Postgraduate Medical Federation (see page 274), the representative of the undergraduate deans on the Council and a dean representing the armed services, compose the Advisory Committee of Deans which is a committee of the Council. This committee recommends to the CVCP the names of the three deans to be nominated as members of the Council. The Committee for Postgraduate Medical Education for Wales nominates a separate representative, normally the postgraduate dean.

The deans meet in another forum – the Conference of Postgraduate Medical Deans and Directors of Postgraduate Medical Education of Universities of the United

Kingdom. It is an unofficial forum with representatives of several other interests co-opted and it meets twice a year.

*Clinical tutors*   The National Association of Clinical Tutors consists of nearly every clinical tutor in the United Kingdom. The members in each region (including the Scottish regions and Northern Ireland) elect one representative to a central council which meets three times a year to discuss matters affecting the tutors' role and responsibilities. Although the National Association is not officially represented on the Council for Postgraduate Medical Education, the Committee of Vice-Chancellors and Principals seeks its advice before nominating two clinical tutors to membership of the Council.

## The profession

*British Medical Association*   The BMA is the professional body which represents and protects the interests of the entire medical profession, although not all practising doctors are members of it. (The great majority of junior doctors do join.) It is governed by a Representative Body consisting of around 600 representatives of divisions (constituencies) and various 'crafts' or sections of the profession, plus the members of the Council (both in office and elected to take office). The Representative Body meets annually to determine policy and deal with amendments to articles and by-laws, and the meeting is held in conjunction with the craft conferences for the different sections – community medicine and health, medical academics, local medical committees, senior hospital medical staff and junior hospital medical staff. Special representative meetings may also be convened.

The Council is the central executive body and is responsible for the management of the affairs of the Association, including the *British Medical Journal*, subject to the decisions of general and special representative meetings. The Trade Union Act 1984 decreed that no members of a principal executive committee or trade union may vote in that body unless elected by members of the union by secret ballot. To conform with this Act the BMA made constitutional changes to its Council in 1986. (Although the Act does not apply to Northern Ireland, the Association has applied the new arrangements to members in the province.)

Forty-four members of the 61-strong Council are now voted for by the membership in three separate annual ballots and only these elected members have voting rights. The three ballots for representation are divided as follows:

a. craft representation – doctors engaged in NHS general practice (six), senior hospital doctors (four), hospital doctors in the training grades (five), community medicine and community health doctors (two), doctors in the armed forces being either serving officers or those in receipt of 'retired pay' but not retired from medical practice (two), and doctors in occupational health (two). The representatives for each category must be members of the Association engaged wholly or mainly in practice, and they are elected by members in the same category

b. regional and country representation – one member representing each of the 14 NHS regions of England and one each representing Wales, Scotland and Northern Ireland, elected by members in the same region or country

c. national representation – four other members elected by all members of the Association.

The chairmen of 'non-craft' committees (unless directly elected in some other capacity), and other ex-officio members who make up the rest of the Council have no voting rights. (This will apply also to the chairman of council and treasurer from 1987.) (British Medical Association, personal communication, 1986)

The BMA Council nominates one member to the Council for Postgraduate Medical Education and also secures nominations of representatives of general practitioners (two), hospital consultants (two) and hospital junior doctors (two) as the main 'consumer' interests.

Doctors employed in the National Health Service are represented by four central committees which, although autonomous, have strong links with the BMA, namely the General Medical Services Committee, the Central Committee for Hospital Medical Services (CCHMS), the Central Committee for Community Medicine and Community Health (CCCMCH) and the Hospital Junior Staff Committee (HJSC). In addition to each central committee there are committees for Scotland, Wales and Northern Ireland to deal with matters of local concern to the profession and the appropriate government department. Some chairmen serve as ex-officio members on the appropriate central committee.[219]

The *General Medical Services Committee* represents practitioners providing general medical services, including trainees. It deals with all matters affecting general practitioners under the National Health Service Acts and watches over their interests. It is recognised by the DHSS as the negotiating body for this branch of the profession. Members of the GMSC are drawn from the Association's Representative Body, from certain committees and groups of members of the Association, from the other autonomous central committees and from a small number of external bodies, two of which are the Royal College of General Practitioners and the Medical Women's Federation. A representative of the regional postgraduate deans is co-opted. The majority of members of the GMSC are, however, nominated on a territorial basis by local medical committees (LMCs) which were formed for the area served by family practitioner committees in England and Wales and for health boards in Scotland. Each LMC is normally composed of local general medical practitioners and general ophthalmic practitioners who have been elected by the appropriate practitioners on the medical and ophthalmic lists held by the FPC. Co-opted LMC members may include nominated hospital medical staff, the district medical officer or an appointee, general practitioner assistants and trainees, and practitioners not otherwise represented.

The terms of reference and constitution of the *Central Committee for Hospital Medical Services* differ from those of the GMSC. Although the Central Committee considers and acts in matters affecting those engaged in consultant and hospital practice, including matters arising under relevant Acts, and generally watches over the interests of all hospital medical staff, it is not the recognised body for negotiating terms and conditions of service. This is done by the Joint Negotiating Committee for Hospital Medical and Dental Staffs which is independent of the BMA. Moreover, the major 'spokesman' for consultants and other hospital staff in consultations with government ministers and the DHSS is the Joint Consultants Committee rather than the CCHMS. The Central Committee has over 80 members of whom two-thirds have voting rights. Those able to vote are appointed by the Assocation's Representative Body, the Regional Committees for Hospital Medical Services in England and the equivalent committees for Wales, Scotland and Northern Ireland, and by bodies representing senior hospital medical officers, associate specialists and hospital dental services. Non-voting members are from specialist subcommittees of the CCHMS, the BMA's Medical Academic Staff Committee and Private Practice and Professional Fees Committee, and from external bodies including the royal colleges of physicians and surgeons and obstetricians and gynaecologists (but not the other colleges for hospital disciplines), the Medical Women's Federation and the Overseas Doctors' Federation. One of the ex-officio members is the chairman of the Joint Consultants Committee.

As its name suggests the *Central Committee for Community Medicine and Community Health* deals with all matters affecting doctors in community medicine in established and training grades, together with doctors in the community health services. This committee, in common with the Central Committee for Hospital Medical Staff, does not negotiate directly with the DHSS on matters relating to terms and conditions of service but through a Joint Negotiating Body. There is also a Community Medicine Consultative Committee which, like the JCC, consults with the appropriate government departments in Great Britain. Membership of the CCCMCH is confined to representatives of community medicine or community health from each of the English regions, Wales, Scotland and Northern Ireland, and of the Trainees Subcommittee, the Community Health Doctors Subcommittee, the Association's Representative Body, the Society of Community Medicine, the Faculty of Community Medicine and the Junior Members Forum. A member without voting rights is appointed by each of the other autonomous NHS committees.

The fourth autonomous committee – the *Hospital Junior Staff Committee* – considers and acts in matters affecting those engaged in hospital practice in the training grades, including matters arising under the relevant Acts, and watches over their interests. The majority of voting members represent the Regional Hospital Junior Staff Committees in England and the equivalent committees for Scotland, Wales and Northern Ireland. The other members are representatives of the Trainees Sub-committee of the GMSC and the Associate Members Group Committee (United Kingdom medical students may apply for associate membership of the BMA), a trainee appointed by the CCCMCH and nominees of the Association's Representative Body. Non-voting members are appointed by the CCHMS, the GMSC, the Medical Academic Staff Committee of the BMA and the British Dental Association.

As the foregoing paragraphs suggest, the committee structure of the BMA is complicated. The annual *Calendar* published by the Association lists for each of many relevant committees – including the autonomous NHS committees and the Joint Consultants Committee and Community Medicine Consultative Committee – the terms of reference and constitution, the names of the bodies represented, and the names and town or city of the current office bearers, members and observers.[219] Some association members serve on a number of committees, so there is continuity in discussions on items common to the agenda of different committees. An account of the origins of the BMA, the General Medical Services Committee, the Central Committee for Hospital Medical Services and the Joint Consultants Committee is provided in the book *Medical practice in modern England* by Stevens.[13]

*Joint Consultants Committee*   When the National Health Service was established in 1948 the JCC was set up as a non-statutory body to speak 'for consultants with one voice'.[13] It jointly represents the United Kingdom royal colleges and medical and dental faculties for the hospital disciplines (14 members in 1985/86), the Central Committee for Hospital Medical Services, the Hospital Junior Staff Committee and the Central Committee for Hospital Dental Services (14 members also). The chairman of the Central Manpower Committee is one of the ex-officio chairmen, and among the observers are two representatives of the Central Committee for Community Medicine and Community Health, two undergraduate deans and a regional postgraduate dean.[219] Under its terms of reference the Joint Consultants Committee formulates policy and considers

'...all matters of policy that may from time to time arise relating to consultant and hospital practice including:
(i) the maintenance of standards of professional knowledge and skill;
(ii) the encouragement of education and research;
(iii) the utilisation to the best advantage of skills and resources...'[219]

It is the final common pathway for advice on such matters to the DHSS, the Scottish Home and Health Department and other appropriate bodies, and it may enter discussions either alone or jointly with other bodies. It is not, however, concerned with the remuneration and terms of service of hospital medical and dental staff 'so that the Committee shall not engage in the pursuit of political purposes'.[219] (The terms of reference for the Community Medicine Consultative Committee are virtually the same.) The Joint Consultants Committee has one representative on the Council for Postgraduate Medical Education.

### National Health Service

The regional and district medical officers (or officers of equivalent status but with a different title) of the health authorities in England and Wales are represented by one member from each group. The DMO is identified after consultation with the Association of District Medical Officers and the RMO is a representative of the RMOs' Group. They comment on the practicality of proposals being considered by the Council in terms of manpower and other resources available to the National Health Service. It is perhaps surprising that the NHS as the major investor in the training of medical staff should have only two representatives on the Council. Moreover, the special health authorities which administer many of the London postgraduate hospitals and which do not have a post of district medical officer status are represented only indirectly. The Council does, however, have a standing committee – the Educational Liaison Group – and the majority of its members hold administrative rather than clinical posts in the NHS.

### Department of Health and Social Security and the Welsh Office

The DHSS and the Welsh Office naturally have a central role in the provision of postgraduate medical education in England and Wales. Estimates of their annual financial contributions are given in chapter 20. Two representatives – one from the DHSS, the other from the Welsh Office – sit on the Council.

### The Armed Services

The medical and dental training programmes in the three armed services are of the same standard as those in the NHS to ensure that doctors and dentists may transfer between the services and civilian practice without jeopardising their careers (page 87). The medical branches of the armed services are represented by one member on the Council and on most of its committees.

### Dental Committee of the Council

The Dental Committee was established in 1972 with the agreement of the Secretary of State for Social Services and representatives of the dental profession to advise the Council on all dental matters and to serve as a central coordinating body for postgraduate dental education. Its membership includes representatives of the Faculty of Dental Surgery of the Royal College of Surgeons of England, universities, the profession (the British Dental Association), and the NHS; and an observer from the armed services attends its meetings.

OBSERVERS ON COUNCIL

### General Medical Council

The 1978 Medical Act extended the General Medical Council's role in relation to postgraduate medical education beyond the pre-registration year and the general function of coordinating all stages of medical education and promoting high standards was assigned to the Education Committee (see the later sections in this chapter). The GMC receives copies of Council's papers and nominates an observer to attend meetings. Usually some representatives on the Council for Postgraduate Medical Education are also members (either elected or nominated) of the GMC, and a co-opted representative of the three Councils for Postgraduate Medical Education serves on the Education Committee.

### Northern Ireland and Scottish Councils for Postgraduate Medical Education

The secretaries of the three Councils for Postgraduate Medical Education usually attend each other's council meetings so that policies may be coordinated throughout the United Kingdom.

### Committees on which the Council is represented

An Advisory Committee on Medical Training in the European Community and a parallel committee for dental training were set up by the European Commission to help to ensure comparability in the standards of basic training and further training of doctors and dentists in the community. Each committee consists of three members and three alternates from each member state and all six nominees from each country attend the meetings, although a member and his alternate cannot both vote on the same issue. The nominees represent the university bodies, the practising professions, and competent authorities. The nominations for the United Kingdom are obtained in consultation with the Committee of Vice-Chancellors and Principals and, for doctors, the British Medical Association and General Medical Council or, for dentists, the British Dental Association and General Dental Council. The Councils for Post-graduate Medical Education in the United Kingdom are also consulted and the alternate to the academic member recommended by the CVCP on each Advisory Committtee is a person recommended by the Councils.[218]

*Committees of the Council*

There are four standing committees. The membership of two – the Advisory Committee of Deans and the Dental Committee – has already been described. The others are the Advisory Committee on General Practice and the Education Liaison Group. The first advises Council on all aspects of the Council's functions which concern or affect general practice. Its membership includes the general practitioners who are on Council, additional representatives of this branch of the profession who are nominated by the Royal College of General Practitioners and by the General Medical Services Committee and representatives of regional postgraduate deans, clinical tutors, hospital consultants and the armed services. The meetings are attended also by observers from the DHSS and the Meeting of Regional and Associate Advisers in England and Wales.

The Education Liaison Group advises Council on the coordination of postgraduate medical and dental education and its membership is dominated by representatives of the NHS – regional medical officers, a regional specialist in community medicine, and district medical and dental officers. The other members represent the regional medical and dental postgraduate deans, and the DHSS and Welsh Office. The chairman of Council takes the chair at meetings.[218]

ACTIVITIES OF THE COUNCIL AND ITS SECRETARIAT

The Council and its standing committees meet three times a year and the committees report to Council at each meeting on matters which have arisen since the previous meeting or in response to a request for advice that was raised at a previous meeting. On some matters the Council may ask all its constituent bodies to prepare a written response, a consultation process which can take months. The documentation prepared and circulated for the meetings is often considerable.

Ad hoc working parties are also established by the Council. Two that met during 1983/84 were the Working Party on the Overseas Doctors Training Scheme (page 97) and the Working Group for the study to explore the feasibility of establishing an information system for hospital medical and dental training posts and trainees in

England and Wales.[11] The Council's secretariat also undertook, at the suggestion of the Council, an evaluation of an Open University course on topics in drug therapy.

The Secretariat, on behalf of the Council or at the request of the DHSS, carries out certain routine administrative activities in addition to servicing Council and its committees. Three are the organising of Safety Net – the system of collecting and distributing information on vacant pre-registration posts and candidates seeking posts (page 190); the organising of hearings by the General Practitioner Trainer Scheme Appeals Committee which reviews the cases of appellants who have not been appointed or reappointed as a trainer (page 157); and the processing of the applications for government support (provided as grants-in-aid) from the royal colleges, faculties and higher training committees. This activity is discussed in chapter 20, page 291). The Secretariat also receives statistical returns on, for example, regional numbers of doctors participating in vocational training for general medical practice and, on an ad hoc basis, regional numbers of time-expired senior registrars (page 180).

The Council receives copies of legislative and policy documents, regulations, guide lines, reports and other publications relevant to postgraduate medical and dental education. Thus it is a resource centre and the Secretariat frequently handles inquiries on many matters. Advice on opportunities for training in the United Kingdom is, however, provided by the staff of the National Advice Centre which shares the same accommodation and is administered by the Council on behalf of the three Councils for Postgraduate Medical Education. The Council, often in association with the councils for Scotland and Northern Ireland or the National Advice Centre or other bodies, collects and prepares material for publication – see for example references 97, 115, 147, 155 and 158.

The two bodies, the Council and the National Advice Centre, are financed by a single annual grant from the DHSS which was approximately £354,000 in 1983/84 and again in 1984/85.[220] The British Postgraduate Medical Federation makes a contribution towards the running of the Advice Centre (about £5000 in 1984/85) in return for services supplied to the Federation. (The Centre took over an advisory service which the Federation had provided for persons interested in studying or training primarily in the London area.) Other income is raised from the sale of publications. Members of Council and its committees may claim travel and subsistence expenses incurred when attending meetings. The claims for 1984/85 totalled £9300.

NATIONAL ADVICE CENTRE

The Centre was set up under the aegis of the three Councils for Postgraduate Medical Education and its first full year of operation was 1977. It provides advice on postgraduate education and training in the United Kingdom to doctors and dentists, most of whom have trained overseas. The advice is given either in replies to incoming letters or during visits made by inquirers to the Centre where the visitors are seen by a medical or dental adviser as appropriate or by one of the administrative assistants or secretaries. Many of the letters request general information on opportunities for training (although the requests are phrased in many different ways). The writers are sent a leaflet outlining current immigration rules; requirements for language proficiency (the PLAB test), registration with the GMC and membership of a medical defence organisation; procedures for applying for advertised posts; and a pro forma letter asking for details of qualifications and experience and for the names of three referees. If the writer has asked for information on courses in a selected specialty, the relevant loose leaf section from the guide on postgraduate medical (or dental) degrees, diplomas and courses [115,221] is forwarded. Letters which cannot be answered in the standard way are answered individually.

Nothing more is done until the doctor (or dentist) replies; many do not. If it is clear that the person intends to travel to the United Kingdom for the purpose of applying for hospital training posts and has completed the pro forma and supplied the names of three referees, the NAC staff will arrange for references to be forwarded to the Centre ready for when the doctor arrives and applies for his or her first job. (The Centre itself does not arrange paid employment.) The doctors are advised to visit the Centre on arrival in the United Kingdom to meet a medical adviser, and many follow the advice. If, instead, the doctor plans to enrol for a course, the Centre can, for some courses, make the booking if copies of references and a curriculum vitae have been supplied. The universities in Australia and New Zealand have a special arrangement with the Centre. They hold copies of the NAC pro forma and, when a doctor plans to visit this country, a completed set of relevant documents is sent to direct to the Centre.

The Centre also receives requests from hospitals in the United Kingdom for copies of references for overseas-trained doctors that are held on file. A doctor may make a single visit to the Centre on arrival in this country and from then onwards enter on each job application form the name and address of the Centre as the source of his references.

Comprehensive statistics on inquiries received and visits made are kept by the Centre. It is unable, however, to record whether doctors who visit the Centre later leave the United Kingdom. Nearly 14,100 written requests for medical information were received in 1985 and, since 1978, the number has always exceeded 13,500.* The 1977-85 trends for the different types of inquiries are shown in Figure 17. The peak

---

* These statistics were provided by the National Advice Centre.

Figure 17  Written inquiries on medical matters received by the National Advice Centre and visits made by doctors to the Centre, 1977-85

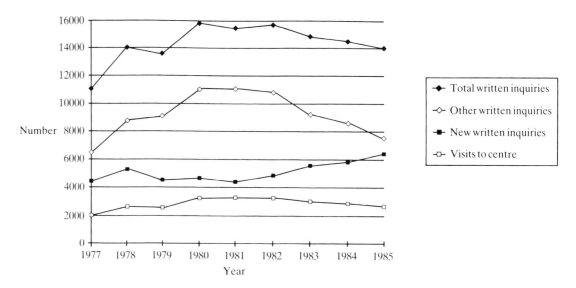

years for written requests of all kinds and for visits to the Centre were 1980-82. The number of new written inquiries was greatest, however, in 1985 and one reason was the introduction of new United Kingdom immigration regulations in April of that year (page 89). Nineteen eighty-five was also the peak year for dental inquiries.

In every year since the Centre opened the area from which the greatest number of new written requests has originated has been the Indian subcontinent (over 40 per cent of the total in 1985). The next most common source of new letters in 1985 was the Middle East (20 per cent). The annual rates of letters received from individual countries in the Middle East, Asia and Central Africa appear to be affected by the political situation within the country. For example, the number of new letters received from Iran more than quadrupled between 1982 and 1984. Over the same period letters from Iraq decreased by almost the same rate. Finally, it is worth noting that the Centre provides its service free of charge, although charges are made for the books and guides which it publishes or distributes.

OTHER BODIES PROVIDING ADVISORY SERVICES

The Overseas Doctors' Association and the Medical Women's Federation also offer counselling to individual doctors. The Overseas Doctors' Association in Manchester aims to protect the interests of overseas doctors and to promote their participation in the decision making processes of the National Health Service. It runs a welfare, information and advisory service concerned with the domestic needs of overseas doctors for which it receives a subvention from the DHSS. The service complements the work of the National Advice Centre and it has been receiving 3000 to 4000 inquiries a year. The Medical Women's Federation promotes the interests of women doctors, both through its own national activities and through women doctors who are members of professional bodies. It is concerned that satisfactory opportunities should exist for women to train as doctors and to work subsequently. The Federation has a member in each region responsible for advising individuals and organisations on the particular needs of women doctors for part-time training posts and part-time career posts. Before the National Advice Centre was set up, the British Medical Association ran an advisory service mainly for non-members. It still provides a service to doctors wishing to practice abroad and to other inquirers. Junior doctors may, of course, turn to their supervising consultants, clinical tutor or regional postgraduate dean for career guidance or advice. The resources available to the deans to develop such services are, however, restricted (refer to pages 301 and 325).

GENERAL MEDICAL COUNCIL AND ITS RESPONSIBILITIES FOR EDUCATION

The year 1858 marks the beginning of the modern system of medical training in Britain for in October a Medical Act was passed which obliged practising doctors to be registered on an official register to be maintained by a council – now the General Medical Council. The Council was also given powers to supervise medical education but not to examine, and to maintain a pharmacopoeia (a function that ceased in 1968). The proposal to regulate the profession caused great controversy and 15 consecutive bills were discussed and rejected by the Houses of Parliament before the 1858 version was passed. (See Stevens[13] and Bhattacharya[222] for an account of the establishment of the first council.) The Council was made independent of the royal colleges and universities although these bodies appoint members to it, and its responsibility was (and still is) to the Privy Council and thus to the Crown.

The Council, by having the power to regulate the standards of existing examining bodies, was able to effect changes in the structure of the examinations for primary and higher qualifying diplomas administered by the royal colleges over the following 30 years. During the 1880s, for example, the colleges of physicians and surgeons in each of the three countries of England, Scotland and Ireland formed conjoint boards to grant medical and surgical primary qualifying diplomas jointly (the English Examining Board was formed in 1884, the Scottish Triple Board in 1884 and the Irish

Conjoint Board in 1886). These arrangements were made in anticipation of another Act passed in 1886 which stipulated that to be eligible for inclusion on the Medical Register all students had to pass examinations in both medicine and surgery from either a university or a conjoint board of professional examining bodies. The Society of Apothecaries of London later transformed its primary diploma into a dual medical and surgical diploma to comply with the requirements of the Act.[13]

The regulations applying to registration after obtaining primary medical qualifications in the British Isles remained unaltered until the Medical Act of 1950 which introduced the 'pre-registration' year. Once a doctor passed the recognised primary qualifying examinations administered by the universities or professional examining bodies, he or she could only be provisionally registered by the GMC. Another compulsory year, providing six months in medicine and six months in surgery in approved hospitals, was required before the doctor could be fully registered. (There was legislative provision for some pre-registration service to be done in midwifery or at an approved health centre.) The Act came into effect in 1953.

### Monitoring undergraduate teaching standards in United Kingdom universities

The Medical Act of 1950 also empowered the Council to visit universities to assess the curricula and standard of training – previously only examinations could be inspected. So between 1953 and 1958 all the medical schools in the British Isles were visited. The English visitors were critical of the schools in the Irish Republic and an Irish visitor was outspoken over the examinations of the University of Cambridge and the English Examining (Conjoint) Board. These bodies were duly revisited and found sufficient.[223] One outcome of the visits was the issuing by the Council of new recommendations on the curriculum for undergraduate teaching. Instead of describing each stage of training, the Council merely indicated to the medical schools the minimum length of the whole period of professional study, declining to specify the period of study alloted to particular subjects or the sequence in which they should be taught. Thus the Council urged the schools as far as possible 'to instruct less and to educate more' (see Stevens[13], pages 175-79).

The practice of visiting the university medical schools to inspect their qualifying examinations lapsed until 1982, with the exception of visits made to the three universities with new medical schools – the Universities of Nottingham, Southampton and Leicester – before they were accepted as licensed to grant medical degrees, and to the new school of clinical studies at Cambridge. However, a new programme of inspection of final qualifying examinations was instituted in 1982 and the Council's Education Committee hopes to complete the inspection of all the universities and non-university licensing bodies, except those mentioned above as recently visited and inspected, by the end of the decade.

The Council also assesses (and visits if necessary) more than 20 overseas universities to ensure that the primary qualifications of these bodies are of a sufficiently high standard to permit holders to be granted full registration by the Council (see page 90 in chapter 7). A system of reciprocity as a precondition for recognition for overseas qualifications was introduced under the provisions of the Medical Act 1886. Thus an arrangement could exist between the governments of the United Kingdom and an overseas country with a medical education system, whereby each country's responsible body (the GMC in the United Kingdom) recognised the other's primary medical qualifications of satisfactory standard for registration purposes. Before 1920 only a few overseas institutions were recognised by the GMC and the system for recognition was based on documentation received from the medical schools concerned. However, during the 1920s the Council found it useful to institute a system of visitation, particularly of universities and medical colleges in India, and the system was later extended to other countries. By the time the Committee of Inquiry into the Regulation of the Medical Profession (chaired by Dr – later Sir Alec – Merrison) met in the early 1970s, 86 overseas medical schools were recognised, 43 having been visited by the Council at least once during the previous 20 years.[2]

At the Merrison inquiry, the GMC expressed its dissatisfaction with the system of reciprocity and it proposed that in future Council should be empowered to grant full registration to doctors holding an overseas primary medical qualification which it recognised as of sufficient standard, irrespective of the country in which the qualification was obtained. The standard would be not less than the minimum standard required for primary qualifications granted in the United Kingdom. The Committee of Inquiry endorsed the recommendation and under the Medical Act 1978 the system of reciprocity was withdrawn with effect from 1 December 1980 and the number of overseas qualifications recognised by the Council for full (and provisional) registration was reduced from 87 to 21. (Doctors holding a qualification from other universities can, of course, apply for limited registration.)

The 21 overseas universities awarding the recognised primary qualifications agreed, as a condition of continued recognition, to be subject to an annual review and to provide information on any changes of substance in the undergraduate medical curriculum, in student numbers and in the facilities, staff and resources available for teaching both pre-clinical and clinical undergraduate students. The universities agreed also that they would be prepared to receive visitors if the Council should believe it to be necessary. Annual reviews of the standards in each of the recognised overseas qualifications have since been made and, in addition, visits were made to the University of the West Indies in 1983 and the University of Malaya in 1984. Certain recommendations were made by the Council delegations which these institutions had to fulfil if their qualifications were to continue to be recognised for full registration. Delegations also visited the newly established medical school of the University of Newcastle in Australia in 1983 and the University of Southern Africa in 1984 because these institutions, supported by the appropriate national regulatory body, had requested that their primary qualification be recognised for full registration.[29] In 1985/86 the number of overseas universities awarding recognised primary medical qualifications was 22.

### Monitoring pre-registration experience

The Council delegates to the universities the responsibility for inspecting and overseeing the standards of the pre-registration posts according to recommendations issued by the Education Committee.[20] The universities provide information on the recognised posts and details of the posts are published at frequent intervals.[163] (The system for regulating the number of HO posts and for recognising them is described on pages 170-173 in chapter 12.) The universities are also responsible for overseeing the progress of the trainees during the pre-registration year and for issuing to them a certificate of experience indicating that an acceptable pre-registration year has been completed satisfactorily. The certificate is then forwarded to the General Medical Council when the provisionally registered doctor applies for full registration. These procedures are covered in greater detail in chapter 13, page 187.

### Postgraduate medical education

The responsibilities of the General Medical Council for medical education were not extended to postgraduate education until the 1978 Medical Act. The Act provided for the establishment of an Education Committee by the Council with the general function of coordinating all stages of medical education and for promoting high educational standards. (There was an Education Committee before the Act but its remit was narrower and it did not have vested legal powers.) This was the fulfilment of a recommendation made by the Committee of Inquiry into the Regulation of the Medical Profession.[2] The Committee of Inquiry had also recommended that the training grades be reorganised – refer to Figure 3 on page 30 – and that the Council (perhaps in a reconstituted form) control standards of specialist education by maintaining a specialist register. The 1978 Medical Act did not explicitly provide for specialist registration but indications of specialist competence could be shown in the Medical Register[82] if the Council decided to do so.[223]

The first full meeting of the new Education Committee was held late in 1979 and in the following February other members of Council joined the Committee to discuss how it might approach the functions of coordination. It was necessary, in particular, to consider how the Council and Committee could best develop a role in relation to the royal colleges and other bodies concerned with postgraduate medical education that would be as satisfactory as the traditional relationship between the Council and the universities and non-university licensing bodies in the field of undergraduate education. In the same month the Council published a document *Recommendations on basic medical education* which, in its draft form, had been widely discussed by the universities, medical schools and non-university examining bodies. Basic medical education was interpreted as pre-medical studies (whether undertaken in school or university), studies up to graduation and provisional registration followed by the pre-registration year leading to full registration. The principal objective of basic medical education is to provide all doctors by the time of full registration with the knowledge, skills and attitudes which will provide a firm basis for future vocational (specialist) training.[224]

The Education Committee then held a series of meetings during 1980 and 1981 with representatives of the royal colleges and faculties, of regional postgraduate deans, of regional medical officers and with other branches of the profession, culminating finally in a conference in February 1982 to which these bodies contributed. A consensus emerged that it would be useful for the Education Committee to consider first the stage of postgraduate medical education (generally described as general professional training) lasting two to three years or so immediately following the pre-registration year. The Committee accepted this guidance, and in 1983 it circulated for discussion a paper containing proposals for 'basic specialist training'.[6]

A fundamental concern of the Committee expressed in the document was the practice of many newly registered doctors of restricting their experience to the specialty of their career choice, although the regulations for the higher qualifying examinations for membership or fellowship of the royal colleges and faculties permit candidates to spend six months or more after obtaining full registration in other disciplines and still be eligible to sit the final examination in the minimum time permitted (see Table 31 on page 124). Thus the Committee proposed that young doctors should spend one year outside their specialty, and that an opportunity to acquire further experience in general practice was desirable for many doctors. The Committee also suggested that the organisation of training posts in the SHO grade should be reviewed and this proposal is discussed on page 38.

Comments on the proposals for basic specialist training were received from many bodies concerned with postgraduate education and training and, on the whole, the ideas were welcomed if they reflected non-mandatory developments. Also arising out of the consultation process was a request from the professional bodies that the period of 'general clinical training' – that is, pre-registration training – should be looked at again with a view to broadening it. (The recommendations for restructuring the training grades made by the Committee of Inquiry into the Regulation of the Medical Profession in the mid 1970s had also been along these lines (page 33). Thus the Education Committee addressed itself to this matter during 1985.[22]

### Maintaining the Medical Register

The regulations for entry to the Principal List of the Medical Register (for fully or provisionally registered doctors) or to the Register of Medical Practitioners with Limited Registration are contained in the Medical Act of 1983. It is the duty of the General Medical Council to administer the regulations. For some, Council can exercise discretion – one example is limited registration. It may be granted, at the Council's discretion, for employment in hospitals or posts in hospitals or institutions which are educationally approved by a royal college or faculty (in England and Wales) and supervised by a fully registered doctor. It may also be granted for employment in posts held in the course of training approved by a university department. Council cannot, however, grant limited registration to overseas qualified doctors for periods which in aggregate exceed five years (page 92). Once doctors have become fully registered they must pay an annual fee – £20 in 1985 – for the retention of their names in the Principal List of the Register unless they have been exempted from the fee on age or other grounds.

The published volumes of *The Medical Register* contain the names of all practitioners who are registered in the Principal List on 1 January in each year.[82] The Council also publishes each fortnight lists of changes in the Principal List. The changes fall into three groups: entries relating to practitioners whose names have recently been entered in the Principal List; changes of address in existing entries in the Principal List; and entries relating to practitioners whose names have been removed from the Principal List, most commonly because of death or non-payment of the retention fee. The register of doctors with limited registration is not published.

The Council, as the body responsible for maintaining the register, must assure itself that those admitted to the Register are competent and it must remove from the Register doctors whose conduct indicates that they are unfit to practise. All complaints or information concerning the conduct of individual doctors received by the Council are screened on up to three occasions and the doctors are given an opportunity to explain the matter. The complaint or information is scrutinised first by the Council's staff. Most cases are then considered by the preliminary screener for conduct cases (the President or a member of Council nominated by the President). A proportion of the cases is referred to the Preliminary Proceedings Committee whose statutory duty is to determine whether a case can be dealt with by the Committee itself or should be referred to the Professional Conduct Committee or to the Health Committee. Cases referred to the Professional Conduct Committee (which numbered 52 in 1984[29]) are heard in public.

The annual reports of the Council contain statistics on the numbers of cases of complaint or information investigated and the outcome, the numbers of doctors trained outside the United Kingdom who were granted registration (full, provisional or limited) under various sections of the most recent Medical Act, and the numbers of attempts made at passing the language proficiency (PLAB) test. The reports also contain accounts of the work of the Council over the previous year and its financial situation and papers on other matters.[29] Annual statistics on the numbers of provisionally registered doctors and fully registered doctors added to, removed from, and remaining on the Register are given in tables in the first of the two published volumes of *The Medical Register*.[82] Bound volumes of the minutes of the Council and its committees and reports of the committees are also publicly available.

## Membership and funding of the Council

The size and structure of the membership of the General Medical Council are determined by the Medical Acts. In 1985 it was made up of 50 members elected by the medical profession, 34 members appointed by the universities, royal colleges and faculties and the Society of Apothecaries of London, and 11 members nominated by the Crown of whom nine were lay (non-medically qualified) persons. Elections are held every five years for the elected members. The United Kingdom is divided into four constituencies (England with 39 members, Scotland with six members, Wales three members and Northern Ireland two members), and all practitioners currently registered with addresses in these countries are entitled to vote. In 1984, when the last elections were held, 113,653 voting papers were distributed and the response rate ranged between 34 per cent for voters in England to 52 per cent for Northern Ireland. Twenty-seven of the successful candidates were sponsored by the British Medical Association.[225]

Over 90 per cent of the Council's annual income is from fees – for registration from UK and EEC doctors, for annual retention (£2.1 million in 1984), and for registration and PLAB tests from overseas qualified doctors (£0.9 million).[29] The remainder is from sales, miscellaneous fees and net investment income. On the expenditure side, nearly half the expenses are directly related to the cost of registering doctors and conducting PLAB tests, maintaining the Register, publishing *The Medical Register* and collecting the annual retention fee. Council is empowered to review the fees and recommend increases to ensure that it can continue independently to meet its statutory obligations. The regulations covering fees associated with the granting of full and provisional registration must, however, be approved by the Privy Council.

# 19 Financial contributions of the universities and research bodies

The pattern of financing postgraduate medical education in England and Wales has developed over the years in a piecemeal fashion rather than being the result of systematic planning. The largest contributions are made by three public institutions: by the universities, whose funding is provided by the Department of Education and Science (DES), with annual allocations to individual bodies being made by the University Grants Committee; by the National Health Service, that is, the regional health authorities and special health authorities which receive annual revenue and capital allocations from the Department of Health and Social Security, and the district health authorities whose annual financial allocations are made by the RHAs, or in Wales, by the Welsh Office; and by the DHSS and the Welsh Office which directly finance the training and continuing education of doctors in general medical practice. The DHSS also supports the Council for Postgraduate Medical Education in England and Wales and the National Advice Centre, and provides grants-in-aid to the royal colleges, faculties and higher training committees; the Welsh Office contributes to the running of the Department of Postgraduate Studies in the University of Wales College of Medicine. Other bodies contribute financially, notably the Medical Research Council which receives an annual grant-in-aid from Parliament via the DES, and the charities and foundations concerned with medical research or education including the royal colleges.

The nature of the commitments by these various bodies is described in this chapter and the next although it is not possible to neatly categorise their different roles and levels of expenditure for two reasons. First, the guide lines on the financial responsibilities for postgraduate medical and dental education contained in the relevant 1973 health circular HM(73)2 (see below) – apart from the arrangements for the salaries of the regional postgraduate deans and advisers in general practice and the honorarium to clinical tutors – were not worked out in detail. Second, the financial accounting procedures covering postgraduate educational activities used by the health authorities are not standardised. (This subject is covered in the following chapter.)

GUIDE LINES ON FINANCIAL RESPONSIBILITIES

The Royal Commission on Medical Education which sat between 1965 and 1968 was asked to review the whole field of medical education and to make proposals 'in the light of national needs and resources' (para 18).[1] In its report, however, the Commission did not discuss in any detail the financial responsibilities implied by its proposals for postgraduate medical education and these included restructuring the training grades along the lines described in chapter 2. Indeed the relevant section on 'financial aspects' was confined to one paragraph (para 195). The Commission drew attention to the tension that existed at the time between the universities and the NHS over the relative shares of expenditure in this field. The UGC with the full support of the DES argued that the universities already devoted 'a very significant part of their resources to professional medical training' which was not part of their primary academic functions; the proper objective for the expenditure of university funds was preparation for higher university degrees. The Commission endorsed this argument and it took the view that training of a more professional rather than academic character ought to be paid for by the NHS. The Service ought also to finance the regional postgraduate committees and the proposed central council and a Scottish committee. Where teaching and facilities for such training were provided by universities the cost should be repaid by the health service. How the reimbursements should be made – by way of fees to individuals, periodic payments on a regional basis or by book-keeping transactions at central government – the Commission chose not to decide.

The Departments of Health in England, Scotland and Northern Ireland, the Welsh Office and the UGC accepted the view of the Commission as broadly reflecting current practice. However, more information on current expenditure was needed. To this end hospital authorities were asked by the Departments of Health to record their expenditure on postgraduate medical education on a routine basis from 1971/72 and the universities were asked by the UGC, on behalf of the Councils for Postgraduate Medical Education, to complete a questionnaire showing university expenditure on professional postgraduate medical education in the financial year 1970/71.[143]

The inquiries revealed a lack of standardisation in both the policies for allocating financial responsibility between hospital authorities and individual universities, and in itemising expenditures within the authorities' accounting systems. At regional level, the general pattern was for the regional hospital boards (now the RHAs) to fund the regional postgraduate committee of which the chief executive officer was the regional postgraduate dean and also part of the dean's salary according to the amount of time given to postgraduate work. In most regions the universities provided the accommodation for the secretariat but the main part of the salaries for the support staff and the running costs were met by the regional boards.[217]

After inquiries were completed and further discussions were held by the health departments, the UCG and other bodies, guide lines were prepared setting the respective financial responsibilities of the NHS and university authorities. They were issued to the health authorities in England and Wales in a health memorandum HM(73)2 in January 1973.[143]

The guide lines applied only to courses, the administrative arrangements for the regional postgraduate deans and their secretariats, and matters relating to research, the reimbursement of clinical tutors and regional advisers in general practice, and the subsistence and travelling expenses of members of regional postgraduate committees. The existing arrangement whereby full-time university teachers who carried out work within the health service were remunerated entirely by the university (except for the cost of any distinction awards which were paid for by the NHS) was to continue, likewise the practice of NHS consultants in teaching hospitals being paid for entirely by the health service although their work involved some teaching. (They may receive an honorarium for their teaching duties. Staff may also hold joint contracts with the NHS and a university, receiving a salary from each.) The supervision of staff in training posts by senior doctors and programmes of clinical demonstrations, clinics, pathological conferences, journal clubs and other discussion meetings were also outside the guide lines, for it was considered not practicable to try to separate, for costing purposes, these activities in teaching hospitals from the care of patients on the one hand, and from undergraduate (and postgraduate) teaching on the other.

These general arrangements between the universities and health authorities for meeting the costs of medical education and training are based on a principle of 'uncosted mutual assistance', more commonly known as a knock-for-knock agreement. The Royal Commission on the National Health Service thought it sensible to accept the existence of this 'grey area' of obligation and accounting between the NHS, the UGC and the universities. 'Rigid definitions of responsibility might lead to neater accounting but would impair good relationships and efficiency' (para 17.24).[3]

The guidance on courses, administration and other matters contained in the 1973 memorandum is still generally applicable in the mid 1980s. However, since under the arrangements it is the health authorities that are expected to reimburse the universities for services provided, the arrangements are covered in the following chapter together with the financial contributions to postgraduate medical education made by the DHSS and the Welsh Office. The arrangements for courses are also discussed in considerable detail in chapter 15. The remainder of this chapter looks at the effects on university clinical academic staffing levels caused by the cuts in university funding during 1981-84, the reorganisation of the medical undergraduate and postgraduate institutions of the University of London, and the financial contributions being made to medical research, teaching and training by the Medical Research Council and major charitable bodies.

THE UNIVERSITIES AND THE FINANCIAL CUTS

The memorandum on the financial responsibilities of the NHS and university authorities pre-dated the period of general economic restraint and financial cuts in public spending that began in the late 1970s. At the end of 1980, the UGC was informed by the DES of likely reductions in university funding and in the middle of the following year a three-year cycle of substantial cuts in grants to be given to the UGC and thus to the universities was announced. The cuts averaged 11 to 12 per cent over the three academic years 1981/82 to 1983/84. The medical schools became particularly anxious. Medical and dental education forms about 20 per cent of university spending and the greater proportion of the expenditure is on salaries. In discussions between the Government departments and the UGC it was agreed that, although clinical medicine could not be excluded in the search for economies, it would not be subjected to the same overall reductions as other disciplines. There would be some variations, however, in the allocations to the medical schools.

Not only was undergraduate medical education threatened by the proposed cuts, but also postgraduate medical education, research, and clinical work in the NHS. As mentioned in chapter 14, clinical academic staff in universities normally hold an honorary contract with a health authority as a consultant if they are a university professor or reader or senior lecturer, or as a senior registrar or registrar if they are on the university lecturer scale. In September 1984 the number of hospital consultants in England and Wales who held honorary contracts was 1534 (11 per cent of all consultants – see Table 8 on page 56), and the great majority were in teaching districts. These doctors are expected to provide the same kind of clinical services to their patients as NHS staff – it has been estimated that in teaching districts they provide over 40 per cent of patient care and in specialties such as pathology, 80 to 100 per cent of the service[226]; they also help to set and maintain high standards of medical practice and professional leadership to junior colleagues in training posts. Traditionally there has been parity in the basic remuneration of NHS medical and dental staff and university doctors and dentists on the clinical academic scale (but not for pre-clinical staff). In the years between 1982 and 1986, however, the relative position of academic staff became increasingly difficult to maintain because of the slowness of the government in providing funds to meet the difference between the annual pay award to NHS medical and dental staff and the award – which is usually lower – to university academic staff.

The Social Services Committee of the House of Commons when examining the subject of medical education during the 1980/81 session noted that recent cutbacks in UGC funding made future prospects in some academic departments less certain and a future career in a medical school might be seen by junior doctors as less secure than an NHS career (para 32).[4] As the Committee presented its report before the effects of the first round of cuts could be observed, it followed up the matter in the 1981/82 session.[227]

On the basis of information received by the Committee from the universities concerned, it appeared that around 300 clinical academic posts of various grades in Great Britain would be lost by the end of the academic year 1983/84. The Social Services Committee was concerned, therefore, about the effects such cuts would have on clinical services and patient care, on shortage specialties and small departments in individual specialties, on medical research, on postgraduate education and generally on the finely balanced knock-for-knock or 'symbiotic' relationship between the universities and health services. The Committee had recommended in its fourth report of the previous session (the Short report) that the Departments of Health should explore with the medical schools ways of developing academic activity and postgraduate training through the funding of academic chairs and senior lectureships (para 208)[4] – this proposal being in line with a recommendation of the Royal Commission on the National Health Service (para 17.31).[3] After considering evidence from the government and university representatives, the Committee accepted that it would, in fact, be imprudent, at least in the current economic climate, for the NHS to assume responsibility for financing academic posts lost in the current UGC cutbacks or for funding newly created academic posts in the short or longer term. Local arrangements might, of course, be made by health districts on an ad hoc basis. The Committee recommended, therefore, that the UGC grant for 1982/83 and 1983/84 be raised (by £5 million approximately in each year) and future allocations of grant by the UGC should contain a measure of protection for clinical medicine.[227]

The government's response to the Committee's 1981/82 report on UGC cuts and medical services was published in November 1982, six months after the publication of the Committee's report. When preparing the response, the DHSS had received new evidence which suggested that the overall effect of the cuts was not likely to be as severe as predicted earlier in the year – fewer than 100 posts with some clinical component had so far been affected in England and Wales.[228] The Department also pointed out that not all clinical academic post-holders performed clinical duties on a regular basis and so patient care would not be affected directly by every academic post lost. The government did not, therefore, endorse the recommendation that clinical academic resources be protected because it believed that the effects on clinical services caused by the reduction in university funded medical posts were likely to be marginal.

The evidence cited in the response of the government had been collected in two surveys which examined the impact of the UGC financial allocations during the academic year 1981/82. One was a survey of the deans of medical and dental schools by the University Hospitals Association (UHA); the other, conducted by the National Association of Health Authorities in England and Wales (NAHA), was of health authorities for districts known to have medical and dental academic staff providing patient services. The two associations repeated their joint surveys in 1983 and again in

1984 to observe the cumulative effect of the reduction of resources over the academic years 1981/82-1983/84.[35]

In England and Wales, over the years 1981-84, 279 clinical academic medical posts were abolished or frozen and 49 posts were unfrozen giving a total of 230 posts abolished or frozen. Seventy-eight new posts were established (of which 28 were 'new blood' posts created in certain specialties by the UGC to compensate for losses and three were created under the University of London's academic initiative scheme). Thus altogether the net loss was 152 posts.[35] Using these survey figures the DHSS then estimated how big the loss was in relative terms. The 152 WTE posts were equivalent to about 10 per cent of the increase in NHS hospital medical staff between 1981 and 1984 and they represented about 6 per cent of the paid medically qualified staff of universities in post at September 1981. Moreover, another 40 'new blood' posts for medicine were allocated by the UGC in 1984/85 and a further 25 posts in 1985/86. (These departmental estimates were published in the 1986 Response by the government to the Third Report of the Social Services Committee from the 1984/85 session. The report was a follow-up to the orginal one on UGC cuts and medical services prepared during the 1981/82 session.[227,229,230]) The joint UHA/NAHA surveys showed, however, that 45 per cent of the net reduction in WTE posts were posts for doctors of trainee status. The pathology specialties experienced the greatest losses. In terms of individuals affected, the numbers were appreciably higher than the WTE figures. There were also substantial losses of pre-clinical academic posts.[35,231]

The information provided by the teaching health authorities, including the special health authorities, in the 1983 UHA/NAHA joint survey suggested that in general patient care had not been noticeably affected. In many districts, however, the staffing of some services was reorganised and, in a few instances, a regional or district health authority had taken over the funding of an academic post. The deans of the medical schools also agreed that service commitments to patients had been sustained and, likewise, undergraduate teaching standards. (One dean is quoted as saying that he 'applauded the increased efficiency' brought about by the cutbacks!) What had been restricted, however, was the time available for personal research by all grades of academic staff and for supervising research projects undertaken by junior staff.[231]

After reviewing the available evidence the Social Services Committee in its follow-up inquiry in 1985 concluded that the effects of the reduction in UGC funding, while more than marginal, had been less than grave.[229] The government early in 1986 also admitted that the position was rather better than it had anticipated in its Response in 1982. Undoubtedly there had been some problems of adjustment in particular places and particular times, but the evidence suggested that the changes in UGC funding had not prevented a significant overall increase in the level of provision of NHS clinical services.[230] The Social Services Committee recommended, however, that the availability of academic jobs across specialties and grades should continue to be monitored.[229] This action would seem to be justified because the universities were told in 1985 to plan reductions in their recurrent spending by at least 2 per cent per annum over the remainder of the decade. Then in May 1986, the UGC introduced a radically new method for distributing funds among the universities based partly on measures of teaching and research excellence. The decisions were made with information supplied mostly by the UGC's own subcommittees but also by research councils, learned bodies, medical charities, and individuals with specialist knowledge.

### REORGANISATION OF THE MEDICAL INSTITUTIONS OF THE UNIVERSITY OF LONDON

At the same time as the universities were implementing the cuts in staffing as the result of the reduction in the UGC revenue allocations, the medical and dental institutions of the University of London were being reorganised. Anyone who has not been closely associated with the University might find the administrative arrangements of the undergraduate medical schools, the postgraduate medical schools and the postgraduate institutes puzzling. Indeed, these bodies were of special concern to the Royal Commission on Medical Education in 1965-68. At that time there were 12 undergraduate medical schools each with an independent teaching hospital group.* The growth of the schools had been rather haphazard, their size varied widely and they were semi-autonomous bodies whose relationship to the University of London was less close than the relationship between universities and their medical schools or faculties elsewhere in Britain. Also, most London schools had little direct contact with a multi-faculty university college. The Commission proposed a series of mergers to reduce the number to six and each would become an integral part of a multi-faculty university institution.[1]

The postgraduate system in London was even more complicated. In 1965-68 there were 14 postgraduate institutes for individual specialties including dentistry. 'Medical schools' attached to certain eminent specialist hospitals or groups of hospitals had been founded – with a few exceptions – in the early 19th century, and in 1945 they were organised as institutions under the British Postgraduate Medical Federation but with each having its own governing authority, academic council and dean. A central

---

*The earliest medical schools were St Thomas's Hospital founded in 606 and St Bartholomew's Hospital in 1123. Teaching began at Guy's Hospital, The London Hospital, Middlesex Hospital and St George's Hospital in the 18th century and at Charing Cross Hospital, King's College Hospital, the Royal Free Hospital, St Mary's Hospital, University College Hospital and the Westminster Hospital in the 19th century.[232]

office for the Federation was established, and the constituent bodies provided higher professional training for doctors demobilised from the three armed services after the Second World War had ended. Two years later the Federation was admitted as an independent postgraduate school of the University of London. Each of the institutes was then recognised by the University between 1949 and 1959 as having the privileges and responsibilities of an integral department of a school of the university.

There was in 1965-68 one other independent postgraduate medical school – the London School of Hygiene and Tropical Medicine. As its name suggests, it serves the fields of community health, epidemiology, occupational medicine and tropical medicine. It is not associated with a hospital group. There was also the Royal Postgraduate Medical School covering all the main hospital medical specialties based at Hammersmith Hospital in west London and associated with St Mark's Hospital in east London. It had been opened as the British Postgraduate Medical School in 1935 and was a member of the British Postgraduate Medical Federation at the time of the Royal Commission. In fact, the Federation developed from the British Postgraduate Medical School. The Royal Postgraduate Medical School became an independent school of the University of London in 1974, and its full-time senior academic clinical staff provide nearly all the consultant staff for Hammersmith Hospital. (St Mark's Hospital is no longer directly linked to the Postgraduate Medical School; it is associated instead with St Bartholomew's Hospital Medical College.)

The Royal Commission claimed that the separation of postgraduate training and research from the main stream of medical education and medical care was 'educationally indefensible as well as uneconomic'. It proposed, therefore, that the special postgraduate teaching hospitals be brought as soon as possible into physical proximity with general teaching hospitals and that their associated postgraduate institutes be integrated with the appropriate undergraduate medical schools (para 15).[1]

Needless to say, the University and, in particular, the governing body of the BPMF was already well aware of the value of providing coordinated postgraduate medical education, but the difficulties were considerable partly because of the geographical distances which separated the institutes and their hospitals. Plans for reorganising and relocating the special hospitals and postgraduate institutes into two groups, one in the Holborn area and the other four miles away in the vicinity of Fulham Road with a few hospitals and institutes remaining outside the two groups, had been announced by the then Ministry of Health in 1961. To consider this proposal further a committee of representatives from the UGC, the University of London and the Ministry of Health chaired by Professor G Pickering was formed and reported in 1962.[233] Recommendations of the Committee were not implemented, however, partly because of a financial crisis affecting the University in 1964/65 and the need to await the report from the Royal Commission on Medical Education which met between 1965 and 1968. A

Table 43    Framework for the reorganisation of undergraduate medical and dental schools and
postgraduate medical schools and institutes within the University of London
proposed in the Flowers report, 1980

| *New medical school and the health region* | *Constituent bodies* |
| --- | --- |
| St Mary's and Royal Postgraduate Joint School of Medicine and Dentistry North West Thames region | St Mary's Hospital Medical School Royal Postgraduate Medical School Institute of Dental Surgery |
| Charing Cross School of Medicine North West Thames region | Charing Cross Hospital Medical School Cardiothoracic Institute |
| University College School of Medicine and Dentistry North East Thames region | University College London Faculty of Medical Sciences (University College London Faculty of Clinical Sciences) (Middlesex Hospital Medical School) (Royal Free Hospital School of Medicine) London School of Hygiene and Tropical Medicine Institute of Neurology Institute of Child Health |
| The Harvey School of Medicine and Dentistry North East Thames region | (St Bartholomew's Hospital Medical College) (The London Hospital Medical College) Institute of Ophthalmology |
| The Lister and St Thomas' Joint School of Medicine and Dentistry South East Thames region | (King's College Hospital Medical School) (Guy's Hospital Medical School) St Thomas's Hospital Medical School Institute of Psychiatry |
| St George's School of Medicine and Dentistry South West Thames region | (St George's Hospital Medical School) (Royal London School of Dental Surgery) Institute of Cancer Research |

Notes: a. Under the framework, undergraduate institutions in parenthesis would no longer have a separate status and the Westminster Medical School would close.
b. Four other postgraduate institutes were to be absorbed into the new general medical schools; the Institute of Dermatology would be taken over by St George's School, the Institute of Laryngology and Otology would be transferred in part to the Institute of Neurology and part to the University College School, the Institute of Orthopaedics would also go to the University College School, and the Institute of Urology would become part of the Harvey School. A fifth institute, Obstetrics and Gynaecology, would transfer to the Royal Postgraduate Medical School.

Source: the Flowers report pages 48–49.[232]

Table 44    Undergraduate medical schools of the University of London and the associated teaching district health authorities, 1985/86

| | |
|---|---|
| Charing Cross and Westminster Medical School* | **North West Thames region** |
| St Mary's Hospital Medical School | Riverside DHA |
| | Paddington and North Kensington DHA |
| The London Hospital Medical College** | **North East Thames region** |
| St Bartholomew's Hospital Medical College** | Tower Hamlets DHA |
| Royal Free Hospital School of Medicine | City and Hackney DHA |
| The Middlesex Hospital Medical School† | Hampstead DHA |
| University College London School of Medicine† } | Bloomsbury DHA |
| Guy's Hospital Medical School†† | **South East Thames region** |
| St Thomas's Hospital Medical School†† | Lewisham and North Southwark DHA |
| King's College School of Medicine and Dentistry‡ | West Lambeth DHA |
| | Camberwell DHA |
| St George's Hospital Medical School | **South West Thames region** |
| | Wandsworth DHA |

DHA = district health authority

  * Charing Cross Hospital Medical School and Westminster Hospital Medical School formed a new school on 1 August 1984 known as the Charing Cross and Westminster Medical School.

 ** The medical colleges of The London Hospital and St Bartholomew's Hospital are still discussing a possible merger.

  † A joint School of Medicine consisting of University College London School of Medicine and The Middlesex Hospital Medical School was formed in 1982. The two schools have retained separate entries to their pre-clinical courses but a joint clinical course has been introduced.

 †† Guy's Hospital Medical School and St Thomas's Hospital Medical School are united as The United Medical and Dental Schools of Guy's and St Thomas's Hospitals. They continue to act as separate admitting institutions for undergraduate students.

  ‡ On 1 October 1983 King's College Hospital Medical School was reunited with King's College London to form the King's College School of Medicine and Dentistry of King's College London.

Source: University Central Council on Admissions Handbook.[235]

second working group under the chairmanship of Professor N F Morris was established by the University of London to re-examine policies for the future of the postgraduate institutes and their associated hospitals. It reported in 1977.[234] The planning of changes arising from recommendations in the second report was, however, overtaken by a general inquiry into the deployment of resources available in London for medical and dental undergraduate and postgraduate education established by the University of London in 1979. The Working Party under the chairmanship of Lord Flowers reported in 1980, the report being commonly known as the Flowers report.[232]

The Flowers Working Party endorsed the view of the Royal Commission on

Table 45    Postgraduate medical schools and postgraduate institutes of the University of London and the associated health authorities and hospitals in 1985/86

| Postgraduate medical school or institute | Associated health authority | Postgraduate hospitals |
|---|---|---|
| London School of Hygiene and Tropical Medicine | — | — |
| Royal Postgraduate Medical School | The Hammersmith and Queen Charlotte's Special Health Authority | Hammersmith Hospital Queen Charlotte's Maternity Hospital Chelsea Hospital for Women Acton Hospital |
| British Postgraduate Medical Federation | — | — |
| Hunterian Institute* | — | — |
| Institute of Cancer Research | The Board of Governors of the Royal Marsden Hospital (SHA) | The Royal Marsden Hospital, Fulham and Surrey |
| Cardiothoracic Institute | The Board of Governors of the National Heart and Chest Hospitals (SHA) | The National Heart Hospital, central London Brompton Hospital, Fulham and Surrey The London Chest Hospital, east London |
| Institute of Child Health | The Board of Governors of the Hospitals for Sick Children (SHA) | The Hospital for Sick Children, Great Ormond Street and Surrey Queen Elizabeth Hospital for Children, Hackney |
| Institute of Neurology | The Board of Governors of the National Hospital for Nervous Diseases (SHA) | The National Hospitals, Queen Square, Finchley and Buckinghamshire Maida Vale Hospital for Nervous Diseases The National Hospitals College of Speech Sciences |
| Institute of Ophthalmology | The Board of Governors of Moorfields Eye Hospital (SHA) | Moorfields Eye Hospital (two units in central London) |

| *Postgraduate medical school or institute* | *Associated health authority* | *Postgraduate hospitals* |
|---|---|---|
| Institute of Psychiatry | The Bethlem Royal Hospital and The Maudsley Hospital Health Authority (SHA) | The Bethlem Royal Hospital and The Maudsley Hospital, south London |
| Institute for Dental Surgery** | The Board of Governors of the Eastman Dental Hospital (SHA) | Eastman Dental Hospital, central London |
| Institute of Dermatology (until mid 1985†) | West Lambeth Health Authority (DHA) | St John's Hospital for Diseases of the Skin, Soho and Hackney |
| Institute of Laryngology and Otology†† | Bloomsbury Health Authority (DHA) | Royal National Throat, Nose and Ear Hospital, Soho |
| Institute of Orthopaedics†† | Bloomsbury Health Authority (DHA) | Royal National Orthopaedic Hospital (main unit Stanmore) |
| Institute of Urology†† | Bloomsbury Health Authority (DHA) | St Peters, St Pauls, St Philips and The Shaftsbury Hospitals, Holborn |
| Institute of Obstetrics and Gynaecology (until mid 1986‡) | The Hammersmith and Queen Charlotte's Special Health Authority‡‡ | (see the first entry in the table) |

SHA = special health authority    DHA = district health authority
  * The University of London withdrew its financial support from the Institute of Basic Medical Sciences in 1984/85 and the Institute has been replaced by Hunterian Institute taking in the previous clinical departments at the Royal College of Surgeons of England.
 ** The Institute of Dental Surgery is part of a North London consortium with University College and The London Hospital Dental School.
  † In August 1985 the Institute of Dermatology merged with the United Medical and Dental Schools of Guy's and St Thomas's Hospitals and it is hoped to rehouse the Institute ultimately on the St Thomas's site.
 †† In 1987 the Institutes of Laryngology and Otology, Orthopaedics and Urology will become part of the single medical school being set up by University College Hospital Medical School and the Middlesex Hospital Medical School.
  ‡ The Institute of Obstetrics and Gynaecology merged with the Royal Postgraduate Medical School in August 1986.
 ‡‡ In 1984 the Hammersmith Special Authority took over the management of the Queen Charlotte's Maternity Hospital and the Chelsea Hospital for Women.
Sources: Annual reports of the British Postgraduate Medical Federation[162], and NHS statutory instruments.[236–238]

Medical Education that it was desirable for the basic medical sciences to be in contact with both teaching hospitals and multi-faculty university colleges but opportunities for creating complexes of this kind (such as the proposed University College complex) might not arise for a very long time, lack of finance being one reason. The Working Party did, however, adopt the Commission's recommendation that there should be a series of mergers between the undergraduate medical schools and that the postgraduate institutes should be integrated with the appropriate undergraduate medical schools. In its deliberations the Working Party took into account the requirements of the health service to reduce substantially the numbers of acute beds in inner London (see the next chapter, page 297). This meant that increasing numbers of undergraduate medical students would have to obtain their clinical experience outside the main teaching hospital groups.

The Flowers report recommended that the present structure be replaced by five schools of medicine and dentistry and one school of medicine only, and that each school consist of one or more of the existing undergraduate medical schools and one or more of the postgraduate institutes. (The proposed framework is shown in Table 43, the existing undergraduate schools (as of 1985/86) are listed in Table 44 and the postgraduate schools and institutes in Table 45.) Under the Flowers proposals, five of the smaller postgraduate institutes would, however, cease to exist as separate entities but be absorbed into the new general medical schools (refer to the notes in Table 43). The Working Party believed also that because the Institute of Basic Medical Sciences in Lincoln's Inn Fields had no clinical commitment and no associated special hospital, it should cease to be maintained financially by the University of London but should see its future, instead, with the Royal College of Surgeons of England. (University funding was later withdrawn and it was reconstituted as the Hunterian Institute taking in clinical departments at the Royal College of Surgeons. It is also worth noting that the University does not fund the Institute of Cancer Research; its funding comes from the Medical Research Council supplemented by grants from cancer research charities, notably the Cancer Research Campaign, and from donations from the general public.)

Once the new management arrangements were completed, the Flowers Working Party believed the British Postgraduate Medical Federation should cease to be a school of the University and its Central Office be closed. The regional postgraduate deans for the four Thames regions would then have to seek new accommodation. The Working Party appreciated that a number of legal problems had to be resolved before the management structures for the new schools could be fully implemented, thus the process would be 'evolutionary rather than revolutionary'.[232]

The Flowers report was the subject of prolonged discussion during the spring and summer months of 1980 and was formally considered by a Joint Medical Advisory Committee followed by a Joint Planning Committee of the University's Court and

Senate.[239] The Committees were able to take account of the cycle of cuts in government funding for universities that was first announced as the Flowers report was due to appear. Although not accepting the Flowers proposals in their entirety, the Committees endorsed the conclusions in the main. The University also established in 1980 a Working Party on Medical Costs which examined the costs of both clinical and pre-clinical departments in the undergraduate medical schools and, with the assistance of a team of management consultants and other experts, prepared a series of options or arrangements of undergraduate medical teaching involving the phasing out of some pre-clinical or clinical departments of individual schools.[240] The Joint Planning Committee was able to take account of this work.

By the mid 1980s a number of changes to the organisation of the undergraduate medical schools had been completed – the most notable being the merger in 1984 between Charing Cross Hospital Medical School and Westminster Hospital Medical School which did not have a pre-clinical school – or were being planned (refer to the footnotes in Table 44). The proposal that a joint pre-clinical school for St Bartholomew's Hospital Medical College and The London Hospital Medical College be built on the site of Queen Mary College in east London – a plan that was first formed in the late 1960s – was so contentious that in 1985, the College Council of St Bartholomew's sought legal advice on ways to avoid the merger. Eventually a compromise was reached – part of basic medical sciences and research will continue to be provided by St Batholomew's. Progress had also been made in reorganising the postgraduate institutes by the mid 1980s, although if the footnotes in Tables 43 and 45 are compared it will be seen that some of the mergers were not in accordance with the Flowers recommendations.

The number of senior staff in the federated postgraduate institutes remained relatively static over the years 1981-84 when the universities were experiencing severe financial cutbacks. The institutes and postgraduate medical schools did, however, experience serious financial retrenchment when, shortly before announcing the cycle of cuts in university funding, the government adopted a policy of requiring overseas students to be entirely self-supporting.[35] In 1980 the British Postgraduate Medical Federation was threatened with losing 44 per cent of its recurrent grant. (About 45 per cent of the students enrolled on courses held at the institutes of the Federation at that time were from overseas.[162]) Cutbacks in staffing in the institutes were, therefore, achieved before 1981 when the undergraduate schools began to suffer. Over the following years the institutes and the Royal Postgraduate Medical School received additional help from the associated special health authorities – which are described in the next chapter – and there was an increase generally in funds received from research grants and charitable foundations. However, in mid 1986, planned moves of three institutes to new premises (the Institute of Child Health, the Institute of Dental

Surgery and the Institute of Neurology) were under threat. The UGC grant to the University of London for 1986/87 had been affected by the change in the distribution policy (page 274), and the University was uncertain whether extra maintenance grants needed by the institutes to cover the removal would be available.

THE RESEARCH BODIES

Although the majority of deans of medical schools and faculties in the 1983 UHA survey reported that the cuts in UGC funding had meant less time being available for personal research by senior staff and for supervising junior researchers, the deans also commented that research in some instances had been sustained by the increase – sometimes substantial – in 'soft money' benefactions and other resources (page 11).[231] The DHSS calculated from published university statistical returns that the rate of increase in university clinical medical departments' expenditure on 'specifically funded' research between 1980/81 and 1983/84 was equal to 23 per cent in real terms.[230] There was, in fact, a shift in the funding patterns of the major agencies involved in medical research during the period of the cuts. The Medical Research Council, the largest contributor, found itself in a 'no growth' situation but this was offset by the ability of certain of the major charitable bodies to expand their commitments to research.

*Medical Research Council*

The MRC, together with the other government research councils, receives most of its finance (95 per cent in 1984/85) from the government as a grant-in-aid. The grant – which is negotiated through the Advisory Board for the Research Councils – is 'cash limited', although it includes an allowance for pay awards and pay rises and these might eventually be higher than predicted. The majority of the money must also be spent within the year for which it was voted. If suitable research applications exceed income the Council must choose which of its areas of expenditure will have to be trimmed or cut substantially.

Slightly over half its income in 1984/85 was allocated to the MRC units – the National Institute for Medical Research at Mill Hill in north London, the Clinical Research Centre at Harrow in Middlesex, about 53 other MRC units, including laboratories in The Gambia and in Jamaica – and to a small number of external scientific staff most of whom are based in university departments. (The majority of the MRC units are situated within or in close proximity to a university or hospital but they are independent of the host institution both in function and administration.) Grants supporting research programmes (normally of five-years duration), research projects (of three-years duration) and research groups absorbed 30 per cent of the budget. Most grants are administered by the grant holder in association with the host institution and it is worth noting that about 28 research groups were set up between 1982 and early 1984 to provide additional support for established medical research teams in universities whose financial support was being curtailed as a result of the cuts in UGC funding. Postgraduate training awards and so on were allocated 6 per cent and the remainder of the budget was spent on administration and central expenses, special grants to institutes – one being the Institute of Cancer Research – and for research, capital equipment and capital building, and international subscriptions.[178,241,242]

Only a small proportion of the MRC budget directly supports postgraduate medical education and training and the proportion is going to shrink. No more than 225 (6 per cent) of the 3946 persons employed directly by the Council in January 1985, including those in the MRC units, were medically qualified. Three-quarters held honorary clinical contracts. The number of medically qualified persons who were recipients of the 1803 scientific salaries, including personal support covered by programme, project and research group support grants, is not known. Nearly 1100 persons held individual training awards or fellowships or studentships in January 1985 (refer to page 195), although again it is not known how many were medically qualified; 385 were holders of intercalated awards made to undergraduate medical and dental students who wish to interrupt their studies to obtain another qualification, usually a batchelor of science degree.[242] In October 1984, however, the Council made a decision to reduce the amount of money for programme (five-year) grants by 25 per cent and project (three-year) grants by 7.5 per cent for the 1984/85 award year commencing in October. (The cut of 25 per cent planned for programme grants was later reduced to 15 per cent when some additional monies were added to the budget.) More drastic still were the cuts planned in the research and advanced-course studentships; these were to be reduced by 30 per cent from October 1985 (from 340 awards in 1984/85 to 235 for 1985/86), and intercalated awards were to fall by 10 per cent (from 380 to 340).[241,242,243] After these decisions were announced the Council learnt that its parliamentary grant-in-aid for 1985/86 was to be £122.3 million, an increase of 4.4 per cent over the previous year and equivalent only to the predicted annual rate of inflation. Its grant for 1986/87 will also be increased by slightly less than 5 per cent. The number of trainee doctors engaged in research financed by the Council is, therefore, likely to fall considerably in the short term.

*Medical research charities*

The direct expenditure on medical research in 1984 by the 35 charities and foundations belonging to the Association of Medical Research Charities was almost £90 million, and it was some £12 million more than was spent in the previous year.[244] The total contribution by the voluntary sector was probably even larger since there are charities supporting medical research outside the Association. Thus the annual expenditure from the voluntary sector compares favourably with that of the Medical Research Council. Over 60 per cent of the contribution from the members of the Association is from three charities – the Wellcome Trust, the Cancer Research Campaign and the Imperial Cancer Research Fund. Taking the Wellcome Trust first, the expenditure of the Trust rose from £24.5 million over the two years 1980-82 to £33.5 million in 1982-84, representing an increase of 37 per cent. The allocation for the 12 months 1984/85 was £18.7 million. Further growth is anticipated.[175,244]

The Wellcome Trust supports most fields of medical research in university departments and hospitals throughout the United Kingdom, with mental health, ophthalmology and toxicology being subjects for special development in the mid 1980s. It also supports research in tropical medicine and infectious diseases, with the research being carried out in the United Kingdom and in Wellcome Trust units in Kenya, Brazil, India, Thailand and Jamaica, in veterinary and comparative medicine, and in the history of medicine (in the Wellcome Institute for the History of Medicine), in associated units and by individual grant holders.

The Trust's other major activity is the financing of research fellowships, senior lectureships and lectureships in basic biomedical or clinical sciences usually with a research component. (The procedures for applying for the various awards are described in chapter 14 page 194.) The lectureship scheme was created in 1982 in response to the financial difficulties facing the universities. By the end of 1984, 21 appointments had been made under the lectureship scheme and more appointments were planned.[175]

The Cancer Research Campaign and the Imperial Cancer Research Fund also substantially increased their expenditure on medical research in these years. In 1984 the Cancer Research Campaign contributed £18 million (including £9.7 million to universities and medical schools and £7.2 million to its laboratories and the Institute of Cancer Research and Beatson Institute for Cancer Research). The 1984 expenditure exceeded that of the previous year by 13 per cent.[245] The Imperial Cancer Research Fund's direct expenditure in 1983/84 was £13.1 million, representing an increase of 22 per cent over 1982/83, and most of the funding went towards its own research laboratories.[182] Like the Wellcome Trust, the CRC and ICRF also finance research fellowships (page 198).

Substantial contributions to medical research are also made by NHS health authorities, boards of governors and special trustees from the trust funds they manage (page 196) – the total expenditure in England in 1983/84 being £12.68 million.[181] The DHSS, mainly organised through the Research Management Division (previously the

Office of the Chief Scientist) and the Welsh Office, provide support for research in the health and personal social services and social security. The Department also supports research and development of equipment, appliances and supplies for the NHS and information technology, including clinical systems, and evaluations of special medical developments. The total research expenditure for 1984/85 was £18.7 million, of which slightly over £11 million was for health, personal social services and social security research. Evaluation of medical equipment and supplies absorbed another £2.4 million. For 1985/86 the planned increase in the budgets for these two areas of research was almost 4 per cent. Following a concordat between the Departments of Health and the Medical Research Council in 1981, the MRC agreed to raise its expenditure on health service research to £2 million a year by 1985/86 (at 1980 prices). The target was reached and will be maintained in ensuing years.[246]

Further expansion in the numbers of lectureships and fellowships created for doctors of senior registrar status by the charitable foundations might be limited if the Joint Planning Advisory Committee decides to place a quota on the number of doctors in England and Wales who can hold honorary senior registrar contracts (see pages 61 and 200). Anxiety over this proposal was expressed in the 1982-84 report of The Wellcome Trust which, as mentioned above, has recently set up a lectureship scheme. 'If too small and inflexible a quota [for honorary senior registrar appointments] is introduced the only effect will be the curtailment of the number of posts funded by non-government funds, which seems to be a nonsensical position when government funds are short' (page 9).[175] The 1986 proposal from a ministerial working group[299] (page 39) that district health authorities should no longer grant honorary contracts at a registrar level but, instead, clinical research posts with honorary registrar contracts should be provided within regional registrar quotas, could also have a restrictive effect on research investment.

# 20 Financial responsibilities of the DHSS, Welsh Office and health authorities

The responsibility for spending money on postgraduate medical and dental education from the annual budget allocated for health services by the Treasury lies, in England and Wales, with the DHSS and the Welsh Office for certain functions, and with the regional and district health authorities and the special health authorities for the London postgraduate teaching hospitals. The family practitioner committees are involved but as agents of the two government departments. The money used by the health authorities is from their revenue accounts, unless there is capital expenditure on constructing a postgraduate medical centre or extending or converting existing accommodation.

This chapter completes the review of the organisation of postgraduate medical education in England and Wales by describing the financial responsibilities of the two government departments and the health authorities. The development of the special health authorities to administer the London postgraduate teaching hospitals, and the SIFT system for compensating health authorities responsible for undergraduate teaching hospitals for the additional service costs of teaching are also discussed. (Although SIFT is only indirectly relevant to postgraduate medical teaching and research, the subject has been included for reference purposes.)

FINANCIAL RESPONSIBILITIES OF THE DHSS AND THE WELSH OFFICE

Since most of the functions for which the DHSS and the Welsh Office are financially responsible are discussed at length in previous chapters, they are only summarised in the following pages. Table 46 shows the estimated expenditure on postgraduate medical education covered by the DHSS in England for 1985/86. Excluded from the table, however, is the central funding for the Midlands and South Western Inter-regional Training Scheme in community medicine which was withdrawn from October 1986 (page 208), and expenditure on doctors returning to general practice after three or more years and prolonged study leave for general practitioners. Approximately 98 per cent of the estimated expenditure of £39 million by the DHSS in 1985/86 was on general medical practice.

1. *Grants to general practitioner trainers and course organisers* (refer to pages 156 and 158). Although there are 2600 or so approved trainers (including those designated as course organisers) in England and Wales, only about 1700 in England and 160 in Wales are responsible for a trainee at any given time. They receive a grant for the period when a trainee is attached and from 1 June 1985 the grant was £3340 per

Table 46    Summary of the items of expenditure on postgraduate medical education in England covered by the DHSS and estimates of expenditure for 1985/86

| | *Estimated expenditure 1985/86 £'000* |
|---|---|
| Reimbursement of grants to general practitioner trainers and course organisers (grant of £3340 per annum from 1 June 1985) | 6,600 |
| Reimbursement of trainers' expenses (telephone charges, and additional motor vehicle allowance of up to £2505 per annum) | 4,000* |
| Trainees' salaries and allowances while in general practice, employers' national insurance and superannuation contributions, and removal expenses (estimated average gross cost per trainee of £15,000 per annum) | 25,500 |
| Section 63 educational courses for general practitioner principals, assistants and trainees | |
|     course expenses budget distributed among regional universities | 1,000 |
|     travel and expenses budget used for reimbursing family practitioner committees | 1,100 |
| Retainer scheme for doctors with domestic commitments (fee £155 per annum in 1985) | 65 |
| Grant to Council for Postgraduate Medical Education in England and Wales and National Advice Centre | 355 |
| Grants-in-aid to the royal colleges and higher training committees | 275 |
| Grant to the Joint Committee on Postgraduate Training for General Practice for carrying out statutory duties | 85 |
| Expenses of standing committees and ad hoc working parties | 15 |
| Total estimated expenditure | 38,995** |

* Based on the assumption that at least 90 per cent of trainers employing a trainee claim the full motor vehicle allowance and most receive reimbursement for telephone charges.

** Excluded is the central funding for the Midlands and South Western Inter-regional Training Scheme in community medicine which was withdrawn from October 1986, and expenditure on doctors returning to general practice after three or more years and prolonged study leave for general practitioners.

Note: See pages 286–291 for the methods of calculating the estimated expenditures.

annum. There is usually at least one course organiser in each health district and the total number in 1986 was 255 in England and 22 in Wales. These general practitioners receive a grant for the duration of their appointment and the annual grant is the same as the grant for trainers. The family practitioner committees with which the trainers and organisers are contracted pay the grants and the committees negotiate with the

DHSS in England or the Welsh Office in Wales for an allocation in their annual budgets to cover the cost. The overall expenditure on grants in England in 1985/86 is estimated as £6.6 million.

2. *Reimbursement of trainers' expenses*  Trainers may receive payment for the costs of installing an extra telephone extension in the surgery and a telephone and an extension in a trainee's home and for the rental charges; they can also claim an allowance if a motor vehicle is necessary for the use of a trainee in addition to any other vehicle or vehicles used for the purposes of the practice. The allowance for a car used on a full-time basis over one year was £2505 in June 1985.[42] If at least 90 per cent of trainers employing a trainee received the full car allowance (discussions with FPC officers suggest that the proportion is probably very close to 100 per cent) and most received reimbursement for telephone charges (the quarterly rental for a telephone extension being nearly £20), then the expenditure on trainers' expenses covered by the DHSS in 1985/86 would have been £4 million approximately.

3. *Salaries of general practitioner trainees while in the general practice phase of their training*  Trainees in general practice are employed on the same basic salary scales as trainees in hospital (page 71). They can also receive a board and lodging allowance for out-of-hours duties which in June 1985 was equivalent to 15 per cent of the basic salary. The trainer employs the trainee but the cost of the trainee's salary is met by the FPC and the trainer also receives reimbursement from the committee for the employer's portion of the national insurance and superannuation contributions. The expenditures of the FPCs in England and Wales are covered by the appropriate government department. The average gross cost per trainee in 1985/86 was around £15,000. This figure included basic salary and board and lodging allowance totalling about £12,350, the employer's national insurance and superannuation contributions which amounted to £1670, London weighting where applicable, and removal expenses which can vary considerably. There were probably 1700 or more trainees in general practice in England throughout 1985/86 and so the cost to the DHSS for salaries and additional payments was in the order of £25.5 million.

4. *Continuing education courses and vocational training courses under section 63 of the Health Services and Public Health Act 1968*  Under the present arrangements for courses for general medical practitioners (principals, assistants, and trainees who are in the general practice phase of their training) in England, money is allocated by the DHSS to two budgets. The first budget covers the costs of running courses. It is divided among the regions and each regional budget is transferred to the relevant university or, for the four Thames regions, to the British Postgraduate Medical

Federation of the University of London. In nearly all regions the budget is admini-stered by the regional adviser in general practice. The cash limit set on the total budget for courses in England in 1985/86 was £1 million (refer to Table 39 on page 211). The second budget is for travel and subsistence expenses of general practitioners including trainees attending section 63 courses. The doctors submit the claims to the FPCs for payment and the committees are reimbursed by the DHSS from this central budget which, in 1985/86, had a cash limit of £1.1 million.

5.  *Retainer scheme for doctors with domestic commitments who are unable to work more than one day (or two sessions) per week but who intend to undertake more substantial work in the NHS when circumstances permit* (pages 111-112)   Scheme members are expected to attend at least seven educational sessions a year and they receive an annual fee of £155 (in 1985/86) from the regional health authorities acting as agents on behalf of the Secretary of State for Social Services. The authorities show these payments in their annual accounts and receive reimbursement.[95] (A similar scheme operates for dentists.) National statistics on the number of doctors participating in the retainer scheme are not published, but the figure may be relatively small. In the Northern region in 1982, for example, there were 27 members[103] and in South East Thames the membership was 23.[15] If a level of participation of 20-30 doctors was common across the regions, the reimbursement provided by the DHSS for 1985/86 would have been less than £65,000.

6.  *The Council for Postgraduate Medical Education in England and Wales and the National Advice Centre*   The constitution of the Council and its functions and the work of the Advice Centre are covered in chapter 18. In 1983/84 and again in 1984/85 the annual grant from the DHSS to cover the expenditure of both the Council and the Centre was in the order of £354,000. Additional services provided by the secretariat of the Council, such as the Safety Net scheme for pre-registration HO posts and the administration of the appeals procedures under the vocational training regulations, are also covered by this grant. (The British Postgraduate Medical Federation makes an annual contribution towards the running of the National Advice Centre.)

7.  *Grants-in-aid to the royal colleges, faculties and joint committees on higher training* As this subject is not discussed elsewhere in the book it is covered in the next section. In 1984/85 the contribution from the DHSS to the colleges and joint committees was in the order of £275,000.

8.  *Grant to the Joint Committee on Postgraduate Training for General Practice* Under the National Health Service (Vocational Training) Regulations the Joint

Committee has the responsibility for assessing the particulars and supporting statements of applicants for a certificate of prescribed experience or the particulars and supporting evidence of applicants for a certificate of equivalent experience. The Committee receives a grant direct from the DHSS to cover its expenditure on these statutory functions. In 1984/85 the grant was £84,000.[247]

9. *Grant from the Welsh Office to the Department of Postgraduate Studies of the University of Wales College of Medicine* The Welsh Office contributes towards the expenditure of the office of the postgraduate dean and meets the expenditure in Wales on doctors and dentists in retainer schemes, on section 63 courses for general practice, on training in community medicine, and so forth.

10. *Departmental standing committees and ad hoc working parties* The two main standing committees in the field of medical manpower and postgraduate training in England and Wales are the Central Manpower Committee which advises the DHSS and Welsh Office on the annual allocations of consultant, senior registrar and registrar posts in the NHS and also SHO posts in the special health authorities (page 41), and the newly established Joint Planning Advisory Committee which is to set national targets and regional quotas, if necessary, on senior registrar trainee numbers (NHS and honorary) in the main specialty groupings and possibly on registrar numbers at some later date (page 61). Two of the DHSS-established ad hoc working parties or committees which reported in 1984/85 were the Working Party on Section 63 Courses for General Medical Practitioners in England[194] and the Advisory Committee on Medical Manpower.[92] This second body was set up jointly by the health departments in England, Scotland and Northern Ireland and the Welsh Office, with representatives of the professions participating (page 307). The combined expenses of such standing and ad hoc committees in England – excluding the costs of servicing them – are probably in the order of £10,000 to £15,000. (As a comparison, the travel and subsistence expenditure by the Council for Postgraduate Medical Education on persons attending council meetings and meetings of standing and ad hoc committees was £13,200 in 1983/84 and £9300 in 1984/85.[220]) Matters concerning postgraduate training and education are on the agenda of other groups that meet regularly with health department officers. These groups include regional medical officers and directors, regional specialists in community medicine with responsibility for medical manpower and medical staffing, and the Joint Consultants Committee.

Finally, account must be taken of the work performed within the DHSS and the Welsh Office: routine tasks such as the setting of regional quotas of pre-registration HO posts and the screening of applications for part-time training under PM(79)3 arrangements; the preparation of directives on new or amended policies; the servicing of standing committees and ad hoc committees; and the preparation of evidence for working parties, committees of inquiry, royal commissions and such like. Senior officers serve on departmental committees and committees established by external bodies. Also, as mentioned in the previous chapter (page 285), the DHSS and the Welsh Office financially support research inquiries in the health and personal social services and evaluations of special medical developments, research and development of equipment, appliances and supplies for the NHS, and the development of information technology including clinical systems.

GRANTS-IN-AID TO THE ROYAL COLLEGES AND JOINT COMMITTEES ON HIGHER TRAINING

In the early 1970s when the earliest of the higher training committees were being formed – the Joint Committee for Higher Surgical Training followed by the Joint Committee for Higher Medical Training (see chapter 17) – the newly established Council for Postgraduate Medical Education in England and Wales recommended to the Secretary of State that financial support in the form of grants should be made to the royal colleges, faculties and JCHTs for meetings held to devise programmes for training, and for the inspection of posts as suitable for training. The Councils for Scotland and Northern Ireland were also generally in favour of financial assistance being given. The Secretary of State agreed that these activities would help to improve medical practice and that they were tasks which could not be properly carried out by the health authorities. It was important, however, that the colleges were clearly seen to be independent of the health authorities. Moreover, public funding involves public accountability, and financial support for the colleges' activities could lead to a diminution in their independence. After considering this and other factors the DHSS decided to make grants to the colleges and joint committees on higher training which would provide substantial help but only after the Councils' advice had been taken.[217]

For many years the grants-in-aid were equivalent to approximately two-thirds of the expenditures recommended to the DHSS; in 1984/85, however, the proportion was 59 per cent and the rate set for 1985/86 was lower at 57 per cent. The colleges and other training bodies which are members of the joint committes on higher training (page 233) contribute the rest of the income of the joint committees. Taking the Joint Committee on Higher Medical Training as an example, nearly 60 per cent of the Committee's income is the grant-in-aid from the DHSS and the remainder is made up of grants from the Royal Colleges of Physicians of Edinburgh, Glasgow, Ireland and London and the Irish Committee for Higher Medical Training.

The system for applying for the grants is as follows.* The Royal Colleges of Physicians (London), Surgeons of England, Obstetricians and Gynaecologists,

Pathologists, Psychiatrists, Radiologists and General Practitioners submit to the chairmen of the three Councils for Postgraduate Medical Education by October in each year an estimate of their expenditure on general (professional) training (see chapter 16) in the forthcoming financial year. The estimate from the Royal College of Surgeons of England covers the Faculties of Anaesthetists and Dental Surgery, and the Faculties of Community Medicine and Occupational Medicine are accounted for in the estimate from the Royal College of Physicians (London). Estimates of expenditure on higher training by the joint committees on higher training or the equivalent college committees are also submitted. The estimates are prepared under headings which cover an honorarium for a director of studies where appointed, and the usual items such as secretarial and administrative staff, postage, telephone and stationery, and accommodation.

The travel and subsistence heading in the estimates excludes expenses incurred by college representatives and representatives of the joint committees on higher training or specialty advisory committees when they are visiting hospitals to inspect posts. Normally these costs have been borne by the health authorities responsible for the posts. Now, quite frequently, the employing authority of the visitor covers the visitor's expenses. The expenses incurred by college and JCHT/SAC representatives when travelling to London to attend meetings on general professional or higher training matters may be met by the representatives' own employing authority. The policy for general practitioner representatives differs because, being independent contractors, they do not have an employing authority. Thus the combined estimates from the Joint Committee on Postgraduate Training for General Practice and the Royal College of General Practitioners include travel and subsistence expenses incurred by representatives.

Guidance on the payment of expenses of hospital doctors and dentists, including university teachers with honorary consultant contracts, while on college and related activities is contained in a letter from the DHSS – DS278/72 – dated 17 November 1972 (and quoted in Davies[217]). No distinction was made in the letter, however, between inspections of NHS posts and inspections of posts for honorary contract holders. It merely suggested that when a single programme of visits to regional hospital board hospitals and hospitals administered by boards of governors – which, at the time the letter was written meant teaching hospitals – takes place, 'it may be most convenient if a single claim is submitted to the regional authority'. Another suggestion in the letter was that it would be reasonable for hospital authorities to grant

---

* This information was provided by the Council for Postgraduate Medical Education in England and Wales.

special leave to NHS and honorary consultants who are members of committees engaged in training.

After the estimates of expenditure for the forthcoming financial year have been reviewed by the chairmen of the Councils, recommendations are sent to the DHSS on the target expenditure for each college and joint committee on higher training. The Department decides what level the grants-in-aid will be for the year and the payments are made direct to the approval bodies at six-monthly intervals. The colleges and joint committees are obliged to inform the chairmen of the Councils after the end of the financial year of their actual expenditure. If an original estimate proves to have been too low the college, or the constituent colleges and other bodies on the joint committee on higher training, bear the additional cost.

The overall expenditure on higher training recommended by the Councils to the DHSS for 1984/85 was £250,600, and the figure for general training was £122,000, and for monitoring standards of training for entry to general practice, £93,000. (The Joint Committee on Postgraduate Training for General Practice also receives a direct grant from the DHSS each year for carrying out statutory responsibilities (refer to item 8 on page 289).) Thus the recommended total figure was £465,600 and the grants-in-aid awarded by the DHSS were in the order of £275,000. The actual combined expenditure of the recipient bodies exceeded the recommended expenditure by 0.7 per cent.

SERVICE INCREMENT FOR TEACHING (SIFT)

The NHS has a statutory responsibility to make available to the medical schools and faculties of the universities, clinical facilities for the teaching of medical and dental undergraduate students. In the mid 1970s a DHSS working party known as the Resource Allocation Working Party (RAWP) developed a formula that is now used by the Department when allocating resources among the 14 health regions of England.[248] (Many regional health authorities also use the RAWP formula when deciding on revenue allocations for district health authorities.) When the Working Party looked at teaching hospital costs the available data showed that first, designated 'teaching hospitals' were on average more costly than hospitals in which no teaching takes place; second, the higher costs of these hospitals bore no relationship to either the size or needs of the populations served by the hospitals; and third, the average costs per student for individual teaching hospital groups varied substantially, with three-quarters of the London hospital groups being above the median. Factors other than the teaching function and the presence of students were also identified as contributing to the higher cost of teaching hospitals: regional specialties tend to be located in teaching hospitals; research work tends to be similarly concentrated; and teaching hospitals have developed in various degrees as 'centres of excellence' over the years. The RAWP working party proposed, therefore, that health authorities in England should receive an allowance 'to cover the additional service costs incurred by the NHS in providing facilities for the clinical teaching of medical and dental students'. This was to be known as the Service Increment for Teaching, or SIFT. (In Scotland a different system for reimbursing health authorities operates and it is known by the acronym SHARE.)

Under SIFT the 14 regional health authorities receive an annual allowance related to their number of clinical medical undergraduate students. The allowance is estimated as being equivalent to 75 per cent of the median excess service cost per student, the median figure being derived from a ranking of the excess costs per student of the teaching hospitals associated with each medical school in England. The RHAs, in turn, distribute the allowance among those district health authorities which provide regular teaching for clinical students, but each RHA decides its own methods for making the allocation.* The numbers of clinical students used in the national SIFT formula each year are projected two years on to allow for any future changes in student numbers. The national rate per student remains constant, apart from an annual adjustment to allow for inflation in costs. The rate in use in the mid 1980s was estimated using cost data for 1976/77 and 1977/78 by the Advisory Group for Resource Allocation which met between 1978 and 1980.[249] (The Advisory Group was established to carry out further work recommended by the RAWP working party.)

The decision of the RAWP working party to adopt the figure of 75 per cent was based on regression analyses carried out by Culyer and colleagues at the University of York. They used data on 268 acute hospitals in England with more than 100 beds, 40 of the hospitals being within teaching hospital groups, to explore different models of the effects of medical students on hospital costs. The model found to be most satisfactory because it gave the best estimates of teaching hospital costs, also gave the lowest estimate of the cost of the teaching function – around 75 per cent of the extra cost per case.[250] The other 25 per cent of the extra cost per case was attributed to other factors including hospital case complexity and length of inpatient stay.

The assumptions underlying the SIFT formula, in particular the continued used of the figure of 75 per cent, have been criticised; one objection is that SIFT takes no account of the research functions of teaching hospitals.[251-253] Postgraduate research students were excluded from the formula by the RAWP working party on the grounds

---

*The calculation of the allowance for dental students differs – it is estimated as being equivalent to 85 per cent of the total national outpatient expenditure of dental teaching hospitals.[249]

that NHS expenditure is not significantly affected by them and their numbers are both relatively small and are fairly evenly distributed among the regions.[248]

As a contribution to the debate, Copeman and Drummond carried out a study in two teaching districts and the associated medical schools – West Lambeth HA which is associated with St Thomas's Hospital Medical School and Birmingham Central HA serving the University of Birmingham – to see if it was feasible to separate the costs of therapy (patient care), teaching and research at a local level.[254] The study confirmed that close interrelationships exist between teaching hospital and medical school activities and, as suggested in the previous chapter, the main joint resource is medical staff time. While it was possible to obtain details of the contracts held by NHS consultant staff and university staff with honorary consultant contracts, to obtain in sufficient detail information on how the staff spent their time and its contribution to teaching, research or patient therapy, required detailed surveillance of their activities. Research activity was measured by estimating the annual expenditure on all grants received from different sources, the overheads that could be fairly allocated to research and by adding up the number of research papers published over a year – over 1000 in each centre. Two costs from research borne by the hospitals were 'spill over costs' during the life of a research project such as extra tests ordered and lengthened inpatient stays to complete research observations, and long-term costs at the end of the project if the research resulted in an extra service or a more expensive treatment technique being introduced.

The researchers found no evidence that the SIFT allowance as currently calculated fails to cover the narrowly defined service costs of teaching undergraduate students. It is the research and developmental activities (and provision of patient therapy) that are so difficult to cost separately by conventional cost accounting methods and which the managers and clinicians in the survey districts felt were being inadequately funded. The feasibility study did show, however, that data can be assembled at a local level to improve the statistical analysis of teaching hospital costs.

SPECIAL HEALTH AUTHORITIES FOR POSTGRADUATE TEACHING HOSPITALS

Until the reorganisation of the National Health Service in 1974 the teaching hospitals in England and Wales were outside the regional hospital board organisation, a situation which the Royal Commission on Medical Education viewed as unsatisfactory from the point of view of medical education. The teaching hospitals including the postgraduate hospitals were administered instead by boards of governors. The Commission recommended in its report in 1968 that a single unified system should be established.[1] Under the 1974 reorganisation, however, it was mainly the teaching hospitals associated with undergraduate medical schools that were incorporated in the new health authority structure – in England their administration was taken over by health districts within area health authorities designated as teaching authorities (AHA(T)s). When the National Health Service was further reorganised in 1982, the tier of area health authorities was removed and the management of the teaching hospitals passed to district health authorities.

When the plans for the 1974 NHS reorganisation were being drafted, decisions on the future management of the London postgraduate teaching hospital groups had not been reached, and so under the National Health Service Reorganisation Act 1973, the boards of governors responsible for these groups of hospitals were 'preserved' until February 1979 and they continued to manage the hospitals. The boards were made individually accountable to the Secretary of State for Social Services who appointed their chairmen and members partly from the nominations of the associated postgraduate institutes and the Thames regional health authorities. They received their finance direct from the DHSS.

During the five years until 1979 the subject of the future of the postgraduate hospitals was considered at meetings within the DHSS, at at least one conference, by a study group set up by the DHSS to consider future financial arrangements and, naturally, by the boards of governors themselves. The Teaching Hospitals Association with financial support from the King Edward's Hospital Fund for London even commissioned a firm of management consultants to review the situation.[255] Eventually, in September 1978, the DHSS issued a consultative document *Future management of the London specialist postgraduate hospitals* which proposed alternative organisational arrangements.[256] The three main alternatives were: each hospital group to become accountable to an existing AHA(T); special health authorities with statutory powers and functions similar to the AHA(T)s and accountable to specified regional health authorities be established; a single special health authority directly accountable to the Secretary of State be set up to administer all the hospital groups.

Two more documents on the future of the postgraduate hospitals became available during 1980. In the meantime, however, the preservation of the 12 boards of governors had been extended until 31 March 1982.[257] One of the new documents was a paper prepared by the chairmen of the boards of governors in response to the Flowers report on the reorganisation of the medical institutions of the University of London (discussed in the previous chapter).[258] The other was a report from the London Health Planning Consortium which simply provided another set of proposals for linking individual postgraduate hospitals with undergraduate teaching hospitals.[259] The Consortium had been established in 1977 by the DHSS, the University Grants Committee, the University of London and the four Thames regional health authorities because these bodies were concerned that the strategic planning for the health services in London should be coordinated as far as possible. The tasks of the Consortium were to identify planning issues relating to health services and clinical teaching in London, to decide who should study them, to evaluate planning options and to make recommendations as appropriate. Study groups were set up to look at the services for certain related specialties and a series of reports were published on, for example, cardiology and cardiothoracic surgery[260], radiotherapy and oncology[261] and neurology and neurosurgery.[262] Another report, *Towards a balance*[263], examined the organisation of the clinical teaching of the London medical schools and the links between the schools and acute hospitals within the metropolitan area. It was published in February 1980, almost at the same time as the publication of the Flowers report on the medical and dental resources of the University of London.[232] The most far reaching of the proposals from the Consortium was that the number of acute beds in the health districts within the geographical area covered by the Greater London Council (GLC) should be reduced by at least 20 per cent between 1977 and 1988.[264] In the years that followed, substantial reductions were made in the annual allocations of revenue to the London districts and the health authorities were forced to close numerous small hospital units and wards in larger units.

The Secretary of State finally turned to the London Advisory Group for its advice on the appropriate arrangements for managing the postgraduate hospitals. The Group had been set up specifically to advise the Secretary on matters of particular concern. Its members were drawn from the University Grants Committee, the University of London, the DHSS, the four Thames regional health authorities (the regional chairmen rather than regional officers who were on the London Health Planning Consortium) and from other bodies such as the GLC, the British Medical Association and the Royal College of General Practitioners. The chairman was Sir John Habakkuk, Principal of Jesus College, Oxford. The Group did not suggest a single policy to be applied to all postgraduate teaching hospitals. Instead, guided by the University of London's plans for the postgraduate institutes, it proposed that six of the larger postgraduate hospital groups should continue to be managed independently by boards of governors and the boards should be directly accountable to the Secretary of State. These groups were the Bethlem Royal and Maudsley Hospitals, the Hospitals for Sick Children, Moorfields Eye Hospitals, the National Heart and Chest Hospitals, the National Hospital for Nervous Diseases, and the Royal Marsden Hospital. As the remaining six groups were likely to be affected by changing circumstances – the termination of the independence of the associated postgraduate institute or the rehousing of a postgraduate hospital in close association with a general hospital – the continuance of the boards of governors in such circumstances was considered by the Advisory Group to be undesirable.[265]

The advice from the London Advisory Group was accepted in principle and on 1 April 1982 when the National Health Service in England was further reorganised, seven special health authorities for London postgraduate teaching hospitals came into operation.[236] The seventh was the Hammersmith Special Health Authority for the Hammersmith Hospital which is associated with the Royal Postgraduate Medical School. (The future of this hospital was not discussed by the Advisory Group.) A final decision over the future of the Eastman Dental Hospital had not been reached in 1982 and it was not made an SHA until 1 April 1984. Also on 1 April 1984, the responsibility for managing Queen Charlotte's Hospital for Women and the Chelsea Hospital for Women was transferred to Hammersmith SHA. The special health authorities and their associated postgraduate institutes are listed in Table 45 on page 278 and it is interesting to note that six have retained 'board of governors' in their statutory title. The other postgraduate teaching hospitals, their associated institutes and the plans for their future are also shown in Table 45.

The chairman and members of each special health authority (or the board of governors) are appointed by the Secretary of State for Social Services after consultation with the University of London and other appropriate bodies, and the authorities are directly financed by the Secretary and are responsible to him. The financial responsibilities of the SHAs towards postgraduate medical education are the same as those of other health authorities. At least one of the members of each special health authority is nominated by the region or district health authority in which a hospital or part of a hospital administered by the SHA is situated. The relevance of this requirement can be seen in the third column of Table 45 – four of the SHAs are responsible for hospitals which are separated geographically by many miles. One other point of note: the regional tables prepared from the DHSS annual 30 September census of hospital medical staff include an annexe covering the London postgraduate teaching hospital groups.[7]

### FINANCIAL RESPONSIBILITIES OF THE HEALTH AUTHORITIES FOR POSTGRADUATE MEDICAL EDUCATION

The 1973 note of guidance on the financial responsibilities of NHS and university authorities for postgraduate medical and dental education was, as mentioned on pages 269-270 in the previous chapter, concerned with areas of activity or responsibility which universities could reasonably expect health authorities to contribute financially towards: postgraduate courses provided by universities and not leading to university higher degrees; administrative arrangements for the regional postgraduate deans and their secretariats; honoraria for clinical tutors and the salary of the regional adviser in general practice; and travel and subsistence expenses of members of regional postgraduate committees.[143] Health authorities are responsible also for a range of other activities: granting study leave and meeting travel and subsistence costs of medical and dental staff attending courses, conferences, examinations and so forth; meeting the administration and running costs of postgraduate education centres and libraries; granting special study leave and reimbursing the travel and subsistence expenses of senior members of staff including honorary contract holders who attend meetings at the royal colleges, faculties and higher training committees on matters relating to training; granting special leave to members of staff who visit other hospitals to inspect posts; and reimbursing the travel and subsistence expenses of visitors who inspect the authorities' own posts.

In 1978 a working party of the Medico-Pharmaceutical Forum reviewed the exercise carried out in the early 1970s to collect information on the current expenditure of health authorities on postgraduate medical education (page 269) and it summed up the situation as follows.

'It is difficult to get accurate and meaningful figures about expenditure on postgraduate medical education. This is because the financial arrangements differ from region to region. For example, the cost of a locum tenens who replaces a doctor attending a postgraduate course may sometimes be regarded as a part of the cost of educating the absent doctor or it may be included with the cost of locums filling service vacancies. The method of financing Deans' offices, and such educational facilities as library services, also vary so much that it is difficult to get directly comparable figures for all regions.'[266] (and reproduced in volume II of the Short report, pages 144-45[4])

To see if the situation was any different in the mid 1980s, a small exercise was carried out while the material for this book was being gathered.

The NHS statutory accounts completed by each health authority in England at the end of a financial year has a heading Postgraduate Medical and Dental Education (sub code 010) on the Other Services Account (statement 12). Authorities can also enter on the Other Services Account under a heading Other Services, individual major items such as 'the expenses of a meeting of medical bodies'. To get an overall figure of the expenditure by the regional health authorities on postgraduate medical and dental education as recorded on the Other Services Account each regional health authority was requested to supply a copy of their published annual accounts or the relevant information from them for the year ended 31 March 1984. They all cooperated, usually by sending a copy of the published accounts. (Information on the local administrative arrangements between the universities and the regional health authorities over the financing of the regional postgraduate deans' offices had been recorded in the interviews with the deans during the fieldwork for the study on the feasibility of establishing a national information system on hospital training posts and trainees[11]

Table 47   Expenditure by regional health authorities on postgraduate medical and dental education entered on the Other Services Account* of the published accounts for the year ended 31st March 1984, and the number of medical trainees in the post-registration grades and the number of dental trainees, 30 September 1984

| Regional health authority | Revenue | Medical post-registration trainees** | Dental trainees† |
|---|---|---|---|
| | £ | No | No |
| Northern | 243,662 | 1272 | 34 |
| Yorkshire | 151,889 | 1252†† | 45†† |
| Trent | 201,776 | 1750 | 51 |
| East Anglian | 154,161 | 669 | 10 |
| North West Thames | 208,249 | 1487 | 27 |
| North East Thames | 249,396 | 1877 | 66 |
| South East Thames | 222,680 | 1434 | 74 |
| South West Thames | 548,578‡ | 945 | 47 |
| Wessex | 324,125 | 852 | 24 |
| Oxford | 165,331 | 921 | 17 |
| South Western | 91,915 | 1024 | 38 |
| West Midlands | 6,588†† | 1809 | 65 |
| Mersey | 220,542 | 994 | 36 |
| North Western | 172,745 | 1728 | 51 |
| Total for 14 regional health authorities | 2,961,637 | 18,014 | 585 |

* Item 7, postgraduate medical and dental education, sub code 010 on statement 12, Other Services Account of the published accounts.
** NHS-employed doctors and holders of honorary contracts in the senior registrar, registrar and SHO grades in the hospital service and community medicine.
† Dental trainees – both NHS-employed and honorary contract holders – in the senior registrar, registrar, SHO and HO grades.
†† The numbers of honorary senior registrar medical and dental trainees was supplied by the Yorkshire RHA.
‡ Expenditure on the office of the regional postgraduate deans by the South West Thames RHA was £277,000.
‡‡ The West Midlands RHA's accounting procedures for items of postgraduate education differed markedly from the procedures followed in the other regions.

Sources: Published accounts of the regional health authorities for the year ended 31 March 1984[267–277], information supplied by North East Thames, South West Thames, South Western and West Midlands RHAs, and the DHSS 30 September 1984 censuses.[7,9,10]

(page 20).) Letters requesting a copy of the 1983/84 published accounts were also sent to the treasurer's department of 11 London teaching district health authorities, seven provincial teaching district health authorities and seven special health authorities for postgraduate teaching hospitals. The outcome of the requests sent to the district and special health authorities is discussed later.

*Expenditure of the regional health authorities*

Shown in Table 47 is the expenditure classified under the heading Postgraduate Medical and Dental Education on the Other Services Account of each regional health authority for the financial year 1983/84. One feature is immediately obvious. The expenditure entered by two regions was markedly different from the other regions: West Midlands entered only £6600 on its account, South West Thames, £549,000. The accounting procedures used in the treasurer's department in each of these regions differed from the procedures adopted in the majority of treasurers' departments. There was nearly a four-fold difference in the expenditure entered by the other regions, the range being from £92,000 to £324,000, but again different accounting procedures provided part of the explanation. For example, the figure for South East Thames of £223,000 covered the costs of the regional postgraduate medical and dental deans' office including salaries and honoraria, plus other contributions to postgraduate education (equivalent to 3 per cent of the expenditure), whereas the similar figure for Mersey covered both the costs of the dean's office and the study leave expenses of senior and junior medical staff employed by the regional health authority.

The largest item of expenditure in a regional health authority budget for a dean's office is the reimbursement to the university of the salaries of the postgraduate medical dean who can hold a full-time, maximum part-time or part-time appointment, the part-time dental dean or adviser if one has been appointed, and the part-time regional adviser in general practice and associate advisers where appointed. The 1973 guide lines on the financial responsibilities of the NHS and university authorities noted that universities were free to treat the salaries of postgraduate deans as being *sui generis* (of a special kind) and to fix them at their discretion, and that the university could seek reimbursement from the regional authority for some part of the salary.[143]

Postgraduate medical deans are appointed from university staff or NHS hospital consultant staff or from other medically-qualified professional groups, and since many carry on regular academic and/or clinical sessions – perhaps five or six sessions per week – as well as their duties as dean, the arrangements made between universities and the regional health authorities over the deans' salaries differ from region to region. There is no relationship between the number of weekly sessions spent by the deans on educational and training matters and the number of trainees within the regions, although there is a three-fold difference in the regional numbers of medical trainees (NHS-employed and honorary contract holders combined) in the post-registration grades – see column 2 in Table 47. Moreover, in 1984 only one of the part-time deans shared his post-registration duties with a senior colleague and another had associates who attended many committee meetings on his behalf. The situation in the Trent region is slightly different. The regional deanship rotates among the three postgraduate deans of the Universities of Sheffield, Leicester and Nottingham and the two associate deans share some of the responsibilities of the regional dean.

In the interviews with the deans during the fieldwork for the feasibility study part-time deans defended the practice of continuing with clinical or academic sessions on the grounds that it enabled them to retain their credibility with their clinical colleagues when discussing matters relating to training. It is unfortunate, however, that the deans should feel that collegial esteem needs to be maintained in this way because the responsibilities of deanship appear to be equivalent to a full-time load or more.

One newly appointed dean prepared a table showing the standing committees and bodies of which he was a member or was expected to attend on occasions, and the frequency of the meetings held over 12 months. Committees under the aegis of the regional health authority of which he was a member (and often the chairman) numbered ten and he might be asked to attend meetings of another committee. University committees numbered eight, and the total number of scheduled meetings of the combined regional/university bodies exceeded 80, which is equivalent to nearly two per week over a working year. In addition the dean was a member of national bodies such as the Advisory Committee of Deans of the Council for Postgraduate Medical Education in England and Wales, the Conference of Postgraduate Medical Deans and Directors of the Universities of the United Kingdom, and committees of his own royal college. Other deans are on various other national bodies including the General Medical Council. The list took no account, of course, of membership of any ad hoc working groups, visits made to inspect pre-registration HO posts, meetings with visitors who are inspecting regional training posts, counselling senior registrars and trainees in other grades, and general day-to-day activities. Moreover, new responsibilities are continually being added to remit of the deans. In 1985, for example, the DHSS issued a memorandum on the hours of work of junior hospital staff (PM(85)1). It recommended that each regional health authority should establish a panel consisting of, amongst others, the postgraduate dean (or deputy) to make recommendations to district health authorities on rota arrangements and to hear cases of grievance from individual staff members.[64] At the end of 1985, regional health authorities were advised to establish a regional mechanism for the purpose of allocating regional quotas of senior registrar posts that may be set by the newly established Joint Planning Advisory Committee[40] (page 61). Again the deans will be involved. If the recommendation from the ministerial working group (which reported in mid 1986[299]) that registrar posts be divided into regional and district posts, is implemented, this will mean even more work.

The level of administrative support available to the deans and regional advisers in general practice varies according to the range of administrative functions carried out by the postgraduate office and the general policy of the local university or regional health authority towards providing secretarial staff. Among the administrative functions that are not performed by all regional offices are overseeing the placement of newly-qualified doctors in house officer posts and monitoring their progress through the pre-registration year (see pages 187-188), administering fully both the section 63 courses for general practitioners and vocational trainees and the budget for the courses on behalf of the university (pages 210-213), and servicing meetings held by the regional postgraduate medical education committee, the pre-registration committee, the specialty training committees, and so forth. The impression gained from visits made to the postgraduate offices is that the relationship between administrative functions performed and staffing levels is weak and that local practice over the financing of the salaries of secretarial and administrative staff by university and regional authorities varies considerably.

Decisions by universities on whether to charge overheads on the regional budget for the postgraduate office which a university administers, and for the maintenance of office accommodation if it is within university premises, are discretionary. (Responsibility for the capital cost of teaching hospital building schemes is apportioned between the NHS and the university concerned according to the Pater Formula devised in 1957. There is not a similar agreement about paying for the running costs of buildings shared by NHS and university departments or for the costs of the integrated teaching hospitals and medical schools which have been built in recent years, although the Royal Commission on the National Health Service noted the need for such a formula (para 17.22).[3]

It is not possible to identify in the published statutory accounts of most regional health authorities the expenditure on study leave expenses of doctors employed by the RHA (hospital consultants, specialists in community medicine, senior registrars and sometimes other trainees), the travel and subsistence expenses of senior staff members when on training visits or at meetings, and the claims of visitors who have inspected regional posts. The payments for hospital medical and dental staff are usually entered on the Administration Account (statement 08) under the general heading of Training and Education (sub code 241). Also entered under this heading are the study leave expenses of non-medical staff. There were, however, at least three exceptions to this practice in 1983/84. North West Thames, South East Thames and Oxford showed study leave expenses for medical and dental staff separately on the Other Services Account. North West Thames spent £57,000 on study leave for medical and dental staff in non-teaching districts who were on the regional pay roll and South East Thames spent £98,000 on this category of staff. Oxford also spent £98,000 but it was from a regionally-managed budget for study leave to which all medical and dental staff employed by the health authorities in the region could apply. The West Midlands RHA has adopted the practice of recharging to the DHAs study leave expenses of RHA employed medical staff along with salary and other expenditures.

### Expenditure of the district and special health authorities

The responses of the treasurers' departments in the teaching districts and special health authorities to the letter asking for a copy of their published accounts were rather surprising. The letters had explained how information was being collected on the expenses of health authorities under the heading Postgraduate Medical and Dental Education (sub code 010) on the Other Services Account for 1983/84. The treasurer's department of one teaching district in South East Thames wrote to say that its accounts did not include an item for postgraduate medical and dental education expenditure because it was an undergraduate teaching authority and another teaching district in the same region did not enter anything under the heading because it did not have a postgraduate teaching hospital. However, the treasurers' or management accounting departments of three special health authorities pointed out that they entered nothing under this heading either. Any relevant expenditure such as study leave was charged to Training and Education (sub code 273) under General Services on the Hospital Services Account (statement 10) – which is a common practice in health districts – or else the costs were borne by the associated postgraduate institute. (The subject of districts' policies for granting study leave and associated expenses is discussed in chapter 15 (page 216).)

An assistant treasurer in a provincial teaching district explained that postgraduate medical training costs were functionally analysed as hospital services and, therefore, had conventionally been merged with other training and educational expenditures. From now on, however, his department would enter them separately on the Other Services Account and he estimated that the sum would be in the region of £70,000. A London teaching district in North West Thames calculated its costs on medical and dental education for 1983/84 as being £65,000, including the running costs of its postgraduate medical centres. Historically the treasurer's department had kept a separate account for medical and dental training although it did not make an entry on the Other Services Account of the published accounts.

Most of the remaining authorities simply forwarded a copy of the 1983/84 published accounts and in two from different regions there was an entry under the heading Postgraduate Medical and Dental Education. One of these two sets of accounts also showed that the health authority had transferred a substantial sum of money to the associated university. Further inquiries confirmed that regional accounting practices do differ on this matter. The majority of district health authorities in the South West Thames and Mersey regions make an entry on the Other Services Account on their annual published accounts and some districts in other regions do the same. However, the actual amounts vary markedly. In South West Thames in 1983/84, for example, the districts' expenditure ranged from less than £4000 in the teaching district to over £40,000 in another London district. Clearly, without having knowledge of local accounting procedures it is not possible to draw any conclusions over the size of the financial contributions made by the health authorities towards postgraduate medical education and training.

# 21    Medical manpower planning

The purpose of writing this book was to describe the organisation of postgraduate education for junior doctors in England and Wales, and to identify the various areas of responsibility and the financial commitments of the government departments, the NHS, the universities, the royal colleges, faculties and higher training committees, and of other bodies – in particular the General Medical Council, the Council for Postgraduate Medical Education for England and Wales and the Medical Research Council. It was never expected at the outset of the writing, however, that it would take 20 chapters to cover these subjects in sufficient depth.

The related subject of medical manpower planning has not been covered in these chapters. Any reorganisation of hospital training grades, for example, would have to be planned within the overall framework of hospital medical staffing, with account being taken of the contribution to clinical practice made by non-medically qualified professional groups. Because these issues are complex it would be appropriate for medical manpower planning to be the subject of a companion book. An account of recently published reports and papers in this field is, however, given in the following pages because the publications raise matters touched on in the preceding chapters.

NATIONAL REPORTS

At the time of writing the most recently published national documents in the field of manpower planning were from the Advisory Committee for Medical Manpower Planning[92] and a working party of the National Association of Health Authorities in England and Wales.[278] Both reports were published in 1985. (The Advisory Committee report was ready for publication a few months before its actual date of publication in March 1985.) Another report published in 1985 was from the Comptroller and Auditor General.[279] During the previous year a team from the National Audit Office had visited four regional health authorities in England and a teaching and non-teaching district in each region, health districts in Wales and health boards in Scotland. Discussions were also held in the appropriate government departments and the views of the Joint Consultants Committee (page 254) were received. The report discussed the national and regional distribution and control of hospital medical manpower, planning mechanisms, the career structure and the system of remuneration. The latest document, published in July 1986, contained a package of integrated proposals from a ministerial working group formed at the end of 1985 (page 310).

The Advisory Committee for Medical Manpower Planning was set up in August 1982 by the health departments in England, Scotland and Northern Ireland and the Welsh Office, with representatives of professional bodies, regional medical officers and the universities appointed to serve on it.[92] The Committee was asked to advise on factors which the government will need to consider when deciding on the future level of student intake to the medical schools in the United Kingdom. Projections were made of the 'supply' of doctors (numbers working or seeking employment) in the United Kingdom over the 30 years to 2010, and the 'demand' (employment opportunities) of health authorities, general medical practice, universities, other public bodies and the private sector over the same period. Factors most likely to affect the supply side were identifed as the annual output of graduates from medical schools, migration rates of UK-born doctors and doctors born outside the United Kingdom, the participation rates of women doctors and the retirement ages of employed doctors.

After considering alternative methods for predicting demand the Advisory Committee concluded that, as for other western nations, it is highly probable that the determinant of demand for medical manpower will continue to be the level of resources available for health care. Moreover, the rates of growth in doctor numbers will be a continuation of the trends in the recent past unless there is a marked change in the availability of resources. The areas of medical practice in which doctors work may, however, differ as patterns of medical care change, and the regional variations in staffing levels (see Figure 5 in chapter 3) may also give rise to different regional patterns of care.

According to the Committee's estimates, if there is a steady fall in the inflow of overseas doctors and the level of intake to the medical schools remains constant at a target of 4230 a year from 1983 onwards*, and the rate of growth in UK job opportunities is less than 1 per cent per annum from 1980 onwards, a considerable oversupply of doctors could result, with the problem being felt most acutely by young trainees. If, however, the demand grows at an average of 1 per cent there will be an apparent surplus of doctors (around 2000 or 1 to 2 per cent of the total number), but the level is not significant given the many uncertainties involved. A growth in demand

---

* Current policy on medical student numbers stems from the recommendation made by the Royal Commission on Medical Education in 1968 that there should be a very significant increase in the annual student intake. The government accepted the recommendation, a long-term target was set and, since then, the annual intakes have gradually increased in size. The policy was endorsed by the Royal Commission on the National Health Service in 1979[3] and by the Medical Manpower Steering Group which was a group set up by the DHSS, the Treasury and the Central Policy Review Staff to look at the supply and demand for medical manpower in relation to the likely availability of resources to the year 2000. It reported in 1980.[280]

of over 1 per cent per annum could lead to shortages of doctors. The future for hospital medical staffing is likely to be particularly difficult. Unless there is a steady increase in the number of hospital career grade posts over the remainder of the present decade, the prospects for junior hospital doctors are discouraging, with excessive lengths of time being spent in training grades and unemployment a possibility. The Advisory Committee believed, therefore, that changes may be needed in the hospital staffing structure and that the subject should receive urgent attention.

There was not a consensus among the members of the Advisory Committee, however, on whether the supply of doctors generally should be regulated by lowering the annual intake of students to the medical schools. Some members, including the majority of those nominated by the professional bodies, were in favour of immediately restricting the intake to less than 4000, which is close to the 1980 level and only 130 fewer than the number actually enrolled in 1983. (It is the policy of the British Medical Association that medical school intake in the United Kingdom should be reduced to the 1979 level in order to prevent an overproduction of doctors in relation to jobs available – refer to the discussion paper Medical manpower in the year 2000.[281] However, the views of the autonomous General Medical Services Committee (page 252) differ on this matter.[282]) Other members of the Advisory Committee – many being representatives of government departments – were not in agreement with the representatives of the professional bodies, even though the size of the suggested reduction of the student intake was little more than fine tuning. They wished to avoid the possibility of a shortage of doctors in the future. This had happened in the 1960s partly because deficiencies in official statistics during the 1950s had obscured the general trends in the supply of doctors (see Stevens[13], pages 244-46). (The national censuses of medical staffing were first held in the early 1960s.) There was general agreement among the members, however, that the level of medical student intake should be reviewed at regular intervals, the next review to take place in about two years time. The Advisory Committee had experienced difficulties also in obtaining adequate data on certain subjects – doctors working outside the NHS, the participation and activity rates of women doctors and, to a lesser extent, migration patterns of both United Kingdom and overseas-born doctors.

The National Association of Health Authorities in England and Wales set up its working party in response to a resolution passed at the Association's 1984 annual general meeting. The resolution expressed the view that medical and dental manpower planning by the DHSS and the development of the consultant grade in particular, should be brought within the framework of mainstream NHS manpower planning.[278] The Working Party concentrated on the difficulties being experienced by health authorities who, at a time of financial restraint, are expected to progress towards providing a hospital service run predominantly by consultants, as recommended by the Social Services Committee of the House of Commons in 1981 (the Short report[4]) but without the full support of the medical profession – at least locally – because of anxieties over the demands that might be made on consultant staff especially if their hours of work were extended. The Working Party was concerned also that medical care is presently being provided by doctors who are either over-trained for the posts they occupy or are undertrained for the work they are doing, and that an (unspecified) number of 'time-expired' junior doctors have no prospect of being appointed as consultants. The lack of opportunities within the present career structure for women doctors who may, in increasing numbers, wish to continue with their clinical careers but not on a full-time basis (or who are unable for domestic reasons to seek employment in other parts of the country where suitable vacancies exist) was also noted. (The policy of allowing unrestricted numbers of women to enrol as medical students was not generally adopted by the medical schools and faculties in the United Kingdom until the mid 1970s. Thus, when the staffing patterns of the NHS were established around 1948, the medical profession was predominantly male and the ratio of men to women doctors was probably not expected to change significantly.)

The NAHA report was much briefer than the report of the Advisory Committee, partly because it did not contain any statistical analyses. The proposals for change listed in the document were developed at meetings of the Working Party – the members of which were lay members of health authorities, and representatives of community medicine, nursing, postgraduate medical education and NHS management – and in discussions held with representatives of the Central Manpower Committee (page 41), the Hospital Junior Staff Committee associated with the BMA (page 254) and individual experts. Some of the proposals were about the planning process. It was suggested, for example, that decision-making over consultant appointments should be greatly devolved to regions and districts, especially as the national difficulties of staffing shortage specialties had nearly been eliminated, but central control over the number of junior training posts should continue. Other proposals were really policy recommendations. If the goal in the longer term is to ensure that a higher proportion of patient care is provided by fully-trained doctors and that doctors spend no longer in training than is necessary then, the Working Party believed, a fundamental review of the medical career structure by representatives of the health services and the medical profession is needed. Urgent consideration should be given to the question of whether there should be a graded career structure with at least two grades of fully-trained staff – both grades having full clinical responsibility for patients but doctors in the lower grades being subject, managerially, to a 'senior specialist' or 'head of service'. The review should also consider whether the system of postgraduate training is meeting the current needs of the health service.[278]

A step has now been taken towards finding solutions to the hospital career structure. In October 1985 the Minister for Health, Mr Barney Hayhoe, wrote to the chairman of the Joint Consultants Committee suggesting that the JCC collaborate in tackling the difficult problem of developing a more rational career structure for doctors in the hospital service. The JCC responded positively to the invitation and a small working group was formed with members representing the JCC, the Central Committee for Hospital Medical Services (page 253), the Hospital Junior Staff Committee, the BMA, the royal colleges and faculties, RHA chairmen, and the health departments. The group met on a monthly basis with the Minister normally chairing the discussions or, in his absence, the Chief Medical Officer of the DHSS. Technical subcommittees were formed to look at specific problems. The working group met for the first time in January 1986[111] and it reported six months later in July.[299] The main recommendations in the report are described on pages 39, 48, 54, 183 and 202.

### REGIONAL AND DISTRICT MEDICAL MANPOWER PLANNING

Regional and district health authorities, including the authorities in Wales, are expected to incorporate in their ten-year strategic plans and short-term operational programmes, objectives for medical and dental staffing in the hospital and community health services, taking account of teaching requirements, available revenue resources, and current government policies on the allocation of career and training posts and priorities for selected care groups such as the mentally ill and the mentally handicapped.

The team from the National Audit Office found on their visits to health authorities in 1984 that the art of medical manpower planning was not very advanced. Only one of the four regional health authorities visited (out of 14) had a long-term medical manpower strategy and had identified the number of consultants likely to be needed over the next ten years. Again, only two of the eight health districts visited in England had drawn up five or ten-year strategies covering medical manpower. The majority had not fully considered manpower implications in their forward planning. One district had, however, begun a programme of examining the health care needs of client groups in the served population and this would enable future doctor requirements to be assessed.[279]

Undoubtedly, one reason regional health authorities have made slow progress in developing medical manpower strategies has been a widespread lack of comprehensive information – held preferably in a computerised database – on the establishment (number and type of posts) in each grade and specialty, district by district. In 1984 only two regions had fully computerised regional establishment files (Trent and South West Thames)[11] but by the beginning of 1985 all other regions were either developing databases or were about to implement plans.[159] The progress made by district health authorities to set up their own establishment files was limited in comparison.

Ad hoc medical manpower studies have been carried out in a few health regions. In the Northern region, the regional specialist in community medicine with responsibility for medical and dental staffing visited the health districts in 1982/83, usually accompanied by the regional postgraduate dean, to collect information on numbers of established posts and sessional commitments and to record the views of representatives of the clinical staff on medical and dental staffing requirements for the next 15 years. Particular attention was paid to consultant requirements. These assessments were based on services needed for patient groups and did not take account of external factors such as the availability of revenue to support the staffing levels or policy guide lines on consultant to trainee staff ratios. The total number of requests for additional consultant posts, excluding posts in dentistry, was 523 and this figure was equivalent to 70 per cent of the whole-time equivalent number which would be created if the recommendation to double the number of consultants by 1996 contained in health circular HC(82)4[25] – which the DHSS issued after the government considered the 1981 Short report[4,24] – was fully implemented in the region. Offsetting the increase in consultant posts would be a reduction in training posts and, depending on assumptions made about the length of postgraduate training, the number of posts lost would be between 282 and 374. The net gain in hospital medical staff (excluding pre-registration house officers, hospital practitioners and clinical assistants) over the 15 years would therefore be between 222 and 314.[283] (If the higher estimate of 314 was realised the average rate of growth would be 1 per cent per annum.)

Sheffield Health Authority has gone a step further in matching staffing requirements to services provided.[284] The district medical officer and a colleague, working under the assumption that the financial resources available for medical staffing will continue to be tightly controlled, developed a district medical staffing model aimed at providing services for patients led by senior staff (consultants and senior registrars). Thus, in outpatient departments, the staffing levels should ensure that all new outpatients are seen by a senior staff member, and all inpatients should be seen by senior staff within 48 hours of admission but preferably within 24 hours. Formulae for the acute clinical specialties were developed taking account of the bed utilisation rates, on-call rota commitments, the special attributes of Sheffield as a teaching district, and doctor-related variables such as time spent in training grades and the retirement ages of consultants. Using the model, Todd and Coyne calculated what the staffing levels in the main clinical specialties ought to be if outpatient and inpatient standards of service are to be met.

Taking the four specialties of general medicine, paediatrics, general surgery and obstetrics and gynaecology together, the model proposed that the total number of posts be virtually unchanged but the number of consultants posts should be increased from 58 to 71.5 with each specialty receiving new posts. The total number of senior registrar posts would remain almost the same but with small losses and gains among the specialties. The total number of SHO posts would, likewise, remain almost the same, although obstetrics and gynaecology would lose five posts (out of 19 posts) and general surgery and general medicine would gain three to four posts each. The largest losses were proposed for the registrar grade – 31 posts across the four specialties would be reduced to 15 with general medicine and general surgery bearing most of the losses. To offset the squeeze on the middle training grade, the health authority was considering whether, for planning purposes, it should treat the normal duration of experience in the SHO grade as being longer than the ideal duration (of about two years). The staffing figures for specialties derived from the model were issued to the appropriate divisions for discussion and at least one, the surgical division, was willing both to accept the offer of more consultants in general surgery and to discuss the numbers and grades of junior staff.[284] If the revised staffing levels for the four specialties were introduced in the Sheffield district, the content of the training in the junior grades would probably be altered.

MANPOWER PLANNING BY THE ROYAL COLLEGES, FACULTIES AND SOCIETIES FOR THE SPECIALTIES

Historically the royal colleges have not seriously concerned themselves with manpower matters. The position changed, however, during the 1970s. The Royal College of Surgeons of England in its first report on surgical manpower and the career structure explained the reason why its Council decided in 1979 to set up a college committee on career structure.

> 'It is no longer possible for the College, as an educational body intimately concerned with the training of surgeons since the establishment of its Fellowship in 1843, to take the once prevalent view that its role is exclusively that of setting and maintaining standards while others have the responsibility of controlling manpower and devising a career structure. It is admittedly true that so far the Royal Colleges have had very little power to affect decisions on manpower planning or career structure, but unless their views are formalised and made known, decisions will continue to be taken without the important and often unique information that the Colleges and their Joint Committees on Higher Training have at their disposal.' (page 1)[285]

This report was followed by a second on the same subject in 1982[286], the preparation of which had been triggered by the publication of the Short report with a recommendation that the imbalance in the ratio of consultants to junior doctors be substantially reduced[4] and by the support given to the recommendation by the government.

The first comprehensive report on manpower from the Royal College of Physicians in London (published in 1977) was almost ahead of its time.[287] It admitted that no longer were specialty committees of the College being realistic in urging the creation of more training and consultant posts whenever a new development in their field of medicine was being promoted. The constraints were both an inadequate supply of doctors and the financial constrigencies operating in the health service. (The Resource Allocation Working Party's formula (RAWP) for redistributing resources among the health regions[248] was adopted by the government around the time that the Standing Committee of Members of the College was drafting the document.) Contained in the report was a critical review of the type of work conventionally carried out by hospital medical staff and a discussion of whether some of it could be performed instead by general practitioners or by non-medically qualified staff. The report asked also whether consultants could not liaise more flexibly with consultant colleagues over resources and, likewise, be more flexible in their approach towards the working arrangements of their junior staff. Among the conclusions reached was that the hospital career structure needed to take account of current views on postgraduate training, and that the deployment of medical manpower should be appropriate to the different needs of individual specialties.

The Royal College of Physicians subsequently set up a manpower advisory panel and, with the encouragement of the Joint Consultants Committee, the other colleges have tended to follow suit. The manpower advisory panels or committees have prepared papers or reports on two subject areas. One has been college policy on the staffing of specialties. The two reports of the Royal College of Surgeons[285,286] are examples and the 1983 report of the manpower advisory subcommittee of the Royal College of Obstetricians and Gynaecologists.[288] In psychiatry the author of a report to the Royal College of Psychiatrists on the future of the consultant in psychiatry was the then president, Professor K Rawnsley.[289] The report expressed the view endorsed by the Council, that the College should prepare for an increase in the proportion of hospitals and units working without trainees. The Royal College of Pathologists has issued guidance on the staffing and management of NHS pathology departments.[290,291]

The other college documents have reported findings from surveys of college members or, as happened in obstetrics and gynaecology in 1982, from a survey of junior doctors (SHOs) working in the specialty in the United Kingdom.[292] For colleges which cover more than one specialty these surveys have usually been carried out by the advisory committee responsible for each specialty or by another agent on behalf of the advisory committee, perhaps the society for the specialty or an academic research team. The purpose of the surveys has been to collect information on the working patterns of senior staff and to work out what should be the appropriate staffing level or target for the specialty (usually expressed in terms of consultants per 100,000 population). Papers giving results of such surveys are normally published in the appropriate college journal or in the journal for the specialty. Four examples are the report on the survey of pathologists practising cytopathology in the *Bulletin of the Royal College of Pathologists*[293], a report from a survey of general physicians in the *British Medical Journal*[294], a report on the third biennial survey of cardiologists and physicians with a special interest in cardiology in the *British Heart Journal*[295] and a survey of physicians with a special interest in gastroenterology in the journal *Gut*.[296]

The Faculty of Anaesthetists intends to become even more involved in medical manpower matters. It has developed a system to record information on the recruitment of doctors to the specialty designed along the lines of the system known as 'fields of recruitment' for hospital specialties which the DHSS ran for many years until 1982/83 (page 59). Faculty assessors who represent the Faculty on consultant and senior registrar appointment committees throughout the United Kingdom have been asked to provide factual information on successful and unsuccessful candidates applying for posts in these two grades. The exercise began on 1 October 1985 and the information is held centrally in the offices of the Faculty of Anaesthetists. Since the Joint Committee for Higher Training of Anaesthetists is concerned with senior registrar training programmes in the Republic of Ireland as well as in the United Kingdom, permission has been sought from Irish authorities to extend the information collection exercise to the Republic. (Professor M Vickers and Mr S Alan, personal communication 1986).

# 22 Review and proposals

The main suppliers of postgraduate medical education in organisational terms are the triumvirate of the health service, the universities and the royal colleges and faculties. In the view of one regional postgraduate dean, Professor N Kessel, the universities are currently the weak link and it will be a tragedy if they cannot play their part in the future.[297] But his suggestion that the universities try to generate additional income to help offset the cuts in government funding for university education by organising comprehensive postgraduate courses for regional trainees with reasonable fees being charged, might not be received sympathetically by health authorities who are themselves financially very constrained. In 1985, for example, district health authorities received no additional revenue to cover the annual salary awards of medical and dental staff which exceeded the general pay limit set by the government and the exceptional awards made to nurses and the professions allied to medicine to compensate for an erosion in their earnings over recent years. Moreover, because of the retrenchment in academic staffing levels, universities are unlikely to have sufficient spare teaching capacity to develop courses, and finance to employ additional staff is going to be restricted at least until the end of the decade. Also, it is questionable whether academic departments can provide the breadth of teaching needed by trainees in some hospital specialties whose careers will be spent providing district-based services but without the technological back-up and other specialised resources found in teaching hospitals.

In the same paper, Kessel expressed impatience over the apparent lack of direction in academic medicine (undergraduate teaching, postgraduate teaching and training, and academic clinical medicine and research) and these views are probably shared by others.

'A large number of national bodies discuss academic medicine: medical sub-committees of the UGC and the Committee of Vice-chancellors and Principals, the metropolitan and provincial committees of undergraduate medical deans, the committee of postgraduate deans, the Council for Postgraduate Medical Education, the Federation of Associations of Clinical Professors, the academic staff committee of the British Medical Association, the Association for the Study of Medical Education, and, vicariously, the education committee of the GMC. None is effective. Because each leaves it to the others, is above the battle, too partial, too official or too weak, each lacks the resolve. That must come from within academic medicine.' (page 901)[297]

The reception given to the proposals in the discussion document 'Basic specialist training'[6] from the Education Committee of the General Medical Council aptly illustrates Kessel's point. Under the 1978 Medical Act the Education Committee was given the statutory autonomous responsibility for coordinating all stages of medical education and for ensuring that standards are high. After receiving guidance from the profession in 1982 on subject areas deserving the Committee's earliest attention, the Committee prepared the document on basic specialist training which embodies the notion that the years immediately after full registration should be a time for understanding the broad base of many diseases and disabilities and for appreciating the importance of being able to communicate with patients and colleagues. The Committee was concerned that many hospital doctors are starting to specialise very early in their careers, even though the regulations for higher qualifying examinations for membership or fellowship of the royal colleges and faculties permit candidates to spend time in other disciplines. If the Committee's proposals (which are described in greater detail on pages 37-39) were to be implemented, they would require training programmes being developed for hospital doctors in the SHO grade along the lines of the schemes for vocational training for general practice.

The document on basic specialist training was circulated to bodies associated with medical education and training and written comments were submitted to the Education Committee. On the whole the proposals were welcomed, provided they reflected a non-mandatory development. The Committee had to accept that proposals of this kind will not become effective unless the regulations for higher qualifying examinations are modified to require all candidates to have experience of another discipline and there is a change in the discouraging attitudes of some appointment committees towards applicants with broadly-based experience.

REGIONS TO INSPECT GENERAL PROFESSIONAL TRAINING POSTS?

One area of postgraduate education for which the universities in association with the health authorities could quite properly assume responsibility is the inspection and approval of hospital training posts for general professional training. When the idea of inspecting training posts was being generally discussed by the royal colleges and newly established joint committees on higher training in the early 1970s, the Council for Postgraduate Medical Education in England and Wales and the then Secretary of State for Social Services felt that in the interests of medical practice these autonomous collegiate bodies should be encouraged to assume the role rather than the health authorities, and government grants-in-aid were introduced to assist the colleges financially. Over the years systems of inspection have been developed, most being based on a five-year cycle of inspections. Seven joint committees on higher training or equivalent college committees are responsible for over 3100 senior registrar medical posts in England and Wales (including those covered by the schemes in psychiatry) and the 16,400 registrar and SHO medical posts are overseen by eight royal colleges and faculties (including the Royal College of General Practitioners in association with the Royal College of Physicians (London)). It is the responsibility for this second very large group of posts which should, in due course, be transferred to the regions.

The effort made by the colleges in setting up the systems ought not to be under-estimated especially when the numbers of posts and hospitals in England and Wales are considered. The Royal College of Physicians in London administers a system covering 5000 posts and the system of the Royal College of Surgeons of England is of a similar size, although it includes posts in hospitals in some overseas countries. The administrative procedures of the colleges' systems are not, however, uniform. Policies vary over the identity of officers to whom final reports on visits or letters containing recommendations should be sent, and not every college ensures that a copy is sent to the district medical officer or the district general manager in the appropriate health authorities. (The policies of some approval bodies were developed in the light of discussions at meetings held under the auspices of the Council for Postgraduate Medical Education in England and Wales.) Inadequacies in communication arrangements can quite easily be overcome, however, given the will.

Disappointment has been expressed that visitors when inspecting posts in hospitals sometimes make recommendations for upgrading the services or increasing the establishment of posts which are not in accordance with the district's operational programme or are unattainable goals for financial reasons. Visitors have also been criticised occasionally for not recommending the withdrawal of approval from posts in which previous holders have had very poor examination successes or which tend to be filled by doctors who have been in the grade for a number of years. If the visitors were thoroughly briefed on every occasion, these criticisms could also be overcome. (The forms completed by hospitals when visits are being arranged often do not include questions on the professional achievements of post holders past or present.)

All health authorities in England and Wales are expected to incorporate objectives for hospital staffing in their ten-year strategic plans and short-term operational programmes, taking account of available revenue resources and current government policies on the allocation of career and training posts and priorities for selected care groups. A planning model developed in the Sheffield Health Authority to determine the ratios of career posts to training posts needed in the acute specialties if the services are to be led by senior clinicians showed that the numbers of registrar posts in general medicine and general surgery would be reduced by over 60 per cent, with some compensating increases in the SHO grade, and that obstetrics and gynaecology would lose five out of 19 SHO posts (page 311). If the Sheffield Health Authority implemented plans along these lines, the content of the training offered in the registrar and SHO posts in the acute specialties would be altered and training in associated specialties such as anaesthetics might also be affected. Other districts are starting to review their staffing patterns in a similar manner, and regional health authorities now want to impose tighter controls on the numbers and distribution of training posts. Moreover, it has been recommended by a ministerial working group that from 1987 registrar posts be divided into regional posts (with contracts held at region) for doctors eligible to seek a consultant career, and district posts (with contracts held at district) for training overseas doctors.[299] If these activities become commonplace, then the colleges' five-year cycles of visits (or four-years in psychiatry) will not be sufficiently frequent to monitor the effects of the changes. Ad hoc visits to hospitals can be arranged, but if many districts were to reorganise their staffing patterns they would generate an extra administrative load for the secretariats of the college training committees and practising clinicians on the panels of visitors would have to spend even more of their time on this activity. (Employing authorities grant special leave to consultant staff when they are engaged on college training activities.)

The way around the difficulty would be to transfer the responsibility for approving general professional training posts to the regional postgraduate medical education committees which are joint university/health service bodies. In Scotland the regional postgraduate committees already perform this function and the monitoring of community medicine registrar and SHO posts in England is done regionally by the subcommittee for community medicine of each RPGMEC in association with the regional faculty adviser. In most of the 14 regions and Wales, the necessary infrastructure already exists or is being developed with the setting up of specialty subcommittees of the RPGMECs. In a few regions specialty subcommittees in the diagnostic disciplines, anaesthetics and obstetrics and gynaecology, are currently monitoring standards of general professional training. Information databases on training posts are also being assembled by the regional health authorities with the help of the regional postgraduate deans' offices and the district health authorities.

The regional postgraduate medical education committees and their specialty subcommittees would be well positioned to devise or oversee the development of district-based programmes of general training incorporating approved posts in specialties which are complementary but within different disciplines and covered by different royal colleges and faculties. In association with district health authorities they could also organise specialist training programmes incorporating NHS-established or supernumerary training posts for overseas qualified doctors who enter the country independently or under sponsorship.

Naturally, there would be administrative costs falling on the regional authorities but these should not be substantial. The actual expenditure by the royal colleges and faculties on existing systems for approving general training posts, including dental posts in hospitals, was £124,250 in 1984/85 (see page 293). If this figure was shared instead among the 14 regional health authorities of England and the health authorities of Wales on behalf of the RPGMECs, the regional expenditure (calculated on a per post basis for both NHS-established and honorary posts) could range from £4500 in East Anglia to £12,000 in North East Thames. If the RPGMECs in North East Thames, North West Thames and South East Thames assumed responsibility for inspecting posts in the special health authorities within their region, the administrative costs would be correspondingly higher.

Undoubtedly, reluctance will be shown by some if not all the collegiate bodies to such a proposal. One reason is that candidates for the great majority of the higher qualifying examinations administered by the colleges are expected to have trained in posts which have been approved by college representatives (Table 31, page 124). The MRCP(UK) is the only college membership qualification for hospital disciplines that does not have this requirement. The Royal Colleges of Physicians rely instead on written statements about the candidates' experience from proposers (of eight or more years standing as college members or fellows). The close involvement of the college or faculty regional advisers in the work of the specialty subcommittees of the RPGMECs should ensure, however, that the standards of training established by these educational bodies are respected. If there were still fears that regional inspectors might not be able to report impartially on all occasions, partly because of their employee status with the regional health authority, the colleges could request that a college representative from another region be appointed to each team of visitors. If the colleges wished to keep their own files on posts or schemes up to date, they could be supplied with copies of reports on visits of inspection. They would also be in the position to monitor regional standards by comparing the examination success rates of candidates from the different regions.

Objections to the proposal might also be voiced by some regional postgraduate deans on the grounds that education and training is their responsibility and medical manpower matters are outside this remit. However, the person with the greatest responsibility for medical manpower planning would remain a health service appointment – a regional specialist in community medicine or the regional medical officer or director according to the management arrangements in the individual regions. It is worth noting that the Social Services Committee of the House of Commons in its 1985 follow-up report on medical education recommended a greater degree of involvement of postgraduate deans in the formal mechanisms of regional manpower planning (para 55).[5]

The transference of the responsibility from colleges and faculties to regional postgraduate medical education committees would need to be carefully planned. Each region and Wales would have to complete the organisation of its own approval machinery and finish setting up an information database on its establishment of general training posts. The appropriate central body to oversee the preparatory arrangements would be the Council for Postgraduate Medical Education for England and Wales whose membership, as constituted in mid 1986, includes representatives of the royal colleges and faculties, the National Health Service and the universities. The Council, however, may wish to delegate the task to a standing committee or an ad hoc committee set up for the purpose. Naturally, the Education Committee of the General Medical Council – which has the statutory responsibility for coordinating all stages of medical education – would have to endorse the proposal. The transference of approval responsibility should not cause any practical difficulties over registration. The Council already accepts, for the purpose of limited registration, employment in hospitals or posts in hospitals or institutions which are educationally approved by a regional postgraduate committee (as happens in Scotland) as well as by a royal college or faculty. The proposal would also have to be acceptable to the Secretary of State for Social Services for statutory reasons. Under the National Health Service (vocational training) regulations for England and Wales, posts selected by regional postgraduate medical education committees for training for a certificate of prescribed experience must be 'approved for the purposes of training in a hospital specialty or in the specialty of community medicine by the Royal College or Faculty for that specialty'.[161] So if the RPGMECs were to take over responsibility for assessing the educational status of hospital posts for specialty training, the regulations would have to be revised accordingly.

DEMAND FOR, AND SUPPLY OF, POSTGRADUATE MEDICAL EDUCATION
AND TRAINING

The chapters of this book have been organised within a 'demand' and 'supply' framework. The demand for postgraduate medical education and training comes primarily from the largest employer, the National Health Service, and from trainees who wish to follow careers in the hospital service, general medical practice or community medicine. The demand for training in occupational medicine and in the armed services has not been overlooked. The NHS also appears on the supply side, together with the universities, royal college and faculties and higher training committees and the medical research bodies. The DHSS and the Welsh Office cover the funding for training for general medical practice in England and Wales. The General Medical Council has statutory powers to regulate educational standards and the Council for Postgraduate Medical Education in England and Wales has the responsibility of providing the government with an authorative source of advice on education and training matters.

The question which must be considered now is whether the supply side is meeting the demand being generated by the health service and by the trainees themselves. If, in the hospital service, the aim of the postgraduate education and training system is to produce sufficient fully-trained doctors to fill the available vacant hospital consultant posts – which number approximately 700 in England and Wales each year – then the system is working reasonably well. In 1984/85, the Central Manpower Committee only restricted the advertising of new consultant posts in mental handicap. In previous years there had been shortages of trained senior registrar candidates in many specialties, notably in the disciplines of psychiatry, pathology and radiology, and in geriatric medicine. In the 'popular' specialties of medicine and surgery, however, there is an oversupply of fully trained candidates.

A mechanism to regulate the flow of suitable candidates was introduced in 1985: the Joint Planning Advisory Committee will set national targets and regional quotas on the number of senior registrar posts (NHS-established posts and posts for honorary contract holders) in the main specialty groups. In the future it will probably do the same for registrar posts (page 61). One effect of this policy, unfortunately, might be the creation of a new crisis point at the junction between the registrar and senior registrar grades, or between the registrar and SHO grades when registrar numbers are eventually tailored to senior registrar training opportunities, unless career opportunities are greatly expanded.

The health service as represented by the National Association of Health Authorities in England and Wales is worried about both the restricted career prospects of trainees and the problems of trying to provide services led by fully trained doctors. NAHA would like urgent consideration to be given to the question of whether a graded career structure should be created with at least two grades of fully trained staff, each having full clinical responsibility for patients but with one being subject 'managerially' to the other.[278] The professional bodies do not accept the idea that there should be a two-tier consultant grade, partly on grounds of impracticability, or a sub-consultant grade below the consultant grade. When the Social Services Committee of the House of Commons was considering the subject of medical education in March 1985, the deputy chairman of the Central Committee for Hospital Medical Services was asked the reactions of consultants to proposals for a sub-consultant grade.

> 'We think it is wrong to train a junior to consultant level and put him in a sub-consultant grade and pay him a sub-consultant salary. That would appeal to the Health Authorities but it is unfair on the junior. If he has the capabilities and the desire to be a consultant, then he should be appointed a consultant.' (page 14)[5]

The 1986 ministerial working group recommended instead that a new non-training intermediate level grade be introduced. Doctors would enter it after completing their SHO experience. Strict regional manpower controls and central monitoring would ensure that growth in the size of the grade would be gradual and in the longer term, the numbers would not exceed 10 per cent of the numbers of consultants. New clinical assistant appointments of six sessions or more would no longer be made.[299]

Turning to the hospital trainees: how successful is the postgraduate medical education and training system in meeting their individual requirements in the mid 1980s? For the 2300 senior registrars with full-time NHS contracts in England and Wales the system is generally working well although there is a duplication of effort by some regional and collegiate training committees. Relatively few of these doctors fail to become accredited or complete the higher qualifying examinations in pathology and the reasons for failure are usually personal. (There is no equivalent 'mechanism' for judging when trainees in psychiatry have completed their training.) Thus the problems surrounding full-time NHS senior registrars who are time-expired are caused mainly by shortages of career opportunities rather than inadequate training. Reports from part-time trainees – nearly all of whom are women – suggest, however, that further attention should be given to the training programmes and career opportunities for senior registrars holding part-time contracts. (There were nearly 300 men and women in NHS part-time posts in England and Wales in 1984.) The same point can be made about the training programmes of many of the 600 doctors with honorary senior registrar contracts.

Training in the pre-registration year is also closely regulated and relatively few of the annual number of 2950 house officers in England and Wales do not become fully registered after one year by submitting a certificate of experience to the General Medical Council. A certificate of experience is granted by the university of the trainees after they have presented certificates of satisfactory service issued by the health authorities for each house officer posts held and which together provide an acceptable pattern of experience. There are not, however, guide lines on how the term 'satisfactory service' should be interpreted. The Education Committee of the GMC is now looking at general clinical training provided in the pre-registration year with a view to broadening the content.

For the 6150 doctors in the registrar grade in England and Wales and the 10,250 in the SHO grade the situation is very different. Probably no more than 1000 to 1500 of the 5450 NHS-employed registrars working full-time are covered by some form of regional system which routinely monitors their progress; the number of senior house officers that are covered – excluding those in the hospital phase of vocational training schemes – is no greater. For the great majority of doctors, therefore, no information is held in the regions on their educational attainments and training experience. South

West Thames is an exception: the regional health authority maintains a computerised information system which covers all post-registration trainees; the office of the regional postgraduate dean in the North Western region was establishing a similar computerised system in 1985.

The information recorded annually in the DHSS 30 September census of hospital medical staff is, naturally, restricted in scope. Moreover, it is not comprehensive in the coverage of doctors holding honorary contracts. The 1984 census did show, however, that four years or more had passed since 1006 or 16 per cent of all registrars had first entered the grade. (Their first job might have been as a locum.) The number of senior house officers in this position was 1354, or 13 per cent of the total, and these numbers and percentages in the two grades were the highest recorded in 15 years. Doctors born overseas were noticeably more likely to be time-expired in the two grades than doctors born in Britain. Overseas-born registrars and senior house officers were also noticeably over-represented in the geriatric specialty and, for registrars, in the psychiatric and obstetrics and gynaecology specialties. Senior house officers from overseas were more likely to enter the surgical and anaesthetics specialties.

What the census data cannot show, however, is whether time-expired doctors in these grades hold a royal college or university higher qualification or have passed the first examination for membership or fellowship of a college. Without information on their examination performances, it is not possible to judge whether they have failed to pass out of each grade because of a scarcity of vacant posts in the higher grade or because they are educationally ill-equipped for promotion. (Examination performance is not, of course, the sole criterion for judging whether a person is deserving of promotion.) Information on education attainment can be collected in two ways: from the royal colleges and faculties which administer the higher qualifying examinations, and from the trainees themselves.

The collegiate bodies are protective of their information. Lists of candidates who have passed the final examination for membership or fellowship or have been admitted as fellows to a college as a consequence of passing a final examination are published in the colleges' journals, with the exception of the passes for the MRCP(UK). The lists – including ones for the MRCP(UK) – are frequently supplied to the *British Medical Journal* for publication but they are not in a format which enables analyses to be easily done. Information on successes in the part 1 or primary examinations for membership or fellowship is less readily available. The Royal Colleges of Physicians do not even make public the percentage pass rates for the two parts of the MRCP(UK).

Trainees are not obliged to inform their employing authority of the outcome of any examinations they sit, even though the authority may have granted weeks of study leave for the purpose and paid for course fees and travel and subsistence expenses but not examination fees. Clinical tutors – who are university appointments – are beginning to hold the districts' study leave budgets for hospital medical and dental staff, and in certain districts the tutors are expected to counter-sign study leave application forms. It would be appropriate, therefore, for the tutors to record the examination results of those who are granted study leave for this purpose. They could then give advice to trainees who are not progressing by passing examinations and any others who are not even studying for examinations. Alternatively, they could refer the matter to the trainees' consultant supervisor. (Professor P Rhodes in his proposed school of graduate medicine for the Wessex region saw one of the first tasks of the clinical tutors to be the compilation of a record on junior and other staff in the districts.[298]) The information on examination performances collected by each tutor could be used also to assess the 'outcome' of the district's expenditure on study leave and, if aggregated with the results from other districts, it could be used to evaluate the regional courses provided by the universities and teaching hospitals. It is worth noting that these suggestions for monitoring progress are broadly in accordance with a recommendation from the ministerial working group that all senior house officers should receive formal careers counselling shortly after entering the grade and regularly thereafter.[299] There was no suggestion, however, as to who would be responsible for the counselling.

Naturally, the administrative load of the clinical tutors and their secretarial staff will increase if they undertake routine assessments of individual trainees. It is not possible to estimate the level of additional costs of providing sufficient administrative backup that would be borne by the district health authorities because information on their current expenditure on postgraduate medical education and training is not available. Clinical tutors are practising clinicians and they receive an annual honorarium of up to £1105 (in April 1986) which is provided by the regional health authorities. It would be appropriate for the honoraria payments to be raised to compensate for any additional work carried out by the tutors, most of whom are already engaged in organising local educational programmes of courses and meetings and overseeing the running of the postgraduate centres, and in liaising with the general practitioner course organisers over section 63 courses and the vocational training schemes. (Course organisers receive a personal grant of £3340 per annum but the cost of this grant is covered by the DHSS.) If the regional postgraduate medical education committees wanted to establish a regional information system covering district-employed trainees (similar to the MEDICS system in South West Thames), this would be another administrative task for the health authorities and possibly a financial charge.

If the regional health authorities offered resistance to proposals which required their budgets for postgraduate medical education to be increased, it would be understandable in view of their present economic circumstances. It cannot be said, however, that the level of their current expenditure is particularly high. For example, the combined expenditure of the four Thames regional health authorities on the offices of the regional postgraduate deans in 1983/84 (salaries, honoraria, accommodation, travel and subsistence, and so forth) was approximately £950,000 (page 300). This was equivalent to about £162 per hospital post-registration medical trainee, hospital dental trainee and trainee in community medicine. Moreover, the expenditure in North West Thames and South East Thames was only 1 per cent of the cash limited revenue budget allocated to each of the two regional health authorities by the DHSS for the authorities' own services.[271,272] It should be noted though, that for community medicine, the regional health authorities in England took over financial responsibility for education and training when the DHSS between 1983 and 1986 withdrew its support from the educational programmes developed by the three consortia of health regions. (There are fewer than 300 trainees in this specialty in England and Wales.)

The funding of training for general medical practice is on a very different scale. Expenditure on grants for course organisers and trainers in England was in the order of £6.6 million in 1985/86, equivalent to £3900 for each new fully-trained doctor. To this overall figure must be added the proportion of the combined budget of £2.1 million for section 63 courses and travel and subsistence that was spent on trainees rather than on general practitioner principals and assistants. If the amount was as much as a quarter[194] the overall cost per trainee, excluding his or her salary and allowances and reimbursements for personal and practice expenses, was over £4000. Account should also be taken of the DHSS grant-in-aid to the Joint Committee for Postgraduate Training in General Practice negotiated through the Council for Postgraduate Medical Education in England and Wales and the separate grant made to the Joint Committee for carrying out statutory responsibilities (page 287). If an equivalent annual amount of £4000 per trainee was spent in England on NHS-employed post-registration medical trainees, and dental trainees working in the hospital service, the total budget would be in the order of £72 million.

The system for training doctors for general medical practice was developed in accordance with certain tenets: the content of the training should be closely defined, trainees should be supervised, and the experience gained should be assessed and be found to be satisfactory. Whether the relatively high annual cost of operating this model is fully justifiable is a difficult question that has never been explored systematically.

Postgraduate deans are exhorted regularly to provide career guidance for trainees. A recent example was in the 1985 follow-up report on medical education from the Social Services Committee.

'We recommend that Postgraduate and Undergraduate Deans should intensify their efforts to provide realistic career advice to medical students and trainee doctors...'(para 55)[5]

The 1986 ministerial working group also believed that health authorities, with professional advice, should review the position of doctors now in the training grades who are judged unlikely to make any further career progress, and arrange for them to receive suitable careers counselling.[299]

The postgraduate deans tend to receive such directives with an air of resignation. The return on time spent in counselling and career guidance is, on the whole, relatively low as one dean explained in an interview for the study on the feasibility of a national information system for hospital training posts and trainees[11]:

'This business of career advice is the most illusive thing. It is very emotive. Everybody says "Nobody gives it. The dean should give it, the medical school should give it and they don't." We have career fairs and try to give out information . . . But people coming to you for career advice don't really want advice, they want a job.'

A proportion of those wanting a job in the hospital service wish to train in oversubscribed specialties. Increasing numbers of men and women are, however, seeking long-term employment which is commensurate with their level of training and their ability to work on a full-time or part-time basis. Until there is an expansion in career opportunities in this service any new investment in the postgraduate education system is not going to benefit the trainees greatly. For the 'suppliers' of education and training the task of highest priority must be, therefore, to collaborate with the government and the professional bodies in developing a new career and training grade structure for the hospital service. Since the number of doctors in training posts in England and Wales is so large, there may be merit in testing the feasibility of any new grades or other proposals in one or two regions before implementing policy nationally.

# Abbreviations

| | |
|---|---|
| AAC | advisory appointments committee |
| AFOM | Associateship of the Faculty of Occupational Medicine |
| AHA | area health authority |
| AHA(T) | area health authority (teaching) |
| BMA | British Medical Association |
| BPMF | British Postgraduate Medical Federation |
| CCCMCH | Central Committee for Community Medicine and Community Health |
| CCHMS | Central Committee for Hospital Medical Services |
| CMC | Central Manpower Committee |
| CPME | Council for Postgraduate Medical Education in England and Wales |
| CRF | Cancer Research Fund |
| CVCP | Committee of Vice-Chancellors and Principals of the Universities of the United Kingdom |
| DA(UK) | Diploma in Anaesthetics of the United Kingdom |
| DCH | Diploma in Child Health |
| DES | Department of Education and Science |
| DHA | district health authority |
| DHSS | Department of Health and Social Security |
| DMO | district medical officer |
| DRCOG | Diploma of the Royal College of Obstetricians and Gynaecologists |
| EEC | European Economic Community |
| ENT | ear, nose and throat (otolaryngology) |
| FA | Faculty of Anaesthetists |
| FCM | Faculty of Community Medicine |
| FFARCS(Eng) | Fellowship of the Faculty of Anaesthetists of the Royal College of Surgeons of England |
| FOM | Faculty of Occupational Medicine |
| FPC | family practitioner committee |
| FRCR | Fellowship of the Royal College of Radiologists |
| FRCS(Eng) | Fellowship of the Royal College of Surgeons of England |
| GLC | Greater London Council |
| GMC | General Medical Council |
| GMSC | General Medical Services Committee |

| | |
|---|---|
| GP | general practitioner |
| GPT | general professional training |
| HA | health authority |
| HJSC | Hospital Junior Staff Committee |
| HM | Her Majesty's |
| HO | house officer |
| HTC | higher training committee |
| ICRF | Imperial Cancer Research Fund |
| JACSR | joint advisory committee for senior registrars |
| JCC | Joint Consultants Committee |
| JCHT | joint committee on higher training |
| JCHMT | Joint Committee on Higher Medical Training |
| JCHPsychT | Joint Committee on Higher Psychiatric Training |
| JCHST | Joint Committee on Higher Surgical Training |
| JCHTA | Joint Committee for Higher Training of Anaesthetists |
| JCPTGP | Joint Committee on Postgraduate Training for General Practice |
| JHMO | junior hospital medical officer |
| JPAC | Joint Planning Advisory Committee |
| LMC | local medical committee |
| LPGTH | London postgraduate teaching hospital |
| MAS | Manpower Advisory Service |
| MCQ | multiple choice questionnaire |
| MD | doctor of medicine |
| MFCM | Membership of the Faculty of Community Medicine |
| MFOM | Membership of the Faculty of Occupational Medicine |
| MRC | Medical Research Council |
| MRCGP | Membership of the Royal College of General Practitioners |
| MRCOG | Membership of the Royal College of Obstetricians and Gynaecologists |
| MRCP(London) | Membership of the Royal College of Physicians (London) |
| MRCP(UK) | Membership of the Royal Colleges of Physicians of the United Kingdom |
| MRCPath | Membership of the Royal College of Pathologists |
| MRCPsych | Membership of the Royal College of Psychiatrists |
| MSc | master of science |
| NAC | National Advice Centre |
| NAHA | National Association of Health Authorities in England and Wales |
| NHS | National Health Service |
| ODA | Overseas Development Administration |

| | |
|---|---|
| OME | Office of Manpower Economics |
| OMP | ophthalmic medical practitioner |
| OPCS | Office of Population Censuses and Surveys |
| PhD | doctor of philosophy |
| PHLS | Public Health Laboratory Service |
| PLAB | Professional Linguistics Assessment Board |
| RAMC | Royal Army Medical Corps |
| RAWP | Resource Allocation Working Party |
| RCGP | Royal College of General Practitioners |
| RCOG | Royal College of Obstetricians and Gynaecologists |
| RCP(London) | Royal College of Physicians (London) |
| RCsP(UK) | Royal Colleges of Physicians of the United Kingdom |
| RCPath | Royal College of Pathologists |
| RCPsych | Royal College of Psychiatrists |
| RCR | Royal College of Radiologists |
| RCS(Eng) | Royal College of Surgeons of England |
| RHA | regional health authority |
| RMAC | regional medical advisory committee |
| RMC | regional manpower committee |
| RMO | regional medical officer |
| RPGMEC | regional postgraduate medical education committee |
| SAC | specialty advisory committee |
| SCM | specialist in community medicine |
| SHA | special health authority |
| SHMO | senior hospital medical officer |
| SHO | senior house officer |
| SIFT | Service Increment for Teaching |
| SR | senior registrar |
| TCTP | Technical Cooperation Training Programme |
| TRAB | Temporary Registration Assessment Board |
| UGC | University Grants Committee |
| UHA | University Hospitals Association |
| UK | United Kingdom |
| UMT | unit of medical time |
| VT | vocational training |
| WMC | Welsh Manpower Committee |
| WTE | whole-time equivalent |

# References

1   Royal Commission on Medical Education 1965-68. (Chairman: Lord Todd) Report. Cmnd 3569. London, HMSO, 1968.

2   Committee of Inquiry into the Regulation of the Medical Profession. (Chairman: Dr A W Merrison) Report. Cmnd 6018. London, HMSO, 1975.

3   Royal Commission on the National Health Service. (Chairman: Sir Alec Merrison) Report. Cmnd 7615. London, HMSO, 1979.

4   House of Commons Social Services Committee. (Chairman: Mrs Renée Short) Fourth report, session 1980-81. Medical education, 4 volumes. HC 31. London, HMSO, 1981.

5   House of Commons Social Services Committee. (Chairman: Mrs Renée Short) Fifth report, session 1984-85. Medical education report: follow-up. Together with the proceedings of the Committee and the minutes of evidence. HC 303. London, HMSO, 1985.

6   General Medical Council Education Committee. Proposals for basic specialist training, in minutes of the General Medical Council, 1983, vol 120, 254-67. London, GMC, 1985.

7   Department of Health and Social Security. Hospital medical staff – England and Wales. 30 September 1984. National tables, regional tables, and annex to regional tables – London postgraduate teaching hospitals. London, Statistics and Research Division, DHSS, 1985 (annual).

8   Department of Health and Social Security. General medical services: some basic statistics. England and Wales. 1 October 1984. London, Statistics and Research Division, DHSS, 1985 (annual).

9   Department of Health and Social Security. Community medicine and community health services medical staff. England and Wales. 30 September 1984. National tables, and regional tables. London, Statistics and Research Division, DHSS, 1985 (annual).

10  Department of Health and Social Security. Hospital dental staff – England and Wales. 30 September 1984. National tables, and regional tables. London, Statistics and Research Division, DHSS, 1985 (annual).

11  Dowie R. An information system for hospital medical and dental training posts and trainees in England and Wales: report of a feasibility study. London, Council for Postgraduate Medical Education in England and Wales, 1984.

12  National Health Service, Department of Health and Social Security. Steering Group on Health Services Information. (Chairman: Mrs E Körner) Third report to the Secretary of State (manpower information). London, HMSO, 1984.

13  Stevens R. Medical practice in modern England. New Haven and London, Yale University Press, 1966.

14  Rhodes P. An outline history of medicine. London, Butterworths, 1985.

15  Ridout A B. Report on hospital medical manpower in the South East Thames region with special reference to current trends. Bexhill on Sea, South East Thames Regional Health Authority, 1982.

16  Ministry of Health and Department of Health for Scotland. Report of the Inter-Departmental Committee on the Remuneration of Consultants and Specialists. (Chairman: Sir William Spens) Cmd 7420. London, HMSO, 1948.

17  Ministry of Health and Department of Health for Scotland. Report of an Inter-Departmental Committee on Medical Schools. (Chairman: Sir William Goodenough) London, HMSO, 1944.

18  Ministry of Health and Department of Health for Scotland. Medical staffing structure in the hospital service: report of the Joint Working Party. (Chairman: Sir Robert Platt) London, HMSO, 1961.

19  Parkhouse J. Medical manpower in Britain. Edinburgh, Churchill Livingstone, 1979.

20  General Medical Council Education Committee. The Medical Act 1956 (experience before full registration) regulations 1979. London, GMC, 1979.

21  Department of Health and Social Security. Government response to the fifth report from the Social Services Committee, 1984-85 session. Cmnd 9701. London, HMSO, 1986.

22  Crisp A H. Medical education, in General Medical Council annual report for 1984, pages 3-7. London, General Medical Council, 1985.

23  Department of Health and Social Security, Medical Manpower Division. Medical and dental staffing prospects in the NHS in England and Wales. Health Trends, 1980, vol 12, 51-54; 1981, vol 13, 57-60; 1982, vol 14, 28-33; 1983, vol 15, 35-39; 1984, vol 16, 25-29; and 1985, vol 17, 45-52.

24  Department of Health and Social Security. Government response to the fourth report from the Social Services Committee, 1980-81 session. Cmnd 8479. London, HMSO, 1982.

25  Department of Health and Social Security. Hospital medical staff: career structure and training. HC(82)4. February 1982.

26  Department of Health and Social Security, Scottish Home and Health Department and Welsh Office. Medical manpower – the next twenty years. London, HMSO, 1978.

27  Department of Health and Social Security. Pre-registration house officer posts: future targets. Letter to regional medical officers, 25 August 1983.

28  Department of Health and Social Security. Pre-registration house officer posts: future targets and Safety Net arrangements for summer 1985. Letter to regional medical officers and district medical officers, 15 April 1985.

29  General Medical Council. Annual reports for years 1978 to 1984. London, GMC.

30  Department of Health and Social Security, Medical Manpower Division. A registrar's prospects of obtaining a senior registrar post, 1973. Health Trends, 1974, vol 6, 54-55.

31  Hall G H. First vacant, first cut. (Letter) British Medical Journal, 1984, vol 289, 696.

32  Department of Health and Social Security. On the state of the public health 1983. London, HMSO, 1984 (annual).

33  Office of Population Censuses and Surveys. Mortality statistics, series DH5 no 11. London, HMSO, 1985.

34  National Health Service. Hospital medical and dental staff (England and Wales). Terms and conditions of service. April 1981 (revised). London, Department of Health and Social Security, 1981.

35  University Hospitals Association (England and Wales) and the National Association of Health Authorities in England and Wales. A survey of academic medical staffing changes in the clinical medical schools and (university) clinical faculties in England and Wales 1981 to 1984. London and Birmingham, University Hospitals Association and National Association of Health Authorities, 1985.

36  Department of Health and Social Security. Resource distribution for 1984-85, service priorities, manpower and planning. HC(84)2. January 1984.

37  Department of Health and Social Security, Hospital Medical Staffing Division. Hospital medical staffing in the National Health Service in England and Wales: fields of consultant and senior registrar recruitment. Health Trends, 1972, vol 4, 66-69.

38  Cookson J B. Post-registration experience of tomorrow's physicians. (Letter) The Lancet, 1984, vol ii, 44-45.

39  Taylor I and Clyne C A C. Senior registrar applications in general surgery in 1982 and 1985. (Letter) British Medical Journal, 1985, vol 291, 143-44.

40  Department of Health and Social Security. Joint planning of training grade numbers. Arrangements agreed in discussions between representatives of health departments, the Joint Consultants Committee, the Committee of Vice-Chancellors and Principals of the Universities of the United Kingdom and the Medical Research Council. London, November 1985.

41  General Medical Services Committee. General practice: a British success. London, British Medical Association, 1983.

42  Department of Health and Social Security and Welsh Office. Statement of fees and allowances payable to general medical practitioners in England and Wales. London, 1974 (with annual amendments).

43  Joint Committee on Postgraduate Training for General Practice. Reports of the work of the Committee – 1984 and 1985. London, 1984 and 1985.

44  Department of Health and Social Security. Recruitment to community medicine: report of a joint working group. London, DHSS, 1980.

45  Department of Health and Social Security. Community medicine staff – posts without a permanent holder. England and Wales. 30 September 1984. London, Statistics and Research Division, DHSS, 1985 (annual).

46  Department of Health and Social Security. Implementation of the NHS management inquiry report. HC(84)13. London, June 1984.

47  Faculty of Community Medicine. Specialist training in community medicine. London, Faculty of Community Medicine, 1981.

48  Anonymous. Report of Joint Working Party on the Training of Clinical Medical Officers in Child Health. (Chairman: Professor J O Forfar) Edinburgh, Joint Paediatric Committee, 1981.

49  Anonymous. Career structure and training of community health doctors. British Medical Journal, 1982, vol 284, 359-60.

50  Joint Paediatric Committee of the Royal Colleges of Physicians and the British Paediatric Association. Training of senior clinical medical officers in child health. British Medical Journal, 1982, vol 285, 955-56.

51  Department of Health and Social Security. Survey of community health service clinical medical staff, England and Wales, Scotland. National tables. 31 May 1983. London, Statistics and Research Division, DHSS, 1983.

52  Department of Health and Social Security. Pay and conditions of service: remuneration of hospital medical and dental staff and doctors in community medicine and the community health service. Advance letters (MD) 1975 to 1985.

53  Central Statistical Office. Monthly digest of statistics, no 478, October 1985. London, HMSO, 1985.

54  Review Body on Doctors' and Dentists' Remuneration. Eleventh report 1981. Cmnd 8239. London, HMSO, 1981.

55  Review Body on Doctors' and Dentists' Remuneration. Twelfth report 1982. Cmnd 8550. London, HMSO, 1982.

56  Review Body on Doctors' and Dentists' Remuneration. Thirteenth report 1983. Cmnd 8878. London, HMSO, 1983.

57  Review Body on Doctors' and Dentists' Remuneration. Fourteenth report 1984. Cmnd 9256. London, HMSO, 1984.

58  Dowie R. National trends in domiciliary consultations. British Medical Journal, 1983, vol 286, 819-22.

59  Daniel G. The allocation of units of medical time in relation to medical staff establishments. Health Services Manpower Review, 1983, vol 9, 13-17.

60  Management Advisory Service. Study of the allocation of units of medical time in relation to medical staff establishments. Final report. Cheltenham, MAS, 1982.

61  Department of Health and Social Security. Junior hospital medical and dental staff: hours of work. PM(82)37. November 1982.

62  Department of Health and Social Security. Junior hospital medical and dental staff: hours of work. Advance letter (MD)3/83, June 1983.

63  Stewart-Brown S. Junior hospital doctors' posts: remaining one in two rotas. British Medical Journal, 1984, vol 288, 503-5.

64  Department of Health and Social Security. Junior hospital medical and dental staff: hours of work. PM(85)1. January 1985.

65  Council for Postgraduate Medical Education in England and Wales. Careers in medicine. London, CPME, 1980 (reprinted 1983).

66  Royal College of Physicians Faculty of Occupational Medicine. Standing orders. London, Faculty of Occupational Medicine, 1978.

67  Royal College of Physicians Faculty of Occupational Medicine. Introductory courses in occupational medicine. London, March 1985.

68  House of Lords. Select Committee on Science and Technology, session 1983-84. Occupational health and hygiene services, vol 1: report. HL (99-I). London, HMSO, 1983.

69  Royal College of Physicians Faculty of Occupational Medicine. Evidence to House of Lords Select Committee on Science and Technology Sub-Committee II – Occupational health. London, Faculty of Occupational Medicine, 1983.

70  Department of Employment. Employees in employment: industry. (Table 1.2) Employment Gazette. 1983, vol 91, no 3, S8-S9.

71  Public Health Laboratory Service. PHLS annual report 1983/84. London, Public Health Laboratory Service Board, 1985.

72  Home Office. Prison statistics. England and Wales 1983. Cmnd 9363. London, HMSO, 1984.

73  General Medical Council. List of hospitals and house officer posts in the United Kingdom which are approved or recognised for pre-registration service. Eleventh edition. London, GMC, 1985.

74  Department of Health and Social Security. Vocational training for general practice: the National Health Service (vocational training) regulations 1979. HC(FP)(80)1. London, February 1980.

75  Central Office of Information for the Ministry of Defence (Army). Doctor in the Army. London, HMSO and Royal Army Medical Corps, 1985.

76  Royal Army Medical College. Year book 1985. London, Royal Army Medical College, 1985.

77  The Navy List 1983. London, HMSO, 1983.

78  The Army List 1984, part 1. London, HMSO, 1984.

79  The Air Force List 1984. London, HMSO, 1984.

80  The British Council. Annual report 1983-84. London, HMSO, 1984.

81  Department of Health and Social Security. Employment of overseas doctors and dentists in the United Kingdom. HC(FP)(85)14 and FPN 394. July 1985.

82  General Medical Council. The medical register 1985, 2 volumes. London, GMC, 1985 (annual).

83  General Medical Council. Limited registration of overseas doctors. Note LR2. London, January 1983.

84  Department of Health and Social Security. Applications from European Community practitioners for medical, dental and nursing posts: knowledge of English. HC(81)7. July 1981.

85  General Medical Council. Note on applications for full registration by doctors who hold or have held limited registration. Note FR8. London, March 1985.

86  Anonymous. Sponsoring overseas doctors. British Medical Journal, 1983, vol 286, 1369-70.

87  Lawson J. Sponsorship of overseas postgraduates by Royal College of Obstetricians and Gynaecologists. London, Royal College of Obstetricians and Gynaecologists, 1986.

88  Strong J A. The GMC should be more concerned with the postgraduate rather than the primary qualifications of overseas doctors. (Letter) British Medical Journal, 1984, vol 288, 1460.

89  Azami M B. The GMC should be more concerned with the postgraduate rather than the primary qualification of overseas doctors. (Letter) British Medical Journal, 1984, vol 289, 52.

90  Hasan M. The GMC should be more concerned with the postgraduate rather than the primary qualification of overseas doctors. (Letter) British Medical Journal, 1984, vol 289, 51-52.

91  Islam N. The GMC should be more concerned with the postgraduate rather than the primary qualification of overseas doctors. (Letter) British Medical Journal, 1984, vol 289, 52.

92  Department of Health and Social Security. Report of the Advisory Committee for Medical Manpower Planning. London, DHSS, 1985.

93   Day P. Women doctors: choices and constraints in policies for medical man-power. King's Fund Project Paper No 28. London, King Edward's Hospital Fund for London, 1982.

94   Department of Health and Social Security. Re-employment of women doctors. HM(69)6. February 1969.

95   Department of Health and Social Security. Opportunities for part-time training in the NHS for doctors and dentists with domestic commitments, disability or ill-health. PM(79)3. September 1979.

96   Jessop E G, O'Brien M and Parkhouse J. Part-time training: experience in the Northern Region. Public Health, London, 1984, vol 98, 134-38.

97   Council for Postgraduate Medical Education in England and Wales. Part-time in medicine. London, CPME, 1981.

98   Anonymous. Review of DHSS training scheme. British Medical Journal, 1982, vol 285, 453.

99   Anonymous. Part time senior registrar training. British Medical Journal, 1985, vol 290, 408.

100  Burke C W and Black N A. Part time senior registrars, registrars, and senior house officers in general medicine and its specialties: a report to the Royal College of Physicians. British Medical Journal, 1983, vol 287, 1040-44.

101  Davidson C A, O'Brien M and Roberts S H. Market research into part time training: consumers' views and regional variations. British Medical Journal, 1986, vol 291, 1736-38.

102  Department of Health and Social Security. Women doctors' retainer scheme. HM(72)42. London, 1972.

103  O'Brien M and Jessop E. The performance of the doctors' retainer scheme. Public Health, London, 1983, vol 97, 296-300.

104  Anonymous. Health service accused of racial discrimination. The Times, 7 January 1984, page 4.

105  Parkhouse J, Campbell M G and Parkhouse H F. Career preferences of doctors qualifying in 1974-1980: a comparison of pre-registration findings. Health Trends, 1983, vol 15, 29-35.

106  Hutt R, Parsons D and Pearson R. The timing of and reasons for doctors' career decisions. Health Trends, 1981, vol 13, 17-20.

107  Department of Health and Social Security and Welsh Office. Hospital medical and dental staff. Notes on completion of forms SBH50 and 50(1), SBH57 and 57(1). London, DHSS Statistics and Research Division, July 1984.

108  Todd G B, O'Brien M and Gooding D. Career structure – the modern doctors' dilemma. British Medical Journal, 1985, vol 291, 755-56.

109  Todd G B and Sheldrick K B. Registrars and senior house officers in post in the Trent region in 1982. British Medical Journal, 1983, vol 286, 1997-98.

110 Smith D J. Overseas doctors in the National Health Service. London, Policy Studies Institute and Heineman Educational Books, 1980.

111 Anonymous. From the JCC. British Medical Journal, 1986, vol 292, 356.

112 Innes Williams D. Overseas doctors and the staffing structure of hospitals. British Medical Journal, 1985, vol 291, 873-76.

113 Department of Health and Social Security. The appointment of consultants and senior registrars. HC(82)10. May 1892.

114 Royal College of Surgeons of England. Criteria for consultants in surgery. College and Faculty Bulletin. Supplement to the Annals of the Royal College of Surgeons of England, 1984, vol 66, no 1, 6-7.

115 Councils for Postgraduate Medical Education and National Advice Centre. Guide to postgraduate degrees, diplomas and courses in medicine in 1986. London, CPME, 1986 (annual).

116 Royal Colleges of Physicians of Edinburgh, Glasgow and London. MRCP (UK). Examination regulations. Edinburgh, Glasgow and London, September 1983.

117 Royal College of Surgeons of England. Regulations relating to the examinations for the Diploma of Fellow (F.R.C.S.Eng.). London, March 1985.

118 Faculty of Anaesthetists, Royal College of Surgeons of England. Regulations relating to the examinations for the diploma of fellow in the Faculty of Anaesthetists (F.F.A.,R.C.S.Eng.). London, November 1983.

119 Royal College of Obstetricians and Gynaecologists. Membership examination regulations. London, April 1983.

120 Royal College of Psychiatrists. Rules for entry to the membership examination (M.R.C.Psych) including the preliminary test. London, July 1982.

121 Royal College of Radiologists. Regulations for training in radiology and examination for the fellowship. London, July 1983.

122 Royal College of Pathologists. Regulations regarding the examinations for membership (medically-qualified candidate). London, April 1984.

123 Faculty of Community Medicine. Community Medicine. Training, examination regulations and syllabus. London, May 1984.

124 Royal College of Physicians Faculty of Occupational Medicine. Regulations for the diplomas of associateship and membership. London, December 1984.

125 Royal College of General Practitioners. Notes on membership, associateship and the membership examination. London, April 1982.

126 Robson J G. Flexibility in general professional training. British Medical Journal, 1982, vol 284, 720-21.

127 Royal College of Obstetricians and Gynaecologists. Fifty-fifth annual report 1983. London, 1984.

128  Royal College of Radiologists. Annual report of council 1983/84. London, 1984.

129  Royal College of Obstetricians and Gynaecologists. Recognised hospital appointments for training for the membership and diploma. London, June 1984.

130  Royal College of Pathologists. Annual report of the council and treasurer's report. London, 1984.

131  Royal College of Psychiatrists. Annual report 1984. London, 1984.

132  Royal College of Surgeons of England. College and Faculty Bulletin. Supplements to the annals of the Royal College of Surgeons of England, 1982, vol 64; 1983, vol 65, 1984, vol 66.

133  Smith R. Becoming a member of the royal colleges of physicians: trial by MCQ. British Medical Journal, 1982, vol 285, 1341-42.

134  Nunn J F. Restructuring of the fellowship examination. (Address by the Dean of the Faculty of Anaesthetists) Annals of the Royal College of Surgeons of England, 1982, vol 64, 210.

135  Lumley J S P, Browne P D and Elcock N J. The MCQ in the primary FRCS(Eng). Annals of the Royal College of Surgeons of England, 1984, vol 66, 441-43.

136  Wilson G M. The M.R.C.P. and F.R.C.S. examinations. British Journal of Medical Education, 1967, vol 1, 103-7.

137  The medical directory. 2 volumes. Edinburgh, Churchill Livingstone, (annual).

138  Ward A W M. Psychiatrists who passed MRCPsych 1975-77. Health Trends, 1984, vol 16, 80-83.

139  General Medical Council. Minutes of the General Medical Council 1983, vol 120, 218-20. London, GMC, 1985.

140  Egerton E A. Choice of career of doctors who graduated from Queen's University, Belfast in 1977. Medical Education, 1985, vol 19, 131-37.

141  Ministry of Health. Postgraduate medical education in regional hospital board hospitals. HM(64)69. London, September 1964.

142  Joint Working Group on Medical Advisory and Representative Machinery. Report on regional management arrangements. London, Department of Health and Social Security, 1981.

143  Department of Health and Social Security and Welsh Office. Financial responsibilities for postgraduate medical and dental education. HM(73)2. London, January 1973.

144  Bussey A. Professional advice to the National Health Service – the medium or the message? British Medical Journal, 1984, vol 289, 204-6.

145  Department of Health and Social Security and Welsh Office. Appointment of regional advisers in general practice. HM(72)25. London, April 1972.

146 University of London British Postgraduate Medical Federation. Doctors' study guide. Thames health regions. October 1985 to September 1986. London, British Postgraduate Medical Federation, 1985 (29th edition).

147 Council for Postgraduate Medical Education in England and Wales and National Association of Clinical Tutors. Directory of postgraduate medical centres. London, CPME, 1972, 1984 and 1986 (biannual).

148 University of Newcastle upon Tyne Regional Postgraduate Institute for Medicine and Dentistry. The role of the clinical tutor in the Northern Region. Newcastle, 1981.

149 Oxford Regional Committee for Postgraduate Medical Education and Training. District postgraduate clinical tutors: their duties and method of appointment. Oxford, 1985.

150 University of Bristol. Postgraduate centre handbook for clinical tutors, administrators and secretaries. Bristol, 1985.

151 Joint Committee on Postgraduate Training for General Practice. Criteria for the selection of trainers in general practice. London, 1980.

152 Gray D J P. Selecting general practitioner trainers. British Medical Journal, 1984, vol 288, 195-98.

153 Schofield T P C and Hasler J C. Approval of trainers and training practices in the Oxford region: assessment. British Medical Journal, 1984, vol 288, 612-14.

154 Department of Health and Social Security. Vocational training for general practice. Payment of training scheme course organisers. London, 1974.

155 Council for Postgraduate Medical Education in England and Wales. Vocational training schemes for general practice. London, CPME, 1984.

156 Trent Regional Postgraduate Medical and Dental Education Committee. Handbook. Sheffield, 1984.

157 University of Oxford, Oxford Regional Health Authority and Oxfordshire Health Authority. Postgraduate medical and dental education information bulletin 1985/6. Oxford, Oxford Regional Committee for Postgraduate Medical Education and Training, 1985.

158 Councils for Postgraduate Medical Education in the United Kingdom. The supervision of higher professional training in medicine and dentistry. London, Edinburgh, Belfast, 1984.

159 Dowie R. A workshop on medical manpower information systems (report of meeting). Community Medicine, 1986, vol 8, 175–77.

160 National Health Service, Department of Health and Social Security. Steering Group on Health Services Information. (Chairman Mrs E Körner). Sixth report to the Secretary of State. (Financial information) London, HMSO, 1984.

161 National Health Service, England and Wales. The National Health Service (vocational training) regulations 1979. Statutory Instrument, 1979 No 1644. (H79-683) London, HMSO, 1979.

162 University of London British Postgraduate Medical Federation. Handbook and annual report. London, British Postgraduate Medical Federation, 1986.

163 General Medical Council. List of hospitals and house officer posts in the United Kingdom which are approved or recognised for pre-registration service. Eleventh edition. London, GMC, 1985.

164 Harris C M, Dudley H A F, Jarman B and Kidner P H. Preregistration rotation including general practice at St Mary's Hospital Medical School. British Medical Journal, 1985, vol 290, 1811-13.

165 Anonymous. Time expired senior registrars: conditions for extension. British Medical Journal, 1983, vol 286, 1369.

166 Rothnie N G. Manpower problems in general surgery. (Letter) British Medical Journal, 1985, vol 291, 973.

167 Glynn M J and Millington H T. First senior house officer job: goal or hurdle? British Medical Journal, 1985, vol 291, 292-93.

168 Joint Committee on Postgraduate Training for General Practice. Training for general practice. London, 1982.

169 General Medical Council. Note on applications for full registration by doctors who hold registrable primary qualifications granted in the United Kingdom and who hold or have held limited registration. Note FR5. London, GMC, June 1984.

170 University of London Academic Council Standing Committee on Pre-Registration. Report on the method of appointment to pre-registration house officer posts in the medical schools of the University. London, January 1984.

171 Mogey G A. The Safety Net and preregistration posts. British Medical Journal, 1978, vol ii, 1136-38.

172 Department of Health and Social Security. Pre-registration house officers: Safety Net. Letter to undergraduate deans. 15 April 1985.

173 Department of Health and Social Security. Junior hospital medical and dental staff: honorary contracts for junior clinical academic staff. PM(84)12. London, July 1984.

174 National Health Service. Standard manpower planning and personnel information (STAMP) system, medical manpower statistics system. User manual (version 7). London, Department of Health and Social Security, 1982.

175 The Wellcome Trust. The Wellcome Trust 1982-84. Fifteenth report. London, The Wellcome Trust, 1985.

176 The Wellcome Trust. Information on Wellcome Trust grants 1983. London, The Wellcome Trust, 1983.

177 Medical Research Council. Support of research and training. London, MRC, 1984.

178 Medical Research Council. Medical Research Council handbook 1984-85. London, MRC, 1985.

179 Medical Research Council. Project grants. London, MRC, 1983.

180 Department of Health and Social Security. Management of NHS trust funds. HC(85)6. London, February 1985.

181 National Health Service Reorganisation Act 1973, National Health Service Act 1977 and Health Services Act 1980. Accounts 1983-84. HC 331. London, HMSO, 1985.

182 Imperial Cancer Research Fund. Annual report and accounts. 1983-84. London, ICRF, 1985.

183 Imperial Cancer Research Fund. Scientific staff. An introduction to career structure. London, ICRF, January 1985.

184 Association of Clinical Professors of Medicine. Academic medicine and the future of senior registrar/honorary senior registrar and 'soft money' posts. March 1984.

185 Council for Postgraduate Medical Education in England and Wales. Desiderata for postgraduate medical centres. London, CPME, 1981.

186 Ministry of Health. Postgraduate medical and allied education. HM(67)33. London, June 1967.

187 Meneces A. Postgraduate medical centres. Health Trends, 1969, vol 1, 16, 18.

188 Russell I, Lally E and Dobson M. Report on national survey of postgraduate medical centres and their administrators. Newcastle, Health Care Research Unit University of Newcastle upon Tyne and National Association of Postgraduate Medical Education Centre Administrators, 1981.

189 Department of Health and Social Security and Welsh Office. Health Building Note 42. Accommodation for education and training. (Draft) London, September 1985.

190 Universities' Statistical Record. University statistics 1983-1984 and 1984-1985, volume one, students and staff. Cheltenham, Universities' Statistical Record, 1984 and 1986.

191 Universities' Statistical Record. University statistics 1982-1983, and 1983-1984 volume three, Finance. Cheltenham, Universities' Statistical Record, 1984 and 1985.

192 University of London British Postgraduate Medical Federation. Specialist courses 1986. London, British Postgraduate Medical Federation, 1986.

193 Department of Health and Social Security and Welsh Office. Hospital medical and dental staff: lecture fees for postgraduate medical education. HM(72)63. London, October 1972.

341

194 Department of Health and Social Security. Report of the Working Party on Section 63 Courses for General Medical Practitioners in England. London, DHSS, 1984.

195 Department of Health and Social Security. Travel and subsistence payments in respect of approved study courses for general medical practitioners (principals, assistants and trainees). HN(FP)(85)11. London, March 1985.

196 Ellis N. What is happening to section 63? British Medical Journal, 1985, vol 290, 1527-28, 1530.

197 Department of Health and Social Security. Doctors in community medicine and the community health service: study leave. PM(84)5. London, February 1984.

198 Department of Health and Social Security. Hospital medical and dental staff: study leave. HC(79)10. London, April 1979.

199 Norton G, O'Brien M and McEvoy M. Who goes where, why and for what? Public Health, London, 1984, vol 98, 43-48.

200 Royal College of Surgeons of England. Pilot scheme for surgical tutors. Annals of the Royal College of Surgeons of England, 1964, vol 34, 70-73.

201 Councils for Postgraduate Medical Education in the United Kingdom. The role of college regional advisers. London, Council for Postgraduate Medical Education in England and Wales, 1984.

202 Royal College of Physicians of London and Royal College of General Practitioners. Report of the Joint Committee on General Professional Training. London, Royal College of Physicians, 1982.

203 Councils for Postgraduate Medical Education in the United Kingdom. Summary of criteria for approval of posts for general training. London, Council for Postgraduate Medical Education in England and Wales, 1984.

204 Royal College of Surgeons of England. Recognised hospitals and appointments. Appendix to the regulations for the diploma of fellow (F.R.C.S.Eng.). London, September 1982.

205 Faculty of Anaesthetists, Royal College of Surgeons of England. Recognised hospitals and appointments including schedule I and schedule II categories. Appendix to the regulations relating to the examination for the diploma of fellow in the Faculty of Anaesthetists (F.F.A.R.C.S.Eng.). London, June 1982.

206 Royal College of Physicians of London and Royal College of General Practitioners. Posts considered for general professional training in the Yorkshire region. London, Royal College of Physicians, 1984.

207 Joint Committee on Higher Medical Training. First report October 1972. London, JCHMT, 1972.

208 Joint Committee on Higher Medical Training. Training handbook. London, JCHMT, 1983.

209  Joint Committee on Higher Surgical Training. Fourth report. London, 1986 (forthcoming).

210  Joint Committee for Higher Training of Anaesthetists. Higher specialist training. London, 1979.

211  Joint Committee on Higher Psychiatric Training. Handbook. London, JCHPsych, 1987 (forthcoming).

212  Joint Committee on Postgraduate Training for General Practice. The Joint Committee on Postgraduate Training for General Practice. London, 1982.

213  Royal College of Obstetricians and Gynaecologists. Regulations for accreditation of completion of higher training of Members of the College. London, RCOG, 1984.

214  Royal College of Pathologists. Postgraduate training in pathology. London, RCPath, 1984.

215  Lister J. Accreditation: who needs it? (Editorial) British Journal of Hospital Medicine, 1985, vol 34, 323.

216  Joint Committee on Higher Medical Training. Specialist certificates in medical specialties. (Office instruction ESC9) London, 1984.

217  Davies J O F. An account of the work of the Council. London, Council for Postgraduate Medical Education in England and Wales, 1975.

218  Council for Postgraduate Medical Education in England and Wales. The Council and bodies concerned with postgraduate medical and dental education. London, CPME, 1984.

219  British Medical Association. Calendar 1985-1986. London, BMA, 1985

220  Council for Postgraduate Medical Education in England and Wales. Accounts for the year ended 31 March 1985. London, CPME, 1985.

221  Councils for Postgraduate Medical Education in the United Kingdom and National Advice Centre. Guide to postgraduate degrees, diplomas and courses in dentistry. Second edition. London, Council for Postgraduate Medical Education in England and Wales, 1983.

222  Bhattacharya S C. The origins and early work of the General Medical Council, in General Medical Council Annual Report for 1982, pages 16-20. London, General Medical Council, 1983.

223  Draper M R. The GMC from 1950 to 1982: a registrar's impression, in General Medical Council annual report for 1982, pages 11-16. London, General Medical Council, 1983.

224  General Medical Council Education Committee. Recommendations on basic medical education. London, GMC, 1980.

225  General Medical Council. Election results. British Medical Journal, 1984, vol 289, 194.

226  Anonymous. Honorary injustice for medical teachers. (Editorial) British Medical Journal, 1985, vol 291, 1300-2.

227  House of Commons Social Services Committee. (Chairman: Mrs Renée Short) First report, session 1981-82. UGC cuts and medical services. HC 191. London, HMSO, 1982.

228  Department of Health and Social Security. Government response to the first report from the Social Services Committee, 1981-82 session. Cmnd 8744. London, HMSO, 1982.

229  House of Commons Social Services Committee. (Chairman: Mrs Renée Short) Third report, session 1984-85. UGC cuts and medical services report: follow-up. HC 397. London, HMSO, 1985.

230  House of Commons Social Services Committee. (Chairman: Mrs Renée Short) First special report, session 1985-86. UGC cuts and medical services report: follow-up. Observations by the Government on the third report from the Committee, session 1984-85. HC 242. London, HMSO, 1986.

231  University Hospitals Association (England and Wales) and National Association of Health Authorities in England and Wales. Joint survey of the effects of reduced funding of universities on medical schools and faculties and the NHS for the academic years 1981-1983. London and Birmingham, UHA and NAHA, 1984.

232  University of London. Report of a Working Party on Medical and Dental Teaching Resources. (Chairman: Lord Flowers) London medical education – a new framework. London, University of London, 1980.

233  University Grants Committee. Postgraduate medical education and the specialties with special reference to the problem in London. Ministry of Health reports on public health and medical subjects no 106. London, HMSO, 1962.

234  University of London. Report of the Working Party appointed to inquire into the postgraduate medical institutes of the University of London. (Chairman: Professor N F Morris) London, University of London, 1977.

235  The Universities' Central Council on Admissions. How to apply for admission to a university. October 1986 entry. Cheltenham, The Universities' Central Council on Admissions, 1985.

236  National Health Service, England and Wales. The authorities for London postgraduate teaching hospitals (establishment and constitution) order 1982. Statutory instruments 1982, no 314, 7 pages.

237  National Health Service, England and Wales. The Hammersmith and Queen Charlotte's Special Health Authority order 1984. Statutory instruments 1984, no 190, 3 pages.

238 National Health Service, England and Wales. The Health Service Commissioner for England (Board of Governors of the Eastman Dental Hospital) order 1984. Statutory instruments 1984, no 124, 2 pages.

239 University of London. Report of the Joint Planning Committee of the Court and the Senate. Medical education in London. Revised proposals: March 1981. London, University of London, 1981.

240 University of London. Report of the Working Party on Medical Costs. (Chairman: Professor L P LeQuesne) 2 volumes. London, University of London, 1981.

241 Noble D. The Council's finances. MRC News, 1985, No 26, 10-12.

242 Medical Research Council. Medical Research Council annual report for 1984/1985. London, MRC (available from HMSO), 1985.

243 Medical Research Council. MRC annual report 1984-85. The Council's financial position and future prospects. (Press notice) London, December 1985.

244 Association of Medical Research Charities. Handbook 1985/86. London, Association of Medical Research Charities, 1985.

245 Cancer Research Campaign. 62nd annual report 1984 and handbook for 1985. London, Cancer Research Campaign, 1985.

246 Department of Health and Social Security. Research and development report and handbook 1985. London, HMSO, 1986.

247 Department of Health and Social Security. Funding health organisations. (Table) British Medical Journal, 1986, vol 292, 504.

248 Department of Health and Social Security. Report of the Resource Allocation Working Party. Sharing resources for health in England. London, HMSO, 1976.

249 Department of Health and Social Security. Report of the Advisory Group on Resource Allocation. London, DHSS, 1980.

250 Culyer A J, Wiseman J, Drummond M F and West P A. What accounts for the higher costs of teaching hospitals? Social and Economic Administration, 1978, vol 12, 20-30.

251 Drummond M F. Teaching hospital costs – the way ahead. Community Medicine, 1979, vol 1, 183-90.

252 Bevan R G. A critique of the medical Service Increment for Teaching (SIFT). Warwick papers in industry, business and administration, no 6. Warwick, Centre for Research in Industry, Business and Administration, University of Warwick, 1982.

253 Perrin J R and Magee M. The costs, joint products and funding of English teaching hospitals. Warwick papers in industry, business and administration, no 8. Warwick, Centre for Research in Industry, Business and Administration, University of Warwick, 1982.

254 Copeman H A and Drummond M F. Funding the activities of teaching hospitals: a case study of two health authorities. Warwick papers in industry, business and administration, no 7. Warwick, Centre for Research in Industry, Business and Administration, University of Warwick, 1982.

255 Wellman F and Palmer P. The London specialist postgraduate hospitals – a review and commentary on their future. London, King Edward's Hospital Fund for London for the Standing Postgraduate Committee of the former Teaching Hospitals Association, 1975.

256 Department of Health and Social Security. Future management of the London specialist postgraduate hospitals: a consultative document. London, DHSS, 1978.

257 National Health Service, England and Wales. The National Health Service (preservation of boards of governors) order 1979. Statutory instruments 1979, no 51, 2 pages.

258 London Postgraduate Committee. The London specialist postgraduate teaching hospitals: commentary on the future management of the hospitals and institutes, arising from the Flowers report and with reference to 'Patients first' and 'Towards a balance'. London, May 1980.

259 London Health Planning Consortium. The service role of the specialist postgraduate teaching hospitals. London, Department of Health and Social Security, 1980.

260 London Health Planning Consortium. Report of the Study Group on Cardiology and Cardiothoracic Surgery. London, Department of Health and Social Security, 1979.

261 London Health Planning Consortium. Report of the Study Group on Radiotherapy and Oncology. London, Department of Health and Social Security, 1979.

262 London Health Planning Consortium. Report of the Study Group on Neurology and Neurosurgery. London, Department of Health and Social Security, 1980.

263 London Health Planning Consortium. Towards a balance: a framework for acute hospital services in London reconciling service with teaching needs. London, Department of Health and Social Security, 1980.

264 London Health Planning Consortium. Acute hospital services in London. London, HMSO, 1979.

265 London Advisory Group. Management arrangements for the postgraduate specialist teaching hospitals. London, Department of Health and Social Security, 1981.

266 Medico-Pharmaceutical Forum. Report of the Working Party on the Role of the Pharmaceutical Industry in Postgraduate Medical Education. London, Medico-Pharmaceutical Forum, 1978.

267 Northern Regional Health Authority. Annual accounts for the year ended 31st March 1984 for regional headquarters and regional services. Newcastle upon Tyne, Northern RHA, 1984.

268 Yorkshire Regional Health Authority. Annual accounts for the year ended 31st March 1984. Harrogate, Yorkshire RHA, 1984.

269 Trent Regional Health Authority. Annual accounts of the regional and district health authorities for the year ended 31st March 1984. Sheffield, Trent RHA, 1984.

270 East Anglian Regional Health Authority. Regional headquarters' and regional services' annual accounts for the year ended 31st March 1984. Cambridge, East Anglian RHA, 1984.

271 North West Thames Regional Health Authority. Annual accounts 1983-84 for the authority's own services. London, North West Thames RHA, 1984.

272 South East Thames Regional Health Authority. Statutory financial accounts 31st March 1984. Bexhill-on-Sea, South East Thames RHA, 1984.

273 Wessex Regional Health Authority. Regional summary of accounts for the year ended 31st March 1984. Winchester, Wessex RHA, 1984.

274 Oxford Regional Health Authority. Accounts for the year ended 31 March 1984. Oxford RHA, 1984.

275 West Midlands Regional Health Authority. Statutory statements of accounts for the year ended 31st March, 1984. Birmingham, West Midlands RHA, 1984.

276 Mersey Regional Health Authority. Statutory accounts for the year ended 31st March, 1984. Liverpool, Mersey RHA, 1984.

277 North Western Regional Health Authority. Annual accounts, statements and financial and costing returns for the year ended 31st March, 1984. Manchester, North Western RHA, 1984.

278 National Association of Health Authorities in England and Wales. Report of the Working Party on Medical Manpower Planning. Medical manpower planning in the NHS. Birmingham, NAHA, 1985.

279 National Audit Office. Report by the Comptroller and Auditor General. National Health Service: hospital based medical manpower. HC 373. London, HMSO, 1985.

280 Medical Manpower Steering Group. Report. London, Department of Health and Social Security, 1980.

281 Bolt D E. Medical manpower in the year 2000. London, British Medical Association, 1983.

282 Anonymous. Ministerial talks on career structure begin. British Medical Journal, 1986, vol 292, 843.

283 Parkhouse J and O'Brien J M. Medical and dental training and staffing in a region – the long and Short of it. British Medical Journal, 1984, vol 288, 1773-75.

284 Todd J N and Coyne A M. Medical manpower: a district model. British Medical Journal, 1985, vol 291, 984-86.

285 Royal College of Surgeons of England. Report on surgical manpower and the career structure. London, RCS, 1981.

286 Royal College of Surgeons of England. Second report on surgical manpower and the career structure. London, RCS, 1982.

287 Royal College of Physicians of London. The deployment of doctors in the medical specialties. London, RCP, 1977.

288 Royal College of Obstetricians and Gynaecologists. Report of the manpower advisory subcommittee of the Royal College of Obstetricians and Gynaecologists. Consultative document. London, RCOG, 1983.

289 Rawnsley K. The future of the consultant in psychiatry: a report to the College. The Bulletin of the Royal College of Psychiatrists, 1984, vol 8, 122-23.

290 Royal College of Pathologists. Medical and scientific staffing of National Health Service pathology departments. London, RCPath, 1982.

291 Royal College of Pathologists. Management of pathology departments in the National Health Service. London, RCPath, 1984.

292 Royal College of Obstetricians and Gynaecologists. Survey of senior house officers in obstetrics and gynaecology in the United Kingdom. London, RCOG, 1983.

293 Hudson E A. Report on the survey of pathologists practising cytopathology. The Bulletin of the Royal College of Pathologists, 1984, no 45, 9-10.

294 Davidson C and King R C. General medicine in the 'eighties. British Medical Journal, 1986, vol 293, 547-50.

295 Chamberlain D A, Bailey L G and Julian D. Staffing and facilities in cardiology in the United Kingdom 1984. Third biennial survey. British Heart Journal, 1981, vol 45, 460-63.

296 Committee on Gastroenterology of the Royal College of Physicians of London. Career prospects in medical gastroenterology in the United Kingdom. Gut, 1981, vol 22, 677-81.

297 Kessel N. Academic medicine in peril. The Lancet, 1983, vol ii, 899-901.

298 Rhodes P. The framework of graduate medical education. The Lancet, 1980, vol i, 356-59.

299 United Kingdom Health Departments, Joint Consultants Committee and Chairman of Regional Health Authorities. Hospital medical staffing: achieving a balance. London, DHSS, 1986

# Index